Second Edition
WORLD PROSPECTS
A CONTEMPORARY STUDY

WORLD

Second Edition

PROSPECTS

A CONTEMPORARY STUDY

John Molyneux
Principal, Castle Frank High School
Toronto, Ontario

Marilyn MacKenzie
Vice Principal, Brockton High School
Toronto, Ontario

Prentice-Hall Canada Inc. Scarborough, Ontario

Canadian Cataloguing in Publication Data
Molyneux, John, date
   World prospects: a contemporary study

2nd ed.
Includes index.
ISBN 0-13-967829-8

1. Social history—20th century.   2. Economic history—20th
century.   3. World politics—20th century.   4.
Industrialization.   I. MacKenzie, Marilyn   II.   Title

HN16.M64 1987   909.82   C87-090047-1

Prentice-Hall Inc., Englewood Cliffs, *New Jersey*
Prentice-Hall International (UK) Ltd., *London*
Prentice-Hall of Australia, Pty., Ltd., *Sydney*
Prentice-Hall Hispanoamericana, S.A., *Mexico*
Prentice-Hall of India Pvt., Ltd., *New Delhi*
Prentice-Hall of Japan, Inc., *Tokyo*
Prentice-Hall of Southeast Asia (Pte.) Ltd., *Singapore*
Editora Prentice-Hall do Brasil, Ltda., *Rio de Janeiro*

ISBN 0-13-967829-8

Project Editor: Judy Dawson
Production Editor/Photo Research: K.C. Bell
Illustrations: Marilyn Boggs
Design: Gail Ferreira Ng-A-Kien
Production: Irene Maunder
Cartography: Geoffrey Matthews
Composition: Q-Composition Inc.
Cover Photo: Imtek Imagineering/Masterfile

Printed and bound in Canada

  6 7 FP 95 94

The publisher of this book has made every reasonable effort to
trace the ownership of data and visuals and to make full
acknowledgement for their use. If any errors or omissions have
occurred, they will be corrected in future editions, provided
written notification has been received by the publisher.

Contents

Preface

The second edition of *World Prospects* is considerably revised and updated from the first edition. Material on development strategies, environmental concerns, the role of women, nuclear energy, trade policies, basic needs, colonialism, deforestation and desertification has been greatly enhanced, while other material has been rewritten to reflect recent developments. A new chapter has been added at the beginning of the book, dealing with issues analysis, and a new Appendix has been added at the end, dealing with ecology and the environment. All data maps and charts have been re-drawn to reflect the latest available information. Photographs are almost all new.

But the purposes of the book remain the same: to help you increase your analytical skills and your awareness of the complex dynamic relationships among the world and its peoples; to encourage you to think critically about your own and other people's values and positions; and to assist you in making reasoned evaluations of the myriad problems and opportunities facing us all in our global environment.

The book itself offers many opportunities — sometimes in the guise of problems — to realize some of these goals. Questions and related activities are numerous, so numerous, in fact, that they cannot all be readily completed within a year. A selection will, therefore, be needed.

It is not necessary to study *World Prospects* by following the order of its chapters. Because its themes are linked it is possible to begin with any chapter. The concluding section of each chapter draws your attention to some linking themes between the chapter ending and the one just following. If your studies follow another order, you may find it useful to make your own thematic connections between chapters.

We have received much support from MaryLynne Meschino, Judy Dawson and K.C. Bell in the preparation of this revised edition, and we would like to thank them most sincerely for their help and encouragement.

John Molyneux/Marilyn MacKenzie
Toronto, 1987

1 GENERAL OVERVIEW

Differences of Opinion

For whatever reason, some people are pessimists; others are optimists. Accordingly, some see the world as beset by problems, even as others see it as full of opportunities. Most people, however, are aware of both the problems and the opportunities. The purpose of this book is to present as impartial an analysis as possible of some of the world topics of major concern to many people and, wherever possible, to examine the future possibilities existing in any given situation.

Hartland

Because of the existence of both problems and opportunities in most, if not all, situations, it is better to think in terms of *issues*, which have at least two sides to them, than of problems or opportunities, which may represent only a single side of an issue. For example, the issue of population may be presented as a problem by using the term "over-population," while describing population as a "resource" presents it as an opportunity. It is a characteristic of all issues that they have at least two sides, and most have many more. The major world issues addressed in this book are population, food, industrialization, energy, quality of life, migrations and geopolitics.

Beetle Bailey

People across the world hold different views on all these issues. Some, for reasons of strategic and military strength, for example, view rapid population growth as a national asset; others, for reasons associated with poverty and hunger, view it as a national liability. Still others see rapid population growth as an opportunity for economic growth, or as a problem in terms of exploited low-wage labour. There are examples throughout this book of such varying points of view, and an attempt is made to present as full a spectrum of views as possible. However, it is important that you be alert for instances of *ethnocentrism*. Ethnocentrism is present whenever someone unnecessarily judges the culture or behaviour of some other society by the standards of his or her own. For example, many of the views presented here are those of the Western press. Many writers in the Western world are supportive of the other parts of the world and, to the best of our ability, their views have been represented. You should also remember that views are held individually. As one example, there is no such thing as a "Canadian view"; there are instead the views of 25 000 000 individual Canadians, never expressed with a single voice. On a world scale — and all the issues in this book are dealt with on a world scale — the possibilities for widely varying views are almost endless. Despite these endless possibilities, many people tend to think similarly about certain aspects of important issues. Many people think, for instance, that continued development of nuclear energy poses unacceptable risks to society and should be stopped. Many others claim these risks are acceptable and that nuclear energy should continue to be developed.

Another essential characteristic of issues is that they do not stand alone. They exist in the meshed web of life. For example, the issues relating to food, its quantity, quality, distribution and availability, do not exist in isolation. They exist in relation to population numbers,

Be alert for instances of ethnocentrism. One form of ethnocentrism would be a tendency to judge personal worth by standards of material wealth.

Unicef/David Mangurian

technology, transportation systems, political will, economic prices, cultural traditions, land-holding practices, past experience and a host of other factors that influence food-producers. In some times and situations, one of the factors may be dominant. The 1985 drought in the area of southern Alberta and southwest Saskatchewan known as Palliser's Triangle drastically cut that area's food production while leaving the rest of the Prairies unscathed. Had you been a farmer thus affected by drought, and seen your crops shrivel and your income disappear, followed a year later by the fall of world wheat prices to their lowest level in years, what would have been in your mind for the following year? Similarly, if you had been a farmer in the Sahel region of Africa during the locust plague of 1986, only just recovering from several years of drought, and you had seen your newly growing crops stripped of greenery by swarms of locusts, what would have been in your mind for the future?

Issues and the Environment

We have just noted that issues do not stand alone; they exist as part of the "meshed web of life," as part of an environment (see Appendix 1). Moreover, each specialized environment (the food environment, the industrial environment, the geopolitical environment and so on) is part of the total global environment. It is characteristic of the environment that actions affecting one part of it ultimately produce reactions elsewhere and that actions at one time subsequently produce reactions in the same place at a later time. Industrial activity in England may cause trees to die in Norway; deforestation in Amazonia may subsequently cause soil erosion in the same region.

The seven world issues presented in this book are inextricably linked. Changes in any one have an impact upon the rest. Think for a moment,

Action and reaction: in Pequerque, Bolivia, fertile land, lost to the new reservoir in the background, must be compensated for by increasing food production on the remaining land. Here, women weed the potato fields.

for example, of the effects on population, food, industry, energy, the quality of life and geopolitics, if all migration were to cease, or to double.

While our seven issues are related directly to concerns over the global environment, there are other cross-linkages to matters of common concern. Global resource use is addressed in one form or another in the chapters on food, industry, energy and quality of life. Population trends are dealt with primarily in the chapter on population, but also are addressed in the chapters on food, industry, energy, quality of life and migrations. The cultural, political and economic aspirations of people are particularly discussed in the chapters on industry, energy, quality of life, migrations and geopolitics, but are noted in the chapters on population and food. The uses of technology are a feature of all chapters except that on migration.

It is probably true to say that the attitudes people have toward the issues discussed in this book are strongly related to the views they hold of the durability of the environment. Some believe that the environment is already under severe pressure and that additional population, increasing industrialization and continuing resource use will cause the environment to become so degraded that the quality of life for everyone on earth will suffer irreparable harm. Others hold that the environment is capable of supporting more people, more industry and more resource use, provided care is taken in keeping the environment clean, and that the quality of life for millions can only be improved by continued growth. Still others maintain that the environment is nowhere near danger point and that unhindered growth is possible far into the foreseeable future (see Appendix 1).

As you study the issues presented in this text, carry with you the idea of the "meshed web of life" and constantly ask yourself how far the elements of each issue indicate that the environment is being put under pressure or whether they indicate that the environment will permit further growth. You will not find easy answers.

Issues Analysis

The essence of issues analysis rests in attempting:

- to identify the various factors that affect people's views;
- to ascertain their relative importance;
- to examine the nature of problems caused by different and conflicting views;
- to distinguish between opinion and fact; and
- to present possible plans for action.

Issues analysis is difficult because many persons in a problem or conflict situation are neither disposed to examine alternative viewpoints nor satisfied to implement plans with which they disagree. Issues enter the realm of politics, the arena where decisions are made.

The seven major issues discussed in this book (population, food, industrialization, energy, quality of life, migrations and geopolitics) are treated separately for purposes of analysis, but wherever appropriate will be cross-referenced to related issues. Each issue will be analyzed with respect to the geographical distribution of its essential components, its relationships with kindred factors, its change through time and its future prospects. For example, industry is analyzed in terms of its general characteristics and global distribution, its effects on natural resources, labour supplies and governments, its existence as part of different development strategies, its reasons for existence and perceived disadvantages, and its part in the changing nature of global employment trends.

Various tools of analysis will be used. Research is the basic tool for all analysis. You should be prepared to spend time in the library using the card catalogues and the hanging files, as well as keeping up-to-date on world issues through the daily news. You also should develop the habit of reading or scanning a number of the more useful weekly and monthly periodicals. Of course, the basic geographical tool is the map, and much use will be made of maps to identify patterns. Particular use is made of graded-shading maps because they are the best of all maps for showing patterns of intensity as well as patterns of occurrence. Any relationships existing among the numerous components of the issues presented may be tested either visually (by comparing maps of different components) or statistically (by comparing the data on which maps are based). For example, any relationship which may exist between population growth rates and food production growth rates may be tested either by comparing maps of these items or by applying one statistical technique or another to the data on which the maps are based.

Such comparisons, or correlations, visual or statistical, may be positive, negative or zero; the two items compared may match well or they may be the opposite of one another or there may be no apparent relationship at all. In any case, they raise questions. Does the existence of one item, for example, cause or deny the existence of the other, or are both items subject to the influence of a third? This is the heart of issues analysis, for without such answers there can be neither understanding nor resolution.

Answering questions posed by graded-shading maps and visual and statistical correlations requires reading and research followed by thoughtful analysis, a breaking-down of the topic into its several components for examination. It demands that different views be explored and, where

Geography is not just about maps, but about people and their relationships to the lands they inhabit.

possible, justified. It should also produce an awareness of possible future scenarios. It necessitates a search for synthesis, a putting together of one's views, based on an evaluation of the evidence and an assessment of likely outcomes.

Issues analysis requires:

- identifying the distribution, intensity and relationships of the components of issues (maps, statistical analysis, research);
- investigating the origins and natures of such components (reading, research, analysis);
- developing an awareness and understanding of the different views (based upon differences in values) held by different people in relation to the components of issues (reading, research, analysis);
- understanding the dynamics of issues and their possible future developments; and
- formulating a synthesis of one's views on the issues, refining one's system of values, and realizing that one's views and values may need to be modified as the future unfolds.

Map Analysis

It has been said that geography is about maps and that what cannot be mapped cannot be geography. Certainly maps are one of the fundamental tools of geography. Accordingly, throughout this book, you will be asked to create many of your own.

Primarily, maps establish spatial patterns that should lead to further inquiry. For example, the map in Fig. 2-3 (Variations in birth rates throughout the world) provides somewhat the same information contained in Column D of Appendix 3, but shows it spatially. The map shows much more readily than the data in Column D that the higher birth rates generally exist within the tropical areas of the world, and that Africa is the continent with the most uniformly high birth rates. The information provided by the map immediately poses questions, such as *What possible causes, if any, exist for the relationship between the tropical areas of the world and higher birth rates?* What other questions can you suggest?

The pattern identified in Fig. 2-3 also shows anomalies, or differences from what might be expected in view of the general situation. For example, Ireland's birth rate is anomalously high for Europe (although only slightly). What other anomalies can you find in Fig. 2-3? Are they positive or negative anomalies; that is, are they above or below average?

Maps may also be used to identify relationships, or correlations. For example, compare the map in Fig. 4-2 (Variations in per capita value of gross manufactured output throughout the world) with that in Fig. 5-6 (Variations in per capita electricity production throughout the world). The relationship is obvious, but there are still questions. Why, for instance, is Canada in the first rank for electricity production, but only in the second rank for gross manufactured output, both on a per capita basis? Conversely, why is West Germany in the first rank for manufactured output but only in the second rank for electricity production? The correlation established between the two maps, while obvious, is not perfect. What other factors could explain the differences?

Correlative mapping may be used to test any possible relationship. For example, in the last few years persistent drought has been suggested as a major cause of famine in the world. This thesis, or unproven assumption, may be tested by comparing Fig. 3-1 (Variations in protein intake throughout the world) with Fig. 3-3 (Arid environments). You should by now be able to suggest what sort of relationship, if any, exists between drought and famine, what anomalies, if any, exist, and what questions can be raised and investigated. For example, if you find a strong relationship, your questions may be about why such a relationship exists and what, if anything, could be done to alter it, assuming that a change would be desirable. If you find only a weak relationship or none at all, your questions may be about the reasons for the widespread acceptance of the thesis (i.e., persistent drought is a major cause of famine), as well as about the alternative causes of famine. There will always be questions to ask, regardless of the type of correlation.

Statistical Analysis

Statistics are useful to lend precision to observable and recordable phenomena, such as the annual number of births in a nation, or the annual quantity of rice harvested in an area. They must, however, be treated with care because the efficiency, accuracy and frequency of data collection varies from country to country. Moreover, different countries do not always count the same things in the same way. For example, Australia excludes from its population count (or census) any of its armed forces stationed overseas, while Greece includes them. France (among others) includes in its total milk production the milk that is suckled directly by young animals, while Spain excludes all milk fed to animals. Further complications occur when the "year" is looked at: not all countries follow a January 1st–December 31st calendar year. Among those that do, there may well be differences between the recording year and the calendar year. For example, Australia (along with many other southern hemisphere countries) uses a July 1st–June 30th recording year for much of its production. For a number of reasons, therefore, the use of statistics as a means of comparison between different countries needs to be approached with caution.

The problems inherent in statistics do not, however, negate their usefulness if caution is used. The main uses of statistics in geographical issues analysis lie in:

- the establishment of correlations between different phenomena;
- the identification of groupings and deviations (anomalies) from those groupings; and
- the recognition of trends.

Predicting the Future

All the issues discussed in this book are highly changeable. They have an origin in the past, a reality in the present and an existence in the future. As the present is different from the past, so the future will differ from the present. It is one of the tasks of issues analysis to present possible futures, which partially explains the presence of the word *prospects* in the title of this book.

Thomas Edison once said, "the phonograph has no commercial

value," which shows how difficult it can be, even for "experts," to predict the future with any degree of accuracy. In most societies even up to the fairly recent past, and perhaps still in some societies today, the difficulties of predicting the future did not matter very much. People were curious about their own personal or family futures, and resorted to such devices as tarot cards, palmistry, astrology, and the reading of a variety of phenomena such as freshly killed animal meat or entrails. But there was little specific interest in the future of society at large. Life in general changed very slowly for most people and, apart from crises such as war, earthquake, flood and plague, the future could be broadly anticipated to be very similar to the present.

The situation, however, has changed. The application of technology to production, transportation and communication has materially altered the way many people live, and continues to do so. News now

People of every country now realize that change and choice are possible. What choices do you think these children in Uelen, USSR, will make about their futures?

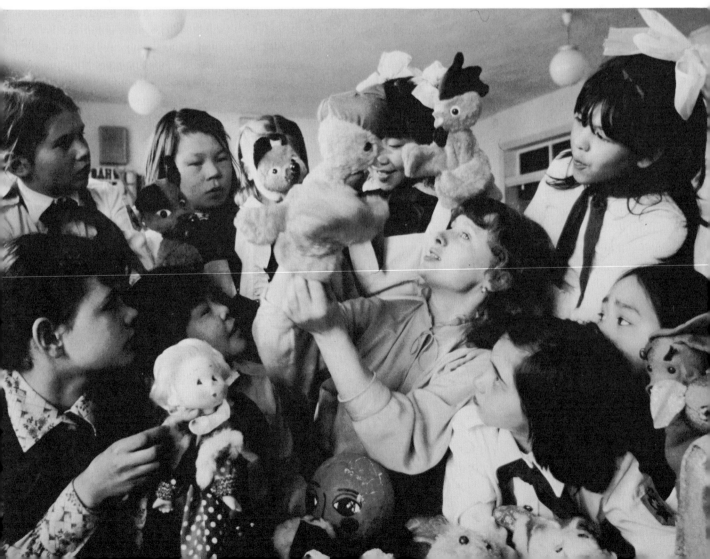

travels around the world almost instantly, and people everywhere are much more aware than they used to be of the differences from one part of the world to another. Changed expectations have accompanied this growing awareness, and much of the world now wants a future different from the past, a "better" future. The people of every country now realize that change is possible, and that choices can be made.

Some countries have even set up specialized "think tanks" to analyze trends and developments in an effort to predict the future. Three important examples in the USA are the Hudson Institute, the Rand Corporation and the Stanford Research Institute, while the USSR has the Section for Social Forecasting of the Academy of Sciences. Examples in Canada include the Fraser Institute and the C.D. Howe Institute.

The techniques of "futures analysis" vary, but fall broadly into four groups:

- "Brainstorming," in which a group is asked to "invent the future" in some particular area, such as food production or employment opportunities. The members of the group make their suggestions, react to each other's suggestions, discuss each person's reasons, accept or reject ideas and continue until consensus is more or less reached.

- "Contextual Mapping," in which established trends are projected into the future in the light of expected changes. This is a common way of "predicting the future," usually based on a series of statistics from the past and present. The difficulties are those of all futurological techniques, namely in the area of "expected changes." One of the best-known examples of contextual mapping is the computer-based study called *The Limits to Growth*, produced for the Club of Rome.

- "Delphi Technique," in which about 40–60 specialists are questioned individually about the likely future in some field. The minority views in each round are eliminated, and the remaining more commonly held opinions are then presented back to the individual specialists for further consideration and choice until a consensus in reached.

- "Normative Forecasting," in which norms, or targets, are set and plans made to reach them. This is a device used by many governments, in such forms as one-year or five-year plans.

Problems arise in the decision-making process as to what should be achieved, and governments throughout the world certainly vary in the ways in which they approach this problem. However, let us look now in more detail at the major issues we identified earlier, starting with population and ending with geopolitics.

2 POPULATION

Introduction

The world's population is increasing rapidly. As it does, concern also increases over the possible problems created by the effects of more and more people on the global environment. More people require more food, more minerals, more energy. As their need for each of these things becomes more pressing, so too does the pressure on them to migrate and to make political changes.

In many countries, these concerns are discounted. Larger populations are thought to promise greater strategic, military, political, economic and cultural power. Other societies, for personal, religious or cultural reasons, consider the creation of new life to be among the highest priorities and accord it preference over concerns about the environment and the future availability of food and jobs.

Nevertheless, rapid population growth is regarded by many as one of the world's most pressing issues. Almost daily we are asked to help starving people around the world. We hear of natural resources that are being quickly depleted by the growing numbers of people and by the growing pressures of economic growth. We read forecasts of "standing room only" in the world of the future. We are told of the desperate need for jobs to employ the world's burgeoning population. Robert McNamara, former president of the World Bank, warns that many countries may "grow beyond the boundaries required for political stability and acceptable socio-economic conditions." He predicts mass unemployment, nightmarish giant cities, environmental destruction, widespread malnutrition, persistent illiteracy and frequent epidemics. His vision of the future is an unpleasant one.

Current statistics about world population growth make McNamara's predictions seem plausible. The world's population, which took thousands of years to reach 1 billion, needed only about another 100 years to double to 2 billion, and only another 50 years to double again to 4 billion, a number reached by the mid-1970s. By 1986 the world's population was reported to be 5 billion, and it was forecast that the global population would reach a total of about 6 billion by the year 2000, and 8 billion by the year 2025.

HERMAN

Every major problem on this planet can be linked to overcrowding.

ANIMAL CRACKERS

If they occur, such large populations will aggravate every social and economic problem facing the world today. The main issues of the future would centre on the feeding, clothing, housing, educating, employing and keeping healthy of growing legions of people.

The following extracts will suggest the size and complexity of the population issue.

In the mid-1980s world population was increasing at an average rate of between 1.6% and 1.7% per year. This means that on a base of 5 billion people, there were an additional 80–85 million each year. On the projected base of 8 billion in 2025, there will be, if the annual rate is maintained, an additional 128–136 million people per year.

Keeping a tight rein on population growth is necessary, according to Chinese leaders, if the country is to be modernized. Education and publicity has focused on linking higher living standards to fewer children and on a sense of patriotic duty.

The importance of population control was underlined by Premier Zhao Ziyang in his speech earlier this month to the first session of the sixth National People's Congress.

"We must persistently advocate late marriage and one child per couple, strictly control second births, prevent additional births by all means, earnestly carry out effective birth-control measures and firmly protect infant girls and their mothers."

Chinese demographers have warned that if every couple continued to have two children instead of one, China's population would not stop growing until it reached 1.8-billion in the year 2025.

The Globe and Mail, Toronto, 1983 6 24

Emmett Cardinal Carter sees a potential for global revolution if starvation and unemployment continue unchecked.

"We cannot keep on going the way we are when a whole large proportion of the world's population lives in starvation, watching their children die of malnutrition, and various other side conditions, while the rest of the world — a smaller proportion — lives in affluence," said the Cardinal, the ranking member of the English-speaking Catholic Church in Canada.

"I don't think this [state] in human affairs can endure," he continued.

"It's just a question of how long it will be before it (a revolution) arrives. So I worry about it, indeed."

The Globe and Mail, Toronto, 1983 12 9

The world's population is inexorably increasing at the rate of 1.7 per cent per year (Population Reference Bureau, Washington, D.C., 1982). So why does Toronto's Emmett Cardinal Carter (Cardinal Foresees A Global Revolution — Dec. 9) want us to give attention only to the effects of this growth — unemployment, malnutrition, possible revolutions and dictatorships — rather than such a major cause of these problems? In 1984, another 80 million will join the present consumers of oxygen, water, food, fuel, materials and space to further reduce our planet's resources, and so on, until there are no more "haves" to help the "have nots." Competition for resources and for markets exacerbates the situation.

The Cardinal is right about the effects he cites, but why does the world ignore a growing cause of these problems?

Letter to the editor, *The Globe and Mail* 1984 1 4

. . . most of the increase, according to a report issued today by the U.N. Fund for Population Activities, will occur in countries least able to afford it.

The fund said the current per capita income in the richest nations was 220 times that of the poorest ones, and that the rising population rate in many underdeveloped countries was "undercutting the quality of life for many millions of people."

From a Reuter report published in *The Toronto Star* 1984 6 13

"The ultimate aim is a population of 70 million, from the present 14.8 million, to fulfill Malaysia's dream of becoming a strong industrial nation by the year 2000. Its argument: A bigger population will create a larger consumer base with increasing power to generate and support industrial growth," Indrani writes.

"Malaysia believes that it can produce more manufactured goods economically only if the domestic market is large or if the developed countries adopt an open policy on such goods. But as it is, the largest consumers of manufactured items are the developed countries, which have become protectionist."

World Press Review 1984 6

SINGAPORE (Reuter) —

Singapore is working out a new family planning program which sets double standards based on the genetic theory that children born to scholars have a better chance of growing up to be good, talented citizens.

Graduates and professionals will be told to go forth and multiply. The less educated will be urged to have no more than two children.

Prime Minister Lee Kuan Yew has thrown his full weight behind the controversial program. Lee and his deputy, Goh Keng Swee, say it is wrong for highly educated women to remain single and waste their genes, robbing the state of a talented generation vital to maintain the island's prosperity.

It will be equally wrong for the less educated to spread their genes without restraint, which Lee and Goh are convinced will lower the island's high standards.

An official spokesman said that for the less academically inclined, the

message will remain the same — two is enough.

Published in *The Globe and Mail* 1984 2 8

Earlier this month Ceausescu [Romania's President] imposed the tax surcharge on single people and childless couples and mounted a massive propaganda drive. Penalties for illegal abortions and black-market contraceptive dealing were stiffened.

Without divulging the current rate, Agerpress, the official Romanian news agency, recently reported that the aim is to raise the birthrate to between 19 and 20 per 1,000 population so that the country will have 25 million inhabitants by 1990. The current population figure is 22.6 million.

That raises a troubling question. How does Ceausescu intend to feed 25 million when his hapless economy already has trouble feeding the current numbers? The food shortages in Romania are the worst, the line-ups to the butcher and grocery stores the longest, throughout Eastern Europe — Poland included.

Another question is where the regime intends to house all the children or let them play. Instead of creating more, the authorities have actually been reducing the number of playgrounds, according to complaints in the Romanian press.

"We used to have swings, but they took them away," several children wrote recently in a letter to the Bucharest weekly Flacara.

In some Bucharest neighborhoods there is 35 per cent overcrowding in public housing. According to the Romanian Laboratory of Sociology, systematic elimination of playgrounds — to make room for vegetable gardens and small factories — has left 26 per cent of the children in Bucharest living at least a half hour's walk from the nearest play area, with half of them having to take a bus to get there.

But the propaganda campaign goes on.

"Having and raising children is a foremost patriotic duty," Ilse Rudolf, a "hero mother" of 12, wrote the other day in Neuer Weg (New Road), the daily for Romania's 800,000 ethnic Germans.

John Dornberg, *The Toronto Star*, 1984 3 25

The average African woman bears 6.4 children, compared to 1.9 in Europe and 1.7 in Japan. The UN says Africa has a "terrifying infant mortality rate"; if that rate could be reduced, Africans could choose the size of their families. But that prospect "seems distant in 1984."

The pro-government *China Daily* of Peking [June 6] takes a different view of Africa's problem. Zhang Tongzhu, a professor at Nanking University, writes, "It is onesided or alarmist to say that population size is the source of all evils. Take the food shortage, for example. On one hand, Africa's food shortage is partially due to excessive population; on the other hand, another major cause is the drought and crop failure of the past twenty years. . . . The so-called land shortage does not exist and most African countries could feed still more people. . . .

"Of course, it is necessary for Africa to control its growth rate. But at the same time, efforts should be made to develop the economy, including agriculture, processing, communications, and transportation. The economic structure should be adjusted."

World Press Review 1984 8

In the body of this chapter we will examine in detail the extent and nature of world population growth, some of its associated environmental, political, social, economic and technological problems, and some of the different developments taking place around the world. Our study will conclude with a look at the population issue as it is developing in one country, Kenya.

Fig. 2-1
Changing proportion of the world's population aged 60 years or over, 1975 (top) and 2025 (bottom, est.)

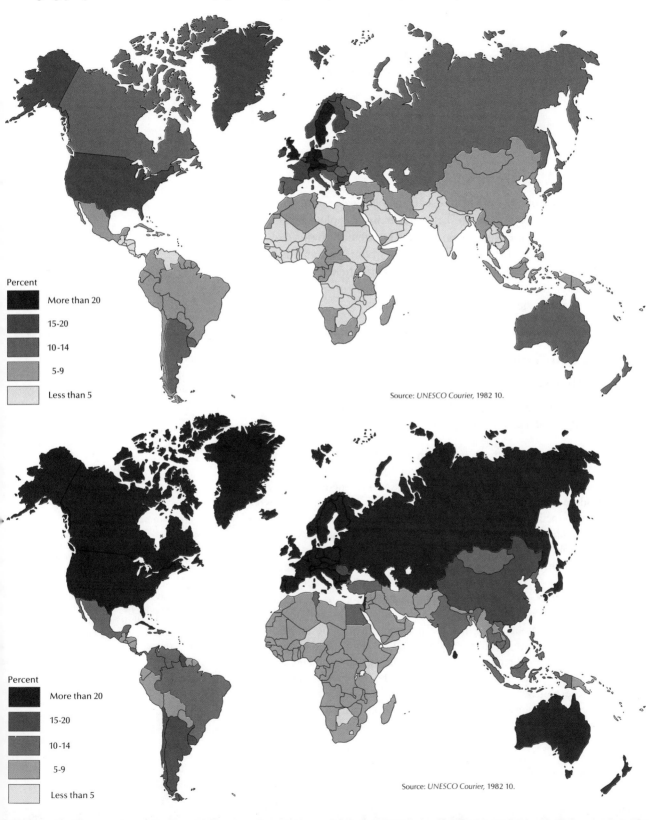

Percent

More than 20

15-20

10-14

5-9

Less than 5

Source: *UNESCO Courier,* 1982 10.

Percent

More than 20

15-20

10-14

5-9

Less than 5

Source: *UNESCO Courier,* 1982 10.

The Apparent Problem

Attitudes to World Population

We have little reason to assume that early people were concerned with the population question. It is unlikely that many people worried about the existence of others, except when the need to defend themselves arose or when they wanted to trade with their neighbours. Gradually, as the numbers grew, some individuals began to concern themselves with population. The reading "From Confucius to Malthus" gives a summary of some of these early views on population growth.

From Confucius to Malthus . . .

Since antiquity men have asked:
"Is there an optimum population?"

Man has been concerned with population problems since ancient times. From antiquity, statesmen and thinkers have held opinions, based on political, military, social and economic considerations, about such issues as the most desirable number of people or the need to stimulate or retard population growth.

Ideas and theories on population have nearly always revolved around the real or supposed problems of individual societies and have stimulated the most response when directed specifically towards those problems. Thus the ideas of the philosophers of ancient Greece dealt mainly with the population questions faced by the city-state with a relatively small population. In the Roman Empire the views on population reflected the populationist outlook of a society in which population was considered a source of power.

The thesis that excessive population growth may reduce output per worker, depress levels of living for the masses and engender strife is of great antiquity. It appears in the works of Confucius and his school, as well as in the works of other ancient Chinese philosophers.

Some of these writings suggest that the authors had some concept of optimum population, as far as the population engaged in agriculture was concerned. Postulating an ideal proportion between land and population, they held the government primarily responsible for maintaining such a proportion by moving people from over-populated to under-populated areas, although noting also that government action was reinforced at times

The *populationist* view holds that an increasing population is an advantage to a state.

Optimum population can be defined as the ideal population size for a specific area. If this number is exceeded, each person will receive a reduced share of the wealth produced. If the population falls short of this number, there will not be enough people to create the area's maximum possible wealth; thus the total wealth and the amount given to each person will be reduced.

A *city-state* is a self-governing and fully independent political unit, much as Singapore is now. City-states were most common in the ancient world of Babylon, Greece and Assyria, and in Renaissance Italy.

Spontaneous migrations occur whenever people in an area feel that their future survival is in jeopardy if they remain.

by spontaneous migration.

These ancient Chinese writers also paid some attention to another aspect which has occupied an important place in subsequent literature on population theory, that is, the checks to population growth. They observed that mortality increases when food supply is insufficient, that premature marriage makes for high infant mortality rates, that war checks population growth and that costly marriage ceremonies reduce the marriage rates, although they paid little attention to the manner in which numbers adjusted to resources. Despite these views on population and resources, the doctrines of Confucius regarding family, marriage and procreation were essentially favourable to population increase.

The writers of early Greece were more concerned with the formulation of policies and rules for population than with theories about it. Plato and Aristotle discussed the question of the ''optimum'' population with respect to the Greek city-state in their writings on the ideal conditions for the full development of man's potential.

They considered the problem of population size not so much in economic terms, but more from the point of view of defence, security and government. The thought was that population should be self-sufficient, and thus possess enough territory to supply its needs but not be so large as to render constitutional government impossible.

The Romans viewed population questions in the perspective of a great empire rather than a small city-state. They were less conscious than the Greeks of possible limits to population growth and more alert to its advantages for military and related purposes. Perhaps because of this difference in outlook, Roman writers paid less attention to population than the Greeks. Cicero rejected Plato's communism in wives and children and held that the State's population must be kept up by monogamous marriage.

The preoccupation with population growth, the disapproval of celibacy and the view of marriage as primarily and fundamentally for procreation was mainly reflected in the Roman legislation of that time. Particularly the laws of Augustus, creating privileges for those married and having children and discriminating financially against those not married, aimed at raising the marriage and birth rates.

The Hebrew sacred books placed much emphasis on procreation and multiplication and, for this reason, unfruitfulness was regarded as a serious misfortune. In general, Oriental philosophers appear to have favoured fertility and multiplication. An exponent of some of the views on population for the period dating back to some three to four centuries B.C. is *Arthasàstra*, a book written as a guide for rulers and attributed to Kautalya. The work discusses such aspects as the desirability of a large population as a source of military and economic power (although recognizing that the population may become too large); the effects of war, famine and pestilence, and the colonization and settlement of new areas.

Early and medieval Christian writers considered questions of population almost entirely from a moral and ethical standpoint. Their doctrines were mainly populationist but less so than those of Hebrew writers. On the one hand, they condemned polygamy, divorce, abortion, infanticide and child exposure; on the other, they glorified virginity and continence and frowned upon second marriage.

The main arguments in favour of celibate practices are found in the teachings of St. Paul. Some early Christian defenders of ecclesiastical celibacy resorted to economic arguments not unlike some of those later used by Malthus. Referring to the growth of the known world's population, they attributed want and poverty to this cause and cited pestilence, famine, war, etc. as nature's means of reducing excess population.

The prevailing tendency, however, was to favour, as in earlier times, population growth. The high mortality which was found everywhere and the constant threat of sudden depopulation through famine, epidemics and wars predisposed most writers towards the maintenance of a high birth-rate. The opposition to birth control, for instance, was based not only on church doctrine but also on a fear of depopulation.

The views of Muslim authors on population resemble those of the Hebrew and Christian authors. Special mention should be made, however, of the interesting but long unrecognized work by Ibn Khaldoun, an Arab author of the fourteenth century. His opinions are noteworthy in two respects.

In the first place, he held that a densely settled population was conducive to higher levels of living since it permitted a greater division of labour, a better use of resources and military and political security.

Secondly, he maintained that a State's periods of prosperity alternate with periods of decline and that cyclical variations in the population occur in rhythm with these economic fluctuations. Favourable economic conditions and political order stimulate population growth by increasing natality and checking mortality. In the wake of these periods of economic progress come luxury, rising taxes and other changes which in several generations produce political decline, economic depression and depopulation.

At the dawn of the modern era, the emergence of the nation-states and the related issue of power led mercantilist writers to emphasize once again the advantages, both political and economic, of a large population. Malthus's contrary theory had its roots in political, economic and social issues which existed during his time. The same can be said of Marxist views on population.

More recent developments in population theories have been influenced predominantly by two factors. The first of these was the upsurge of population growth, especially in the developing countries. This fact has created a need for a better understanding of the factors in population growth. Secondly, the nearly universal preoccupation with the problems of development has called for a considerably more penetrating theoretical framework for assessing the interrelations between population and economic and social development.

The search for an acceptable population theory has thus gained importance. If such a theory could be elaborated, it would provide a better insight into the development process, and could constitute a basic element in policy-making and planning for development.

UNESCO Courier 1974 7-8

Mercantilism is the doctrine that a country's economy is important and should be strengthened by protecting industries through tariffs, increasing foreign trade and emphasizing manufactured exports. The possession of colonies as a source of raw materials is seen as an advantage, and the operation of armies to maintain these colonies a necessity. According to this doctrine, large populations are an asset, for they provide a labour supply, markets and troops as demanded.

Malthus believed that populations tended to grow too fast to be supported adequately by available resources. He forecast eventual disaster if populations kept on increasing.

Marxist population beliefs are guided by the principle that wealth is the product of the efforts of the workers, and that if more wealth is required then more workers are also required. These beliefs are broadly populationist in nature.

DISCUSSION AND RESEARCH

1. Which philosophers and writers argue in favour of population growth? What are their reasons?
2. Which philosophers and writers argue against population growth? What are their reasons?
3. What factors appear to influence a society's attitudes toward population growth? Give examples with your answer.

China's efforts to control its population growth have led to its controversial "one-child policy."

Marilyn MacKenzie

About the year 1800, some European countries began to count their citizens. However, many census-takers were unable to count everyone accurately, and sometimes they did not go to remote places. Accordingly, early census figures were only approximately correct. Even today, no one knows exactly how many people there are in the world, and census-taking is still somewhat inaccurate or infrequent in many countries. For example, China has had only two full censuses this century. The first one (in 1953) reported a population of 574 205 940, while the second one (in 1982) reported a population of 1 008 175 290, several million more than Chinese experts predicted. Most countries still use "best estimates" instead of accurate counts in many instances. Fig. 2-2 gives the accepted UN and other estimates of world and continent populations since 1800.

Earth's population estimated to hit 5 billion today

WASHINGTON (AP) —
Somewhere on Earth today, the world's five billionth person will be born, say experts at the U.S.-based Population Institute.

If true, the new milestone will come just 10 to 12 years after the fourth billionth person checked in. But not all experts agree today is the day.

Carl Haub, a demographer at the private Population Reference Bureau, noted United Nations estimates indicate the five billion mark won't be reached until about next March. Other statisticians have said the milestone may have already quietly passed, since many countries simply do not keep very good track of their populations.

Associated Press, 1986 7 7

Fig. 2-2
Population totals, 1800-1980, and estimates, 1990-2000

	1800	1850	1900	1920	1940	1960	1970	1980	1990*	2000*
Africa	95	98	130	141	176	270	344	470	635	853
Asia	596	698	886	966	1212	1645	2056	2579	3058	3549
Europe (1)	192	274	423	487	573	639	705	749	789	822
Latin America	21	33	63	91	131	213	283	364	459	566
North America	6	26	82	117	146	199	228	248	274	299
Oceania	2	2	6	9	11	16	20	23	26	30
World Total	**912**	**1131**	**1590**	**1811**	**2249**	**2982**	**3632**	**4433**	**5241**	**6119**

(1) includes USSR

* = estimate

Source: For information up to 1900, an average of:
   Carr-Saunders, *World Population*, 1922; and Willcox, *Studies in American Demography*, 1940;
   For information after 1900:
   UN, *Demographic Yearbook*, 1962; UN, *Statistical Yearbook*, 1973; and UNESCO, *Statistical Yearbook*, 1983.
Note: all figures are millions

STATISTICAL ANALYSIS

4. Obtain some 4-cycle semi-log graph paper (see Appendix 4), and plot on it seven time-series graph lines, one for each of the six continents and one for the world total, as shown in Fig. 2-2. For clarity use seven different colours, and label each line with its correct name directly against the end of each line. Do not use a legend.

What are the chief points that emerge from the graph?

What explanations can you suggest 1) for recent differences in slope (and therefore in growth rates) among the different lines, and 2) for the changes that have occurred over time in each of the lines separately?

5. Taking 1900 as the base year, so that we get figures for the twentieth century only, use the data in Fig. 2-2 to calculate index numbers (see Appendix 4) for 1980 for each of the six continents and for the world total. For example, the index number for the growth of Africa's population from 1900 (1900 = 100) to 1980 is (470/130) × 100, or 362. Index numbers tell you more precisely than a line graph just how quickly the populations of the different continents have been increasing this century. Why do you think North America has grown at a faster rate than Asia? Why do you think Europe has grown so slowly?

The Reasons for Present-Day Concern

World population figures show that the population of the world is quickly increasing. Rapid population growth is a major concern today. This concern exists for several reasons. Perhaps the most basic reason is that the world seems unable to feed its present population satisfactorily, and a growing population will increase the problem. Some people foresee massive food shortages and disastrous famines on a global scale.

There are several other causes of concern. It is feared that more people will mean more industry, leading to exhaustion of the world's resources, especially minerals and fossil energy. Some people are worried that there will be too few jobs and too many unemployed people if population growth continues. Others foresee mass migrations as people move from areas that seem to offer little to areas that appear to be wealthy. There may even be conflict as different parts of the world attempt to

There is an old African proverb, "Land feeds people, people eat land." What do you think it means?

Fig. 2-3
Variations in birth rates throughout the world

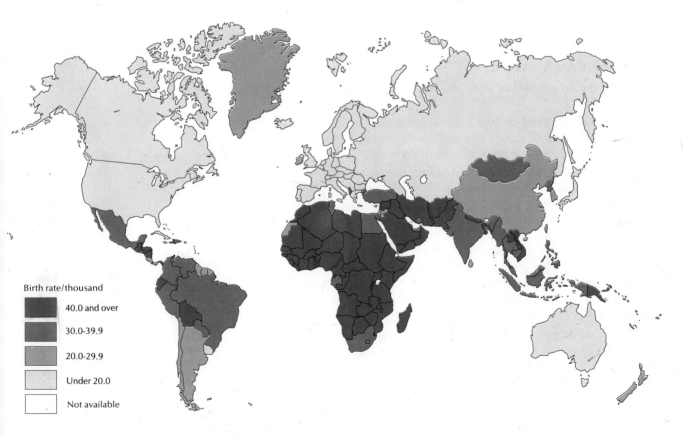

Birth rate/thousand

- 40.0 and over
- 30.0-39.9
- 20.0-29.9
- Under 20.0
- Not available

protect their wealth. Taken together, these worries constitute a basic concern about the quality of life on a global scale.

In later chapters we will discuss in detail quality of life and other population-related concerns such as food, jobs, migration, energy supplies and world development. For the moment, it is sufficient to be aware that these issues are related to rapid population growth. In the next section we will examine some factors leading to population growth.

The Causes of Population Growth

The most obvious cause of population growth is a high birth rate. Column D of Appendix 3 shows you the latest available data regarding birth rates for the world's countries. You can see that the figures vary considerably, from a high of 53.8/1000 (53.8 births per thousand people per year) for Kenya to a low of 10.1/1000 for West Germany. The map in Fig. 2-3 also shows these data. It is an example of a "graded-shading" map, where the graded intensity of the shading represents the pattern of variations in the data being mapped.

There are many reasons for high birth rates throughout much of the world. A basic reason is security. Many countries have no pensions

STATISTICAL ANALYSIS

6. a. Write an account of what you notice about the distribution plotted in Fig. 2-3.

  b. Explain in terms of your existing knowledge of the world what you think might be the causes of high birth rates in so many countries and the causes of low birth rates in others.

7. The *Rule of 72* is a useful formula for calculating the time it takes a quantity to double. The formula is $d = (72/i)$, where d is the number of years for doubling to occur, 72 is the formula constant, and i is the annual percentage rate of increase. For example, if a country has an annual population increase rate of 1.6%, then its doubling time is $d = (72/1.6)$, or 45 years. By using this formula and the population increase rates in Column H of Appendix 3, decide which countries will most likely double their populations before the year 2025. When you have identified the countries, shade them in on a world map similar to that in Appendix 4.

  a. What do you notice about the plotted distribution?

  b. What sort of relationship is there between your map and the map in Fig. 2-3?

  c. Are there any anomalies that need investigation? If so, research the possible explanations.

or social security systems to support their older citizens. In these societies, people must depend upon their children to support them in their old age. The need to ensure that some children will survive long enough to support their aging parents does much to guarantee higher birth rates in such cultures.

Another reason for higher birth rates is the desire to have extra help in the fields or an extra wage-earner in the family. Much of the world does not have a high level of mechanization, and extra help in the fields is often valuable, especially if it is an unpaid member of the family. Equally useful are family members who can work as extra wage-earners and raise a family's standard of living. Other reasons for high birth rates in some parts of the world are the traditional domestic regard in which women are held in many societies and the often accompanying male view that large families indicate both virility and the ability to provide. Also, in some countries, there are religious reasons for large families, while in others military or strategic considerations cause governments to favour large families.

While high birth rates (over 40/1000) seem to be the main cause of rapid population growth, they do not by themselves explain the population explosion. Indeed, birth rates were high for centuries in all societies around the world and yet there was no population explosion. Population growth has become a concern only in the last two hundred years and, ironically, it is also during this period that many countries have for the first time reduced their birth rates. Clearly, there is more to population growth than just high birth rates.

Attempts to improve the economic and social status of women throughout the world have so far had their most significant impact in both Western and Eastern Europe and in North America. Elsewhere, they have had much less impact. For example, Islamic inheritance laws allow a female only one-half of the share allowed to a male.

At 44.8/1000, Mozambique has one of the highest birth rates in the world. These children are participating in an educational project sponsored by the International Red Cross.

Canadian Red Cross/Bob Shearer

For thousands of years, birth rates were high; but because death rates also were high the world's population grew only slowly. If a couple had ten children, three might die at birth or in infancy, another three of childhood diseases and two more of plague or warfare. This would leave only two to look after their parents and carry on the generations. Large families were therefore the norm. If a few more children were able to survive into adulthood, the population would still grow slowly.

There was a slight increase in the birth rates of most early industrializing countries about two hundred years ago, caused perhaps by better food and health care. However, the basic reason for the start of the population explosion was not that people began to have larger families but that more children lived to be adults and have families of their own. Death control, brought about by better health care, better hygiene, and better food all helped more young people to survive to child-bearing age. In the example above, therefore, of the original ten children born perhaps only one or two would die as children. Meanwhile, the improved health care, hygiene and food supplies that were available to children were also available to adult women, extending for many of them their own lives and child-bearing years, so that many more women were able to have

Urban families, like their rural counterparts, often have more children to share in family work and support. These children – called *guambras* – in Quito, Ecuador, sell candy, newspapers and other goods at the city's bus terminal.

The first country to apply technology to industrialize on a large scale was the UK. It was quickly followed by Germany and the USA.

more children. Such changes occurred first in Europe and North America, but now have spread to every country in the world.

When the birth rate remains high while the death rate declines the population begins to grow rapidly. It continues to grow rapidly just so long as birth rates remain significantly higher than death rates. In every country of the world, death rates have historically declined before birth rates, creating a situation popularly called the "population explosion." In some countries, where death control occurred over 100 years ago, birth rates have subsequently declined, and the population explosion has been contained. These countries are mainly in Europe and North America.

In many other countries, where death rates have only recently declined, birth rates remain high. The gap between birth and death rates is technically called the *natural increase rate*, expressed as so many (additional) people per thousand of the (existing) population. The larger it is, the faster the population is growing. Europe and North America experienced their periods of fastest population growth from 50–100 years ago; much of the rest of the world is experiencing it now.

STATISTICAL ANALYSIS

8. Examine the death rate data in Column E of Appendix 3. In nearly all cases it is lower than the birth rate. The difference, the natural increase rate, is given in Column F. Draw a graded shading map to illustrate the world pattern of natural increase (NI) data, in five classes:

30.0/1000 and over	very bright red
20.0/1000–29.9/1000	bright red
10.0/1000–19.9/1000	pale red
0.0/1000– 9.9/1000	very pale red
under 0.0/1000	pale blue

What explanations can you suggest for any differences you find between this map and the one in Fig. 2-3?

9. The map that you drew in assignment 8, showing where population is exploding the fastest, does not give you a full picture. It omits any reference to the size of the population.
   An extra 32.0/1000 in Nigeria, which has a population of 91 178 000, will produce more people in a year than the same rate of 32.0/1000 will produce in Malawi, which has a population of only 7 056 000. Indeed, Nigeria will produce an additional 2 917 696 people (91 178 × 32.0), which is almost thirteen times as many as Malawi's 225 792 (7 056 × 32.0). What we need, therefore, is a map showing absolute quantities, so that we can see where absolute population growth will be largest. This will complement the map in assignment 8 and help to give you a fuller picture. First, calculate the *population impact factor*

(i.e., the approximate number of additional people who will be created annually in each country), using the data in Columns A and F of Appendix 3. To do this, multiply the number of thousands in the population by the NI rate, as shown above for Nigeria and Malawi. Recognize the limited accuracy of these figures, for as the base enlarges over the years so will the number of additional people; but you would need a computer to do these calculations. When you finish, group your results into four classes and draw a graded shading map.

a. What should the title of this map be?

b. What do you conclude regarding the distribution of impact?

10. A country with a very high rate of natural increase will tend to have a high percentage of young children in its population. The exact percentage can be well illustrated by a *population pyramid*, as shown in Fig. 2-4(b). In a population pyramid, the bottom bar shows the percentage of the population that is under five years old, the next bar the percentage of the population between five and ten years old, and so

Fig. 2-4a

Age and sex percentages for six selected countries (M = male, F = female)

	A		B		C		D		E		F		
	Kenya		South Korea		Japan		East Germany		?		?		
Age	M	F	M	F	M	F	M	F	M	F	M	F	Age
85	0.3	0.3	0.0	0.1	0.2	0.1	0.2	0.6	0.1	0.1	0.3	0.6	85
80	0.3	0.3	0.1	0.2	0.5	0.4	0.6	1.3	0.1	0.2	0.5	0.9	80
75	0.2	0.2	0.1	0.4	0.8	1.0	1.3	2.3	0.3	0.3	0.8	1.3	75
70	0.2	0.2	0.4	0.7	1.1	1.5	1.7	3.0	0.4	0.5	1.3	1.7	70
65	0.7	0.5	0.7	1.0	1.5	1.9	1.6	2.9	0.6	0.6	1.7	2.2	65
60	0.7	0.7	1.0	1.2	1.8	2.2	1.4	2.4	0.7	0.8	2.1	2.4	60
55	0.9	0.9	1.4	1.6	2.1	2.7	1.9	3.1	1.0	1.0	2.4	2.7	55
50	1.2	1.2	1.6	1.9	3.0	3.1	2.7	3.1	1.3	1.3	2.5	2.7	50
45	1.4	1.5	2.3	2.4	3.4	3.5	3.2	3.2	1.6	1.6	2.4	2.5	45
40	1.6	1.8	2.9	2.8	3.6	3.6	4.0	4.0	2.0	2.0	2.5	2.6	40
35	1.9	2.1	3.0	2.9	3.9	4.0	2.8	3.0	2.4	2.4	3.0	3.3	35
30	2.6	2.7	3.5	3.3	4.6	4.6	3.3	3.0	2.9	2.9	3.8	3.9	30
25	3.4	3.5	4.1	4.1	3.9	3.8	4.0	3.8	3.6	3.5	4.3	4.3	25
20	4.2	4.5	5.5	5.3	3.4	3.3	4.2	3.9	4.5	4.4	4.7	4.7	20
15	5.6	5.8	5.7	5.5	3.6	3.5	4.2	4.1	5.4	5.3	4.7	4.6	15
10	6.9	6.7	6.1	5.7	3.9	3.7	3.6	3.5	6.5	6.2	4.1	3.9	10
5	8.2	8.1	6.1	5.7	4.4	4.2	2.7	2.7	7.6	7.4	3.8	3.6	5
0	9.4	9.3	5.8	4.9	3.7	3.5	3.4	3.3	9.4	9.1	3.7	3.5	0

Source: UN *Demographic Yearbook,* 1984.

on, with the percentage of the very oldest people (85 and over) in the top bar. Using the data for Country E in Fig. 2-4(a), construct a population pyramid.

a. What relationship does the shape of your pyramid have to those already drawn in Fig. 2-4(b)?

b. Which named country is it most similar to?

Fig. 2-4b
Four sample population pyramids illustrating an evolutionary sequence

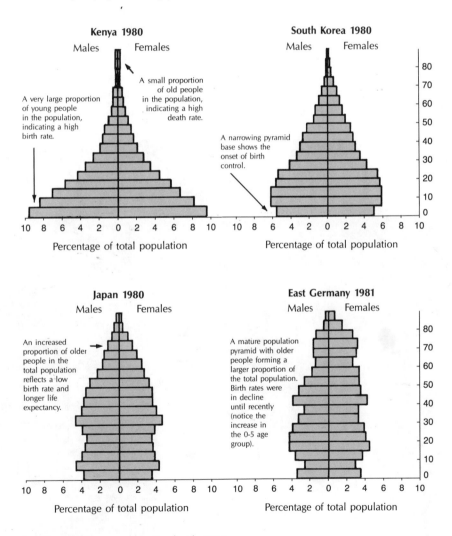

Source: UN *Demographic Yearbook*, 1984.

Malthusianism

About 1800, industrialization began to take hold in Europe; agriculture was becoming modernized, and people increasingly left their farms and villages to live in towns and work in factories. The migration to the towns, a movement still occurring around the world, produced for the first time highly visible concentrations of people. Some theorists began to worry about population growth and, partly as a result of this, census-taking grew in popularity.

Some present-day world cities are incredibly huge by past standards. For example, Mexico City has about 17 million people, most of whom have come from the rural areas of Mexico.

Among the most important of these early theorists was the Englishman Thomas Robert Malthus, who wrote a book forecasting the possibility of widespread starvation. Malthus believed that the birth rate would grow faster than food supplies could increase, and that the surplus people would die from one cause or another. Malthus held that the population would tend to increase at a *geometric rate*, which means that they would multiply by a constant factor (for Malthus, the factor was 2) in each successive generation. Meanwhile, food supplies would increase at only an *arithmetic rate*, thereby merely adding the same quantity over each

"A highly visible concentration of people." A street scene in Jaipur, India.

John Molyneux

comparable time period. The following chart shows how geometric population growth would outstrip the arithmetic growth of food production.

	Periods of time (*e.g.*, *generations*)				
	A	**B**	**C**	**D**	**E**
population (*geometric*)	1	2	4	8	16
food (*arithmetic*)	1	2	3	4	5

Obviously, this situation could not continue for long. During Periods A and B, the food supply would keep pace with the growth of the population. By Period C, however, some people would be going hungry, since there would be enough food for only three-fourths of the population. By Period D, even more people would be hungry, and some would die of starvation.

DISCUSSION AND RESEARCH

11. In a Period C situation, which sectors of the population do you think will go hungry? Or do you think everyone will be just a little bit hungry?

12. When death by starvation is common, what else is likely to happen?

Famines can occur in large or small countries, wherever the population outgrows its food base (or the food base is damaged for some other reason). The Sahel region across the northern savannas of Africa has periodic but devastating famines, worsened by the unreliability of precipitation in what is naturally a marginal area for food production anyway.

The suggestions you made in answer to question 12 may be the same that Malthus thought of when he first put forward his theory: famine, disease or plague, riots, looting, warfare and the overthrow of governments. They are commonly called the *Malthusian checks on population growth*. These factors effectively prevent a Period E situation from developing; as soon as Period C or D is reached the Malthusian checks kill enough people to return the population to a Period A or B situation. This happened in Ireland between about 1750 and 1850.

Ireland's population grew from about 2 500 000 in 1767 to about 5 400 000 in 1804, and to about 8 100 000 in 1841. According to Butlin ("Prologue to an Irish tragedy," *Geographical Magazine*, 1976 11),

> the causes of this growth, which was not unduly spectacular by contemporary West European standards, are disputed, but explanations include a fall in the age of marriage and a consequently higher birth rate, and a fall in the death rate, variously explained by improved food supplies as a result of the increased cultivation of potatoes and the effect of widespread inoculation against smallpox.

As the Irish diet became more dependent on potatoes as the primary source of nourishment, it also became more vulnerable. When the potato crops of 1845, 1846 and 1848 were destroyed by blight, widespread famine followed.

By 1851, Ireland's population had fallen to about 6 600 000, with death and emigration almost equally responsible for the decline of about 1 500 000 in ten years. Continued emigration has since taken many millions from Ireland and, although its birth rate has been unusually high for Western Europe, it has failed to replace the population it has lost through emigration. Ireland's present population is well below 4 000 000.

As he developed his theory, Malthus considered the problems of famine and plague common in Europe at the time. He failed, however, to foresee the eventual elimination of these problems as the economies of these areas grew. For example, famine and plague have been virtually eliminated from Europe and North America. Recently, two countries which have historically suffered much from famines, India and China, have become largely self-sufficient in food production. Nevertheless, famine and plague are still common in parts of the world, and Malthus's early warnings are widely believed by many Neo-Malthusians today. Read the following article by Isaac Asimov, called "Let's suppose . . . ," and compare it with the extracts from "Population problem" by Donald Warwick.

India has been supplying food aid to the Sahelian countries in recent years.

Let's suppose . . .

A tale for the year 3550 A.D.
by ISAAC ASIMOV

Suppose the whole world became industrialized and that industry and science worked very carefully and very well. How many people could such a world support? Different limits have been suggested, but the highest figure I have seen is 20 billion. How long will it be before the world contains so many people?

For the sake of argument, and to keep things simple, let's suppose the demographic growth rate will stay as it is now at two per cent per annum. At this rate, it will take 35 years for the population to double, so it will take the present world population of 3.8 billion 70 years to reach the 15.2 billion mark. Then, fifteen more years will bring the world population to our 20 billion. In other words, at the present growth rate our planet will contain all the people that an industrialized world may be able to support by about 2060 A.D. That is not a pleasant outlook for only 85 years from now.

Suppose we decide to hope for the best. Let us suppose that a change *will* take place in the next 70 years and that there will be a new age in which population can continue rising to a far higher level than we think it can now. This means that there will be a new and higher limit, but before that is reached, still another change will take place, and so on. Let's suppose that this sort of thing can just keep on going forever.

Is there any way of setting a limit past which nothing can raise the human population no matter how many changes take place?

Suppose we try to invent a real limit; something so huge that no one can imagine a population rising past it. Suppose we imagine that there are so many men and women and children in the world, that altogether they weigh as much as the whole planet does. Surely you can't expect there can be more people than that.

Let us suppose that the average human being weighs 60 kilogrammes. If that's the case then 100 000 000 000 000 000 000 people would weigh as much as the whole Earth does. That number of people is 30 000 000 000 000 times as many people as there are living now.

It may seem to you that the population can go up a long, long time before it reaches the point where there are 30 000 000 000 000 times as many people as there are today. Let's think about that, though. Let us suppose that the population growth rate stays at 2.0 per cent so that the number of people in the world continues to double every 35 years. How long, then, will it take for the world's population to weigh as much as the entire planet?

The answer is — not quite 1 600 years. This means that by 3550 A.D., the human population would weigh as much as the entire Earth. Nor is 1 600 years a long time. It is considerably less time than has passed since the days of Julius Caesar.

Do you suppose that perhaps in the course of the next 1 600 years, it will be possible to colonize the Moon and Mars, and the other planets of the Solar system? Do you think that we might get many millions of people into the other world in the next 1 600 years and thus lower the population of the Earth itself?

Even if that were possible, it wouldn't give us much time. If the growth-rate stays at 2.0 per cent, then in a little over 2 200 years — say, by 4220 A.D. — the human population would weigh as much as the entire Solar system, including the Sun.

We couldn't escape to the stars, either. Even if we could reach them; even if we could reach *all* of them; population would reach a limit. If the growth-rate stays at 2.0 per cent, then in 4 700 years — by about 6700 A.D. — the human population would weigh as much as the entire Universe.

So you see we can't go on forever at the rate we are going. The population rise is going to have to stop somewhere. We just can't keep that 2.0 per cent growth-rate for thousands of years. We just can't, no matter what we do.

Let's try again, and let's be more reasonable. Suppose we go back to considering the density of population on Earth.

Right now, the average density of population on Earth is 25 per km^2. If the population of the world doubles then the average density of population also doubles, since the area of the world's surface stays the same. This means that at a population growth-rate of 2.0 per cent per year, the average density of population in the world will double every 35 years.

In that case, if the growth-rate stays where it is, how long will it take for the average density of population to become 18 600/km^2? Such a density is almost 750 times as high as the present density, but it will be reached, at the present growth-rate, in just about 340 years.

Of course, this density is reached only if human beings are confined to the land surface of the world. Perhaps human beings will learn to live on the bottom of the ocean, or on great platforms floating on the sea. There is more than twice as much ocean surface as there is land surface that would give more room for people.

That wouldn't do much good, however. At the present growth rate, it would take only 45 additional years to fill the ocean surface, too. In 385 years, the average density of population would be 18 600/km^2 over land and sea both. That would be by about 2320 A.D.

But a density of 18 600/km^2 is the average density of population of the island of Manhattan.

Imagine a world in which the average density everywhere, over land and sea alike — *everywhere* — in Antarctica and Greenland, over the oceans and along the mountains, over the entire face of the globe — was equal to that of Manhattan. There would have to be skyscrapers everywhere. There would be hardly any open space. There would be no room for wilderness or for any plants and animals except those needed by human beings.

Very few people would imagine a world like that could be comfortable, yet at the present growth-rate we will reach such a world in only 385 years.

But let's not pick Manhattan. Let's try the Netherlands. It is a pleasant, comfortable nation, with open land and gardens and farms. It has a standard of living that is very high and yet its average population density is 400/km^2. How long would it take for our population to increase to the point where the average density of the surface of the world, sea and land, would be 400/km^2?

The answer is 200 years, by about 2175 A.D.

You see, then, that if we don't want to go past the average population density of the Netherlands, we can't keep our present growth-rate going even for hundreds of years, let alone thousands.

In fact, we might still be arguing in an unreasonable way. Can we really expect to have a world-wide Netherlands in the next 200 years?

No one really believes that mankind can spread out over the ocean bottom or the ocean top in the next 200 years. It is much more likely that man will stay on land. To be sure, there may be some people who would be living off shore in special structures, on the sea or under it. They would make up only a small fraction of all mankind. Almost everybody will be living on land.

Then, too, not every place on land

is desirable. It isn't at all likely that there will be very many people living in Antarctica or in Greenland or in the Sahara Desert or along the Himalaya Mountain range over the next 200 years. There may be some people living there, more people than are living there now, but they will represent only a small fraction of the total population of the Earth.

In fact, most of the Earth's land surface isn't very suitable for large populations. At the present moment, most of the Earth's population is squeezed into that small portion of Earth's land surface that is not too mountainous, too dry, too hot, too cold, or too uncomfortable, generally. In fact, two-thirds of the world's population is to be found on a little over 1/13 of the land surface of the planet. About 2 500 000 000 people are living on 11 000 000 km² of land that can best support a high population.

The average density on the 11 000 000 square kilometres of the best land is 230/km², while the average density on the rest of the land surface is just under 10/km².

Suppose the population continues to increase at the present growth-rate and the distribution remains the same. In that case, after 30 years, the average population density of the less pleasant parts of the Earth will reach the 19/km² figure, but the density of the 11 000 000 square kilometres of best land will be 400/km².

In other words, we will reach a kind of world-wide Netherlands density-figure, for as far as we can go, in only about 30 years.

But will all the world be as well-organized and as prosperous as the Netherlands is now? Some of the reasons why the Netherlands is as well off as it is now, are that it has a stable government, a highly-educated population, and a well-organized industrial system.

This is not true of all nations and they need not expect to be as well off as the Netherlands when they are as crowded as the Netherlands. Indeed, if they have an agricultural way of life and a poorly-educated people, who don't have long traditions of stable government, then a population as dense as that of the Netherlands now is, would only bring misery.

In other words, the world can't keep going at the present growth-rate, even for tens of years, let alone for hundreds or thousands.

The matter of a population limit is not a problem for the future, then. We might just as well realize that the world is just about reaching its population limit *now*.

Of course, this entire argument is based on the supposition that the population growth-rate will stay the same as it is now. If the growth-rate drops, that obviously will give us more time before the limit is reached. If it drops to zero, the limit will never be reached. Even a 1 per cent per year population increase, however, is enough to bring disaster. So we can't just sit back and do nothing. We will have to do something.

This article is taken from *Earth: Our Crowded Spaceship*, New York: John Day Co., 1974. Reprinted by permission of the author.

Population problem

by DONALD P. WARWICK

Population doomsayers commonly present statistical descriptions about the current population situation, project them into the future and argue that the likely pattern in the year 2000 constitutes a "population problem." Such discussions often duck the question of just what makes something a problem, and why the projected demographic growth qualifies under that rubric. Any statement about a "problem" involves at least three elements: *facts*, such as statistical data on the present and past size of the world's population; *values*, or desired states which may be threatened or which may fail to materialize as a result of a given set of developments; and *assumptions* about the relationships between a given set of facts or projections and one or more values.

To make a convincing case that demographic growth is a problem, the analyst must present solid facts or reasonable projections about present and future numbers of people, indicate the values, such as survival, freedom, or economic growth, that will be jeopardized by such growth, and show just how population growth will affect the values at stake. It is not enough simply to pronounce that a doubling of the world's population will automatically imperil human freedom, cause revolutions, or produce mass famines. If one wishes to pass from scare-mongering to responsible social predictions, it is imperative to document the specific connections between population size or distribution and a given value, such as survival. We know from other efforts at social forecasting, including earlier predictions about the dire consequences of stabilized population growth, that these exercises easily lend themselves to the projection of one's fears or fantasies onto a far-removed landscape. Further, the task of those who would argue for a "population problem" is not complete until they show why, from a moral standpoint, it is undesirable for a given value to be threatened. There is not much debate on the desirability of avoiding famines, but when it comes to the preservation of the political stability of authoritarian regimes, the value is very much open to question. In short, it is a form of intellectual sloth to proclaim the existence of a population problem without stating concretely the facts, values, and assumptions that underlie this assertion.

The greatest drawback to most discussions of "the population problem" is a failure to set forth the values threatened by demographic growth, and to show why such threats are problematic. Most of us would agree that the carrying capacity of the earth is finite, and that there would be an ultimate threat to the survival of the species if population should continue to double every thirty years. But since we are nowhere near that limit, and since it is very unlikely that the present rates of growth will continue for the next several hundred years, a breakdown in carrying capacity is usually not the issue. The values more commonly cited to demonstrate the existence of a problem include economic growth, nutrition, the ability of governments to provide such services as schools and housing, maternal and child health, and political stability.

But careful research into the relationships between population growth and almost any one of these values raises doubts about the existence of a straightforward problem even at the factual level. For example, despite dozens of treatises to the contrary, it is by no means evident that rapid population growth has a negative effect on economic growth. The debate continues among economists working in the field, but at this time it would be fallacious to argue that the bulk of the evidence clearly supports one or another position. The most we can say with any surety is that the relationships between population and economic growth are complex, and may well vary according to region, the type of political system, and similar noneconomic factors. The same is true for the relations between population growth and political stability. Rapid growth may indeed increase the pressures on a political system, for example, by raising the demands for public services in urban areas, but whether this turns out to be a healthy challenge or a crippling crisis depends on many other factors, including the legitimacy of the government, its economic resources, and the capacity of the rulers to govern. Similar ambiguities arise with almost every area of value used to define a problem.

A related fallacy is seen in the tendency to approach population questions in global rather than national terms, or to choose those national examples which best fit one's preconceptions about a problem. Again, when the question is the ultimate carrying capacity of the earth, a global focus is essential, but this has not been the predominant emphasis. To the extent that population problems are experienced, they are experienced mainly at the level of the nation-state. And it was clear at the World Population Conference at Bucharest that the countries of the world present a great diversity in population structure. Partly because this country neatly fits the preconceptions of those who would have us believe in a "population crisis," India has been by far the most common example in the population literature. Recently it has been joined by Bangladesh. If Bucharest did nothing else, it helped to show these two countries do not, in fact, represent the wide range of conditions found in Asia, Africa, and Latin America. Argentina, for example, is, like India, a large country, but most observers, including its own government, would consider it underpopulated in certain respects. To speak of impending demographic catastrophes for this country, which has experienced extensive rural depopulation in recent years and which is now actively seeking immigrants, is almost laughable. Similarly, within the African continent there are several countries or parts of countries whose "problem," especially as defined by the families involved, is sterility rather than excessive fertility. To lump all of these variegated situations together in all-encompassing statements about a "world population problem" is to show symptoms of demographic simple-mindedness.

Reprinted by permission of the author.
The Chelsea Journal 1975 12

DISCUSSION AND RESEARCH

13. For what reasons could the author of "Let's suppose . . ." be described as a modern Malthus?

14. "We will have to do something," says Isaac Asimov. What do you suggest?

15. While Asimov believes we have to do something about the growing numbers of people in the world, Donald Warwick says that talking about world population is "simple-mindedness," and that each country must be considered separately. Is either one of these authors right? Are they both right? Give reasons for your answers.

16. Donald Warwick notes that some values, such as political stability, may be threatened by continued population growth. He thereby defines the problem primarily as an attack on existing values rather than as a matter of survival. Of the values he mentions, which do you think would be the first to be abandoned as population pressure mounts? Which do you think would be the last? Would your answers be the same for different societies? If so, why? If not, why not?

17. Why can't people simply move from overpopulated parts of the world into underpopulated parts? Give examples of the problems that might arise.

Is There a Population Problem?

The challenge offered by population growth in the near future will concern the ability of the earth and its people to provide enough resources to support a steadily growing population. This challenge will also extend to the ability and willingness of society to organize itself and its use of resources to provide more than a deteriorating quality of life for its members. In this sense, global population growth presents a moral as well as a technological challenge. If these cannot be met, there will certainly be a crisis.

Is such a crisis likely to occur? Are our future options limited to choosing between an overcrowded famine-prone world or a world whose population is restricted but well-fed? We shall return to this general topic later in this chapter. First, let us look at some possible solutions to the population problem.

It is in remembering that statistics represent the lives of individual people that we perceive technological challenges become moral challenges as well.

They are demonstrably not being met in all parts of the world.

Possible Solutions

Reduced Birth Rates

Malthusian checks are one answer to the problem of population growth, and they are at work in some parts of the world today. However, while famine and disease kill millions of people, they do not affect the population growth of every country. A look at Column F of Appendix 3

Fig. 2-5
Selected examples of birth rates, 1780-1980

Year	Canada	France	Italy	Japan	Sweden	UK	USA
1780	—	—	—	—	35.7	—	—
1790	—	—	—	—	30.5	—	—
1800	—	32.9	—	—	28.7	—	—
1810	—	31.8	—	—	33.0	—	—
1820	—	31.7	—	—	33.0	—	55.2
1830	—	29.9	—	—	32.9	—	—
1840	—	27.9	—	—	31.4	32.0	51.8
1850	45.0	26.8	—	31.0	31.9	33.4	—
1860	40.0	26.2	38.0	31.0	34.8	34.3	44.3
1870	37.0	25.9	36.8	32.0	28.8	35.2	—
1880	34.0	24.6	33.9	34.0	29.4	34.2	39.8
1890	30.0	21.8	35.8	34.0	28.0	30.2	—
1900	30.0	21.3	33.0	35.0	27.0	28.7	32.3
1910	29.0	19.6	33.3	35.0	24.7	25.1	30.1
1920	25.0	21.4	32.2	35.0	23.6	25.5	27.7
1930	21.0	18.0	26.7	35.0	15.4	16.3	21.3
1940	25.0	13.6	23.5	37.0	15.1	14.1	19.4
1950	28.0	20.5	19.6	19.5	16.5	15.8	24.1
1960	27.0	17.9	18.1	17.0	13.7	17.1	23.7
1970	17.4	16.7	17.6	13.0	13.5	16.3	18.4
1980	15.5	14.8	11.2	13.7	11.7	13.5	16.2

Note: 1. Reliable data are unavailable for some of the earlier years.

2. There are no data for the less developed countries, so none can be included in the table.

Source: B.R. Mitchell, *European Historical Statistics, 1750-1970*; *Japan Statistical Yearbook, 1977*; *Historical Statistics of the US*, Bicentennial edition; Urquhart & Buckley, *Historical Statistics of Canada*; *The World Almanac*, 1982.

reveals that many countries which are not unduly affected by famine and disease still have very low rates of natural increase. Examine the birth rates for these countries in Column D. Lower birth rates explain the low rates of natural increase in these countries.

The histories of the birth rates of several countries indicate that when they have changed they have usually declined. For example, Canada's birth rate was 45/1000 in 1850, while it was down to 15.5/1000 in 1980. More details are shown in Fig. 2-5.

The reasons for declining birth rates are complex and not fully understood. Some of the possible causes include better birth control methods, better education, more job opportunities for women, more machinery to replace human labour, better pensions, later marriages, easier divorce, and preferred childless lifestyles.

The following articles illustrate some of the reasons people give for a falling birth rate.

One of the great population debates of the last 20 years has been whether to sponsor family planning as a stand-alone policy, or to build family planning into a complete strategy of socio-economic development. In some places a policy of family planning has not been agreed upon as a national goal. The current trend is toward the development of comprehensive strategies.

STATISTICAL ANALYSIS

18. Plot the data in Fig. 2-5 as a multiple line graph (see Appendix 4). What do you notice?

NEW DELHI (AP) —
Easwari Subramaniam, a farmer's wife and mother of two children in a remote south Indian village, is "the envy of all women" in the country, the government says.

For one thing, 32-year-old Subramaniam cannot have any more babies. She was sterilized in return for the official payment of $16 and five state lottery tickets — a newly created incentive of India's revived birth control program.

Then, when the July ticket was drawn, Subramaniam won the $10,000 first prize.

Subramaniam's own reaction to her good fortune has not yet reached New Delhi, 2,090 kilometres (1,300 miles) from her home village of Mankuttaipalayam. But the Health Ministry was quick to declare her a symbol of "a new era in the family welfare program."

Associated Press, 1986 7 13

The World Fertility Survey is one of the best examples of carefully structured research work showing the complex interrelationships between one aspect of population and other variables. The Survey demonstrates the truth of several assumptions — that fertility goes down as status in society goes up, for example — and refines some others. Employment for women and low fertility have generally been found to be linked, but the World Fertility Survey showed that women who had worked at some time had fewer children than those who had never worked, and that the type of occupation is important. Agricultural work apparently has little effect on fertility compared with blue-collar employment, while white-collar and professional women have the smallest families.

Literacy and level of education affect not only the number of children a woman has but their chances of survival. Children of illiterate women in Latin America, for example, have a risk factor 3.5 times that of children whose mothers have had ten or more years of education. The probability of death between birth and the age of two declines steadily as the mothers' level of education rises.

Research and experience in the 1970s seem to show that the aim of reducing both birth and death rates in developing countries is best served by paying attention to the education and employment of women, to access to health and family planning services and to changes in attitudes to family formation.

UNESCO Courier 1982 8 9

Kingsley Ferguson, a psychologist at the Clarke Institute of Psychiatry, says it isn't instinctive to want children. It's a learned attitude encouraged by historical necessity, societal pressures and strong religious beliefs, he says.

Because of high infant mortality before this century, couples often had as many children as possible to guard against not having enough children to farm the land or work to help feed the family. Even if a couple didn't want children, birth control methods weren't reliable. And for some couples, a belief that each child was a "soul for Christ" discouraged any thoughts of conscious childlessness.

Most of us still conform. People still yearn for immortality through their children.

But circumstances have changed. Couples today have choices. And there are those, like the Chambers and Ken and Wendy Melbourne, who make conscious decisions to remain child free.

Married for 17 years, the Chambers made their decision gradually. After they married they began to save for a home, and when they had enough for a down payment, they bought a condominium where children weren't allowed. Years later, when they had enough money to buy a house with a yard, they bought a cottage on a cliff instead. They started getting hooked on travelling, and got used to a free, easy and exciting lifestyle that gave them immense pleasure.

"After a while we realized we were doing things that weren't conducive to having children," says Donna, who has one sibling. Buying a condo with white shag carpet is a case in point.

"We realized that we had a happy lifestyle, and we didn't feel having children would make it happier. We like our life the way it is."

Reprinted with permission —
The Toronto Star Syndicate 1986 4 5

DISCUSSION AND RESEARCH

19. The birth rates in some countries have been falling. From your reading of the different articles, what values have helped to cause this decline?

20. It is also clear from the clippings that birth rates have not changed in isolation; other aspects of life have also changed. Identify some of these "other aspects," and try to decide through discussion and research which, if any, must change if birth rates are to fall.

The Birth Control Controversy

Arguments about birth control range over its essential desirability and over the techniques for its implementation.

On one side are those who regard birth control as unnecessary, and perhaps as undesirable. Their views are often called *pronatalist*. Individuals, groups and nations who hold such views may do so for religious, military, political or economic reasons. For example, Islamic and Roman Catholic societies generally oppose birth control because it is contrary to their essential religious beliefs. Many pronatalists equate military or political power with a larger population, as is the case in Brazil. In much of Africa, political power is closely related to tribal size. Economically, some pronatalists, as in Malaysia, believe that a larger population provides both a larger labour force and a larger market.

There is also a widespread view among many of the developing countries that birth control is a continuing form of colonialism or imperialism. Such countries consider birth control a "Western" idea, being urged on the developing countries in an attempt to maintain Western dominance in world influence and resource use. They assert that the real problem is underdevelopment, not overpopulation, and that large populations produce more as well as consume more. In general, therefore, pronatalists view additional people as a benefit to society.

Opposing the pronatalists are those who support birth control. They see a world headed for disastrously increasing overuse of resources. They see a deteriorating quality of life in many of the world's famine areas. They see populations too large ever to employ, educate, or provide with adequate health care and other basic needs. They see social and political unrest and, ultimately, they see a world headed for collapse. In some countries they view the question so seriously that they promote government enforcement of birth control measures (e.g., compulsory sterilizations and vasectomies). Such policies, however, raise concerns over individual human rights.

The contrast between the pronatalists and those who support birth control may be seen in more depth in the following articles.

Samir Amin, an Egyptian, is recorded as saying, "When the Portuguese came to the Congo for the slave trade, they estimated there were a million people there. Three hundred years later, they estimated there was a population of about 300 000. Black nations think of oppression on many levels, both past and present. If the whites ask black nations to reduce their population now, what are blacks to think?"

Ms Rian, midwife at Dong Klang, visits her friends and patients with newly born babies. Thailand adopted a national population policy in 1970, with the aim of reducing the birth rate.

Unicef/Na Pombejr

BANGKOK —

Tek Kor's days as Thailand's one-man population explosion are not over yet.

The 41-year-old meatball vendor and father of 22 arrived here yesterday to undergo a much-publicized operation at a free "vasectomy festival" organized by Thailand's leading family planning campaigner.

But he changed his mind at the last minute, claimed he had been tricked into believing he would be paid a million baht (about $48,000) and drove off with six of his seven wives with a vow to marry No. 8 soon and produce still more children.

Meechai Viravaidya, the organizer of the free vasectomy clinic, had hoped that the conversion of Thailand's "family planning enemy No. 1" would help dispel fears among many Thai men that a vasectomy would result in sexual impotence.

But he denied having offered him any money and said he had no idea where the meatball vendor got the impression he would be paid.

Tek Kor, whose real name is Saisupat Terrapabsakulwong, is from Nakhon Pathom near Bangkok, where he is also known as the Nakhon Pathom Casanova.

He said he had been influenced by letters and cables sent to him by the U.S.-based Club of Life.

The Club of Life, which claims 50,000 members in 40 countries, had told him he would become a "tool" for Meechai's "genocidal" and "treasonous" family planning program.

Tek Kor seemed to echo some of the group's arguments when he declared before leaving the vasectomy clinic set up in a ballroom of a luxury hotel here, "I think ambitious, hard-working people like me should be encouraged to have lots of children to help build the nation."

His first wife, Siem-ung, said that although she was "furious" when a month after marrying Tek Kor, he took a second wife, she learned to live with the situation.

Tek Kor, who says he sleeps with his wives in a rotation system, now plans to marry a farmer's daughter he met eight years ago when he married wife No. 5, who also introduced him to No. 6 and No. 7.

Tek Kor said he needed many children to help him with his meatball business, but he has rejected suggestions that having a large family is merely a clever way of obtaining cheap labor.

From *The Washington Post*, reprinted in
The Toronto Star 1985 7 5

Seventy-three-year-old Raimundo Carnaúba and his wife, Maria Madalena de Sousa, are from Brazil's impoverished northeastern state of Ceará. Maria Madalena has had thirty-two pregnancies, five of which ended in miscarriage. Five children died; twenty-two survive.

"If I had it to do over I would have the same number of children," she says. Her husband, told that the Brazilian government may finally begin to promote family planning in 1984, raises his voice: "The government is stupid. The only one who can determine the number of children in a family is God."

World Press Review 1984 2

A country of continental dimensions such as Brazil, with fabulous natural resources, abundant wealth, and without prejudice in matters of race, colour, or religion, needs a population sufficient to occupy and defend its territory from international greed.

The demographic policy implicit in anti-natalist campaigns judged by some to be absolutely necessary for our development, would result in the stagnation or regression of the growth of our population — we who already exist in such small numbers in a country so large and with inexhaustible resources. A policy of stimulating births thereby assuring more economic development will permit us to have more Brazilian workers, technicians and scientists. In addition to producing consumer and producer goods, with Brazil industrialized, our technicians and scientists will be able to transform our heavy industry partially into an industry capable of producing military goods.

From the military point of view, population is power, and in Brazil, in spite of Malthusian campaigns, population growth has historically served the country in that we have more rapid economic growth than that of countries with low natality, such as Argentina, Chile, and Uruguay.

From *The Brazilian Demographic Problem*,
Escola Superior de Guerra, quoted in Daly,
"Marx and Malthus in N.E. Brazil,"
Reprinted by permission.
Population Studies 1985 7

. . . rapid population growth is a central development problem. Continuing rapid growth on an ever larger base will mean lower living standards for hundreds of millions of people. The main cost of such growth, borne principally by the poor in developing countries, has been, and will continue to be, lost opportunities for improving people's lives.

. . . Why does it put a brake on development? There are three main reasons.

First, it exacerbates the difficult choice between higher consumption now and the investment needed to bring higher consumption in the future. As population grows more rapidly, larger investments are needed just to maintain current capital per person, both physical and human capital — that is to say, a person's education, health, and skills. Otherwise, each worker will have less equipment and skills to work with, and productivity and incomes will stagnate or even fall. Every effort is thus required simply to maintain the status quo . . .

Second, in many countries, increases in population threaten what is already a precarious balance between natural resources and people . . . Where populations are still highly dependent on agriculture, continuing large increases in population can contribute to overuse of limited natural resources, such as land, mortgaging the welfare of future generations . . .

Third, rapid population growth is creating urban economic and social problems that risk becoming wholly unmanageable. Cities in developing countries are growing to a size for which there is no prior experience anywhere . . . The rise in urban population, 60 percent of which is due to natural increase, poses unprecedented problems of management even to maintain, let alone improve, the living conditions of city dwellers.

No one would argue that slower population growth alone will assure progress. But the evidence . . . seems conclusive. Poverty and rapid population growth reinforce each other. Therefore, the international community has no alternative but to cooperate, with a sense of urgency, in an effort to slow population growth if development is to be achieved. But it must be slowed through policies and programs that are humane, noncoercive, and sensitive to the rights and dignity of individuals.

World population has grown faster, and to higher numbers, than Malthus would ever have imagined. But so have world production and income. If we can correct the current mismatch between population and income-producing ability, a mismatch that leaves many of the world's people in a vicious circle of poverty and high fertility, we may yet evade the doom which Malthus saw as inevitable. It is *not* inevitable that history will vindicate his dire prediction of human numbers outrunning global resources. We have a choice.

But that choice must be made now. Opportunity is on our side. But time is not.

From "Address to the National Leaders' Seminar on Population and Development," by A.W. Clausen, President of the World Bank, Nairobi 1984 7 11

A recent review of World Fertility Survey findings in 29 developing countries shows that fertility levels are highest in Africa, where the average total fertility rate (TFR) is 6.7 compared to [an] average TFR of 4.8 in Asia and Pacific countries and 4.6 in Latin America. The average number of children desired is 7.1, in Africa, compared to 4.0 in Asia and Pacific countries and 4.3 in Latin America.

How can this be explained? Why has fertility remained high, or in some cases even risen, in the face of rising education, falling mortality, and some urbanization, factors that caused fertility to decline in other parts of the world? Why is preferred family size universally so high in Africa? What factors explain high fertility and preference for large families? Are the fertility determinants in Africa different from those in other parts of the world?

Based on a study of available social-anthropological and other literature, we wish to put forward two working hypotheses. The first is that the security motive (i.e., search for physical survival of family, clan and tribe) makes for a larger ideal family size in Africa. Some support for this hypothesis can be found in the notion that large numbers in a family or clan may be the only guarantee of security in fragmented, traditional societies where governments have not yet established the protective cover via the rule of law enforced effectively by a mobile, non-partisan, police force. The second hypothesis is that high fertility in Africa reflects the predicament of women. There is strong social pressure on women to marry and produce children, thus extending the kinship network. An intense desire is created for family roles by community praise of the wife and mother and severe censure of the unmarried or childless woman.

From R. Faruqee & R. Gulhati, "Rapid Population Growth in Sub-Saharan Africa," *World Bank Staff Working Paper No. 559* 1983

"In Mexico City, especially among middle-class residents, sexuality . . . has recently been brought into the open to an extent unprecedented in this conservative, Roman Catholic society."

In rural areas in 1975, 15.9 per cent of married women used some form of birth control. By last year that figure had risen to 38 per cent. In urban areas the use of birth control by married women has risen from 45.7 per cent in 1976 to 57.9 per cent last year.

Mexican middle-class women are caught in a tug of war between strict social and religious norms and contemporary ideas about the independence and equality of women.

World Press Review 1983 12

For those people and societies who have decided that birth control is desirable, there often remain many problems, mostly of a social, economic or religious nature. The high rate of infant mortality is one of the greatest barriers to a wider use of birth control in many countries where governments have decided to favour its practice. Until individual parents are convinced that their first two or three children will survive into adulthood, they will likely continue to produce large families. They will also likely continue to produce large families so long as they do not have ready access to birth control facilities. Large families are also likely to continue where they remain the social norm, where boys are more highly regarded by society than girls, and where a family's economic welfare is not harmed by more children. Large families may also continue to exist wherever religious beliefs limit the practice or the types of birth control permitted.

For a variety of reasons, many societies prefer sons to daughters. This causes the birth rate to be significantly higher than if sons and daughters had equal standing, since families produce children until they have the desired number of sons. What reasons can you suggest for the preference for sons? How do you suppose such beliefs can be changed?

The children in this picture are two-year-old twins; the one on the left, a girl, the one on the right, a boy, both raised at home in southern India. The difference in their condition is due to the fact that the boy was nursed first and fed first, his sister getting what was left over.

Unicef

A few of the problems facing the implementation of birth control practices are illustrated in the following articles.

Egypt is facing population bomb

by Vincent J. Schodolski

CAIRO, Egypt —
There are times in this dusty, eroding city of 11 million that the streets become so crowded you secretly hope no one else leaves his house.

Yet by the end of this century, pro-jections say there will be at least 18 million people in Cairo. Egypt's population of 47 million, which grows by 1 million every 9 months, will double in the next 26 years, forecasts say.

"Short of famine and civil war, there is no way of stopping this," said a Western population expert. "I don't even want to think about Egypt with 90 million people." Neither does President Hosni Mubarak.

"If we continue this way, we will have terrible famine, unemployment and terrorism," Mubarak said recently at a conference in Cairo on population control.

Hindered progress

While the country has had a family-planning program for years, the vastness of the problem coupled with the crushing weight of the Egyptian bureaucracy has hindered progress.

In addition, there is a major debate within Egypt about the proper philosophy regarding population control.

Many feel the best way to limit the size of families is to raise the standard of living to the point where people decide on their own that they just want fewer children.

Western experts helping the government with population planning say that this is one means of limiting the number of people, but not the one for Egypt. "This is a very, very, very, slow process," said one. "Egypt just does not have the time for it."

However, a variety of economic, social and religious reasons lead many Egyptians to disagree.

"Large families are one of the requirements of poverty," said Heba Handoussa, a professor of economics at the American University of Cairo. "It is not right to ask a family to have fewer children when they are faced with losing family members they need to survive."

Another element in the debate is the influence of religious and social factors. Islam prohibits certain types of birth control, and abortion is strictly illegal.

While the government has adopted a halfway approach that combines efforts to promote birth control and boost family income, officials concede that time is running out.

"I don't think we can wait until family income rises to a point where they (Egyptians) stop having so many children," said Helmi Bermani, director general for planning at the health ministry. He feels that the efforts the government has undertaken are working.

The government operates thousands of clinics that provide information on family planning in addition to routine medical care. There also are separate clinics run by the social affairs ministry, unions and private organizations.

State-run

However, a study commissioned by the U.S. Agency for International Development (USAID), said that only about 2.4 per cent of Egypt's eligible population of married couples at reproductive age were receiving family-planning help through state programs.

At the moment, the average family has 5.4 children, and to reach the goal of a two-child family that experts feel would give the country a real chance at population control, 70 per cent of Egyptians would have to have access to such services.

While Egyptians are presently able to endure the difficulties of poverty with seemingly endless patience, many Western experts and elements within the government believe that unless something is done quickly to stem the growth of the population, that endless patience may run out.

LONDON —
At a conservative estimate, about 3,000 baby girls are being murdered in China each day. Only the bravest optimist would believe that the situation is not going to get worse.

This holocaust, moreover, is largely the consequence of social engineering run wild: the Chinese government's determination to restrict families to only one child.

There has always been a high incidence of female infanticide in the Chinese countryside, because of the greater value peasant society places on boy children. A recent survey in Anhui province found that there were 3 million more men than women between ages of 25 and 35, and the 1982 census revealed that in the country as a whole there are 106 men to every 100 women.

That means that even in normal times almost half a million little girls were killed each year in China. But these are not normal times.

A recent study published by the Chinese Women's Federation found that in some areas of Anhui province the ratio of female to male babies surviving to one year old has now plummeted to one-to-five.

The researchers found one village where over 40 female babies had been drowned in the past two years. In another village, out of eight babies born in 1982, the three boys had survived, three of the five girls had been drowned, and the other two had been abandoned.

The long-term implications of this are just beginning to dawn on the Chinese authorities. Two years ago Prime Minister Zhao Ziyang called publicly for the protection of "infant girls and their mothers," and the China Youth Rally sagely observed that if the present sex imbalance continued, "there will be a serious social problem in 20 years when a large number of young men will be without spouses." Poor things.

The implications are in fact far greater than the Chinese government has yet publicly acknowledged. It is very likely that the rising tide of crime in Chinese cities, which has led to 7,000–8,000 executions in the past year, is closely connected with the huge pool of 20 million urban youths who are unemployed, mostly male — and, in millions of cases, doomed to life-long celibacy because of the existing sex imbalance.

How violent and unstable a society China will be in 20 years' time if it has 100 million young men in that situation simply beggars the imagination. And there is, moreover, the real prospect of population collapse. The numbers of the next generation depend solely on the number of girls born in this generation.

If the female infanticide rate continues to get worse, it could mean an abrupt and drastic drop in the number of young people coming along to feed and support the teeming millions of older Chinese. No large human society has ever gone through experiences similar to those the Chinese are now preparing for themselves, nor would any sane society want to.

Yet the Chinese are caught in a grim dilemma, for neither do they want to have a population of 1.4 billion by the end of the century — which is what even their present, relatively modest population growth rate of 1.3 per cent would give them.

In the old days, a peasant family whose first child was a girl would usually accept her grudgingly, and go on to try again for a boy. But now only one child is permitted: You can only try again if the little girl dies. And so, in a horrifyingly large number of cases, she is killed.

So far, the "one child" rule is only laxly enforced in the more remote rural areas. Most peasant families still go to two children, and 20 per cent of all rural births last year were third children. But if enforcement improves and more and more peasant families are faced with really severe penalties for going beyond one child, the death rate for female babies is likely to go through the roof.

China must find some way of limiting its population. But a method that leads to a million little girls floating dead in village ponds each year is not the right one.

Gwynne Dyer, *The Toronto Star* 1985 2 17

Not all governments pursuing birth control policies have found the problems impossible to overcome. Sri Lanka is a case in point. As elsewhere, Sri Lanka's first approach to the problem was medical, based primarily on the distribution of contraceptives by doctors and clinics. Not enough people went to the clinics, however, even though the government set up a wide network. The Family Planning Association of Sri Lanka also ran a mobile vasectomy clinic, but clients were few in number.

The next step, as elsewhere, was a massive publicity campaign, trying through appeals to national and self-interest to motivate people to limit their families. The third step was to introduce a commercial marketing element to the first two steps. This wider strategy is now highly successful. It started in 1973 and sells contraceptives and the idea of birth control in the same way most other products or ideas are sold: openly and with ready availability, backed by intensive and ongoing advertising. Small stores were persuaded to carry contraceptives the way they carry soap or tea. The product name chosen, Preethi, means "happiness" in both Sinhalese and Tamil, and it has come to be applied to the entire program.

DISCUSSION AND RESEARCH

21. How would you respond to a person who asserts that (a) the world, or (b) a particular country, needs more people?

22. Suggest the sorts of evidence needed to support the claim that a particular part of the world is overpopulated.

23. How would you define "overpopulation"?

24. Does Canada need more people? Give reasons for your answer.

25. In what ways do your own values differ from those noted in the articles relating to pronatalism and birth control?

National Population Policies

In the *World Development Report 1984* it was noted that 95 nations out of 116 listed provided some form of support for family planning. This support was described as "very strong" or "strong" in only 11 of them: "very strong" in China, Singapore and South Korea, and "strong" in Colombia, El Salvador, Hong Kong, India, Mauritius, Mexico, Panama and Sri Lanka.

There is little agreement about controlling population growth, either in the need for it or in the techniques for implementing it. There are so many different opinions, all backed by strongly held values, that birth control may never become a universal policy. To gain a further sense of the strength of the feelings involved, look at the next reading. It is a statement by the Chinese Ambassador to the United Nations, Li Luye, in response to charges made in the US House of Representatives on 1985 7 10 that China's population policies involved "crimes against humanity."

Population is a serious problem facing the developing countries. China's population has exceeded one billion. For several years in the past, the annual net increase in China's population was over 20 million. Such a sizable increase would have exerted a tremendous pressure on any country, not to mention a developing country still relatively backward culturally and economically. In order to develop our economy and improve the people's living standard, China has, since the early 1970s, pursued a policy of bringing the population growth rate under control in a planned way.

China bases its family planning policy on the actual realities in the country and, in order to show the im-portance it attaches to this policy, has included in its national constitution a provision to the effect that both husband and wife have the duty to practice family planning. Our family planning program is aimed at controlling the population growth rate, improving the quality of the population, making the population growth commensurate with the economic and social development and in harmony with the development of resources and the protection of the environment. This policy is in the interest of the Chinese people and is also in conformity with the plan of action, declarations, and recommendations adopted by the two world population conferences held in 1974 and 1984 respectively. China's family planning policy enjoys the support of its people and has also won the understanding and general support of the international community.

In the past dozen years or so, in accordance with the principle of combining state guidance with popular voluntariness, China has conducted education on population issues among the broad masses, explaining the interrelationship between population and social and economic development, popularizing knowledge about contraception and supplying couples of reproductive age with various kinds of contraceptives free of charge. China has thus achieved some results in the control of population growth, and the annual population growth rate has dropped from 17 per thousand in 1974 to 10.81 per thousand in 1984.

Beginning in 1979, the Chinese Government has called for "One child for one couple." This is a call issued in light of specific conditions of the current historical period and is based on the reality that the base figure of China's population is big and the absolute population growth is high. This is not a state decree or a mandatory rule by the Government. According to the statistics collected at the end of 1984, of the 150 million married women of reproductive age, 28,170,000 (i.e., 18.25 percent) of the total, have only one child and have already received an "Only Child Parents' Certificate." We commend and give awards to families having one child; we advise those couples who wish to have two children to arrange the births with proper intervals. In other words, we encourage late marriage, spacing births, and fewer children. In implementing our family planning program, we emphasize contraception and also allow abortion when contraception fails. There are, of course, unplanned births, but the babies thus born are equally protected by law.

It would have been inconceivable to implement such an unprecedented family planning program in a country with a huge population and achieve considerable success without the voluntary cooperation of hundreds of millions of couples. In such a gigantic undertaking, shortcomings are unavoidable. But once they are brought to our notice, we openly expose and correct them in good time. However, out of ulterior motives, one big power has seen fit to distort and vilify China's population policy by wilfully exaggerating some individual cases of violation of our policy and has even put forward some unreasonable demands interfering with China's internal affairs. We categorically reject these demands. In fact, as we all know, this big power where abortions are not uncommon faces very serious social problems itself with such social crimes as drug traffic and addiction. It would be just as absurd if anyone should conclude from these facts that all these activities are supported by the government of that country.

China is a developing country. In building up the national economy and promoting social progress, it relies mainly on its own efforts while seeking international assistance and support. What makes us feel glad is that the cooperation between the Chinese Government and the United Nations Fund for Population Activities has been very fruitful. We highly appreciate the contribution made by UNFPA under the leadership of Mr. [Rafael M.] Salas toward solving the world population problem. I would also like to take this opportunity to express our heartfelt thanks to all countries, organizations, and personages who have sympathized with and supported our population policy.

I wish to reiterate here that the Chinese Government will as always continue to strengthen cooperation with UNFPA in the field of population and will join the international community in a common effort to overcome all difficulties on the road of advance and will do our part in stabilizing the world's population.

Reprinted from *Population and Development Review 12*, No 1 (March 1986): 162-163

Demographic Transition

As societies provide greater social benefits, such as old age security and more paid jobs for women, they will gradually address many of the reasons people give for having large families. It may be true, as many have asserted, that "development is the best contraceptive."

If so, we might foresee a general reduction in birth rates based on individual choice rather than government policy. This will hold true, however, only if technological and economic development produce the same pattern of social results in each case.

By observing the behaviour of past birth and death rates, researchers have constructed a theoretical "model," called the *demographic transition model*, which projects birth and death rates for a certain period of time.

Fig. 2-6
The demographic transition model

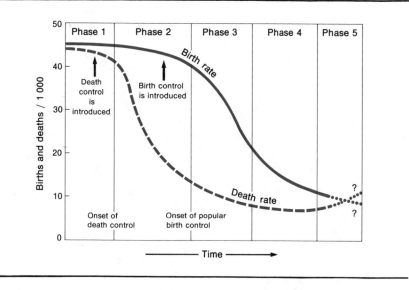

Inductive analysis means taking a series of individual observations and trying to build a general theory using them. Induction builds from particular facts up to a general theory. Its opposite is *deductive analysis*, which means putting forward a general theory and then seeking evidence to test its validity.

The onset of death control means that people generally live longer. Life expectancy is increased, and population pyramids show increasing proportions of older people in the population. In Colombia, for example, life expectancy rose from 45 in 1975 to 63 by 1985. Similar dramatic increases have occurred in other countries in Phases 2 and 3.

The construction of the model (see Fig. 2-6) involves some inductive analysis, and requires testing against the most recent birth and death rate data.

As future birth and death data become available, they may require that the model be modified. Past experience in many parts of the world justifies our present use of the model, and so, for the moment, we will accept it as a framework for analysis and a means of making cautious predictions about the future.

In the demographic transition model, Phase 1 occurs when both birth and death rates are high and apparently uncontrolled. There are no countries still in this phase, since medical aid generally has succeeded in bringing death rates under some form of control.

Phase 2 is marked by a reduction in the death rate as people in a society live longer, and deaths form a diminishing proportion of the total population picture. However, birth rates usually remain high by custom, and the result is a growing difference between the two rates. This is the beginning of the population explosion, which increases in intensity as the difference between the two rates grows. The explosion intensifies because death control does more than permit children to reach child-bearing age; it also allows them to survive right through their fertile years. Phase 2 is thus characterized by rapid population growth as well as by a markedly decreasing average age for the population as more and

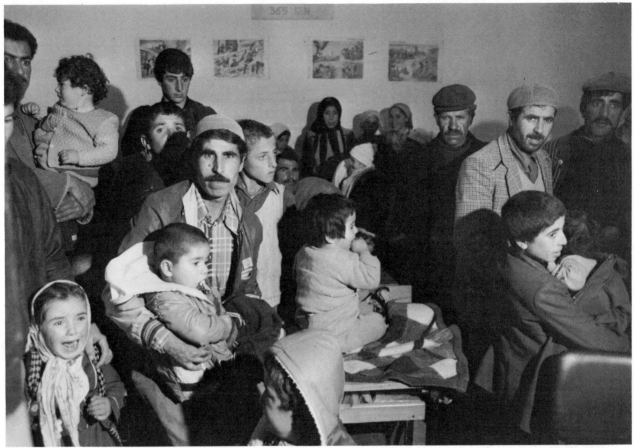

Unicef/John Isaac

more babies are born. The longer Phase 2 lasts, the larger the population becomes.

Phase 3 begins when birth control becomes common enough to cause a significant decline in the birth rate. Then the death rate will usually remain fairly low because the medical aid that originally caused its decline continues. However, the death rate cannot decline forever; death can be postponed, but not escaped. During Phase 3 the population explosion continues, but decelerates as the gap between the birth and death rates diminishes. Note that a slower rate of natural increase may not necessarily reduce population pressure on a country's resource base, because the population base, which exploded through Phase 2, is now much larger.

In Phase 4 both birth and death rates tend to be low and steady. The death rate may rise slightly, because older people now form a larger proportion of the total population. But this is not necessarily true; there may even be "baby booms." Although the details of the situation vary

In three ten-day periods, more than 80% of Turkey's 5 million under-fives were immunized against the diseases that were killing more than 500 Turkish children every week. How will this affect Turkey's population growth rate?

Thailand is an example of a country entering Phase 3. In the mid-1970s its birth rate was close to 43/1000, but by mid-1980s it had dropped to about 32/1000. One reason is the government's determination to extend health care and family planning to all rural areas.

In 1950 there were only about 215 million people over the age of 60 in the world. By 2025 there are expected to be about 1.2 billion.

from country to country, the general trend in Phase 4 is toward low birth and death rates and slow total population growth.

It is possible that Phase 5 will develop more strongly in the future. Death rates may climb above birth rates because of the continued aging of the population, causing a declining total population. West Germany, Denmark and Hungary are already beginning to move into Phase 5, and many other countries, especially in Eastern Europe, are getting close. In *Population Studies* 1985 3 an article titled "Rising Mortality in Hungary" states that the Hungarian government has been trying for 20 years to raise the country's population growth rate and that, while it has had some success in raising the birth rate, these increases have been more than offset by a rising death rate. The article notes that rising death rates also characterize the populations of the USSR, Bulgaria, Poland, Romania and Czechoslovakia, and cites increasing deaths from cancer, heart, respiratory and digestive problems and suicide as the chief reasons. A declining and aging population clearly does not mean the end of worries about the population problem, as the following articles indicate.

One aspect of Britain's changing population structure, the growing proportion of retired and elderly people, is shared by all developed countries. This will progressively extend to the developing world if mortality continues to decline and fertility falls. In traditional societies some five per cent of people are over 65, but modern societies with controlled mortality have 16 per cent or more. In stationary populations that proportion rises to around 30 per cent. In Japan, the rapid fall in fertility is producing an aging population in which the over-65s will increase from nine per cent in 1980 to over 20 per cent by 2020, while Western Europe's over-65s could form 30 per cent of the population by 2030.

In the UK, over 11 million people are over 60. The over-75s are increasing rapidly, from 2.5 to 3.5 million between 1971 and 1996. Many live alone. They are highly concentrated in such 'retirement' areas as North Wales and South Coast, in parts of which they form over 30 per cent of the population; but large numbers are also left in decaying inner city areas. Their particular needs — housing, transport, medical and welfare services especially in the home — are the type of challenge offered by many 'population problems' which should be high on the agenda of national and local government policies.

Reproduced courtesy of *The Geographical Magazine*, London, 1983 8

Many European governments are now concerned about the effects of a diminishing and aging population as they head toward the 21st century.

East Germany pays . . . $450 for the birth of a child. . . . Hungary and Czechoslovakia have put . . . restrictions on their abortion laws. . . .

The U.S.S.R. . . . began encouraging more births in the mid-1970s.

World Press Review 1984 4

- People are growing old faster than children are being born to support them in their old age. In 1950 there were 19 people over 60 and 45 children under the age of 15 for every 100 adults aged 15-59. By 2025 there are expected to be 40 over-60s and only 35 children for every 100 active adults.
- The ILO predicts that there will be 270 million "economically inactive" over 55-year olds in industrialized countries by 2020. That will mean 38 older dependents for every 100 workers — twice as many as in 1950.
- In Austria there is already one pensioner for every two workers.
- The "dependency ratio" in East Asia is expected to double by 2025, when China will have one person over 60 for every three active adults.

UNESCO Courier 1982 10

Fig. 2-7
Canada's birth and death rates, 1850-1980

Year	Births/1000	Deaths/1000
1850	45.0	22.0
1860	40.0	21.0
1870	37.0	19.0
1880	34.0	18.0
1890	30.0	16.0
1900	30.0	13.0
1910	29.0	12.0
1920	25.0	11.0
1930	21.0	10.0
1940	25.0	9.0
1950	28.0	8.0
1960	27.0	7.5
1970	17.4	7.0
1980	15.5	7.2

Source: Urquhart & Buckley, *Historical Statistics of Canada;*
Canada Year Book, 1968 and 1976-77; The World
Almanac, 1982.

DISCUSSION AND RESEARCH

26. What are problems associated with a declining population? Consider the social, political and economic aspects.

STATISTICAL ANALYSIS

27. Using the data in Fig. 2-7, construct a graph according to the demographic transition model, and mark in the phases which you think Canada has passed through since 1850.

28. Using the data for Country F in Fig. 2-4(a), construct a population pyramid. What does it tell you about the rate of population growth in the country? How does it compare with the pyramid you drew for assignment 10? After examining the two pyramids, decide which country you would rather live in. What are the reasons for your choice?

If the transition model holds true, then we should regard the present population explosion as a unique phenomenon, caused by the historic fact that death control has taken effect faster than birth control has. If this is so, then any country in Phase 4 may be safely through the worst

Birth control costs money. The World Bank thinks about $8 billion may have to be spent before the year 2000 to achieve significant declines in birth rates. Contrast this with the estimated $1 000 billion the world currently spends on armaments each year.

of its explosion. For countries in Phase 3, the end of the explosion should be in sight, because their rates of increase are to some extent under control; it will be just a matter of time before these countries reach the relative safety of Phase 4. From the standpoint of population problems (food, housing, jobs, education, health care, social security), the least fortunate countries are those in Phase 2, where death control is well established but birth control is not.

We should now ask ourselves again the question raised earlier in this chapter: is there a population problem? Or is there a problem of development? Who most accurately describes the situation: Asimov or Warwick?

STATISTICAL ANALYSIS

29. Assess the demographic phase of each country in Appendix 3 according to the following criteria:

	Birth rate	**Death rate**
Phase 1	uncontrolled, >40/1000	uncontrolled, >40/1000
Phase 2	uncontrolled, >40/1000	becoming controlled, <40/1000
Phase 3	becoming controlled, 20-40/1000	controlled, <20/1000
Phase 4	controlled, <20/1000	controlled, <20/1000

The figures are guides only. A few countries may not fit neatly into the categories, so use your discretion. When you have decided which phase each country is in, isolate the countries with exploding populations and plot them on a world map. Use a more prominent shading for Phase 2 countries than for Phase 3 countries. You will now be able to see where the population explosion is occurring in the world, which parts are still experiencing the worst effects (Phase 2) and which have passed through the worst (Phase 3). What do you notice about the distribution?

CASE STUDY
KENYA: Population Trends

Kenya's population is currently growing faster than that of any other country in the world. At 39.4/1000 (or almost 4%) per year, Kenya's rate of natural increase is almost twice the world average of 2% per year. The ten countries listed in the 1985 *World Development Report* as having the fastest rates of natural increase are:

Kenya	39.4/1000
Zimbabwe	39.2/1000
Syria	37.5/1000
Honduras	35.3/1000
Guatemala	34.7/1000
Liberia	34.7/1000
Nicaragua	34.4/1000
Iraq	34.0/1000
Belize	33.7/1000
Kuwait	33.6/1000

These ten countries represent the three fastest growing areas of world population: Tropical Africa, the Middle East and Central America. All ten countries are either in Phase 2 or just entering Phase 3 of the demographic transition, which means that their death rates are falling significantly faster than their birth rates (see Fig. 2-8).

In all countries the percent of decline in their death rate between 1960 and 1980 was much larger than the percent of decline in their birth rate. In four countries (Kenya, Syria, Liberia and Iraq), still clearly in Phase 2 of the demographic transition, the decline in the birth rate was very small. Under these conditions population growth in these countries will likely continue to be very rapid for many more years. The World Bank estimates that,

because the age distribution in these countries is such that they will have an increasingly large fertile population far into the future, it will be the twenty-second century before most of them achieve a stable population. Kenya is expected to be last, reaching a population of about 157 million in the year 2130.

At the time of Kenya's 1948 census, its population was 5 406 000. The 1962 census, counted 8 636 000, indicating that Kenya had an average annual growth rate of 3.3%. During the 1960s the growth rate accelerated slightly to an average of 3.4% per year, giving a total population at the 1969 census of 10 943 000. In 1978 the population was 14 700 000, in 1981 it was 17 400 000, and in 1984 it had reached just over 20 000 000. The 3.4% average annual growth rate of the 1960s had climbed to almost 4.0% by the 1980s, and the World Bank estimates that it will rise to as much as 4.5% by the 1990s. If this rate of increase continues in Kenya, its population will double every 16–18 years. Present estimates are that Kenya's population will reach 40 000 000 by the year 2000.

Kenya's high population growth rate is not, however, uniform across the country. It is higher in the traditional rural areas than in the towns, and is highest in the areas that are already the most densely populated. There are three areas of high population density (see Fig. 2-9): one in the west near the shores of Lake Victoria, another northeast of Nairobi, and a third along the southeast coast. These are agriculturally fertile areas, and both attract and support continuing population growth. They are also the home areas of Kenya's major tribes. These tribes are the Kikuyu, who live northeast of Nairobi, and the Luo and Luhya, inhabiting the

Fig. 2-8
Ten countries with the fastest rates of natural increase, 1960-1980, with percentage change

	Births/1000			Deaths/1000		
	1960	1980	% change	1960	1980	% change
Kenya	55	54	−1.8	24	14	−41.7
Zimbabwe	55	47	−14.6	17	8	−52.9
Syria	47	46	−2.1	18	9	−50.0
Honduras	51	47	−7.8	19	12	−36.8
Guatemala	48	42	−12.5	18	7	−61.1
Liberia	50	49	−2.0	21	14	−33.3
Nicaragua	51	47	−7.8	19	12	−36.8
Iraq	49	47	−4.1	20	13	−35.0
Belize	47	39	−17.0	7	5	−28.6
Kuwait	44	38	−13.6	10	4	−60.0

area near Lake Victoria. These large tribes are among the fastest growing groups in Kenya, as are several other fairly large tribes in the vicinity of these population centres.

Other tribes, such as the Somali, Galla and Turkana, who inhabit the thinly populated and less productive areas of northern Kenya, are actually declining in population. The Masai, on the edge of the Serengeti Plains south of Nairobi, have a more or less stable population. There is thus a general trend for the larger tribes to become even larger, and for the smaller tribes to become smaller, either in real numbers (e.g., the Somali), or in relation to the sizes of other tribes (e.g., the Masai). In a land where tribal size is often closely linked to political power, this situation is of some importance.

The causes of Kenya's high population growth rate are varied. The immediate cause is the very high total fertility rate (TFR), i.e., the total number of children that a woman bears throughout her reproductive period. In Kenya, the average TFR is about eight and rising. In 1948, Kenya's average TFR was just over five. The increase is attributed to better food and health care over the last few decades, and to cultural factors that favour a high birth rate. There is a tradition of having at least four children, to be named in honour of the four grandparents, but most Kenyans want more than four children. Children are a source of help in the fields, and offer a future guarantee of care during their parents' old age. The potential benefits of a large family are thought to be much greater than the costs. There are also very strong community pressures on couples to have children, for reasons of social acceptability and tribal status. It is noteworthy that high average TFRs are among the less well-educated rural people belonging to the major tribal groups. The lowest TFRs, on the other hand, occur among the more educated urban people who have largely forsaken traditional lifestyles, and among less well-educated rural people who belong to smaller tribes in the less productive agricultural areas.

The desire of Kenyan women to have children to help them in the fields is a product of Kenyan sex-roles as they relate to food production. Traditionally, women worked in the fields while men

Fig. 2-9
Kenya: areas of high population density and locations of main tribes

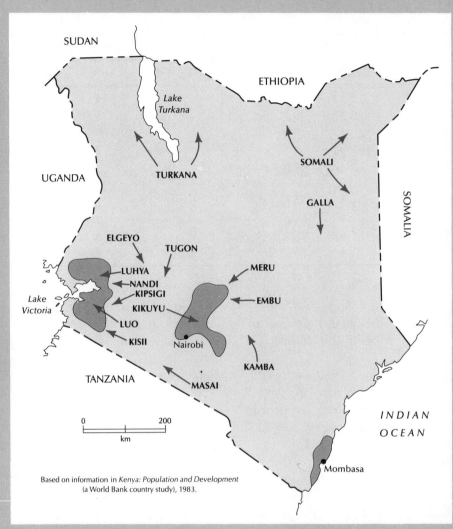

SUDAN

ETHIOPIA

Lake Turkana

UGANDA

SOMALI

GALLA

SOMALIA

TURKANA

ELGEYO

TUGON

MERU

LUHYA

NANDI
KIPSIGI

EMBU

Lake Victoria

KIKUYU

LUO

KISII

Nairobi

KAMBA

TANZANIA

MASAI

INDIAN OCEAN

0   200
km

Mombasa

Based on information in *Kenya: Population and Development*
(a World Bank country study), 1983.

cleared the land, hunted and protected the tribe and its lands. However, as the Kenyan economy has modernized, and men have left home to work in the towns, women have taken over more of the rural jobs previously done by men. The situation is aggravated by the practice of polygamy, which encourages each man to have several wives, each with a separate household. Since this leaves many women with no adult assistance in the running of their homes and farms, children become impor-

tant sources of help and security to their mothers.

Another factor contributing to high TFRs in Kenya is the practice of "bridewealth," by which the father of a daughter who marries is given a quantity of wealth (money, land, cattle, etc.) by the groom as part of the marriage arrangement. This encourages the father both to have many daughters in order to increase the amount of bridewealth he receives and to arrange his daughters' marriages as quickly as possible. The traditional

Women and children of the Samburu tribe in northern Kenya. Many factors contribute to Kenya's high rate of population growth.

tendency to early marriages increases the likelihood of a high TFR.

Against the background of an extremely high annual population growth rate, the Kenyan government is trying to pursue a number of socio-economic goals. These were set out in 1965 in the government document titled *African Socialism and its Application to Planning in Kenya*. In essence, the planning goals are freedom from want, disease, ignorance and exploitation. The means to achieve these goals are rapid economic growth, the development of a mixed (part public and part private) economy and the support of a variety of self-help initiatives. The latest five-year plans (1979–83 and 1984–88) are intended to provide basic services and the income to purchase such services. The fundamental goal is an attempt to raise the standard of living for the Kenyan population.

Achieving the goals of the Kenyan government is made more difficult by Kenya's very rapid population growth. Already, for example, there is considerable pressure on the better food-producing lands, which cover less than 20% of Kenya's total area. The population density on Kenya's agricultural land is about 275 people/km², which compares with the African average for agricultural land of about 50/km², and with India's nearly 350/km². Given Kenya's rate of population growth, the World Bank concludes that, unless population growth slows dramatically by the year 2000, the Kenyan development problem will become critical.

Among the problems usually associated with high population densities — housing scarcity, lack of sanitation, and epidemic disease — the most serious is the problem of food availability. During the 1960s and 1970s, Kenya's increases in food production generally kept pace with increases in population. However, the rate of increase in

Mzee Pembe and Kipanga, Kenya's top radio comics, broadcast a family health show combining education with entertainment.

population is now accelerating while the rate of increase in food production is decelerating due to diminishing returns from marginal land. During the growth period from 1960 to 1980, many small farmers moved into areas largely unsuited to farming. While yields were initially adequate, they cannot now be sustained using present techniques. Much marginal land has been seriously damaged by nutrient loss and by the destruction of the protective cover once given it by the surrounding natural vegetation. The International Food Policy Research Institute has accordingly indicated that Kenya will soon face worsening food deficiencies, to the extent of about 1 000 000 tonnes per year (t/y) by 1990 and 2 000 000 t/y by 2000.

Accelerating population growth is already posing problems in the job market too. Job creation is occurring more slowly than population growth, and the government is planning to try to absorb the unemployed work-force in food-producing enterprises on the marginal lands. Unfortunately, uncontrolled use of some of these lands throughout the 1960s and 1970s resulted in much soil erosion, and the government will have great difficulty making the increasingly barren land more fruitful.

The government will also face future difficulties

Unicef/Bill Campbell

At the other end, Kenyan villagers gather to listen to Pembe and Kipanga's messages about health, agriculture, nutrition and education.

providing other basic needs, such as education, health, water and housing. Such objectives are relatively easy to define, but extraordinarily difficult to achieve. For example, adult literacy in Kenya is still lower than 50%, and any attempt to improve that figure must compete against demands for other educational resources, such as more schools for more children and more technical training for unemployed labour. As well, government efforts to eradicate many communicable diseases are hindered by the overcrowding caused by rapid population growth. The government faces serious problems in almost every direction.

To many people, both inside and outside of Kenya, birth control seems to be an obvious means of removing one of the obstacles to social development strategies. But the introduction of large-scale social programs of birth control is not simple. In 1967, Kenya was the first African country south of the Sahara to adopt an official family planning program. The government's increasing concern over the rapidly growing size of the population was highlighted in the fourth Five-Year Plan (1979-83) when President Moi identified rapid population growth as one of the highest priority problems to confront. The Plan itself notes that by the "end of the century the structure of the population will be more balanced than it is now and the standard of living will be improving more rapidly." However, we have already noted the widespread desire of Kenyans to have large families, as well as some of the underlying socio-economic forces that foster that desire. Therefore, the government's first concern could be to attempt to alter the Kenyans' traditional attitudes towards family size. Surveys in Kenya indicate that there, as elsewhere, higher levels of education for women tend to reduce birth rates. More education alone will probably not be sufficient, since there are also problems with farm-workload and old age security to be addressed.

It will take time for any of the possible solutions to be effective. In addition, there are problems with the availability and acceptance of contraceptives. At the moment, according to Kenya's Ministry of Health, fewer than 5% of Kenyan women in the reproductive age group use any form of contraceptive device. The comparable figure for men is not known. Moreover, existing socio-economic pressures for high TFRs may be reinforced by a preference for economic development over birth control as a means to deal with the problems created by rapid population growth. Present thinking, especially after the 1984 International Population Conference in Mexico City, favours combining the two approaches so that countries may move less stressfully into Phase 3 of the demographic transition.

At a seminar at the University of Nairobi in 1980, jointly sponsored by the government of Kenya and the University of Nairobi, Rashid Faruqee of the World Bank noted that

> Kenya today stands at a watershed. For the near-term its population will grow rapidly, no matter what policy is followed. This demographic momentum is the result of past trends which cannot be altered. But decisions regarding population policy made today can have a very significant impact on the country's future in the year 2000 and beyond. The total population is not very large in absolute size but the rate of its expansion is extraordinarily high. This will impose a serious burden on agriculture and on public finance. It will make more difficult the provision of basic needs services and the creation of gainful employment opportunities for all Kenyans.

Conclusion

Population growth is one of the most difficult issues facing the world. We know that the world population is currently increasing by some 80–90 million each year, with the prospect that, if the rate does not slow down, the increase in real numbers will become larger with each passing year. Does this increase signify a crisis? Will there be enough food for us all? If millions are starving today, what will happen in ten years? In one hundred years?

We have looked briefly at some of the problems facing Kenya, a country where the population explosion threatens to outstrip both food production and the country's ability to provide other adequate basic needs services (education, health care, food, housing, water). In spite of strong economic growth, Kenya's problems also are growing. In this regard, Kenya typifies the situation of many other countries in Africa, Asia and Latin America.

If there are grounds for hope in this situation, we may find them in the examples of other countries with large and growing populations but without the massive technological assistance available in the Western world. Such countries as China, India and the USSR all have decreasing rates of population growth, and their food production appears to be adequate. Moreover, assuming that demographic transition occurs, the population explosion is not expected to last. The UN predicts that world population will stabilize around the year 2100 at about 11–12 billion.

This is, of course, a huge number. Can the world be expected to feed so many people? The next chapter examines the food issue.

3 FOOD

Introduction

Food is a basic resource for the world's population. Its production depends upon a number of related factors. One factor is environmental, such as the availability of fertile soils and suitable climates (see Appendix 1). Another is technological, such as the availability of synthetic fertilizers, pesticides and irrigation waters. Economic and political factors also are important, including the availability of satisfactory distribution networks and suitable pricing arrangements.

The message, however, from the 1984 United Nations World Food Conference held at Addis Ababa was that food availability is one of the world's most serious issues. Famine has always stalked human societies, and the majority of people have suffered the pains of hunger and the threat of starvation. What makes the lack of food serious now is its impact on historically large numbers of people and its potential for social and political turmoil. The United Nations Food and Agriculture Organization (FAO) estimates that at least 500 000 000 people around the world suffer from hunger, and that about 1 500 of them die every day from starvation. The FAO estimate is cautious. The World Bank estimate is 780 000 000, and the International Labour Office estimates that more than one billion people are going hungry.

The FAO says that the main reason for the food problem is the high rate of population growth over much of the world. In the developing countries, where hunger is most common, the rate of population growth is at least twice that of the developed countries, where hunger is less common. In the developing countries, the population appears to be outstripping the local food supply, as Malthus forecast.

Another view of the problem has been put forward by Roger Revelle, Professor of Population Studies at Harvard University. In the *UNESCO Courier* of 1974 7-8, he writes:

> The principal cause [of large-scale hunger] is the low level of agricultural technology in most parts of the world. Instead of the 6.4 metric tonnes grown on a hectare in Iowa, the average Indian or Pakistani farmer produces only a little more than one tonne of wheat or rice.

Developing countries generally feel that it is the developed countries that are largely responsible for the population explosion, since they introduced death control through medical aid without also introducing the accompanying social and economic factors that assist in reducing birth rates.

Output is relatively low in India not only on a per hectare basis but also on a per person basis. For instance, India produces about 150 000 000 t of all foodgrains a year by the labour of the about 250 000 000 people directly engaged in farming. In contrast, the USA produces about 225 000 000 t from the direct work of only about 5 000 000 people.

Other scientists say that enough food may be grown, but that losses to pests keep enough from reaching the people who need it. For harvested and stored crops alone, Lester Brown, in the *UNESCO Courier* of 1984 4, suggests that developing countries lost about 70 000 000 t of cereals to rodents and insects in 1982.

Another reason for the food problem was given by Willy Brandt, Chancellor of West Germany, in an article in *World Press Review* 1984 6:

> The relationship between arms and development has yet to be studied in depth. But the world military bill is approaching $800 billion a year, while official development aid worldwide is less than 5 per cent of that amount. . . .

> It is a tragic irony that the most rapid transfer of highly sophisticated equipment and technology from rich to poor countries has been in the machinery of death. There certainly is no military solution to energy or food shortages, or to hunger, poverty, or social unrest.

Colombia's Ambassador to Italy, writing in the *UNESCO Courier* of 1975 5, also traced the causes of the food problem to political and economic causes:

> The world is approaching the point where as many people die daily of hunger or malnutrition as were killed every 24 hours during World War II. The wielding of the world's economic power by a handful of nations has made it impossible to guarantee the majority of our fellow human beings even the most elementary human rights.

This point of view was also stressed by delegates to a 20-nation food conference at Montréal in 1984 6. They noted that the insistence of the International Monetary Fund (IMF) and the World Bank on the repayment of loans was forcing many developing countries into recession and causing the poorer people in them to go even more hungry. In 1984 7 the Bolivian government, already four months behind on debt repayments, declared that the matter was a choice "between paying our obligations or feeding our people."

Other people assert that the lack of food in some countries results from the patterns of landholding in the developing countries. They argue that in many developing countries a few wealthy landowners control vast areas of land. This pattern is most common in Latin America, but exists in many other parts of the world and produces less food than would many smaller individually owned farms. Evidence available from many land-reform movements is mixed but, on the whole, tends to support this view.

Leonard Broadbent of Bath University's School of Biological Sciences in England notes that about 35% of the food grown in Britain and about 65% of the food grown in the tropics is lost to pests and diseases at some stage between planting and eating.

FAO experts from Yugoslavia (right) and Iran (left) consult with a farmer at Dastena, near Isfahan, Iran. Using the most suitable tools and techniques for ploughing in particular soil conditions improves food production and conserves topsoil.

In its *Global Report 1985–1986*, the Canadian Red Cross Society lists some other factors contributing to world hunger. It notes, for example, the use of some of the best agricultural land for cash cropping for export markets, low food prices and poor distribution methods. Another problem is government emphasis on imported technologies such as deep ploughing in soils that suffer erosion if deeply disturbed or machinery that cannot easily be maintained. The *Global Report* says that the production of cash crops for export such as cotton, coffee and fruit, often diverts resources needed to produce food for local use; instead these crops are used to feed already well-fed countries even better. The *Report* also says that local government action is keeping food prices down to ensure cheap food for city dwellers, which creates little incentive to the farmers to produce more than they need for themselves. Also, many farmers must sell their produce to government-run marketing agencies which cannot always store or distribute the food adequately and therefore waste much of what is produced. Finally, the *Report* points out that many government policies (e.g., access to credit, the promotion of new techniques) favour large commercial farmers over the multitude of small farmers who form the bulk of rural populations.

The story of Muthoka, a small farmer in Africa, shows fairly typically many of the problems relating to food production in the developing countries. The story is reported in *The Washington Post* of 1984 12. Muthoka's first concern is obtaining seeds. His last year's crop failed to produce enough surplus to carry over as seed stock, so he needs to buy seeds. He buys them from the local co-operative, which in turn buys them from the government's seed board. The seeds he needs cost about $15, but he is short of money because of the poor crop the previous year. His farm is small (just over one hectare) and therefore he cannot qualify for government credit. However, by taking other jobs he and his family of five have managed to save about $5, enough to plant about one-third of his farm. He now faces another problem; there is a nation-wide shortage of seeds. The only seeds available are regular corn seeds and not the new hybrid corn seeds that survive better in the short rainy season of October and November. There is also a fertilizer shortage. Chemical fertilizers are imported and expensive, and Muthoka does not consider buying them. He has had to sell his cows to earn money to stay alive after the previous year's poor harvest, so natural fertilizer also is scarce.

Not all developing countries need to import fertilizer. Zimbabwe, for example, produces 15 different types of fertilizer within its own borders.

Even if he grows his partial crop, and even if the rains come and his crop does well, Muthoka will face the problem of getting any surplus to market. His farm is isolated, the roads are poor and he does not have a truck. He has to get his surplus to market however he can, and when he gets there he is required to sell his crop to the government corn-buying monopoly. The price he gets is only about 20% of what he might get elsewhere, because the government corn-buying monopoly deliberately keeps prices low in order to supply cheap food to the towns. Once he has sold his surplus corn, Muthoka will likely wait up to six months for the government monopoly to pay him. He often questions whether growing food is worth the risk and trouble, and wonders if his whole family might not be better off looking for work in town.

Many varied technological, environmental, political and economic reasons exist for inadequate food production. Nevertheless, some parts of the world have huge food surpluses. The European Economic Community (EEC), for example, has vast stockpiles of surplus foodstuffs: almost 10 000 000 t of grain, 500 000 t of beef, 750 000 t of butter, 1 000 000 t of powdered milk, along with "mountains" of other foods. Europe produces these surpluses because government-set prices are high enough to keep even the less efficient farmers in business, so farmers produce far more food than the local market can use.

It is also true that people in the more economically developed parts of the world often use food in what some consider a self-indulgent fashion, both by overeating and by giving large amounts of food to pets. Potential agricultural inputs such as land and fertilizer are sometimes treated in

It is not only in the developed world that economically unproductive animals are allowed a share of available food. In India, cows wander the streets and browse off vendors' displays as they wish and ceremonial monkeys are almost always fed by visitors to temples and other holy places.

The member countries of the European Economic Community (EEC) have amassed large stockpiles of surplus foodstuffs. This Danish farm suggests the general well-being of the EEC countries.

the same way. In Ontario, for instance, it is estimated that 250 000 hectares of land are used to pasture horses whose use is primarily recreational.

In this chapter we will examine the world food situation in more detail. We will look at the importance of food and its general availability; we will also investigate standards of nutrition and explore ways of improving the situation. A case study of food production in tropical Africa follows the general discussion and illustrates some of the points made there.

DISCUSSION AND RESEARCH

1. What causes of the world food problem are suggested in the introduction? What other causes can you suggest?
2. To what extent are the dire predictions of Malthus being proved correct?
3. What arguments can you suggest for having the more developed nations share their food surpluses with the developing nations? What are your arguments against the idea? Which do you favour?

Danish Tourist Board

The Present Situation

The Importance of Food

Why do we eat? The obvious answer, "to remain alive," is too general to be very helpful. Food serves many cultural and psychological needs. Most basically food provides material for cell growth so that decaying cells can be replaced by new ones.

Replacing dying cells is just one way in which our bodies use the energy made available to them by food. The human body "burns" *kilojoules* of energy produced from food.

The greatest amounts of energy are usually needed for the maintenance of basic body functions (called *basal metabolism*), which include breathing, blood circulation, the maintenance of body temperature and muscle action. The energy required for this purpose varies according to climate: more energy is needed in the colder parts of the world than in the tropics. The amount of energy used in basal metabolism varies from about 6 000–8 000 kJ/d.

Energy also is essential for physical growth. Physical requirements vary during a person's lifetime, peaking at about 15–17 years, and then tapering off. Such regular activities as walking and talking require relatively little energy, about 1 000 kJ/d, or about 10% of our daily needs. Energy is also required for other activities, such as work. The amount needed varies with the type of work done: a job requiring much physical labour obviously demands more kilojoules than a desk job.

The kilojoules we need to produce energy come from three main sources: carbohydrates, fats and proteins. Carbohydrates and proteins both yield 16.8 kJ/g, but a gram of fats can yield up to 37.8 kJ. This means that fats are the most concentrated form of food energy. Foods which are rich in fats are butter, lard, liver, egg yolk and vegetable oils.

The less productive carbohydrates are widely available, either in the form of sugars or in starchy foods such as rice, wheat, corn and potatoes. Starchy foods are easy to grow and therefore form the staple diet for billions of people throughout the world.

Proteins come chiefly from meat, milk products, eggs and fish. Some plants, notably cereals and soybeans, are also good sources of protein.

Food energy has traditionally been measured in Calories. It is now measured in kilojoules. The conversion rates are:

1 Calorie (kilocalorie) = 4.2 kJ
0.238 Cal = 1.0 kJ

A kilojoule is the amount of energy needed to move a mass of one kilogram a distance of one metre at an acceleration of one metre per second each second.

The major sources of proteins are often expensive and scarce throughout the world. The average person requires about 56 g/d of protein, one-third of which should be animal protein.

In addition to proteins, fats and carbohydrates, the human body needs supplies of minerals, vitamins, whole grain cereals and water, which is even more important than food.

These varied needs are met by different foods. The aim of good nutrition is to eat the correct quantities of a variety of different foods so that the body's needs are fully met. Since no single food can supply everything (milk is the most closely ideal single food), different foods must be consumed to ensure a balanced diet and good nutrition.

Malnutrition is a condition caused by a lack of nutrients; it arises from an imbalance in the variety of foods eaten. Starvation is the most severe form of malnutrition. It occurs when the body receives so little food that it begins to break down its own cells to get the energy it needs to survive. On the other hand, people can eat all the food they want and still be malnourished. Thus malnutrition is a problem connected to the improper quality of food intake, whereas starvation is connected to the improper quantity.

In North America and Europe people may suffer from malnutrition through eating an imbalanced diet. In Canada alone, for example, data published in 1986 indicates that as many as 600 000 hospitalizations a year are related to health problems due to malnutrition. The following article describes some of the results of malnutrition in various parts of the world.

Nutrition in the developing world

Two-thirds of the world's children live in the developing countries and for most of them malnutrition is a fact of existence. The consequences may be death, blindness, irreversible mental retardation due to protein deficiency, or physical impairment, so that they are incapable of employment and of contributing to their countries' progress.

Nutrition as a reliable science is relatively young. The first vitamin to be identified was vitamin A, in 1913; the last, vitamin B_{12}, was not discovered until 1945. Nutritionists now know that about fifty substances must be present in the diet to sustain life and promote health. They can prescribe fairly accurately the necessary minimum allowances of these substances, but they still do not know the full consequences of excessive consumption of certain food elements.

Nevertheless, we know that while about a quarter of the world's people eat too much for their own good, the other three-quarters eat too little. Whereas North America produces 116% of the kilojoules needed by its population, Asia produces only about 90%, so that in that densely populated area of the world there is an overall "energy gap." Moreover, in every part of the world some people have plenty to eat while others have barely enough to sustain life.

The protein gap

The discrepancy in quantity between the diet of the "haves" and that of the "have-nots" is great, but the discrepancy in quality is even greater. In affluent countries, meat, milk, eggs, and other high-protein foods — valuable as elements of a balanced diet but having potentially dangerous concentrations of animal fats unless used in moderation — are consumed in amounts far in excess of recommended allowances. Indeed, they have practically become dietary staples, and in certain income groups a ''meatless meal'' is considered a genuine deprivation. In poorer countries, animal protein foods are often in such short supply that, except in the homes of the rich, they may be served only on special holiday or ceremonial occasions. The diet typically available to children in those countries is grossly deficient not only in high quality protein but in certain minerals and vitamins that animal protein foods provide.

There is good reason to suppose that malnutrition, in one form or another, is the most serious problem now facing the human race. On the one hand, an affluent few are inviting arteriosclerosis (an accumulation of hardened fatty deposits in the arteries) by consuming too much food rich in animal fats — a steady diet of fatmeat hamburgers, ham-and-mayonnaise sandwiches, ice cream, and the like. On the other hand, perhaps as many as two billion people are prey to infection and deficiency diseases because their diet does not give them the needed minimum of proteins, minerals, and vitamins. Among the latter, it is the children from one to five years old who suffer most.

Deficiency diseases

Where hunger and malnutrition exist, an unusually high percentage of babies born alive have a low birth weight and incidence of prematurity is higher. It is also considered that in any country a high mortality rate in the one-to-four-years age group indicates widespread malnutrition. While the immediate cause of death may not be a nutritional (deficiency) disease, malnutrition lowers the resistance to infectious diseases and the ability to recover. Even without infection, deficiency diseases can stunt, cripple, and kill. They claim many victims every day.

Kwashiorkor

Kwashiorkor is the African name for a major deficiency disease of childhood in many less developed countries. It attacks infants who are weaned to a rigorous diet of starch foods which are often too coarse for the child's digestive system, with the result that he suffers from moderate kilojoule deficiency as well as grossly deficient protein intake. A child with kwashiorkor becomes puny, his hair and skin grow pale, his arms and legs become thin, and he develops a potbelly. In the acute disease, the child's face, hands, and legs may swell, his skin may break down as if burned, and he becomes apathetic: when this stage is reached, the disease is usually fatal. In earlier stages, the addition to the baby's diet of food rich in protein will clear up the condition.

Marasmus

The condition known as marasmus is a form of starvation not specifically related to protein. It may develop in a child after an attack of diarrhoea when the digestive system is unable to handle the food available. This disease takes the form of wasting; the skin becomes thin and wrinkled but does not break down and the child does not refuse food or become apathetic. As in the case of kwashiorkor, marasmus victims can be returned to health if they are treated soon enough.

Some of the other diseases of malnutrition are *Beri-beri* which is caused by lack of vitamin B_1 (thiamine); *Xerophthalmia*, a disease of the eyes brought on by lack of vitamin A, causing blindness, and curable by the inclusion of green leaves in the diet; *Pellagra*, caused by a deficiency of niacin found in meat, fish and whole grains and pulses; *Scurvy* resulting from a lack of vitamin C; *Rickets*, a bone disease caused by a lack of vitamin D; *Anaemia*, an iron-deficiency disease.

In addition to the diseases caused by specific deficiencies in the diet, lack of food — hunger — is an all-too-common condition among the poor of the world. In many areas, population is increasing at a rate that is greater than the available food supply can support. Lack of transportation facilities in the developing countries hampers transfer of food from areas of plenty to areas of need. People are leaving the traditional rural economy and crowding into the cities where they can afford only the cheapest and least nourishing food.

Canadian UNICEF Committee 1971 10

DISCUSSION AND RESEARCH

4. Research the causes of malnutrition in North America.

5. Many of the effects of food deficiency are described in the previous reading. Most of them are physical effects. Suggest some of the social, economic and political effects caused by food deficiencies.

Food Availability

Variations in the quantity of food available can be measured by kilojoules. However, the quality of food available is less easy to measure. In North America and Europe common dietary imbalance results from an excess of fats and carbohydrates. In the rest of the world most unbalanced diets can be traced to protein deficiencies. In this book, we will use proteins as a measure of nutritional quality, bearing in mind that protein is only the most obvious of the requirements for a good diet.

Fig. 3-1
Variations in protein intake throughout the world

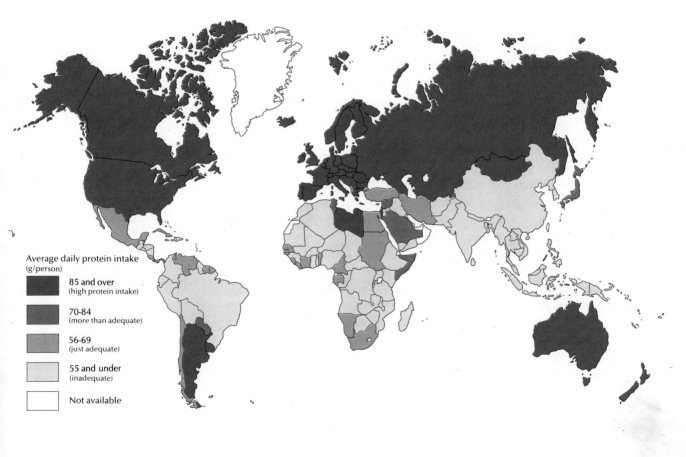

Average daily protein intake
(g/person)

85 and over
(high protein intake)

70-84
(more than adequate)

56-69
(just adequate)

55 and under
(inadequate)

Not available

STATISTICAL ANALYSIS

6. Using the data in Column I of Appendix 3 draw a graded shading map of the average daily per capita availability of kilojoules throughout the world. You might consider using a grading scheme such as:

12 000 and over kJ/person/d	very bright green
10 000 –11 999 kJ/person/d	bright green
8 000 – 9 999 kJ/person/d	pale green
under 8 000 kJ/person/d	very pale green

What do you notice about the distribution of the countries having a food availability below 10 000 kJ/person/d? How does it compare with the population growth maps in Chapter 2, assignments 7 and 8?

7. To find the energy-producing capacity of the food consumed in different nations, calculate the kilojoules per gram (kJ/g) for each country from the data in Columns I and J of Appendix 3. For example, Afghanistan's data are 7 909 kJ and 842 g, and the resulting kJ/g figure is 9.4 (7909/842 = 9.4). Group your answers into four classes and draw a graded shading map to show the world picture. How do you explain the result when you compare it with the kilojoule map in assignment 6?

8. The graded shading map in Fig. 3-1 shows the average per capita daily protein availability in the world's countries. How does the pattern compare with the ones you have just drawn in assignments 6 and 7?

North Americans and Europeans, among others, generally have more kilojoules and proteins than they need. According to the map in Fig. 3-1 and that which you made in assignment 6, there are, however, large populations that get far fewer kilojoules and proteins than they require. In these areas, starvation and malnutrition are widespread.

There are two basic reasons for the lack of sufficient food: greater need than local food production can meet and a lack of alternative commodities to trade for food produced elsewhere. There are many reasons for inadequate food production, several of which are alluded to in the introduction to this chapter. The most serious are probably the reliance on "low" technology, small and scattered landholdings and food losses to insects and other pests.

Farming which must depend on such low technology as animal and human muscle power, shallow wooden ploughs, water wheels, hand seeding, low-quality seeds and inadequate fertilizers cannot produce enough food to support quickly growing populations. For example, compare for

When crops are seeded by hand, the seeds are usually scattered haphazardly over the ground. The plants therefore grow haphazardly, rather than in rows, and are accordingly difficult to harvest.

a few countries the use of fertilizer in kilograms per hectare (kg/ha) as reported by the World Bank in 1985:

Burundi	1.0
Chad	1.7
Ethiopia	2.6
Sudan	4.4
Haiti	5.1
Nigeria	6.5
USA	86.7
Japan	412.1
Switzerland	413.9
Netherlands	738.1
New Zealand	946.8

Infrastructure is the complex web of supporting facilities and services that enable something to thrive.

Despite the high correlation between the use of low technology and the lack of adequate food production, there are strong arguments to continue using low technology in less economically developed countries. These reasons are chiefly related to the infrastructures of such countries. For example, supplies of electricity, gas and diesel oil may be unreliable, the machinery prone to disrepair and the soils unsuited to deep ploughing. Each of these conditions would make the introduction of higher technology even more risky than the existing low technology. Moreover, such economic systems cannot always absorb the small farmers likely to be displaced from their land by higher productivity. Alternative employment opportunities may be scarce and alternative housing difficult to obtain. These are real problems, faced in Europe at the time of its agricultural revolution 100–200 years ago. In 1816 in eastern England, for example, uprooted small farmers roamed the countryside with banners inscribed "Bread or Blood." The dispossessed and underprivileged small farmers of France became a powerful instrument in the overthrow of the monarchy in the French Revolution (1789). Several years later Karl Marx's observations of the degraded quality of life of the poor and destitute in Germany and England moved him to publish the *Communist Manifesto* in 1848 and *Das Kapital* in 1867. The fact remains, however, that the use of low technology is among the main causes of inadequate food production. The question, therefore, is how to raise the level of technology and implement its use with the minimum disruption to the accepted economic and social fabrics of the countries involved.

Small and scattered landholdings create another problem. When plots of land are scattered, farmers spend time travelling from one plot to another. The small size of each plot also makes large-scale machinery useless or impractical. The problem of small landholdings is common in many countries. One reason is the *gavelkind* inheritance laws of many countries, whereby children share equally in the division of their deceased

A former cotton plantation and hacienda in Southern Peru. The land has been expropriated by the government and awaits distribution to small farmers.

parents' land. In time, this system produces a multitude of tiny plots scattered among the remaining descendants. France began to consolidate its many small plots in the 1950s, when it planned to join the European Common Market. At about the same time India also began to plan for inheritance law reform.

Another reason for the existence of many small plots is the governmental break-up of large estates (often called *latifundia*) and the distribution of the land to landless farmers. In most countries small farmers historically have not owned the land they worked, and have had little or no reason to improve farming conditions. In the case of "absentee landlords" the owner also has often had little incentive to improve the land as long as the rents were paid. It has always been one of the first aims of revolutionaries in agricultural societies to confiscate the large holdings and parcel out the land to landless farmers. However, this has not happened in all countries and has not been completed in many. Moreover, unless the new owners are supported by credit, technical assistance and marketing, food production may not increase.

Confiscations took place in Italy under Mussolini, in China under Mao, in Russia under Lenin, in Cuba under Castro and in Japan under MacArthur. In other countries, such as Brazil and India, change has been less revolutionary.

A third major problem is the loss of food to insects and other pests, caused by poor pest control and storage facilities. Pest control is itself a contentious issue, since it usually involves the use of chemicals regarded by many people as hazardous to the environment. The classic example is DDT, which has been banned in the countries which do not really need to use it, but which is still used in many other countries. Less hazardous pesticides have been developed, but these are more expensive than DDT and pose other problems for developing countries.

Provided they have the money to pay for it, countries that cannot adequately feed themselves can always buy food from nations with a surplus, as several European countries do. However, most countries with food deficits also have little money and few ways of earning it. Some of the reasons for this are:

They may receive money as aid. This money often is available in the form of credits which permit the aid-receiving countries to purchase food from the aid-donors by going into debt to them. Most developing countries are very heavily in debt. For example, in 1984 the Latin American nations alone had foreign debts totalling US$ 350 billion. The debt situation is widely regarded as at the crisis point.

– They cannot produce and sell manufactured goods competitively with larger industrialized nations in order to earn enough money to pay for food imports. (There are important exceptions to this, e.g., Taiwan, Korea, Brazil, and — more recently — Indonesia and Malaysia.)

– They cannot earn enough money from their exports of raw materials to buy food on world markets. (There are important exceptions here also, e.g., Malaysian tin, Jamaican alumina, Bangladeshi jute and Zambian copper, but note that international commodity prices are not always as high as the selling countries wish.) There have been several attempts to make selling arrangements that would produce higher prices, most notably by OPEC, but none has ever been very successful for any great length of time. The world's wealthier nations are often accused of rigging international markets to keep the prices of raw materials as low as possible for the major buyers (i.e., themselves), thereby denying increased incomes to the exporting nations.

World copper prices were high until about 1975, and Zambia benefited greatly by being able to push forward many development plans. However, prices have fallen since then and Zambia is now hard-pressed.

In any society, global or otherwise, it is generally true that sellers want higher prices and buyers want lower prices. Countries are no different.

– They do not earn enough money from "invisible exports" to pay for imports of food. Invisible exports are moneys earned through providing services to other countries rather than from the sale of goods. There are a number of important exceptions here, too. For example, Singapore earns invisible export income through the sale of banking, insurance and shipping services; most Caribbean countries earn similar income from the provision of tourist services; and India and Pakistan benefit from money sent back by emigrants working in high-wage countries. The case study at the end of Chapter 7 deals more extensively with the matter of migrant labour and migrants' remittances.

Generally, the lower the percentage of the population employed in agriculture, the greater the efficiency.

Fig. 3-2 shows a scattergraph (see Appendix 4) of the data in Columns L and M of Appendix 3. Column L contains the percentage of each country's population employed in agriculture. These data are widely employed as a test of agricultural efficiency. Column M gives information about the size of each country's international monetary reserve, which is a test of its trading ability. An international monetary reserve is the money held by a country's central bank in the currencies

Fig. 3-2
Relationship between international monetary reserves and percentage of population in agriculture

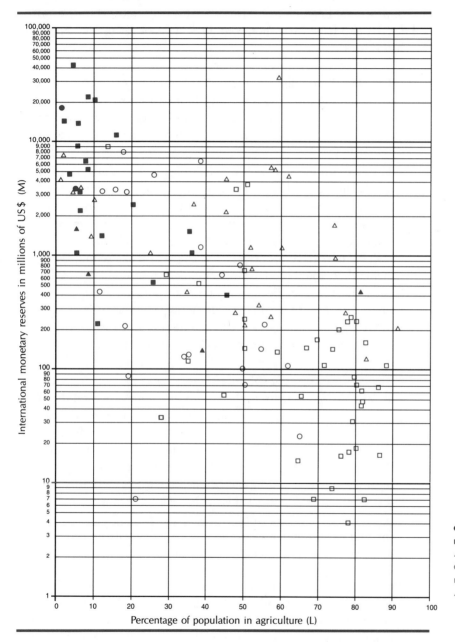

of other nations. In Canada, for example, the Swiss francs, Japanese yen, US dollars and so on that are held by the Bank of Canada form the country's international monetary reserve. Normally this money is largely at the disposal of the government, which may use it for foreign purchases.

STATISTICAL ANALYSIS

9. What do you notice about the relationships shown in Fig. 3-2? What do you think are the chief causes of these relationships?

10. Select one of the data sets, L or M, and relate it to the quantity of food available in each country as expressed in kJ in Column I of Appendix 3. Use the *phi (φ) coefficient* technique as outlined in Appendix 4.

   a. What sort of relationship do you get for your data set (I and L *or* I and M)?

   b. Describe the relationship that you would expect to obtain between I and the data set you did not choose (either L or M).

11. The Food and Agriculture Organization of the United Nations (the FAO) suggests that a large part of the food problem is attributable to the high rate of population growth in the developing countries. This view is shared by others, as the following item from the *UNESCO Courier* of 1975 5 demonstrates:

   > The major problem facing the developing countries . . . lies in the increased rate of population growth . . . due to faster population growth. A vicious circle of malnutrition, leading to higher death rates, which, in turn, motivates large families, is also set up.

   The quotation suggests that a high rate of population growth (Column F of Appendix 3) not only correlates well with food deficits (Column I), but also helps to cause them. We can test this idea mathematically by calculating the *coefficient of determination*, as shown in Appendix 4. It would be laborious to do this for all the countries listed without the help of a computer, so use only the sample of starred (*) countries in Appendix 3, namely Algeria, Brazil, Canada, etc. The number of countries in the sample = n.

   Your answer will lie between 0.0 and 1.0. A number close to 0.0 indicates that only a small degree of i (food availability) can be explained in terms of f (rate of population increase), while a number close to 1.0 indicates that a large degree of i is attributable to variations in f. The figure you have calculated also tells you the mathematically exact percentage of i caused by f. For instance, if your answer is 0.62, then, mathematically, 62% of the variations in i can be accounted for by variations in f.

   a. What is your answer?

   b. What does it tell you about the causal relationship that exists between food deficits and the rate of population growth?

c. Can you explain it?

d. What percentage of food deficits remains to be explained by factors other than rate of population growth?

e. What could these other factors be?

f. How would you test whether or not the factors that you suggest are really part of the cause?

The world food situation is of great concern. There are great inequalities in kilojoule and protein availability. Starvation and malnutrition exist despite the surplus foods being produced. There are conflicting views about the causes of hunger, and there are many different views as to what should be done. Before trying to formulate our own views, we need first to know more about basic nutritional standards.

This photo shows why high technology food production is in some ways incompatible with small landholdings.

Standards of Nutrition

Diogenes, an ancient Greek writer, is reported to have said that if you are rich you eat when you want to, but if you are poor you eat when you can.

It is hard to say how much we should eat. Most of us know when we feel hungry, though we may not always know whether our hunger has its source in our bodies or our minds. We also know when we have eaten too much, but few of us know when we have eaten just what we need for good health. It is still more difficult for us to set standards for others, especially billions of others.

There are no officially recognized standards of nutrition. One early proposal was the Standard Nutrition Unit, formulated by the geographer L.D. Stamp. He took the basic requirement to support an average person for one year as 4 200 000 kJ, deducted about 10% for wastage, and divided the remainder by 365 to arrive at a daily figure of about 10 350 kJ/person. We can round this figure to 10 000 kJ/person/d and call it the Modified Standard Nutrition Unit. This figure is an average for the population as a whole; babies and older adults generally need less than the average number of kilojoules, while adolescents and active younger adults need more. A glance back at the map for assignment 6 will tell you how various countries relate to the Modified Standard Nutrition Unit. Some exceed the standard, but many fail to reach it. This suggests that in the latter countries a few people may be well fed but most are hungry.

Attempts to rank countries according to universal food standards usually meet the criticism that countries in tropical climates need less food than temperate countries and, therefore, will always appear as deficit areas when plotted against a universal standard. This is true. It is also true that medical research indicates much starvation and malnutrition in tropical countries.

Column N of Appendix 3 shows that low latitude countries generally have lower food intake requirements than high latitude countries. The lowest requirement is 9 072 kJ (Burma, Indonesia, Vietnam), while the highest requirement is 11 382 kJ (Finland), a difference of about 20–25%.

To produce a more refined set of norms the Food and Agriculture Organization of the United Nations (the FAO) has calculated an individual norm for each country based on that country's climate, prevailing individual human body size and the age composition of its population. The norms, expressed in kJ, are given in Column N of Appendix 3. The extent to which each country exceeds or falls short of its calculated FAO norm is listed in Column O.

STATISTICAL ANALYSIS

12. Using the information in Column O of Appendix 3, construct a map to show the countries that meet or exceed their FAO norms.

OR

Construct a *linear dispersion diagram* (as shown in Appendix 4) to illustrate the data in Column O. Use a different colour for each continent. Compare the graph to your map in assignment 6 and explain the results.

The nations of the world can now be seen to vary in their ability to meet either absolute food quantities (assignments 6 and 8) or individually tailored food norms (assignment 12). Whichever method is used to calculate basic nutritional standards, we can see that many countries now exist below their necessary minimum levels of food availability.

This butcher shop displays its meat on the open street, without refrigeration and exposed to dirt and insects.

Unicef / Bernard Wolff

Improving the Situation

Food is one of humanity's basic resources. It is also a renewable resource, and increasable. There are growing numbers of people in the world, all wanting enough food. Until all areas of the world can feed themselves adequately, however, we need to look at better ways of redistributing existing global food supplies.

Redistributing Existing Food Supplies

Domestic surpluses exist in several countries. In most cases the surpluses are produced to meet expected trade demands on world markets. For example, Danish bacon is produced in far greater quantities than the Danes can consume. It is sold to buyers in Germany and Britain. Like cars, it is a trade item and, if it could not be sold, would not be produced. Truly surplus food is different; it is usually produced in response to government price-supports and not to market demands. It is sometimes possible for farmers to grow too much in error. It is then called a glut on the market. It too is truly surplus food since there is no market for it. A "market" is defined as a trading situation where some are prepared to sell and others are prepared to buy, the essence being that the buyers have enough money to pay. Many developing countries which lack the ability to pay are outside the market.

Some countries produce food surpluses, and deal with them by destroying or stockpiling them, trading them or dispensing them as food aid. Canadian milk has been poured down old mine shafts, English tomatoes bulldozed into the sea, American cows killed and buried and French fruit allowed to rot. Food is destroyed to prevent it from reaching the market and increasing the supply, which would cause prices to fall. If farmers receive unprofitably low prices they may not grow sufficient crops in the future. The amount of food produced is often controlled in order to control prices. Farmers often are persuaded to underproduce food by governments using official advice, quotas, price support systems, banning edicts and fines. Land is left fallow, and herds and flocks are culled to maintain profitable prices for what is produced.

Some people strongly believe that surplus food should not be destroyed but should instead be redistributed to countries in need of it. Others argue that surpluses should be stockpiled as emergency international reserves to be used in countries experiencing famine. There are powerful reasons for surplus-producing countries to continue providing food relief on an emergency basis, as has been done with sub-Saharan Africa throughout the 1980s. However, there is a growing consensus in the international community that the redistribution of food in this way is counter-productive to any long-term solutions. Recognizing this, delegates at a 1984 food conference in Africa unanimously declared that it was their countries' responsibility to feed themselves. "The world does not owe us a living on a plate," said the Ugandan delegate. The following article by Gwynne Dyer, in a 1983 issue of *The Toronto Star*, explains one view of the situation.

LONDON —

"You can tell the agencies in Europe to send trucks or coffins," said a relief worker in the famine-wrecked Tigre region of Ethiopia, where the main problem is getting the food into a region devastated by years of war.

"There exists a disaster of major proportions, the gravity of which has only recently become apparent to the outside world," said Michael Behr, Oxfam's field director, returning from Goza and Inhambane provinces in Mozambique, 3,000 km south of Tigre, where an estimated four million people face starvation.

About 1,500 km to the west, on the Zambia-Angola border, the United Nations High Commission for refugees is supplying emergency food aid to an influx from the fighting in Angola. In West Africa, Ghana is struggling to feed its people after a year in which a million Ghanaians were abruptly expelled from Nigeria.

The food crisis in Africa is general. After three years of drought across much of the continent, the UN's Food and Agriculture Organization reports that 24 African countries, containing a total of 155 million people, are critically short of food.

From Mali and Mauritania in the northwest to Botswana and Zimbabwe on South Africa's borders, people are hungry. The FAO estimates that Africa will need 3.4 million tonnes of food aid this year, and so far its member countries have pledged only half that amount.

The amount is not beyond the bounds of feasibility; the world grain trade in 1980 totalled 209 million tonnes and it obviously must be provided. You can't just let people starve. But for the longer term, it would help if African countries were to pay a little more attention to feeding themselves.

Ten years ago Africa was a net exporter of food, but food production in sub-Saharan Africa has not kept up with population growth. While population expanded during the 1970s at 2.7 per cent a year, the highest rate of any continent, food output grew by only 1.5 per cent. It has actually been falling recently, from 19.7 million tonnes of cereals in 1981 to only 16.2 million tonnes last year.

Political factors have made matters worse — refugees surging across borders; and whole areas like southern Angola, central Mozambique and much of Ethiopia where prolonged guerrilla warfare has devastated agriculture. But the fact remains that Africa has plenty of land. It has the lowest population density of any continent except Australia, and the vast majority of its people are peasant farmers.

Nor are they shortchanged in foreign aid. The Sahel, one of the most affected regions, received $44 (U.S.) per person in foreign aid in 1981. Even in the rest of Africa it is $20 a year, versus $9 per person in Asia. Yet African farmers are growing less food, and the continent has so little margin of safety that relatively minor political and climatic disturbances can plunge it into a full-scale famine.

The true cause for this inexorably growing disaster is the policies of African governments. It's not just the huge bureaucracies stuffed with the endlessly proliferating relatives and political clients of government ministers which maladminister agriculture in so many countries, but the actual policies they seek to apply. For the power base of most African governments lies in the cities, and the urban masses demand low-priced food.

Unfortunately, keeping people in the cities contented with cheap food means that the prices paid to farmers must also be low. In many places they are so low that the peasants find it is simply not worth growing more than they need to feed their own families. Over much of Africa the peasants are reverting to subsistence agriculture, which leaves them with scant reserves themselves when weather or politics disrupt the normal growing pattern. The urban populations become more and more dependent on imported food, and every disaster in the countryside swells the population of the cities.

It is a vicious circle whose causes are mainly political, and the solution is political too. What is needed are governments with the courage to pay higher prices to the peasants, so they will have an incentive to stay on the land and raise more food, even if that means the urban populations have to pay more for it.

Otherwise, Africa will never recover the ability to feed itself, and it will face recurrent and ever more serious crises.

Gwynne Dyer, *The Toronto Star* 1983

Regular emergency food aid is being distributed through the UN World Food Program. Payments are made in food to local populations for their work on rural development projects. For example, workers on an irrigation ditch are paid in food. The idea is to provide emergency support while at the same time trying to improve the future capacity for local food production. The USA is the chief donor, providing about 75% of all food aid to the program. Canada provides another 15%, followed by Australia, West Germany and Japan (which has delivered rice from surplus stocks since 1970). Aid is also supplied from non-governmental sources, as the following article explains.

Canadian farmers start aid bank

Sometime this month, Norm Brown and about 30 other southern Manitoba farmers will tackle the back-breaking task of bagging some 1,200 tonnes of Canadian wheat and loading it on rail freight cars.

From the bagging process at a seed cleaning plant in Plum Coulee, the wheat will be transported to the Vancouver docks, where it will become part of an 8,000-tonne shipment bound for India.

Four hundred and fifty bushels of that shipment comes from Brown's 640-acre farm, about 120 kilometres (75 miles) southwest of Winnipeg. The wheat donation and the voluntary hours he works are his contribution to a "Christian response to hunger," called the Canadian Foodgrains Bank, involving farmers, churches and the federal government.

Bank organizers looked to the Old Testament story of the first food bank when Joseph gathered grain during the good years and distributed it during the lean years.

"The Joseph story as a model is a good one," Brown said in an interview from his home. "It recognizes the cyclical weather patterns and stores up food in the good years."

Brown said that, as a Mennonite, the bank helps meet what he sees as Christ's challenge to minister to the needy.

"It's one way of doing it. There are others."

The bank also helps ease some of the frustration he feels at the world's food imbalance, where food is produced in abundance to feed people who are often overfed while millions go hungry.

There is also the farmer's sense that drought can hit anywhere in the world: There may come a time "when we will need their help."

The idea of a food bank seeded in the early 1970s as a backdrop of global food shortages and economic emergencies.

Mennonite field workers returning home to Canada after trips abroad suggested such a bank to help ensure a supply of food for distribution during the lean years. The idea was to involve all the churches in a sizable program that would draw on the resources of Canadian farmers to help alleviate emergencies abroad.

The complexity of the wheat trade determined that the bank be on a smaller scale than originally proposed.

"When they went around the grain-controlling agencies like the Canadian Wheat Board and the Canadian Grain Commission, it was realized that the movement of grain — the selling, marketing and movement of grain — is very highly regulated in Canada," said Wilbert Loewen, executive director of the Canadian Foodgrains Bank.

"Finally, it was decided it could be a complicated thing if they went too big. They went back to the Mennonite Central Committee, which agreed to try it first within the Mennonite constituency."

The Canadian International Development Agency promised $2.50 for every dollar raised. (CIDA now contributes $3 for every $1 raised.)

Loewen said it took three to four years to work things out before the bank became fully operational. In the years under Mennonite control, the bank shipped 45,000 tonnes of wheat to Asia, Africa and Central and South America. In the last year, under Mennonite supervision, about $1.2 million, including CIDA donations, was raised.

Two years ago, the Mennonites decided to broaden the base and invited other denominations to join. The Baptist Federation of Canada, the Canadian Lutheran World Relief, the Christian Missionary Alliance, the

Christian Reformed World Relief Committee of Canada, the United Church of Canada and the Pentecostal Assemblies of Canada joined, and the Canadian Foodgrains Bank was established last year.

"We're not anticipating immediately multiplying $1.2 million by seven," Loewen said. "It may take three to five years before it takes off. The important thing is that all partners have control over their own resources. It's like a bank. Each partner has protection and they get monthly printouts of what they have in the bank.

"What we think is a real plus for the program, and also why the Canadian government is so excited about it, is that we will not just ship the wheat without having thoroughly investigated the situation by the field staff who will monitor its distribution."

The bank's main objectives are to provide food for emergency relief, provide food while reconstruction and rehabilitation programs are underway and for long term development.

The bank gets its grain two ways. Farmers market the grain in the nor-mal way and send the cash to the bank, which uses the money along with CIDA funds to buy wheat from the Canadian Wheat Board.

Farmers can also donate grain produced on their farms, which is collected through specially organized drives and stored at 15 collection depots. The grain is then bagged and transported to the dock before being shipped abroad. In all cases, donors can designate contributions to a member church agency, and the amount is credited to the agency's account.

The bank also receives cash donations from farmers and non-farmers to buy wheat and pay for its transportation.

Take the case of the request for 8,000 tonnes of wheat received five weeks ago from Mennonite field staff in India.

Of the total, 2,500 tonnes will come from collection depots in Manitoba and Alberta and will be bagged there because only the Canadian Wheat Board can transport in bulk. The rest will be bought in bulk from the board.

Once the shipment reaches India, it will be distributed by the Canadian Lutheran World Relief and Casa, an Indian organizaton representing 20 Christian denominations.

The wheat will be used as food for work-development projects as farmers work their own land on catchment schemes, the deepening of wells and other programs.

Loewen estimates there are now about 3,000 farmers involved in the food bank program. He said much of the activity is focused in western Canada — the bank, with a staff of three, has its headquarters in Winnipeg. He hopes the program will be expanded into eastern Canada and the bank program will be used to ship corn and other grain abroad.

Loewen also said that administration costs are cut to a minimum by the amount of volunteer help the program receives. It's in the area of self-help that the program may be most effective as it supplies food to people struggling for independence.

"We'd like to work ourselves out of a job," he added.

Reprinted with permission of Toronto Star
Syndicate 1984 3 3

DISCUSSION AND RESEARCH

13. What are some of the advantages and disadvantages of the different solutions to the causes of hunger?
14. Give several of the arguments for and against the destruction of food by governments in food surplus countries?
15. Should farmers in food surplus countries be discouraged from producing more than a certain amount of food, as Ontario milk producers and US wheat growers often are?

Food is more than just nourishment; it is part of each culture's valued tradition. The cultural values attached to certain foodstuffs lead to constraints in the availability of food supplies. Most culturally-based food taboos have little to do with nutrition. For example, most North Americans will not eat snakes or dogs, although these protein-rich foods are delicacies in other parts of the world. In southern India people will not eat wild greens, rich in vitamins and iron. Other examples are the avoidance of beef by Hindus and of pork by Jews and Moslems. Food taboos sometimes cause people to refuse healthful food that would otherwise be available to them.

Rice, wheat and corn are foods acceptable to most cultures, but even these cannot always be substituted one for another. People who usually eat rice as a staple will not, for example, switch readily to wheat or corn, even in an emergency. Meats and dairy foods also have a generally high acceptability, but some taboos are still attached.

The chief trouble with the most widely accepted staples is that they provide a very limited diet. Therefore, to solve the problem of malnutrition, other acceptable and nutritious foods are being introduced through food redistribution programs. Donors often experiment to see what is acceptable. Some successes include *incaparina*, containing 25% high quality vegetable protein that can be mixed with local flour and water; milk biscuits, which provide whole milk to children in areas where there is no water; and superamine, consisting of a 20% protein mixture of wheat, lentils, peas, milk powder and vitamins.

Meanwhile, experiments continue with fish flour, which contains over 70% protein but remains an unappetizing, tasteless grey powder. There are also food analogues, in which substitutes for natural foods are made artificially. Researchers are also studying the use of bacteria for food. Bacteria are rich in protein and they multiply at a fantastic rate. It is estimated that 1 000 kg of bacteria could produce as much as 100 trillion kg of protein daily. Social acceptance might present a problem, but the benefits would be substantial.

Incaparina is a mixture of corn, sorghum, cottonseed, yeast, calcium and Vitamin A. It was developed by the Institute for Central American Nutrition.

Increasing the Quantities of Food Available

"Give a man a fish," runs an old proverb, "and you give him a meal. Teach him how to fish and you give him a living."

Many people now agree that the best way to help the world's hungry to eat better on a long-term basis is to help in providing the education, appropriate technology and capital to increase food production. Several years ago (*UNESCO Courier* 1975 5) the Minister of Agriculture for Mauritius described some of the requirements for increasing food production:

If you want to increase food production in the developing countries, the necessary facilities for which we have been asking for decades now must be provided. The constraints which lie in our way should

Unicef/Bill Campbell

"Teach a man to fish . . . ." Somali nomads weigh their morning catch at the Brava fisheries centre. Their training in fishing and fish processing is part of a program to give nomads from Somalia's drought-stricken northern areas a new living.

be removed or mitigated. What are these constraints? Shortage and high cost of fertilizers, high cost of pesticides, high cost of farm machinery, lack of trained personnel, lack of finance, and, most important of all, of a reasonable level of income for the farmers. This can only be achieved by guaranteed and stable markets and reasonable prices for farm products.

Accordingly, the international community has organized many agencies whose goal is to assist in increasing food production. They do this by means of environmental studies and consultation, technical and financial help and organized research into appropriate farming methods and farm inputs, all in addition to the emergency food relief mentioned earlier. The main channel for this aid is the Development Assistance Committee (DAC) of the Organization for Economic Co-operation and Development (OECD). About 90% of the world's financial aid comes from DAC members, with 40% coming from the USA.

The members of the DAC are Australia, Austria, Belgium, Canada, Denmark, Finland, France, Italy, Japan, Netherlands, New Zealand, Norway, Sweden, Switzerland, UK, USA and West Germany.

The DAC has targeted government assistance from its members at a level of 0.7% of each member's Gross National Product. For the last several years, the achieved level is about half of that. However, there is a huge additional flow of technical, financial and research assistance from organized groups of private citizens (e.g., Oxfam, the Red Cross) as well as from commercial companies within the DAC countries. The combined aid flow from all sources, official, private and commercial, reaches about 0.8% of the GNP, compared with a target for all aid flows of 1%. Assistance also comes from a variety of other countries that are not members of DAC, chiefly the USSR, South Africa and Spain.

The following articles suggest some ways in which people believe the aid should be used. As you go through the articles, list the things that would help to increase food production.

Possible Solutions

1. Support for small-scale farmers:

- Price incentives as well as government programmes to provide agricultural credit, training, and marketing assistance to farmers are required to increase staple food production. Land reform programmes could increase levels of food production in many areas of Africa.

- Throughout most of Africa women produce 80% of food crops. Women should be granted equal status in all aspects of food and agricultural production.

- Subsistence farmers and small producers have been discriminated against by banking institutions. Ghana has experimented with a new rural banking system: nearly half of all loans and advances go into food crop farming and small farmers have proven themselves creditworthy, with a default rate of less than 5%.

2. Marketing and distribution:

- Regulation of the domestic market in staple foods can help solve the problem of drastic seasonal price fluctuations. Government-supported regional cooperatives are now being tried in Burkina Faso, Mali and Niger. The cooperatives buy grain at a controlled price and sell it at the same price throughout the year. This prevents market speculation.

Canadian Red Cross Society, *Global Report 1985–1986*

At the beginning of the 1960s, a group of experts on a field assignment drafted and carried out a soil recovery project in the Sahelian region of Upper Volta. Accurate measurements and calculations showed that the erosion caused by a torrential rainstorm lasting about twenty minutes amounted to some 14 tonnes of fine topsoil per hectare. This calculation gave eloquent proof of the interest of the project, for which farmers were recruited to help dig small dikes along contour lines to control rainfall. To the experts the value of this laudable project was evident. Unfortunately, however, the promoters failed to ensure that the farmers also understood the advantages it offered them. Because they were neither consulted nor paid to maintain the dikes, the farmers soon lost all interest in the "white man's ditches." It was only some years later, when those dikes that had not collapsed controlled the rainwater flow, bringing more water to the wells and improving neighbouring fields, that some of the farmers began to understand the value of the project. Those farmers who recognized the benefits to be obtained requested no financing whatsoever to repair or rebuild their dikes.

This experience and many others observed in the field provide proof that even the best rural development projects, designed by experts and backed with all the material, technical and financial resources needed, are destined to fail if the farmers in whose interest they are purported to be carried out do not feel sufficiently concerned to offer their unreserved participation and if they lack the assurance that the projects are for their own benefit.

It is important, therefore, to seek methods of approach that involve farmers as much as possible rather than insisting on taking decisions for them and imposing solutions on them without taking the precaution of soliciting their opinion. This is an essential prerequisite to obtaining their collaboration. Without the farmers' wholehearted involvement no profound changes can take place. Their participation cannot be obtained by presidential decree or ministerial decision. Tangible, coordinated measures are required which will progressively create a favourable environment, working at a pace acceptable to the farmers and not racing ahead at the speed of technicians and politicians. The farmer must be assured that the land he needs as well as seeds, equipment and other inputs, of adequate quality, will be made available to him at the right time and in sufficient quantity. Furthermore, he must have some guarantee that, when production begins, he will not be despoiled of the fruits of his labour.

UNESCO Courier 1984 4

Increasingly, the energy used in agriculture will be in the form of chemical fertilizer. As population grows, cropland per person shrinks and fertilizer requirements climb. And erosion that has robbed soils of nutrients is forcing farmers to use more fertilizers. Even urbanization is raising demand, since as people move to cities it is harder to recycle the nutrients in human and household waste. Yet the combination of rising energy costs and diminishing returns on the use of additional fertilizer raises doubts that

adequate food supplies can be produced in the future at prices the world's poor can afford.

The central importance of the population/land/fertilizer relationship is a recent phenomenon. Before 1950 increases in food output came largely from expanding the cultivated area, but with the scarcity of fertile new land and the advent of cheap chemical fertilizer this changed. Between 1950 and 1983 world fertilizer use climbed from 15 million to 114 million tons, nearly an eightfold increase within a generation. In effect, as fertile land became harder to find, farmers learned to substitute energy in the form of chemical fertilizer for land. Fertilizer factories replaced new land as the principal source of growth in food production.

This substitution of energy for land is graphically evident: In 1950, when world population totaled 2.51 billion, the harvested area of cereals per person was 0.24 hectares. As growth in population greatly outstripped that of cultivated area, the area per person fell steadily, declining to 0.15 hectares by 1983. While the amount of cropland per person declined by one third, the fertilizer consumption per person quintupled, climbing from just over 5 kilograms in 1950 to 25 kilograms in 1983.

The hybridization of corn and the dwarfing of the wheat and rice varieties that have been at the heart of Third World agricultural advances over the last two decades figured prominently, of course, in the growth in world food output. So, too, did the doubling of irrigated area. But the effectiveness of all these practices depends heavily on the use of chemical fertilizer. Without an adequate supply of plant nutrients, high-yielding

cereal varieties hold little advantage over traditional ones. Likewise, an increase in irrigation is of little consequence if the nutrients to support the higher yields are lacking.

UNESCO Courier 1984 4

Rivers must be dammed for electrical power and water control; deep tube-wells must be sunk; . . . land must be shaped for irrigation; canals and drainage channels must be dug; a whole new organizational pattern must be built among the cultivators; and new agricultural supply, credit and marketing structures must evolve.

The Globe and Mail 1974 4 12

A grain with more nutrition than wheat, similar baking qualities, and hardy enough to grow where wheat cannot survive — that's what scientists are perfecting. It's called Triticale (a name coined from combining the generic names of its parents, rye and wheat) and it could have a major impact on world food supplies during the coming years of shortages.

Cooperation Canada 1974 9

But growing more food is a less effective answer than saving the food that is already grown. If attacks on waste were to save only 10% more of the wheat harvest, for instance, that would add nearly 30m tons to world supplies, making (in theory) nearly one-third more wheat available for international trade. The developing countries' food needs exceed actual supplies by more than 6% only in exceptional circumstances, and it would take only a small improvement in grain storage and processing to eliminate that gap.

But it is immediately after harvesting that the biggest savings can be made. Up to a third of a cereal crop can be lost in post-harvest handling, processing and distribution, and even higher proportions of perishable foods like fruit and vegetables.

At the Rotterdam conference, Dr. H. A. B. Parpia, of the FAO, gave some measures of the damage done by rats, insects and various micro-organisms. Six rats can eat the food of one man; and in a year a pair of rats can produce up to 70 offspring that survive to maturity. A state of emergency had to be declared in Mindanao, in the Philippines, in 1953, when rats destroyed nearly 70% of the crop. When the rat population reaches a density of 0.78 per square metre, as has happened in a food warehouse in Calcutta, the problem is worse than an emergency.

Less pests — more crops

	Pesticide (grams)	Crop yield (kilograms)
	per hectare	
Japan	10 790	5 480
Europe	1 870	3 430
USA	1 490	2 600
Africa	127	1 210
India	149	820

The threat from insects is less obvious, but just as damaging. The pulse beetle passes through eight overlapping generations in a year, and the progeny of 40 eggs can halve the weight of infested grain in six months, as well as contaminating what is left.

But waste of this sort is difficult to deal with in developing countries; about three-quarters of their basic food crops never enter western-style storage, processing and distribution channels, so there is little control over handling.

The Economist 1975 3 22

There are certain plus-factors which can justify a measure of optimism. Foremost among these are the under-estimated versatility and skills of the African farmer. His readiness to innovate is clear from the fact that many of the food and export crops most widely grown have been introduced from outside Africa in modern times. Furthermore, traditional cropping systems are frequently elaborate and — within their limits — efficient. The difficulty is that they were developed over many generations to feed an approximately stable population, and do not lend themselves to sustained increases in productivity. Indeed, no fully satisfactory approach has yet been found for continuous and intensive cropping under the agroecological conditions that prevail in much (though not all) of tropical Africa. There is a technological gap, particularly with regard to soil management and labour productivity, which must be filled before the African farmer can cope with the food needs of the continent.

Technology, however, is not all. Agriculture can prosper only in a favourable policy environment. At the time of their independence, many African countries appear to have seriously under-estimated both the importance and the difficulties of the agricultural sector. As a result, domestic food production has seldom been given the priority it needed.

In a broader context, a bias against agriculture generally, and food production in particular, has become built into the socio-economic structure of many African States, and affects such fundamental issues as exchange-rate and taxation policies, relative price levels, and priorities for the development of infrastructure. It is reflected also in the relatively low prestige attached to work in the farm sector. If food production is to find a new vitality, many countries will have to alter profoundly the attitude toward agriculture held not only by planners and politicians but also by the population as a whole.

The international community, for its part, must find new ways of helping Africa to help itself. Investment and technical assistance are vitally needed, but a multiplicity of small projects, each with its own administrative requirements, can place disproportionate demands upon government services which are desperately short of trained people. Ways must be found of helping governments to redress the balance of economic power in favour of food producers, without precipitating a revolution in the cities. And it must be recognized that, if the African food crisis has been developing for twenty years, it may well take just as long to resolve.

The gravity of the situation has been fully recognized within Africa, for instance in the Lagos Plan of Action adopted in April 1980 by the members of the Organization of African Unity. A framework for action within Africa and by the international community is contained in FAO's Regional Food Plan for Africa. Many studies have been made by other organizations, notably the World Bank, and there is no shortage of analysis and prescription. However, there is as yet no clear evidence that the tide has started to turn. Africa south of the Sahara remains the world's principal food-problem area.

There is no simple explanation of why efforts to eradicate hunger have lost momentum or why food supplies for some segments of humanity are less secure than they were, say, 15 years ago. Declines in food security involve the continuous interaction of environmental, economic, demographic, and political variables.

Some analysts see the food problem almost exclusively as a population issue, noting that wherever population growth rates are low, food supplies are generally adequate. Others view it as a problem of resources — soil, water, and energy. Many economists see it almost exclusively as a result of under-investment, while agronomists see it more as a failure to bring forth new technologies on the needed scale. Still others see it as a distribution problem. To some degree it is all of these.

The issue is not whether the world can produce more food. Indeed, it would be difficult to put any foreseeable limits on the amount the world's farmers can produce. The question is at what price they will be able to produce it and how this relates to the purchasing power of the poorer segments of humanity. The environmental, demographic, and economic trends of the 1970s and early 1980s indicate that widespread improvements in human nutrition will require major course corrections. Nothing less than a wholesale re-examination and re-ordering of social and economic priorities — giving agriculture and family planning the emphasis they deserve — will get the world back on an economic and demographic path that will reduce hunger rather than increase it.

DISCUSSION AND RESEARCH

16. Group the recommended courses of action into those of a purely mechanical nature and those requiring cultural and value decisions. For example, bringing new land into cultivation may be a simple mechanical matter requiring only the will and resources to do it, whereas land reform entails cultural decisions about the sort of society that will emerge after reform. The decision whether to use pesticides concerns other values. Which decisions do you think it is easier for a government to act on? How do you suggest action be taken on the more difficult changes?

There are many different proposals for increasing food production and easing the various cultural, social and political constraints. We shall now consider some of these possibilities in more detail.

The Introduction of New Technologies

The introduction of new techniques is often considered a vital step towards increased food productivity. In the *UNESCO Courier* of 1984 4, Yuri Ovchinnikov of the USSR Academy of Sciences writes that "It is impossible today to achieve an increase in production yields per hectare of land, per head of cattle, or per tonne of raw material unless advantage is taken of the latest scientific discoveries."

International activity in this area is feverish and extremely varied. It includes work in the development of machinery appropriate for use in

Opened in 1986, a research farm in North Saanich, British Columbia, is experimenting with the raising of dairy cows in a controlled setting. Feed is grown hydroponically on conveyor belts, cut by robots and fed into a computerized mixing system, which feeds precisely the correct amount to each cow, identified by a computer reading of its electronically encoded collar. Up to 500 dairy cows are kept on an area of 15 ha, whereas a herd this size would normally need about 100 ha.

New technologies of food production can be introduced to the very young. Students at this day-care nursery (*hogares infantiles*) in Guayaquil, Ecuador, are learning to grow vegetables.

developing countries and the practical use of research in the biochemistry of plants and animals. It involves applying the results of research into controlling the environment. It also deals with problems related to the transmission, adaptation and acceptance of ideas and techniques already successfully established elsewhere. Consider the following examples of work already in progress. They illustrate the amazingly diverse and imaginative ways in which food production problems are being addressed.

In northeast Tanzania, Canadian large-scale wheat technology is used by a number of large state-run wheat farms. The government, with Canada's help, started large-scale wheat production in the area as early as 1970. A research program to develop locally suitable strains of wheat using locally appropriate farming techniques was first established. Then two state farms were cleared to test and demonstrate developments. A research breakthrough in 1976 promised a tripling of yields. There are now six farms under cultivation, all run by Tanzanians, many of whom trained in Canada. Canadian personnel are now limited to one adviser and one mechanic per farm. More Tanzanians are being trained, but now on the state farms themselves. About 90% of Tanzania's wheat is produced by these six farms, satisfying about half the country's demand. Work is expected to continue to expand the number of state farms in the area.

An Ottawa engineering firm has designed a special solar-powered grain dryer. Experiments in Guatemala proved very successful; a manufacturing facility for the solar dryers now operates there. According to the manufacturers, the dryers pay for themselves in two or three years from the fuel that is saved.

The International Fund for Agricultural Development (IFAD) directs its assistance entirely to the small farmers and landless labourers who are the heart of food production in much of the developing world. In Bangladesh, IFAD has funded the construction of wells for irrigation, enabling small farmers to triple their output of rice. Also in Bangladesh, many landless labourers have been helped to buy cows and goats to improve their income opportunities. In Kenya and Nepal, rural women are receiving IFAD aid in the form of agricultural training and access to credit.

Artificial insemination is meant to improve livestock genetically and to increase the rate of reproduction among animals. The genetic improvements brought about in beef cattle in the USA between 1950 and 1980, for example, raised beef output by 70%, while the number of beef cattle increased by only 17%. Also, using Canadian Holstein bulls, Mexico has used artificial insemination to improve quickly its milk yields from specially-bred cows. About 80% of Mexico's milk comes from 20% of its cows, indicating the amount of potential growth available.

Improvements in pest control are another means of increasing available food supplies. According to the World Health Organization (WHO) a single rat can devour up to 30 kg and spoil an additional 150 kg of foodstuffs per year. There are several billion rats in the world. Pheromones (the biochemical attractants used by animals and insects) are a recent discovery, and their use makes the catching of rats several times more efficient.

Other work is being done to replace canal irrigation by sprinkler or drip irrigation; to replace hand seeding by the use of seed drills; to develop hydroponics, whereby crops are raised in water; to apply weather control techniques such as cloud seeding and frost avoidance; to research

Some people object to the farming of beef cattle because they are relatively inefficient converters of crops to meat. These people argue that the land would be better used to grow crops for direct human consumption.

Sprinkler irrigation uses pipes and sprays rather than open ditches. This method reduces water losses by evaporation and to weed growth along ditch-banks. The quantities of water applied and the times of application can be more carefully regulated. In advanced systems of sprinkler irrigation, humidity sensors in the soil next to the plants are connected to computers that turn the water flow on and off according to the sensor readings. Fertilizers and/or pesticides can also be mixed with the irrigation water for easy and cost-cutting application. Drip irrigation, in which dripping water is fed to individual plants by plastic tubing, is even more economical on water; since only the crops receive water, few weeds grow.

Every drop of water in the desert must be conserved. At Al-Jihasi in the Yemen Arab Republic, water is enclosed in pipes to prevent evaporation before it reaches its point of use.

into multicropping, in which an area of land may be made to yield two different crops a year instead of one; and to produce genetically-engineered crops (called "hybrids") with higher yields and more resistance to pests and plant diseases.

These are just some of the hundreds of new techniques, many still experimental, being applied around the world. Much of the experimental work is done by UN agencies, chiefly the FAO and UNESCO, but also by many independent international groups such as the OECD and the Colombo Plan countries. The research is often carried out by university personnel or by people working for major charitable foundations.

Probably the most spectacular event in the application of new plants and techniques has been the "Green Revolution." The term describes the interconnected series of changes resulting from the expanding application of new technologies and seeds throughout the world. Starting in the early 1960s, the International Maize (corn) and Wheat Improvement Centre, called CIMMYT (for Centro Internacional de Mejoramiento de Maiz y Trigo), based in Mexico, and the International Rice

Research Institute, called IRRI, based in the Philippines, have worked profound changes in the world's agricultural scene. Almost one-third of Asia's rice is now produced from IRRI's high-yielding varieties, and almost half of the area planted to wheat uses CIMMYT varieties.

IRRI has produced semi-dwarf rice plants with strong, stiff stems that hold plants upright even with greatly higher yields. The new plants also have more foliage, enabling them to collect more sunshine and increasing photosynthesis. These new varieties are not affected by variations in length of daylight, so farmers in many latitudes can grow them. Some of them also resist pests even without chemical protection. A prime example of increased production is India where, prior to the introduction of high-yielding varieties of rice and wheat in 1965, rice output was about 46 000 000 t/y and wheat output was about 12 000 000 t/y. By 1984 India had reached 83 000 000 t/y for rice and 59 000 000 t/y for wheat (increases of 80% and 392% respectively). During the 1970s India changed from a receiver of food aid to a provider of food aid to its neighbours. It is one of the remarkable successes in food production.

IRRI and CIMMYT have succeeded so well that they are used as models for similar research organizations. They now form part of a family of 13 independent international agricultural research centres supported by the Consultative Group on International Agricultural Research (CGIAR), an informal association of governments (including Canada), international and regional organizations and private foundations, established in 1971.

Most of the research centres funded by CGIAR work with cereals, chiefly rice, wheat and maize. They focus on breeding varieties that produce high yields under different environmental conditions, e.g., length of day, altitude, climate, soil quality and water availability, while also being as resistant as possible to pests and disease. The centres also try to improve local farming systems to increase total productivity. Among such means are the development and use of appropriate farming and post-harvest technologies, the use of crop rotation and the application of natural fertilizers. Much effort also goes into training scientists from the developing world and helping to develop national agricultural research systems.

Despite the work and the successes of the CGIAR centres there is still much to be done. The centres are now directing increasing efforts to help farmers who have limited resources and farmers living in areas with adverse environments. The centres also are paying more attention to the social, economic and political factors that possibly limit the use of improved technologies and the equitable distribution of benefits. Another goal is to encourage the development of national research centres equipped to deal with the local conditions in the developing countries.

IRRI has produced many different varieties of rice. The most famous in getting the Green Revolution started were IR5 and IR8, representing respectively the successful results of the 5th and 8th experiments by IRRI.

Despite the production of surpluses, India still has millions of malnourished people. Remember, a surplus exists where there is no market for it, and a market requires that the potential buyers be able to pay for what they want. Many in India are too poor to be part of the market, as are those receiving food stamps in the USA.

Crop rotation means changing the crops in an orderly pattern from year to year so that the land has a chance to remain fertile. Some crops, such as wheat, are very exhausting to a soil, and when grown year after year gradually deplete the soil's fertility. It is desirable every so often to grow a crop such as clover, which nourishes the soil.

Although the application of new technologies to food production may be desirable as a means of increasing the quantity of food available, their introduction can sometimes cause problems elsewhere in society. The displacement of farmers is one example of the type of socio-economic problem that can result from the application of new technology. Green Revolution technology is beyond the present reach of some farmers. For example, farmers need to use the new hybrid seeds, they need more irrigation water and, usually, more fertilizer. Therefore, it often is only the richer farmers who have easy access to Green Revolution technology. Accordingly they grow richer, often buying out the poorer farmers to obtain still more land.

In India, this consolidation of holdings into fewer hands runs counter to the national policy of land reform, which has aimed since independence in 1947 to divide the larger holdings and transfer land to a multitude of small farmers. The government has established maximum sizes for farms to prevent both consolidation and the creation of large numbers of landless people who then migrate to towns for jobs which do not exist in sufficient number. The government also has fostered the growth of many co-operatives for small farmers so that they might have improved access to the new technologies through bulk purchases and better credit. The government also favours the widespread development of cottage industries to provide alternative employment in the rural areas, slow the migration to the cities and stimulate small-scale industrial activity.

New Organizations

Various organizations have been formed to increase food production. Some, like farmers' unions, co-operatives, land banks, agricultural credit and loan societies and competitive shows, are primarily economic in purpose. Others, such as communes and kibbutzim, also serve social and political purposes. Communes, for example, were the main instrument by which the Chinese government sought from 1949 to 1979 to organize rural production. During the rule of Mao Zedong (1949–76) significant progress was made in attaining local self-reliance. Communes were encouraged to organize all production on a co-operative basis, using the full resources of the local community. Each commune organized its use of fields, irrigation, collection and application of fertilizer, planting, harvesting and distribution of collective income so that everyone was involved in production and everyone got a fair share of food to eat. The level of food availability to all improved greatly.

Since Mao's death in 1976, however, and the subsequent introduction in 1979 of ideas of profit and individual initiative within a new collective framework, internal food production has increased dramatically. The annual per capita availability of rice in China increased from

Rice paddies near Guangzhou are part of China's self-sufficiency in food production.

136 kg in 1977 to 173 kg in 1984. Similar figures for wheat are 44 kg and 85 kg respectively, and for meat, 8 kg and 15 kg (data from *Population and Development Review* 1986 3). China is now virtually self-sufficient in food. Its present farm "responsibility system," building on the successes of the Mao era, allows collectives to contract out land for farming to small groups and even to individual households. Bonuses are paid to those who exceed production targets, while penalties are imposed to discourage shortfall. These changes are supported at the government level by the importation of such new technologies as land reclamation and satellite crop monitoring. Satellites also show the beginnings of soil erosion and the onset of plant diseases and the spread of pests, enabling early preventive action.

Many of these new rural organizations (co-operatives, credit and loan societies, communes and kibbutzim) serve primarily to equalize production opportunities for all farmers by giving them equal access to machinery, credit, technology and marketing resources. In some cases the resistance of the large landowners has had to be overcome by government action, as in South Korea, where the government instituted the Saemaul Movement in 1970. This movement encompassed massive

An area's food production can be increased by forming gardening co-operatives. These villagers in Botswana have just finished planting a communal garden.

land reform along with the creation of a variety of co-operatives, and all farmers were provided with training in the new system of organization.

Elsewhere, the organization of small landowners for increased food production is assisted by outside agencies, such as the Participatory Institute for Development Alternatives (PIDA). Approaches that involve the organization of smaller farmers alone, rather than of whole communities, are called grass-roots initiatives. The article on page 100 describes how a group of small farmers in the village of Ranna, Sri Lanka, became organized.

Agribusinesses are another sort of food-producing organization. They are usually headquartered in developed countries, buying or renting farmland and hiring managers to run the operations as business enterprises. Some, such as Kraft Foods of Chicago, or Unilever of Rotterdam, are very large, with branch operations in other countries. Some branch operations are in the developing countries, where plantations may be operated to produce various items such as oil-seeds and fruit.

Such production in the developing countries is almost entirely export-oriented and denies the local populations access to the product as well as to the land itself. This is hotly criticized in the developing countries,

The impact of participatory action research

As a PIDA action researcher my experience in working with small farmers has proved that organized small groups of about 10–15 farmers are capable of breaking the vicious cycle of poverty through self-reliant methods.

In the village of Ranna, twenty five vegetable cultivators (small producers) formed a group and analysed their poverty situation. As a result they realized that unless they reduced the expenditure in cultivation, they would not break the cycle. Therefore, they started sharing labour, rather than hiring it from outside and eliminated the hired labour cost, totally. In this way they were able to save Rs.[rupees] 25.00/–per season, as a group. This experience was so encouraging, that the farmers started a small collective farm which they cultivated as a group in their leisure time. The income generated from this farm helped them to build up a common fund. They decided to deposit the money in a bank. They discussed with the bank also the possibilities of breaking away from the money lenders, and [made] strong arguments as to why the banks should support the process and assist the poorest groups such as themselves. At the end of the discussion the Bank which had hitherto not been doing so had to agree that they could provide their services to this category of farmers. The result was that for the first time they were able to raise Bank loans for cultivation purposes at the rate of Rs. 2,000/– per person. In order to manage with their limited resources, they jointly explored all the possibilities for reducing their expenditure. As a result, on one hand they bought all agricultural inputs in bulk on wholesale price, on the other they reduced their household expenditure, by purchasing the consumer items in bulk at wholesale rates. . . .

S.P. Wickramaarachchi *is Action Researcher with the Participatory Institute for Development Alternatives (PIDA), Sri Lanka.*

Society for International Development, Rome 1984 2

but there is also much support for such plantations based on the jobs and incomes as well as the export earnings they provide. Different developing countries pursue different policies with regard to the continued existence of plantations. Some, such as Cuba, have nationalized the land and taken over production locally. Others have, like Jamaica, developed mixed economies, with some plantations permitted to exist while others are broken up and their production scattered among small farmers. Still others, such as Panama, allow plantations to exist without restrictions.

Land Reform

Land reform is regarded by many governments and farmers as a significant step toward increasing food supplies. Land reform may involve the consolidation of small and scattered holdings into a single unified holding (as in the *remembrement* movement in France and the collectivization activities of communist states). Usually it involves the breakup of large estates into a number of smaller farmer-owned holdings. The process of land reform is often lengthy and inevitably entails a restructuring of local rural society.

Land reforms of all types generally reduce the influence of the landlords. New possibilities arise for formerly dependent workers. There is more security, more status, more mobility. Local leadership is encouraged; self-worth is enhanced. And output may increase. There is strong evidence from the FAO to indicate that small farms are usually more productive per hectare than larger farms (although less productive per worker). Given that smaller farms, often family-owned, usually support more people, the higher yields per hectare are beneficial in providing not only more total food but also more rural employment. However, there is little clear evidence to indicate that land reform itself causes increases in output.

Research in Bolivia over a 20 year period (1955–1975) most clearly demonstrates increases in output, but it is difficult to isolate the effects of land reform from the positive effects of other related factors such as improved technology, more favourable price policies and so on. Nevertheless, there are enough countries where output has increased following land reform to regard the changes as positive. This is especially true if it is accepted that, in order to succeed, the process of land reform requires both the redistribution of landholdings and the provision of credit, technology and marketing systems. Such integrated strategies are the heart of most current rural development programs.

The concentration of landholdings into a few hands and the consequent potential need for land reform, can be measured using the *Gini coefficient*. This coefficient is a measure of the concentration of landholdings based on the difference between an existing distribution of holdings and the theoretically even distribution that would occur if 1% of the owners held 1% of the holdings, 20% of the owners held 20% of the holdings and so on. The coefficient ranges from 0.0 to 1.0, with the higher figures indicating high concentrations of ownership in few hands. Generally, the highest Gini coefficients occur in Latin America, the lowest in North America, Europe and Japan. However, Gini coefficients should be treated with care, for they ignore the quality of the land. Small holdings of irrigated land in Tunisia, for example, will provide higher incomes than much larger holdings of some arid or mountainous land. Nevertheless, they are one useful indicator of prevailing conditions.

Prior to the implementation of land reform measures in Mexico, its Gini coefficient was 0.96, indicating an extremely high degree of concentrated land ownership. Land reform began after the revolution of the early 1910s, occurred most swiftly during the 1930s and culminated in 1976. During that period nearly 100 000 000 ha were redistributed among about half the farmers, and the Gini coefficient fell from 0.96 to 0.69. Though the Mexican government ceased redistribution in 1976, inequalities remain in Mexican land ownership.

Taiwanese land reforms started in 1949 and ended in 1953, changing the Gini coefficient there from 0.65 to 0.46. In that short time the proportion of families owning their own land rose from 33% to 59%, and secure long-term leases were arranged for the remaining tenant farmers.

South Korea's changes are even more remarkable. Reform started after World War II, and resulted in the rapid redistribution of about 25% of the total farmland to about 70% of all the farmers. Before the reform, it was estimated that 19% of the farmers owned 90% of the land and that more than 50% of the farmers were in fact landless tenants. Afterwards, 69% of the farmers owned the land on which they worked and another 24% were part owners, while only 7% were tenants.

The issues surrounding political and economic equality are complex. It is, for instance, possible that in a given situation some farmers are more productive than others. In such a case it seems that the common good may be best served by allowing them to collect more land. On the other hand, some larger farmers have become more productive because they have had prior advantages in health, wealth or power over their peers. Since at no known point did all people begin equally, the mere fact of land possession says nothing definite about individual productivity.

Development of Marginal Lands

Another way to increase food supplies is to bring more land into cultivation. For centuries, people simply cleared away the forest or plowed the grassland whenever they needed more land for farming. Today, most of the suitable land is already in use. The last great development of arable land occurred in the early years of this century with the settlement of the Canadian prairies. About as much land as is already cultivated remains to develop, but it is less suitable for use. This is called marginal land. Marginal lands usually have some environmental and economic disadvantages. They are too cold, wet, dry, hilly or remote. However, these lands will be used if the potential farming income from them can be made to repay the cost of bringing them into production. These costs often exist because of the need to apply technology, but probably will not be incurred until the selling price of the marketed food becomes high enough to cover them. Heated underground pipes, artificial sunlight, greenhouses and special fast-ripening seeds permit extensions of farming into colder areas. Water-resistant crops and controlled drainage schemes make possible the farming of marsh areas, while irrigation and drought-resistant crops allow farming to occur in arid and semi-arid environments.

In an economic sense, *marginal* means on the edge of being used or not used; it does not necessarily imply physical remoteness.

Wheat farming in Canada was extended northward because of the production of a faster ripening variety called Marquis. More recently (1983), Columbus wheat was introduced, offering prairie farmers a 5% higher yield per hectare and better harvesting characteristics.

Cultivation of the Sea

The sea is a rich source of food. However, most fishing today is still a form of hunting, even with the use of sonar spotters and other technological aids. To get the best yields from the sea the techniques of farming, namely planting, tending and harvesting, are useful. Fish hatcheries are already common in inland waters, where tending and harvesting are much easier than in the sea. Sheltered ocean bays and estuaries offer good locations for future sea hatcheries, especially where continuous supplies of warm water are available.

DISCUSSION AND RESEARCH

17. The Green Revolution has produced a variety of social, economic and political pressures.
    a. Research what these pressures are.
    b. How can these pressures be minimized?
    c. What difficulties can you foresee in applying your suggested solutions?
    d. Which do you think is more important: more food or less socio-economic pressure? Or does it depend upon your viewpoint?

18. In the 1950s and 1960s China successfully began to feed its people largely from its own resources. One of the alleged costs of this greater output was the loss of much individual freedom. From your perspective, would increased agricultural output justify a loss of individual freedom? Give reasons for your answer.

19. Should a country such as Canada grow more food to give or to sell abroad or should it admit some of the world's hungry people into its territory? Should it do both?

20. Research what preconditions are required for land reform:
    a. to be perceived as necessary; and
    b. to be implemented successfully.

21. Grass-roots initiatives can be called a "bottom-up" approach to rural development in contrast to many aid schemes that have a "top-down" approach.
    a. What do the terms "bottom-up" and "top-down" mean as used here?
    b. Research the prevailing philosophies of each approach.
    c. Is there a place for both approaches in rural development in developing countries? Give reasons.

Coping with Dry Conditions

Heat and moisture are the basic requirements for crop growth. Many areas in the world are warm enough for good growth, but lack the necessary moisture. One way to increase food supplies is to increase the quantity and reliability of water supplies to farmers. People have, however, always had some limited success in farming desert or semi-desert lands. Some of their systems worked well for a stable population, but no longer can meet the demands of a population explosion. Older technologies that used to bring water into water-deficient areas include the water wheel, the foggara tubes, the shaduf and the flooded field. Nomadic herding and cistern storage are traditional methods for coping with infrequent or seasonal drought. Modern technology, when available, broadens the range of possible solutions to the problems of farming dry areas.

This Vietnamese field suggests how difficult can be the development of marginal lands. Here, the dry season converts the land into parched blocks, while the rainy season turns it into a swamp.

Foggaras, or *quanats*, are tunnels driven into a hillside to trap and channel the water that percolates through the ground within the hill. *Shadufs* are simple balances, weighted with stones at one end to facilitate the raising of a bucket filled with water from a river at the other end.

Fig. 3-3
Arid environments

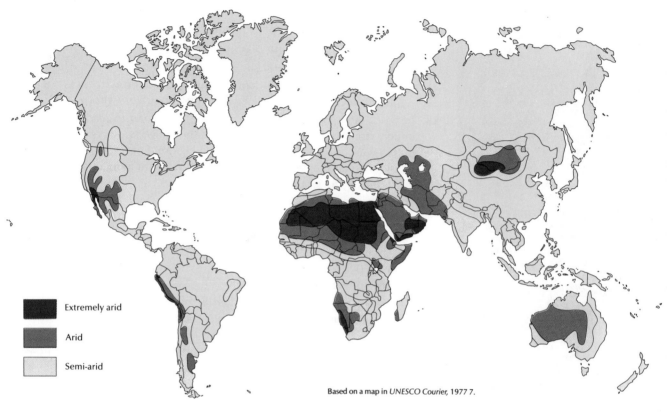

Extremely arid

Arid

Semi-arid

Based on a map in *UNESCO Courier,* 1977 7.

Bringing Water to Water-Deficient Areas

There are several potential sources of water for a water-deficient region. The nearest source is often underground, although such water may be difficult to find and, when found, its use may be restricted to animals because of its extremely high mineral content. Much farming in Australia and the USA depends on modern wells drilled deeply into underground aquifers. Egypt also has recently discovered a huge underground supply of sweet water capable of yielding enough for farming for several decades. The chief problem with such underground water is that it is replenished very slowly by percolating rainfall in surrounding regions. Often it is used much faster than it can be replenished. In the Santa Clara valley of California, underground water was pumped out so fast that unusable sea-water seeped in to replace it, while in another part of the western USA the great Ogallala Aquifer has begun to dry up.

Rivers whose sources are outside dry areas are another major source of water to water-deficient environments. They are called "exotic rivers" because they are foreign to the arid regions. The Nile is the classic example. Its waters have shaped the development of Egypt. The Nile, along with such other exotic rivers as the Colorado and the Indus, has dams, reservoirs and water distribution schemes to help bring water to areas previously without a regular supply.

Like other such projects, the Nile's Aswan High Dam creates problems as well as benefits. It is blamed for increased erosion along Egypt's Mediterranean coast, since it no longer carries much silt down to its delta. It also is held responsible for the decline of the off-shore sardine fishery, the spread of the devastating disease of *bilharzia* (carried by snails that proliferate in the irrigation ditches), the loss of fertile silt downstream from the dam, the increased salt of delta lands as the sea percolates in against a reduced river flow (the river water having been used up in irrigation upstream from the delta), and for increased erosion of bridge piers and river banks as the silt-free waters acquire increased erosive energy. On the other hand, the High Dam has made it possible to harvest more than once a year. Egypt's rice production has more than doubled since the High Dam was built. The electricity generation associated with the dam has also permitted widespread rural electrification and the expansion of Egyptian industry. Many assert that without the dam Egypt would not have escaped the African famines of the 1970s and 1980s.

Any benefits gained by watering naturally arid lands must be measured against the problem such projects create. Exposed reservoirs almost always lose vast amounts of valuable water to evaporation from the water's surface. They also provide breeding grounds for mosquitoes and possible shortages of water near the river mouth where shrunken amounts of water flow. Despite these problems, the promise of a regular water supply in otherwise barren regions is almost irresistible, and some of the world's largest "environment-molding" projects are water transfer plans based on the concept of exotic supplies. The Israeli National Water Plan, summarized in Fig. 3-4, is an example of this. The more extensive California Water Plan is illustrated in Fig. 3-5.

Desalination, the removal of salt from sea-water, is another method of bringing usable water into arid regions. At present there are only three practicable ways of desalinating sea-water: *distillation, electrodialysis* and *refrigeration*. Distillation is the most common, with several large plants around the world, as in Hong Kong, Saudi Arabia, Kuwait and Venezuela; there are also numerous distillation plants in the USA. Electrodialysis, the separation of salt and water by electricity, is rarely used because it is slow and requires too much fuel. Refrigeration is used mostly in Israel, where the Zarchin method of separating ice crystals as they begin to form in the cooling process was developed.

At the moment, all desalination methods are expensive, and the

In the desert, the nearest source of water is often underground. These Yemeni villagers maintain the pump that brings them most of their water.

costs and problems of distribution remain. California has frequently proposed towing icebergs from Antarctica to obtain a large supply of fresh water, and Saudi Arabia actually imports shiploads of water from New Zealand.

Rain-making is another method of obtaining water, although it has never been proven that cloud seeding works; weather is unpredictable, and it is difficult after the fact to know how much rain might have fallen without the seeding. Rain-makers also risk lawsuits from farmers downwind who feel their natural and rightful supply has been taken from them by upwind rain-makers.

Adjusting to Water Shortages

Much time and effort is invested in developing plants that will grow well in very dry areas. These plants may be bred to have any one or more of the following: long root systems to tap underground water supplies, waxy skins to restrict evaporation losses, short stems to minimize unnecessary plant growth, hairy leaves to tap any possible overnight condensation and juicy insides to permit water storage.

In addition, researchers are exploring the development of salt-resistant plants, since arid soils usually contain high levels of salt. Some plants, such as cotton, barley, asparagus and dates, naturally tolerate salt well. Others, such as beans, celery, lemons and oranges, are intolerant. Research aims to extend tolerances and reduce intolerances so that new plant varieties with higher yields can grow in dry areas.

Research also is underway on methods for increasing the condensation of overnight dew. In the dry southern Negev of Israel, farmers plant their crops in slight hollows lined with loose stones so that the stones, which cool rapidly at night, will chill the air around them and encourage condensation. They also cover plants with a polythene sheet pegged horizontally above the plants but weighted slightly in the centre by a pebble (see Fig. 3-7). Moisture from the plants, which is normally lost by evaporation, condenses on the underside of the sheet, while the slight depression caused by the pebble causes the moisture to trickle down the underside of the sheet and drop back on to the plants. The same principle is followed by people who put polythene bags over their houseplants when they leave on holdiay.

Summer fallowing is another useful technique for combating dry conditions. Fallowing leaves the ground unplanted for a year, though it is ploughed and ploughed to prevent rainfall from seeping away. As a result, some water is saved and, when a crop is planted the following year, there is some moisture to help plant growth. This method allows farmers to plant their fields every second year, so that at any one time

Fig. 3-4
Israel's National Water Carrier Plan

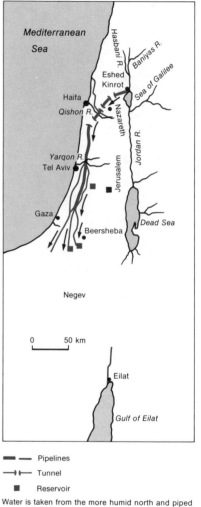

■ ━ ━	Pipelines
→┤├━	Tunnel
■	Reservoir

Water is taken from the more humid north and piped southward toward the Negev Desert. The major irrigation works are between the Yarqon River and Beersheba, although farming continues to push south into the Negev.

An alternative to frequent ploughing is to leave the ground covered with straw or stubble, which restricts evaporation, reduces the risk of soil erosion by wind and provides a measure of fertile humus to help fertilize the following year's crop.

Fig. 3-5
The California Water Plan

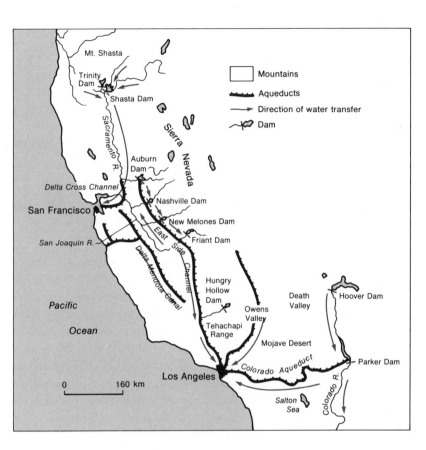

Heavy precipitation, much of it as winter snow, throughout the mountains in the northern parts, especially the Shasta Mountains and the Sierra Nevada, is impounded at a series of dams and channelled southward toward the Mojave Desert. The main recipient of water is Los Angeles.

Irrigation is widespread in the Central Valley and the Los Angeles embayment. Farm productivity is very high under the computerized systems employed, and California ranks first among US states in farm income.

Fig. 3-6
Desalination plants in Saudi Arabia

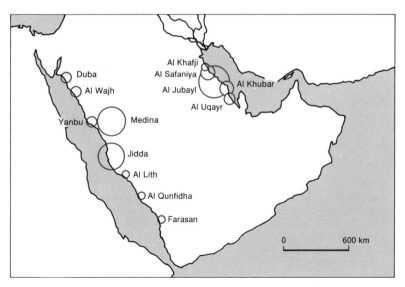

(Circles indicate relative size only.)

Fig. 3-7
A method of conserving plant water

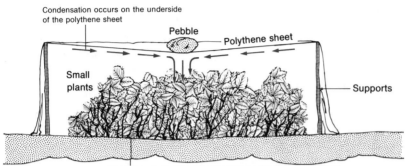

Condensation occurs on the underside
of the polythene sheet

Pebble

Polythene sheet

Small
plants

Supports

Slight slope to channel any water there may be toward the plants

only half the ground is being cultivated. Summer fallowing is very common in the drier parts of the prairie wheatlands in Canada and the USA.

These wheatlands are undoubtedly one of the world's major food surplus areas, and their yields can still be enormously expanded. Farmers in these areas are periodically asked *not* to grow more wheat in order to keep the price of wheat profitable. If prices fall too low, many farmers would be driven out of business. Consumers in developed countries can generally afford these higher prices, though many grumble about them. People in developing countries, however, often cannot afford them. Where many people cannot afford higher food prices, farmers have little incentive to produce for a wide market, and a vicious circle is established. Many changes are needed to approach equity in global food supplies.

In the following case study we will take a more detailed look at some of the particular environmental considerations facing food production in tropical Africa.

The Club of Rome notes that about 40 000 000 ha of prime agricultural land have been deliberately taken out of production in the USA and now lie idle.

TROPICAL AFRICA: Food Production

For centuries, farmers in Tropical Africa have co-existed with their environment and have been able to supply food on a fairly regular life-sustaining basis to their small, stable populations. In recent years, however, populations have increased dramatically, threatening the balance between food needs and the environment. Nevertheless, the potential exists for increases in food production. It is estimated, for example, that as much as one third of the land in Tropical Africa is potentially cultivable, though only about 6% of it is currently cultivated. Moreover, compared with other tropical areas, yields of staple crops are relatively low in this region. This indicates that food production could be increased through higher yields without bringing additional land into cultivation. For example, yields of roots and tubers, such as yams and cassava, are about 7 000 kg/ha in Tropical Africa, compared with yields of about 10 000 kg/ha in Tropical Asia and 11 000 kg/ha in Tropical Latin America. Similarly, yields of such cereals as corn, rice and wheat average about 1 000 kg/ha in Tropical Africa compared with almost twice that amount in similar climates elsewhere.

The general development issues concerning Tropical Africa, including food production, are acknowledged by many observers to be among the most pressing in the world. The following data, based on the *World Development Report 1985*, illustrate the extent of the reasons for concern. Of the 37 countries in the area, 27 are among the 40 poorest countries in the world as measured by per capita GNP. Similarly, as many as 22 of the 40 countries with the world's fastest rates of population growth are in Tropical Africa. The 40 countries with the world's shortest life expectancies include 32 from Tropical Africa, while 25 countries from the same area are among the world's 40 most under-nourished nations. In addition, the 40 countries with the world's slowest growth in total food production include 16 from Tropical Africa and, on a per capita basis, there are as many as 19 from the region. When measured against population growth, only 10 countries out of the 37 in Tropical Africa have sustained increases in food production which either equal or exceed their increases in population.

Potential solutions to the problem of increasing food production, either by opening up new farmland or by increasing yields from the existing farmland are not easy to achieve. Only a small fraction of any new farmland can be reclaimed at low cost. Much of the rest will necessitate heavy expenditures on clearing dense vegetation, installing irrigation and/or drainage systems and initiating a variety of soil conservation measures. In addition, to change farming from a low-input, low-yield pattern to a high-input, high-yield pattern necessitates the use of more fertilizer and the planting of high-yielding varieties of crops. At the moment, fertilizer consumption is generally low throughout Tropical Africa because of high import costs and the general lack of animals and local fertilizer manufacturing capacity. For example, Zimbabwe, the country with the highest fertilizer use in the region (53.2 kg/ha), still uses less than such tropical countries as Costa Rica (113.4 kg/ha), Cuba (172.6 kg/ha), Indonesia (75.0 kg/ha), Malaysia (102.1 kg/ha) and Sri Lanka (71.3 kg/ha). Less than 10% of the cereals planted in Tropical Africa are high yielding varieties, compared with nearly 40% in Latin America and close to 50% in Asia.

The FAO (The Food and Agriculture Organization of the UN) recently completed a major project called "Land Resources for the Future." It compares potential population-supporting capacities, as determined by soils, climatic conditions and levels of farm technology, with actual and projected populations. The calculations for Tropical Africa as a whole confirm that even with existing subsistence farming technologies there is enough arable land to support a population nearly three times the size of the present population. However, the FAO notes that the situation varies greatly among individual countries. Some are already at or close to their food limit using existing farm technology. These countries are Botswana, Burundi, Ethiopia, Kenya, Malawi, Mauritania, Namibia, Niger, Nigeria, Rwanda, Senegal, Somalia and Uganda (see map in Fig. 3-8).

Other countries, chiefly in central Africa, still possess extensive areas of land that can be developed for farming. According to the FAO project, the Central African Republic and the Congo People's Republic can support populations twenty times as large as their existing populations using present farm technology. In Gabon, the

multiple reaches almost 100. Such variations in population-supporting capacity make it possible to look also at the part migration could play in relieving the pressure in the already "filled-up" countries. There are, however, political and social problems associated with migration, and two of the countries already at the limits of their identified capacities have recently expelled foreign nationals (Uganda expelled the East Asian community, Nigeria expelled the Ghanaian community). For reasons of peace and stability, it may be more useful to concentrate on finding internal solutions to the problems of increasing food production.

A number of environmental factors, related mostly to climate, soils and health, resist easy developmental solutions.

The climates of Tropical Africa range from hot desert climates at the northern and southern edges to a full equatorial climate at its heart. The broad pattern is a massive West-to-East rain belt shifting in its entirety either north or south with the seasons. Thus the rain belt moves northward as

The semi-arid edges of the savanna lands support little vegetation and offer small prospect of easy cultivation.

Dorothea Manson

Fig. 3-8
African countries at or near the limits of their population supporting capacity with their present farming technology

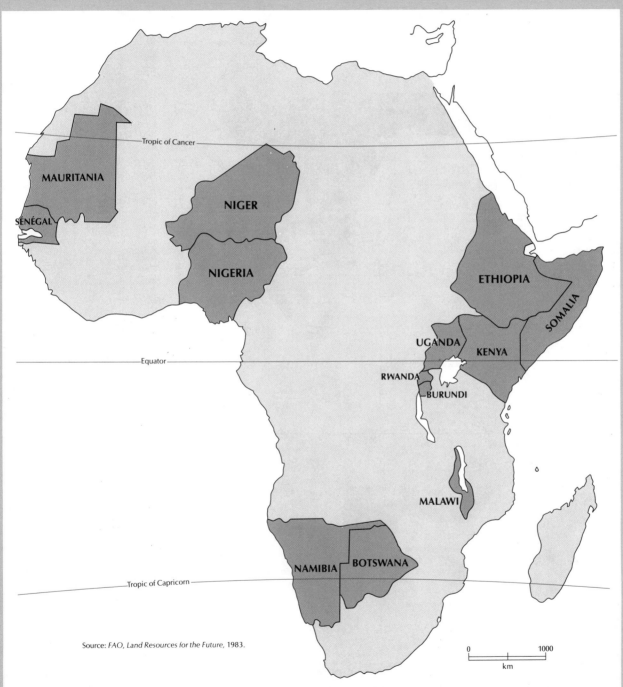

Source: *FAO, Land Resources for the Future*, 1983.

Fig. 3-9
Africa: major precipitation characteristics (simplified)

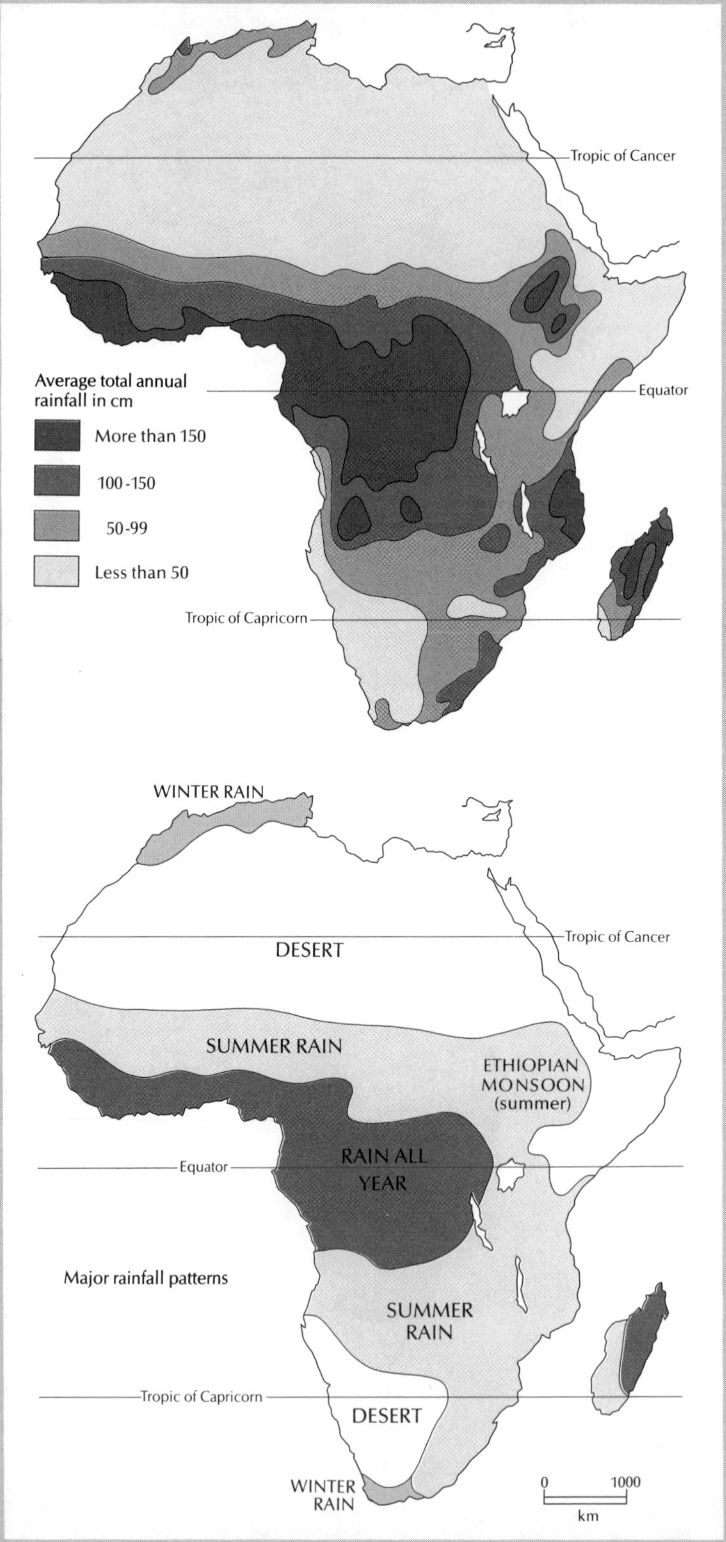

Tropic of Cancer

Average total annual
rainfall in cm

More than 150

100-150

50-99

Less than 50

Equator

Tropic of Capricorn

WINTER RAIN

DESERT

Tropic of Cancer

SUMMER RAIN

ETHIOPIAN
MONSOON
(summer)

Equator

RAIN ALL
YEAR

Major rainfall patterns

SUMMER
RAIN

Tropic of Capricorn

DESERT

WINTER
RAIN

0   1000

km

the overhead sun travels from Capricorn to Cancer, and southward again as the overhead sun returns from Cancer to Capricorn. The rain belt never reaches either Cancer or Capricorn because it moves more slowly than the overhead sun and is "rolled-back" before it has chance to reach the lines of the actual Tropics. Therefore, Cancer and Capricorn lie across areas of desert, while the rain belt never entirely escapes from the tropical heartland around the Equator, where it produces rain through all seasons.

Rainfall reliability is closely connected to rainfall quantity. Rainfall in the equatorial heart is very plentiful and reliable. Toward the outer edges of the rain belt, however, there is much less rainfall. Its reliability diminishes, too, so that the lands at the outer edges of the rain belt receive rain in some years, and in other years do not. Periodic and unpredictable droughts are a characteristic feature of these border zones (e.g., the Sahel).

In Tropical Africa there are three broad climatic zones: a region of persistent rain at and near the Equator; a region on each side of this of summer rain and winter drought; and a region at the northern and southern edges afflicted by drought. In all cases these climates are modified in the eastern parts of Tropical Africa by the mountains and monsoons. The map in Fig. 3-9 shows the major precipitation characteristics.

None of these regions have their seasons determined by temperature. Temperatures are high all year, although they are slightly higher when the sun is overhead. What determines the season is rainfall; and farmers in the region look for the onset of the rainy season rather than for the beginning of spring warmth.

The persistent heat of the tropics, especially when moist, has an enervating effect on human activity. Since there are no killing frosts, the constant heat also fosters the rampant growth of a wide variety of different life-forms, all competing to survive. Attempts to generate new sources of food production often fall prey to the same positive conditions for growth we might think would guarantee their success. For example, a multi-million dollar chicken raising scheme in Gambia failed when a disease wiped out the chickens. In Senegal a rice growing project was severely hindered by thousands of weaver-birds, which descended on the fields as the crop ripened. Such problems are not confined to Tropical Africa, but they are intensified by the proliferation of life forms and the intensity of the competition among them to survive.

It is estimated that the loss of yield for most crops in Tropical Africa runs about 50%. Because of the continuous heat, weeds, insects and bacterial infections are more devastating to plants than elsewhere. Even after harvest, a crop cannot be secured from further losses. Rats, mice and a variety of insects attack stored harvests, and there are particular problems associated with locusts and tsetse flies.

Locusts have been a plague throughout history. A swarm may cover many thousands of square kilometres and each day can eat enough to feed 10 000 people. Serious efforts to control locusts have been made, especially in East Africa and parts of the Sahel. But the difficulty of maintaining international co-operation and the growing resistance of locusts to chemical insecticides are severe problems. The effects of the tsetse fly are perhaps even more serious. The tsetse fly carries disease-spreading trypanosomes (single-celled microbes that enter the bloodstream during the bite of a tsetse fly). In domestic animals, the disease is called "nagana"; its human equivalent is called "sleeping sickness." Both are varieties of the disease trypanosomiasis. The effects on both animals and humans are similar: increasing lethargy leading to death.

Over 10 000 000 km^2 of Tropical Africa — an area larger than Canada — are affected by one or other of the 24 different species of tsetse fly (see map in Fig. 3-10), which effectively bars large numbers of cattle and people from this land. Since cattle can provide protein, manure for fertilizer and power for farm work, the lack of cattle in such

Fig. 3-10
Africa: areas of tsetse fly infestation (simplified)

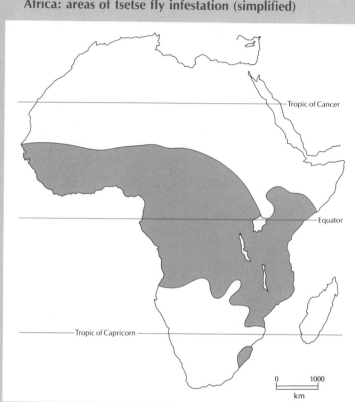

a large part of Tropical Africa poses a major problem. Eradication of the tsetse fly would help to increase food production and to improve diets.

Each of the 24 different species of tsetse fly, however, has different habits and requires different types of country to survive. Nevertheless, none can exist without regular bloodmeals. They also lose moisture from their bodies (dehydrate) very rapidly, and require moist, shady areas to live in. Destruction of forest and clearance of bush may remove the protective shade needed by the flies, but they also expose the soil to a variety of erosive agents. Accordingly, attempts at eradication are directed more toward the use of pesticides. Chief among these are DDT and dieldrin, against which tsetse flies seem to have developed no immunity, and whose environmental side effects are accepted as a necessary cost. Meanwhile, research continues

on the production of equally effective but environmentally safer methods of tsetse eradication.

The soils of Tropical Africa pose another problem. They are unlike the soils of temperate areas. Soils are largely products of their climates, and tropical soils are different from temperate soils because the climate is different. The great heat of the tropics tends to bake the soils, while the rainfall leaches them. The combined heat and moisture tend to produce very deep soils because the surface rock is rapidly broken down by chemical weathering. Unfortunately, the soils also become infertile as rapidly as they are formed because their nutrients are leached out by rainfall. The luxuriant natural vegetation of the equatorial rainforest is not, in fact, an indicator of soil fertility. The roots of trees are shallow and virtually no nutrients are obtained from the soil. The vegetation survives on its own humus

In the Sahel region, the unshaded tropical sun bakes the soil and turns it into laterite, more suitable for making bricks than growing food.

waste, which is plentiful. If the vegetation is cleared, then the source of humus is removed and the natural infertility of the soils becomes obvious.

The traditional farming response has been shifting cultivation. A cleared plot is used for only a few years, during which yields continually decline until a new plot must be cleared and the original plot allowed to revert to bush. To sustain production without repeatedly clearing new land requires the heavy use of fertilizer. Another problem with cleared land is that, lacking natural shade, the soil bakes hard under the sun, turning gradually into laterite. While laterite makes good bricks, it makes very poor soil. Light ploughs can only scratch its surface, while heavy-duty ploughs expose it to increased leaching as well as to increased erosion by water and wind.

One of the nutritional results of the nature of tropical soils is a protein-carbohydrate imbalance in the food produced. Carbohydrates are easily produced by a natural synthesis of water and atmospheric carbon dioxide. Protein production relies mainly on nitrogenous material in the soil and is retarded by the lack of such material in the soil. Therefore, both the nitrogen poor soil and the lack of animal protein in areas afflicted by nagana combine to create serious protein deficiencies in Tropical Africa. Current research is attempting to develop and make available a variety of leguminous crops that can synthesize their own nitrogen from the atmosphere, and thus provide an improved protein supply.

The soil picture is not entirely gloomy, however, for there are large expanses of volcanic and alluvial soils which are naturally fertile. There are also, especially in East Africa, large areas of upland where altitude moderates the harmful effects of heat. For example, there are stretches of alluvial soil near the lakes of Uganda and Kenya, as well as between the Blue and White Niles in Sudan. There are also many areas of good volcanic soil in Burundi, Cameroon, Ethiopia, Kenya, Malawi, Rwanda, Tanzania and Uganda.

Nevertheless, there are additional complications caused by disease in Tropical Africa. The heat fosters the growth of many organisms harmful to humans, and where there is also moisture the problems are even more severe. Lack of good health affects a person's attitudes and capacities, making hard and sustained work difficult. Throughout much of Tropical Africa, good health is rare, and there is a general scarcity of compensating health care facilities. An indication of this is the relatively short life expectancies of the people here, compared with those of other areas. Life expectancy figures are generally in the 40s, with only a few countries reaching the 50s.

In Tropical Africa, shorter average life spans usually are accompanied by much disease. Many people suffer the debilitating effects of one or more serious diseases during their relatively short lives. Studies show that human beings in Tropical Africa carry more parasites than do people in other parts of the world, with an average of two infections per person. The range of diseases is too great to list, but the chief ones are schistosomiasis (bilharzia), trypanosomiasis (sleeping sickness), malaria, leprosy, hookworm, onchocerciasis (river blindness), yellow fever and dysentery.

The combination of concerns presented by climate, soils, plant and animal pests and human disease certainly presents great obstacles to development in Tropical Africa. However, as pests, predators and diseases are controlled, and as the application of water to crops is improved by drainage and irrigation schemes, the rapid growth characteristics of the tropics could make tropical farming more productive than temperate farming.

Conclusion

The global food picture is extremely varied. Some areas have great surpluses, while others suffer from serious scarcities. These variations are not haphazard. We can detect definite patterns in food surplus and deficit regions. Comparisons of population growth and food production generally reveal that countries with very slow population growth also have abundant food supplies. Nations with rapid population growth are usually those with food scarcities. These close correlations lead us to certain questions. For example, is slow population growth a reason for abundant food supplies, and rapid population growth a reason for food scarcities?

Such questions are complex, and we would oversimplify the matter if our answers considered only food supply patterns and rates of population growth. We should also consider other factors that may be responsible for the high negative correlation between population growth and food supplies. One factor may be technology. If a country has a high level of food production technology, it also is likely to have, for example, the technology for effective birth control. The most visible sign of technology is industrial development. In the next chapter, therefore, we turn to an examination of the varying degrees of industrialization throughout the world.

4 INDUSTRY

Introduction

To most people industry means factories, and industrialization the process of acquiring factories. As a process, industrialization is the application of technology to the production of goods. Industrialization is, however, much more complex than this. A society that industrializes usually experiences great changes in its social and economic order: mechanization and large-scale production are introduced; urbanization often occurs as workers migrate to the cities in search of jobs; and existing social systems and values are pressed to change.

In the eighteenth century, the original industrial *hearth regions* were located in Western Europe. Aided by vast numbers of migrants industrialization spread rapidly to North America, diffusing later throughout the rest of Europe and, with gathering speed, in Japan. Recently industrialization has occurred in a number of newer centres such as Hong Kong, Singapore, Taiwan, South Korea, Brazil, India and, most recently, Indonesia and the Philippines. Meanwhile, the original industrial hearth regions are becoming "post-industrial" or service-oriented societies, heavily involved in the diffusion technologies of communications, information, research and finance, with manufacturing still playing a large but proportionately ever-diminishing role.

All phases of the industrialization process are viewed positively by many governments, which actively encourage the development and maintenance of industry, largely for reasons of job creation and economic growth. Encouragement takes many forms, such as sponsorship of trade shows, low industrial taxes, tariff protection against competition from imports, cash grants and the building of technical colleges and vocational schools. Governments of developing as well as of developed countries are concerned to promote the growth of industry. Two countries now in the process of apparently successful industrialization are Brazil and the Republic of Korea (more often called South Korea). The following article, from the *World Development Report 1983*, illustrates the powerful role government can take in industrial growth.

BRAZIL
Flexibility and pragmatism in managing industrialization

Between 1950 and 1980 Brazilian manufacturing grew at an average of almost 10 percent a year, with GNP growth of about 7 percent a year. During this period, per capita income (in 1980 dollars) increased from about $600 to more than $2,000 and, despite continuing problems of poverty in some regions, the overall incidence of poverty declined significantly.

Industrialization was clearly the goal of Brazil's development strategy, although priorities were not set in any systematic or detailed way. Growth followed a typical, and in some sense natural, sequence: first came import substitution of consumer nondurables and then consumer durables; intermediate goods and capital goods followed. The pattern of protection was adjusted flexibly and gradually. Whereas in the 1960s the protection rate was high for consumer goods, medium for intermediate goods, and low for capital goods, by the early 1980s this pattern had been fully reversed.

Brazil's style of growth did not, of course, occur accidentally. Government decisions about exchange rates, tariffs and other import controls, public investments, investment subsidies, and export incentives strongly influenced the allocation of resources. The basic logic followed until the mid-1960s by both private investors and public officials was import substitution: anything imported was potentially a candidate for domestic production. Beyond this, public officials had some ideas about priorities to be given to some sectors, especially in steel, automobiles, and petrochemicals. But indirect promotional policies — such as trade protection and fiscal and credit subsidies — owed their design at least as much to the entrepreneurs who stood to gain or lose from them as to the public officials' view of what was "best" or "efficient" for the nation. Indeed, one reason for the "miracle" growth in the late 1960s and early 1970s was precisely that government listened to the private sector and largely accommodated its wishes.

Consultation and consensus also prevailed during the 1950s, notably in the "Executive Groups" formed to promote growth in five industrial sectors. These groups, made up of senior officials from all relevant agencies, negotiated with private investors to achieve a package that gave the government what it wanted in terms of import substitution, domestic procurement of inputs, and so forth, but that also gave the investors what they needed to be profitable. The government negotiated hard, but the policy package was designed jointly. The automobile industry, one of the five, is a classic example. Costs were high at first, but by the late 1960s at least one firm was producing at internationally competitive costs — perhaps the only one in any developing country at that time. Since then costs and prices have come down in other firms, and today the industry produces competitively and exports a large part of its output.

In the mid-1960s, when the initial phase of import substitution was largely completed, Brazil switched to an export-oriented strategy with major adjustments in its real exchange rate and in financial policy. This was followed by a boom in exports and economic growth that lasted nearly a decade. Since the mid-1970s the government has expanded its share of industry and played a bigger role in the choice of new investment. It has promoted a new wave of import substitution in the few activities where this remained possible. Some sectors (such as steel) may have been overexpanded, and many of the new industries (such as sophisticated machine tools and computers) have complex and rapidly evolving technology; being capital goods, their cost and quality will affect the whole economy. Whether these new activities will become internationally competitive remains to be seen.

World Development Report 1983

DISCUSSION AND RESEARCH

1. Suggest reasons that might lead governments to wish to develop industry.
2. What are some of the problems that might be faced by a developing country wishing to industrialize?
3. What can governments do to hinder or help industrialization?

Despite the general wish of many governments to foster industrial growth, there are many people who express concern about the nature and extent of industrialization. These people are concerned about pollution, resource depletion, a widening gap between the rich and poor and the quality of life in its non-material aspects. We will touch on some of the matters of concern later in this chapter, and examine the quality of life issue in more detail in Chapter 6.

In this chapter we will start by examining the reasons for industrialization and then try to assess the global extent of industrialization. Following that we will look at the factors assisting the process of industrialization and at some of the possible development strategies for promoting industrialization. We will finish this section with an examination of some of the problems associated with the existence of industry. A case study of South Korea, a country whose government chose to industrialize, concludes the chapter.

A modern plant in Jutland, Denmark. In highly industrialized countries, agriculture and industry compete for the available land.

Royal Danish Consulate General / Toronto

Why Industrialize?

Industrialization changes a society. The following are perhaps its most important benefits: the production of material wealth, the creation of a money economy, the widening of personal choice, the creation of jobs and the securing of economic independence.

Industrialization is a process, not a single event. It may take many years for the process to occur.

The Production of Material Wealth

Before any society becomes industrialized the vast majority of its people live by farming. Despite images of rustic bliss, life tends to be quite hard: harvests are variable, storage of buffer stocks is difficult if not impossible, technology is limited, yields are low, output per worker is low, per capita income (usually not in money) is correspondingly small, and disease is usually endemic. Thomas Hobbes, a seventeenth century English philosopher, envisioned life in a lawless society as "nasty, brutish, and short." Life in preindustrial England was not much different.

Industrialization stimulates technological development, challenges old social structures, creates new opportunities and generates higher per capita output. It raises the standard of living as it satisfies the varied needs and desires of the population. Some people benefit sooner than others, thus creating a gap between the newly-rich and the still-poor. It may take a long time, depending upon government policies of wealth distribution, for the still-poor to gain significantly from the process of industrialization. In England the still-poor gained little from the benefits of industry for many decades. In Brazil, an estimated 35–40% of the population still lives outside the money economy. Government policy in Brazil has so far been concerned more to create wealth than to share it equitably. Similarly, according to Du Runsheng, China's top government adviser on rural industrialization, quoted in *Time*, 1985 9 23, "Our government promotes the policy that some will get rich first. Then others will get rich. Our final goal is that all people will be rich."

The wealth that industry creates is most noticeably material wealth: houses, hospitals, transportation systems, energy grids, fertilizers, farm machinery, radios, cameras, newspapers and so on. The list is almost

In *The Bleak Age*, the Hammonds note that in the first several decades of English industrialization, the poor were regarded as people who worked, slept and ate, but lacked the will to succeed and prosper. This was thought to explain why the benefits of industrialization were gained only by the existing elite and the new entrepreneurs.

The large scale of industrial production is vital. It would cost an enormous amount of money to produce just one car, for instance; but if many thousands are produced the costs of plant and machinery can be spread over them all, and each car costs less.

endless. Industrialization generates wealth on a large scale, gradually making goods accessible to many instead of just the privileged few. Nowhere, however, has industrialization yet succeeded in making material wealth available to everyone.

Other developments usually accompany the increase in material wealth. Improved medical care, increased schooling, improved transportation systems and wider choices change life in many ways other than the purely material. Yet these changes are made possible by material development.

The Creation of a Money Economy

The material wealth created is largely responsible for the growth of a money economy throughout a society. In a non-industrial society it is possible for most people to live with little money; subsistence is the norm and there is little need to trade. As industry develops, specialization begins on a large scale. Most industrial workers cannot eat or otherwise directly use the products of their labours and trade becomes essential. Trade may take the form of direct barter, but money makes the process both easier and more flexible. Thus a money economy is generated and people can become richer in monetary as well as in material terms.

Even in a simple economy, barter is not easy. A person who repairs shoes but wants bread has to find a person who bakes bread and has shoes needing repair. Such a *coincidence of wants* is often difficult to find.

The Widening of Personal Choice

In non-industrial societies most people live directly from agricultural work. There may be a few other jobs in trade, administration, religion and craftwork, but they are limited. Moreover, farming techniques do not yield enough surpluses, even *exacted surpluses*, to feed more than a small number of non-agricultural workers. Industrialization changes this. It not only provides a battery of new techniques and materials with which to increase farming surpluses, it also provides a widening choice of jobs not available before. Furthermore, although industrially specialized workers must now buy most of the products they need, they have more money to spend, and a gradually increasing variety of products to buy. Freedom of choice as a consumer is a welcome quality for most people. Their freedom is increased by improved transportation and communication networks, which become available in the early phases of industrialization.

Exacted surpluses are those that are taken from agricultural workers by force, taxation or tithe.

The Creation of Jobs

Industry creates jobs that cannot be provided by farming alone. Not only are there jobs in factories and workshops, but also in a variety of supporting services, such as transportation, energy production, finance and

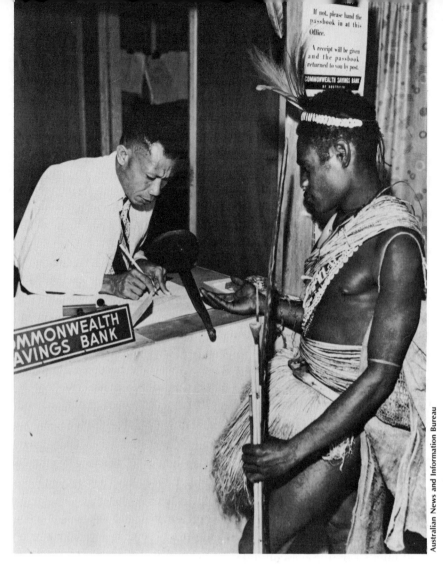

The introduction of a money economy is an early stage in the transition to a more specialized society. This man from the Eastern Highlands of Papua-New Guinea is making the first deposit in his new savings account.

Australian News and Information Bureau

marketing. As technology is introduced into societies, farming also becomes more productive through the use of new methods, tools and fertilizers. Farms require less labour and the rural unemployed seek jobs in neighbouring cities, and in the industrial and infrastructural sectors associated with industry.

Today the need for jobs created by industry is a matter of increasing concern, especially as the world's population increases and more people move to the cities for work. Many developing countries want more industry to employ their populations. Developed countries want to keep the factory employment they already have, which is now endangered by companies expanding into other parts of the world where cheap labour is plentiful.

The director-general of the International Labour Office has noted

'We have 100% unemployment at the
moment, but things can only improve'

The Financial Post, 1984 6 9

(1984) that industrialization would need to create one billion new jobs by the year 2000 if the world is to have full employment. "Short of war and peace," he said, "the most critical problem today and in the foreseeable future is that of work."

The purposes of industrialization have gradually come to be to provide jobs, to generate income, to reduce poverty, to produce material wealth, and to do all these things on as broad a population base as possible, so that the benefits accrue to the many rather than the few.

The following extract illustrates the experiences of Taiwan. It is from *Levels of Poverty*, published in 1980 7 by the World Bank.

The recent history of Taiwan demonstrates the great importance of employment expansion in poverty removal. Within 10 years, the proportion of visible unemployment fell from 6.3% of the labour force to 3.7%. But perhaps more importantly, hidden unemployment and underemployment both showed sharp declines. For example, unpaid family workers fell from being 28.5% of total employment to 15.9%. It is the expansion of employment at a reasonable wage that has permitted the poorer Taiwanese to feed, clothe, and house their families, and send their children to school, as well as to enjoy a steady increase in the availability of consumer goods.

The successful expansion of exports has also been a major factor behind this employment-led prosperity. There is evidence that the export industries provided greater scope for labour utilization than the manufacturing sector in general and the existing import-replacing industries in particular. As far as the role of government is concerned, there is clear evidence of the importance of government policy measures in determining the character of economic development in Taiwan, especially in the promotion of exports.

Securing Economic Independence

Every time we import goods that we could manufacture if all the conditions were available, we are continuing our economic dependence and delaying our industrial growth. It is just these conditions that we are planning to provide . . . to build up our body of knowledge, techniques and skills, to make us more self-confident and self-sufficient, to push towards our economic independence.

Kwame Nkrumah,
President of Ghana, 1963

The industrialization of Africa . . . constitutes a fundamental option in the total range of activities aimed at freeing Africa from underdevelopment and economic dependence.

Lagos Plan of Action,
Organization of African Unity, 1982

Many of the world's developing countries were at one time colonies and, although colonialism has now largely been replaced by local political independence, there still exists a clear need for economic independence, especially to reduce reliance on imported goods that could be made locally instead. Colonies were usually treated by the colonizing country as suppliers of raw materials and as markets for goods manufactured in the colonizing country. Industrial development in the colonies themselves was generally discouraged, and where it was permitted on a limited basis it was generally owned by outsiders. Local populations gained little experience in industry. In addition, the infrastructures created by the colonizing country were aimed at supporting the export-import trade. Railways were built from mines or plantations to ports, but not between areas important to local populations. Education systems, where they affected local populations at all, were designed to provide workers for professional and public service jobs. Little was done to encourage the development of local entrepreneurial and managerial skills.

The practice whereby colonial powers sought raw materials in their colonies and then sold manufactured goods back to them is called *mercantilism.*

In general, when colonies gained political independence the patterns of economic dependence remained as before. They still suffered from economic dependence. Manufactured products had to be imported and raw materials exported. The former colonies lacked local know-how, so technology had to be imported. Managerial and entrepreneurial skills had not been developed and foreign capital had to be imported since little had accumulated locally. The emphasis on industrialization in the ex-colonies after independence was largely a reaction against these types of dependence.

DISCUSSION AND RESEARCH

4. When examining employment, we find that the relationship between farming and industry is very strong.
   a. Describe the relationship.
   b. How does it relate to population growth?
   c. How does it relate to food production?
5. What sorts of industries do you think would be best for newly industrializing countries? Why?

Who Is Industrialized?

There are two basic levels of industry: manufacturing industry and cottage industry. The term "industrialized" refers only to economies characterized by manufacturing industry. Economies characterized by cottage industry are called "preindustrial" or "non-industrial" economies.

In cottage industry economies individual workers or small groups of workers are widely scattered through the locality. These artisans, or skilled workers, supply a very personal level of input, with much skill and muscle power, but few mechanical aids. They earn relatively little for their effort, because their output is limited by the scarcity of power and machinery.

Manufacturing industry is very different from cottage industry. It takes place in factories, using a wide variety of mass production techniques and a great deal of mechanical assistance. When larger inputs of power and machinery are employed we find that industry has a natural tendency to concentrate where power and machinery are most available; this tendency is called *point concentration*, or *agglomeration*. Therefore, most early industrial development has occurred in either already existing or specially built cities. Increasingly, however, there is a trend in all countries to foster the development of industry in rural areas. This is called *dispersion*. It may occur naturally because of the increasingly high operating costs in cities or as part of a deliberate policy of rural development.

Because industrialization is an on-going process it is not easy to say when a nation has become industrialized, and it is correspondingly difficult to know which countries have become industrialized, and which have not. Any single factor can be misleading unless we check it against others, so we will take electricity generation as our prime potential indicator and check it for validity against the value of gross manufactured output, both factors on a standardized per capita basis.

STATISTICAL ANALYSIS

6. We are going to try to obtain a correlation coefficient between per capita electricity generation (Column P of Appendix 3) and per capita value of gross manufactured output (Column Q). This will tell us the degree to

The quality of the work done by artisans is not a major factor in determining how much they earn. As always, good quality commands a higher return than poor quality, but the return is still low in terms of the time, skill and effort put into the product.

Electricity generation is measured in the same standardized units throughout the world, whereas many other possible criteria are measured in different units or in units not readily comparable. What examples can you suggest?

Cottage industry: pots made for the local trade in Bhaktapur, Nepal.

which the two variables are related to each other. A close relationship will indicate that either data set (P or Q) may be used to indicate the extent of industrialization. However, neither data set can explain the causes of the *level* of industrialization.

Use the grouped data technique for obtaining a correlation coefficient, as shown in Appendix 4. Then:

a. Suggest why the relationship is less than perfect.

b. Comment upon the reliability of using either criterion as a meaningful test of the extent of industrialization throughout the world.

c. Suggest or research reasons for the variations in extent of industrialization throughout the world.

7. The scattergraph in Fig. 4-1 shows the relationship between per capita electricity generation and per capita value of manufactured output in graph form. The "line of best fit" shows the main trend.

a. Describe the main features of the graphed distribution.

b. Why do you suppose a few countries are located so far from the line of best fit?

c. If a country wanted to achieve a per capita manufactured output level of about $500, following the general world pattern, how much electricity should it plan on producing on a per capita basis?

8. Examine Fig. 4-2 on page 130 and suggest reasons for the very uneven world distribution of manufacturing activity.

Cottage industry: locally made camel baskets for sale in a Moroccan market.

Fig. 4-1
Relationship between per capita electricity generation and per capita manufactured output

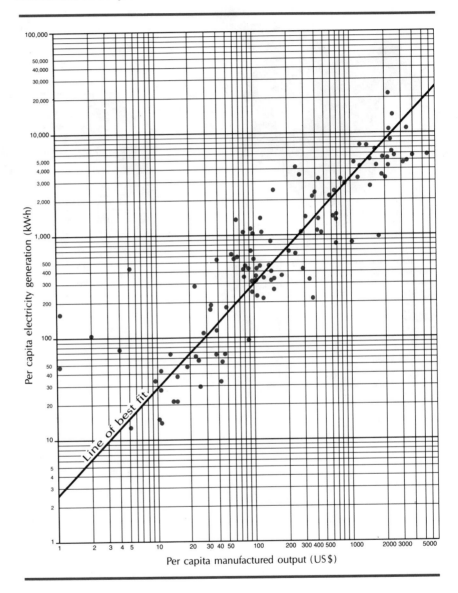

Fig. 4-2
Variations in per capita value of gross manufactured output throughout the world

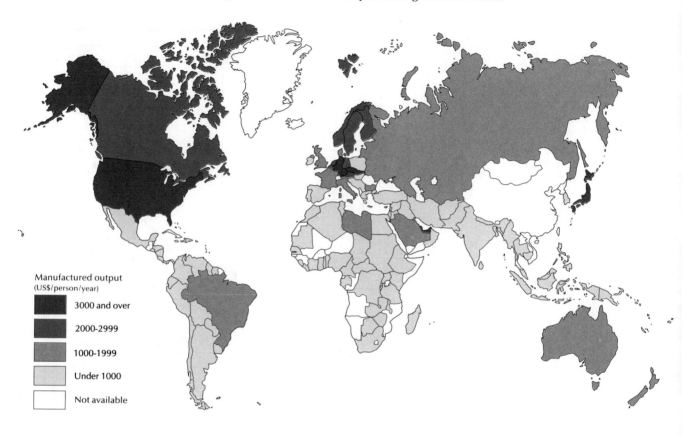

Manufactured output
(US$/person/year)

3000 and over

2000-2999

1000-1999

Under 1000

Not available

What Are the Chances of Becoming Industrialized?

The chance a non-industrial country has of becoming industrialized depends on the degree to which a country's general circumstances favour development. For example, one nation may richly possess mineral resources but lack good transportation systems, while another may have a large supply of labour but inadequate capital for construction. We will examine some of the major factors favouring industrialization and some of the factors hindering industrialization.

Factors Favouring Industrialization

Natural Resources

All industries rely to some extent on natural resources. The degree to which this is true generally varies according to the bulk and, consequently, the transportation costs of the raw materials needed. For example, while pulp and paper industries are usually located near timber areas, watch-making companies need not be situated close to sources of iron ore.

The amount of energy available is often another factor determining whether industry can grow in a particular area. Relatively cheap and plentiful supplies of hydroelectricity in Québec and British Columbia favoured the development of aluminum industries in these provinces, though the raw material is imported from Jamaica, where hydro-electricity is neither plentiful nor cheap.

Natural resources do not consist only of raw materials and energy supplies. They include landscape, climate and position. Landscape can facilitate or hinder industrial growth; flat land makes transportation easy, deep-water channels make good harbours and deep valleys allow for the construction of hydroelectric dams. A good climate also offers advantages. In some places the warmth means that factory heating costs may be eliminated, snow clearance minimized and operating costs thereby reduced. The southern USA, the so-called "sunbelt," offers a good example of the attractions of warmth. In recent years there has been a noticeable trend for industries to move into the southern states.

The raw material is initially bauxite, a red soil-like material produced by the tropical weathering of rock. It is very bulky to transport, and so is partly processed (into alumina) before shipment to Canada.

Warmth is not the only attraction of the sunbelt. State labour legislation is usually less restrictive and labour unions are fairly weak.

As far as location is concerned, the best situations for industrial growth are on or near major transportation routes. For example, Singapore, located at the junction of South Asia and the Far East, has always had good industrial potential.

Labour Supply

In the past rapid industrialization has usually been based on an equally rapid growth of population, enabling an expanding industry to draw successfully upon an adequate supply of relatively cheap labour (cheap because its supply was plentiful). This was the case in England in the eighteenth and nineteenth centuries when the growing population supplied England's developing industries, formed the empire-building armies and helped colonize North America, Australia, South Africa and elsewhere. The influx of ten million refugees from Eastern Europe and the millions of guest workers from southern Europe helped West Germany's post-World War II industrialization. It was also helped in Japan when, following World War II, the industrial labour supply was augmented by millions of people pouring into the cities in a wave of new urbanization sponsored by the government. Hong Kong, also benefited industrially from the tide of refugees from China during the 1950s and 1960s.

The present non-industrial world (see Fig. 4-2) has plentiful labour for the most part, and industrialization is a potentially major provider of jobs for the large populations. Not all countries, though, possess sufficient labour for extensive industrialization. The population data in Column A of Appendix 3 show that several non-industrial countries have very small populations. For example, Belize has a population of 161 000, Botswana 1 075 000, Cyprus 670 000, Equatorial Guinea 282 000, Gabon 988 000 and Gambia 672 000. On the other hand, there are many non-industrial countries with large populations and much "cheap labour." This term is used to describe a labour supply greater than the existing demand for it and which often lacks industrial skills.

Labourers in preindustrial countries work for lower wages for a number of reasons. Alternative methods of earning a living often pay even less, and competition for too few jobs forces wages down. And if wages were higher, employers would turn increasingly to machinery, reducing the number of jobs available. Further, developing countries pursuing a policy of industrialization hold wage rates low to keep product prices at an affordable level. Thus wage rates in non-industrial countries tend to be much lower than in industrialized countries. Although a large pool of inexpensive labour may challenge the country possessing it to create employment for it, it presents obvious advantages to firms able to use it.

In a market economy, the price of labour (i.e., its wages) depends like the price of everything else on the relationship between supply and demand. If supply exceeds demand, prices are low.

Guest workers (or *gastarbeiter*) came to West Germany from countries in southern and southeastern Europe. The high wages enabled many to send money back to their families and, in several cases, to return home and retire. Others remain in West Germany, though the demand for their services has now eased.

DISCUSSION AND RESEARCH

9. Do you approve of firms from industrialized nations setting up operations in a developing country to take advantage of lower labour costs? Who benefits from such a move? Who loses?

Favourable Government Action

Potential industrialists can fairly readily see the natural resources and the supply of labour in a preindustrial country. Less obvious are the invisible advantages of political stability and favourable economic policies. Governments of both industrial and non-industrial countries often advertise their policies in order to compete with other areas and most countries offer generous government assistance to attract industry. Singapore offers a variety of tax advantages to new companies for five years, extended to a further fifteen years if they expand their operations. It permits earnings from exports to be taxed at 4% instead of the usual 40%, allows unlimited employment for foreign nationals, and grants tariff protection against imported competition and free repatriation of profits. To compete, South Korea offers five years at zero taxes, followed by three years at half taxes, no raw material import duties, permanent income tax exemption for foreign nationals, unrestricted repatriation of profits and export promotion by the Korean Trade Corporation. If you were an industrialist seeking to expand, which would you choose?

Repatriation of profits means that firms operating in another country are able to send home the profits they make in the other country. What do you suppose are the advantages of this arrangement to both countries? Are there any disadvantages?

In consequence of this sort of government help, more and more of the labour-intensive manufacturing in the world is shifting gradually to a growing number of developing and highly ambitious countries.

Favourable Attitude Toward Multinational Companies

The term *transnationals* is sometimes used.

Multinationals are firms with their home base in one country and operations in many other nations. They are usually owned by stockholders, although some are owned by governments. Many multinationals are among the largest companies in the world, and a number of them manufacture more than do some entire countries. Of the 100 largest economic units in the world for which an annual balance sheet is published, about half are nations and about half are multinational companies (see Fig. 4-3).

Consider this indication of the multinational shift in manufacturing: in 1901 the USA had 47 firms with overseas manufacturing subsidiaries; by 1950 the number had increased to 988; in 1959 there were 1 891; in 1967 the number was up to 3 646; and it is estimated that by 1991 there will be well over 10 000 firms in the USA with manufacturing subsidiaries overseas. As one Ford executive said, "It is our goal to be in every single country there is. We at Ford Motor Company look at a world map without any boundaries." The present forces of industrial dispersion (or spreading out) are the opposite of the earlier trends to agglomeration, and represent

Fig. 4-3
The world's 100 largest economic units with public balance sheets

Economic Unit (M = Multinational)	Total GNP/Sales	Economic Unit (M = Multinational)	Total GNP/Sales
1 USA	3 059 467	51 Egypt	31 465
2 Japan	1 215 043	52 Chile	30 280
3 West Germany	825 211	53 Malaysia	28 822
4 France	671 767	54 GE (M:USA)	27 947
5 United Kingdom	510 688	55 Hong Kong	27 933
6 Italy	393 275	56 Standard Oil (M:USA)	26 949
7 China	326 361	57 Chevron (M:USA)	26 798
8 Brazil	305 254	58 ENI (M:Italy)	25 798
9 Canada	289 617	59 Portugal	25 407
10 Spain	217 868	60 Atlantic Richfield (M:USA)	24 686
11 India	198 252	61 New Zealand	24 347
12 Mexico	179 240	62 Toyota (M:Japan)	24 111
13 Australia	173 491	63 Peru	23 719
14 Netherlands	170 967	64 IRI (M:Italy)	23 354
15 Saudi Arabia	140 515	65 Hungary	22 407
16 Sweden	123 986	66 Unilever (M:Netherlands)	21 599
17 Belgium	117 758	67 Israel	21 125
18 Switzerland	113 138	68 Morocco	20 862
19 Exxon (M:USA)	90 854	69 Shell Oil (M:USA)	20 701
20 South Africa	89 928	70 Elf Oil (M:France)	20 662
21 Indonesia	88 951	71 Matsushita (M:Japan)	19 993
22 Shell (M:Netherlands)	84 865	72 Chrysler (M:USA)	19 573
23 General Motors (M:USA)	83 890	73 Pemex (M:Mexico)	19 405
24 Venezuela	80 686	74 Ireland	18 917
25 Nigeria	79 325	75 Hitachi (M:Japan)	18 486
26 Turkey	78 939	76 US Steel (M:USA)	18 274
27 Argentina	78 244	77 French Petroleum (M:France)	18 159
28 Austria	77 453	78 Philips (M:Netherlands)	17 835
29 South Korea	72 493	79 Nissan (M:Japan)	17 513
30 Denmark	67 030	80 Petrobras (M:Brazil)	17 087
31 Yugoslavia	64 630	81 Siemens (M:West Germany)	16 638
32 Norway	58 476	82 Syria	16 364
33 Romania	58 242	83 United Technology (M:USA)	16 332
34 Mobil (M:USA)	56 047	84 Volkswagen (M:West Germany)	16 035
35 Ford (M:USA)	52 366	85 Phillips Petroleum (M:USA)	15 537
36 Finland	52 268	86 Occidental Petroleum (M:USA)	15 373
37 BP (M:UK)	50 662	87 Daimler-Benz (M:West Germany)	15 274
38 Texaco (M:USA)	47 334	88 Bayer (M:West Germany)	15 108
39 Algeria	47 134	89 Kuwait Petroleum (M:Kuwait)	14 997
40 IBM (M:USA)	45 937	90 Nippon Oil (M:Japan)	14 785
41 Greece	44 518	91 Tenneco (M:USA)	14 779
42 Philippines	44 097	92 Hoechst (M:West Germany)	14 555
43 United Arab Emirates	41 478	93 Sun Oil (M:USA)	14 466
44 Thailand	40 579	94 Bangladesh	14 383
45 Colombia	39 802	95 BASF (M:West Germany)	14 184
46 Kuwait	39 083	96 Mitsubishi (M:Japan)	14 057
47 duPont (M:USA)	35 915	97 ITT (M:USA)	14 001
48 Pakistan	34 944	98 Venezuelan Oil (M:Venezuela)	13 598
49 AT&T (M:USA)	33 188	99 Fiat (M:Italy)	13 547
50 Libya	32 828	100 BAT (M:UK)	13 461

Source: Appendix 3 for GNP and *Fortune* 1985 8 19 for sales.

Note: All figures are in billions of US dollars

a later phase in the sequence of industrial development.

Multinationals offer advantages to non-industrial countries, as well as posing certain problems. It is because of the advantages, however, that many governments adopt favourable attitudes toward multinationals. The global companies can provide jobs and introduce new technologies. They can bring new ideas, new methods of organization and new contacts. They may provide training in management skills as well as in such trade skills as welding and fitting. They can promote international trade and contribute to the integration of industrially developing nations into the mainstream of the world community.

Multinationals can also pose certain problems to newly-industrial host countries. By removing local resources to the factories of developed nations, they can deprive the host of additional jobs and incomes involved in processing the raw materials. They may inhibit the development of other domestic industries by competing for scarce industrial inputs other than labour and by competing with domestic industries for a share of the limited market. They can hinder the development of domestic research activities by conducting much of their development work in the industrialized countries rather than in the host country. At times their interests may run counter to the interests of the host country (e.g., a multinational may choose to close a factory, although the host nation prefers it to remain open). Such problems can create an element of uncertainty in the plans of host countries. This uncertainty arises essentially out of concerns about sovereignty; who has final authority: the country or the company? Many countries wishing to become more industrialized welcome the benefits brought by multinationals, but often feel obliged to set down certain conditions designed to limit their power. For example, India insists on a measure of local participation in any foreign enterprise operating in the country; the Philippines requires 60% local ownership, and foreigners are restricted to 5% of the total labour in any job category; Peru has decreed 51% local ownership; Investment Canada judges cases individually on the basis of their anticipated benefits.

Canada, nevertheless, is also the home of several multinationals, including Abitibi, Alcan, Canadian Pacific, George Weston, Inco, Moore Corporation and Seagrams, among others. The Varity Corporation is typical of Canada's multinational companies.

Varity is headquartered in Toronto. Until 1986 it was called Massey-Ferguson. It is among the world's largest manufacturers of farm and industrial machinery and diesel engines. The company's products are made in 31 different countries, half of which are developing nations, and sold in almost every country in the world. Combines and balers are made by a subsidiary company at Brantford, Ontario, and sold across the world, with a 17% share of the world market. Combines are also manufactured in Australia for the local market. Tractors are made in 21

Abitibi is the world's largest manufacturer of newsprint; Alcan is a major producer of aluminum; CP operates railroads, airlines, hotels, paper mills and mining companies in many countries; George Weston is one of the world's leading food companies; Inco is the world's leading producer of nickel; Moore Corporation is the world's largest manufacturer of business forms; Seagram's is the world's major distilling group.

different countries, namely Argentina, Brazil, France, Guyana, India, Indonesia, Iran, Italy, Japan, Kenya, Libya, Morocco, Pakistan, Poland, Saudi Arabia, South Africa, Spain, Turkey, the UK, Uruguay and Zimbabwe. Tractor sales accout for about 17% of the world market also. Diesel engines, under the name of Perkins, form another major component of Varity. In 1985, over 10 000 000 diesel engines were manufactured, chiefly in the UK, but also in Brazil, Mexico and Peru, making Perkins the world's largest manufacturer of diesel engines. In addition, construction machinery of various types is manufactured in the UK, and hydraulic equipment in West Germany. Varity runs this global manufacturing network from Toronto, using computer and satellite technology to assist its organization. Although Varity also does most of its research and development work in Toronto, it prides itself on being in constant touch with its numerous product users throughout the world and in encouraging them to suggest improvements. For example, the new 2005 Series tractor, introduced in 1985 to replace the 2000 Series tractor, incorporated 30 new features, of which 20 were suggested by farmers in different parts of the world who had been using the earlier model.

Farm and industrial machinery account for about 75% of Varity's sales, with diesel engines making up the other 25%. The chief markets are in Europe and North America, but sales are increasing in Latin America and Africa.

Varity did not escape the effects of the world-wide economic recession of the early 1980s. Total world sales fell from a peak of US$3 132 000 000 in1980 to a low of US$1 288 000 000 in 1985. Such a large decline caused the company many problems, including closing factories, laying-off workers and selling subsidiaries. From 1977 to 1985 Varity's world-wide labour force fell from 58 000 to 18 000.

Despite its problems, Varity enjoys benefits that are not shared by all multinational companies. It has generally escaped hostile government action, partly because of its widespread employment of local labour and management, but also because government policies in many countries favour businesses that encourage increased farm productivity.

This information is based on the *Massey-Ferguson Annual Report,* for the years 1983 and 1985.

Factors Hindering Industrialization

We have seen that natural resources, plentiful labour, government assistance and an acceptance of multinationals can help industrialization. We will now look at some of the drawbacks that reduce significantly the chances of successful industrialization.

Among the most powerful disadvantages are illiteracy and lack of infrastructure because new industry depends upon these to establish. From the start, therefore, development plans usually include elements of literacy and technical training, along with numerous other infrastructural improvements such as road building, telephone installation, creation of banking facilities and, of course, the construction of factories. To succeed, everything must work together.

An example of the infrastructural difficulties facing developing countries was noted by the World Bank in 1983. Road maintenance was cited as a major problem, to the extent that the road building boom of the 1960s and 1970s threatened to become the road maintenance crisis of the 1980s and 1990s. Roads in many developing countries had deteriorated beyond the point where normal maintenance could be effective. This was caused partly by climate (heat and heavy rainfall) and partly by the expense of maintenance. Ironically, the problem was aggravated by spending money building new roads while the older roads

Infrastructure is the word used to describe the various support services that help to make an operation run successfully. For industry, it will include transportation and communication media, financial markets, education and health facilities, power utilities, employment exchanges and so on.

Movement into an industrial society requires an increased level of literacy. For these apprentices in Chucuito, Peru, becoming skilled mechanics means they must also be able to read plans and written instructions.

International Labour Office

Fig. 4-4

Development criteria and data for developing countries with less than US$75 per capita value of gross manufactured output

Country	MO	A	B	C	D	E	F	G	H	I	J
Egypt	74	48.41	38.2	.003	.012	.104	16.47	0.020	.002	0.04	0.82
Turkey	71	51.26	68.8	.005	.042	.113	28.32	0.031	.008	0.51	0.76
Liberia	61	2.23	21.0	.003	—	.150	3.43	5.869	—	2.40	—
Zimbabwe	55	8.95	68.8	.009	.028	.157	18.55	0.137	.006	1.11	—
Afghanistan	49	14.79	20.0	.001	.002	.028	16.75	—	—	0.50	0.18
Pakistan	48	99.84	20.7	.001	.004	.048	8.52	—	.001	0.22	0.33
Indonesia	44	167.83	56.6	.004	.003	.272	33.31	0.286	.001	1.04	1.94
Rwanda	41	6.04	49.7	.001	.001	.008	34.95	—	—	0.99	—
Haiti	38	5.92	22.3	.001	—	.025	4.71	—	—	0.98	—
Cameroon	34	9.77	40.5	.007	—	.039	9.75	—	.0001	1.15	0.48
India	32	762.51	34.1	.001	.004	.052	6.94	0.038	.001	0.32	0.70
Peru	29	20.27	72.5	.009	.027	.181	66.14	0.204	—	0.26	0.32
Senegal	28	6.76	10.0	.004	.008	.028	1.55	—	.004	0.48	1.82
Sri Lanka	27	16.21	86.0	.004	.006	.028	21.81	—	.0003	0.51	0.12
Togo	26	3.00	15.9	.003	.004	.013	56.09	—	—	0.26	0.93
Sudan	24	21.68	32.0	.001	.003	.016	0.90	—	—	1.82	0.21
Bolivia	23	6.20	63.2	.005	—	.086	16.89	0.001	—	0.77	—
Mauritania	23	1.66	17.4	.003	—	.033	96.43	3.173	—	0.36	—
Burundi	19	4.83	26.8	.001	.001	—	14.02	—	—	0.18	—
Madagascar	19	9.91	50.0	.006	.004	.011	0.56	—	—	0.68	0.27
Tanzania	16	21.90	73.5	.003	.005	.014	1.03	—	.0005	1.89	1.54
Ethiopia	15	32.72	4.2	.0004	.028	.014	8.30	—	—	0.76	—
Sierra Leone	13	3.91	15.0	.002	.004	.010	4.48	—	—	2.18	—
Burma	12	38.89	65.9	.001	.001	.013	6.33	—	—	0.74	0.01
Central African Republic	12	2.66	33.0	.002	—	.013	29.36	—	—	1.28	0.09
Chad	12	5.25	15.0	.001	.001	.008	1.54	—	—	1.69	0.13
Nepal	11	17.00	19.2	—	.001	.005	13.45	—	—	0.91	—
Bangladesh	10	102.74	25.8	.0003	.001	.011	1.52	—	.0004	0.12	0.05
Ghana	5	14.25	30.2	.004	.007	.075	12.27	—	—	0.80	0.05
North Yemen	5	6.07	8.6	.002	—	.018	161.95	—	—	—	0.32
Malawi	4	7.06	25.0	.002	.005	.017	8.02	—	—	1.64	0.15
Benin	2	4.03	27.9	.0003	.005	.004	16.48	—	—	1.08	—
Kenya	2	20.18	47.1	.005	.021	.031	13.31	—	—	1.58	0.43
Lesotho	1	1.51	52.0	.005	—	—	31.39	—	—	0.22	—
Uganda	1	14.73	52.3	.001	.004	.012	1.25	—	—	0.43	—
Zaire	1	33.09	54.5	.003	.001	.065	5.76	—	—	0.39	—

Source: *UN Statistical Yearbook*, 1981; *UNESCO Statistical Yearbook*, 1983.

MO Per capita value of gross manufactured output (US$)

Development criteria

A	Population in millions	F	International monetary reserves in US$/person
B	Literacy rate percentage	G	Iron ore production, iron ore content in t/person
C	Commercial motor vehicles in use/person	H	Phosphate fertilizer production in t/person
D	Telephones installed/person	I	Roundwood production in m³/person
E	Electrical generating capacity in kW/person	J	Research and development funds in US$/person

fell apart. *Time*, on 1984 1 16, noted that Zaire had over 90 000 km of good roads in 1960, but by 1984 only 10 000 km were considered to be passable. Badly maintained roads increase greatly the operating costs of the traffic through increased fuel consumption and more frequent vehicle repair and replacement.

What possible development strategies can a country use to industrialize? Before we try to answer that question in the next section, let us assess the potential a country has for industrial development.

STATISTICAL ANALYSIS

10. We are going to try to assess an index of development potential. The problem of selection of criteria is, of course, ever-present, so we will use those in Fig. 4-4. The countries listed are those for which data are available that have the least manufacturing industry as shown in Column Q of Appendix 3, that is, those with a per capita value of gross manufactured output less than $75. They are listed in order from Egypt with $74 down to Zaire with $1. Information relating to ten criteria is also given.

Devise an index of development potential to help industrialists choose the future location of their new factories. There is no single correct method of formulating such an index. Try two or three different methods and see if you get comparable results. If you get strikingly different results from different methods, what do you say to the industrialists awaiting your report?

11. Design an industrial development brochure for the nation you found to have the highest index of development potential.

12. Each of the criteria in Fig. 4-4 is important because it represents a sector of the country's economy. Try to explain what each criterion represents and why it was selected.

13. Before deciding to invest, an industrialist may require information on other aspects of the country. What are some of these other aspects?

Industrial Development Strategies

Different Possibilities

There are many differing theories about how development should be implemented. It is difficult to suggest that one way is superior to another. Certain strategies have worked in the past for some countries, but not for others. Industrialization designed to achieve national independence may have a very different character from industrialization designed to provide a wide variety of consumer goods. Industrialization designed to satisfy export markets may differ markedly from industrialization designed to help meet the basic needs of the domestic population. Similarly, industrialization meant to raise employment may differ substantially from industrialization intended to raise overall national wealth. There will always be some overlap among these strategies, and the overlap will tend to become larger and the differences smaller as industrialization spreads. A mature industrialized country is able to serve all the initially competing aims. There is as yet no country in the world that has this maturity, but a few, such as the USA, Japan, West Germany, France, the UK, Canada and Italy seem close. The newly industrializing countries must choose, however, to emphasize some goals (e.g., full employment) over others. Their choices generally lie in the following areas:

- market planned or centrally planned development;
- agglomerated or dispersed development;
- import substitution or export promotion development;
- basic needs or megaproject development.

Industrialization occurs over time. The same country may well find different alternatives to be fitting and desirable at different times. Moreover, some countries find they can combine suitable elements from several alternatives into a single successful strategy. We will look at examples as we go along.

Market Planning and Central Planning
One of the choices facing newly industrializing countries is whether to

Critics regard market economies as unplanned. Some assert that the market is a jungle. Supporters, however, argue that a market economy favours a lot of decentralized planning by individuals and groups, especially in response to price signals.

opt for a market system or a centrally planned system, or some form of combination of the two. Market planning means that manufacturers plan what to produce, how much to produce and where to sell it according to their views of market demand. The cost of production, the demand for goods and people's ability to pay for goods determine the type and scale of production.

In centrally planned economies, manufacturers are told what and how much to produce and where to sell it according to the views of government planners on the abilities and needs of the total economy. They are also constrained by the operating budgets allocated by the central planners. Central planning determines the type and scale of production.

The political and economic philosophies supporting market economies are generally those of the Western world, while support for centrally planned economies comes mostly from the Communist world. Both can point to successes; both have their failures. And the chief protagonists of the two systems — the USA and the USSR — would each like to persuade the developing nations of the benefits of their own system. The developing world has responded diversely. Some countries have opted largely for the market model (such as Brazil, Taiwan, Mexico and Singapore). Others have opted mainly for the centrally planned model (such as Cuba, Vietnam, China and Tanzania). Still others have opted for mixed modes of development, including India, Sri Lanka and Indonesia. Japan and South Korea also have industrialized using a combination of central and market planning. The South Korean example is more fully examined in the case study at the end of this chapter.

Reprinted in *World Press Review*, 1985   11

Agglomeration and Dispersion

Another option open to newly industrializing countries is to agglomerate or disperse the newly developing industries. Market forces tend to favour agglomeration in the early stages of industrialization, while dispersion is encouraged in the later stages. A centrally planned economy, on the other hand, has the ability to favour either agglomeration or dispersion at any stage.

The advantages of agglomeration lie chiefly in the savings available through the nearness of the newly developing industries. Transportation costs between different sectors of industry are minimized, trained labour is more easily gathered together, infrastructural support services are more readily provided, and industrial investment is more efficiently attracted. For these reasons — called the economies of agglomeration — many newly industrializing countries are experiencing extremely rapid growth in their industrial "core" areas, usually the capital city and/or major ports. The main cities thus tend to grow very rapidly since they act as

magnets to the rural population. In Ecuador the core area of Quito/ Guayaquil grew from 30% of the total population in 1952 to 42% in 1982. In Panama the population of the core area around the capital increased from 31% to 46% between 1950 and 1980. Such growth rates are unsustainable in the long term because overcrowding, pollution, high prices, overstretched services and a general decline in quality of life result. Eventually *diseconomies* of agglomeration become apparent. Some cities in the developing world are already at or near this point. Examples are Jakarta, Sao Paulo, Cairo and Mexico City. The solution is to try to spread industrial development throughout the non-core areas of the nation, called the "periphery." This requires an equal non-core distribution of the various industrial support services, such as transportation, education and other infrastructural aspects. By reducing the comparative advantages of the core, the periphery can compete in providing jobs and raising living standards, which slows or reverses the flow of migrants to the cities.

Centrally planned economies have more power to specify how many and for what jobs people will be trained. These Soviet students from the Provideniye District are being trained to fill the jobs that industrial development in their area requires: reindeer herders, all-terrain vehicle drivers and radio operators.

The term *diseconomies* is used to indicate a situation where the costs outweigh the benefits.

In a market economy industry usually does not disperse into the rural periphery until a certain threshold of economic growth has been reached in the core: otherwise the momentum of growth is slowed. The example of Sri Lanka illustrates this point. The government set out to provide a wide range of infrastructural services such as education, health care, equal access to food and basic transportation throughout the entire country. Although still a relatively poor country in material terms, Sri Lanka now has an exceptionally high life expectancy, a high literacy rate, a low infant mortality rate and very little malnutrition in comparison with its material peers. Disparities between the core and the periphery have been so lessened that the proportion of the total population living in the core area around Colombo actually fell from 21.3% in 1946 to 20.8% in 1980. However, there has been a price in economic growth, witnessed by Sri Lanka's average annual growth rate for manufacturing industry from 1970 to the mid-1980s of only 2.4%, compared with similar growth rates for Bangladesh (10.4%), Haiti (7.5%), India (4.5%), Indonesia (13.4%), Libya (14.7%), Pakistan (5.0%) and Tunisia (11.6%).

Sri Lanka's example highlights a very real problem facing developing nations. The choice between agglomeration, which promotes rapid economic growth but unevenly rising standards of living, and dispersion, which promotes a more evenly rising standard of living but slower overall economic growth, is a very difficult one. Centrally planned countries face the same difficult choices, but have generally opted for different solutions. The authority of the state is used to limit the size of the core areas; people are not allowed to move in without permission. Such policies have worked. For example, Havana's share of Cuba's population is almost exactly the same now as it was at the time of Castro's revolution. In Vietnam, Ho Chi Minh City is smaller than it was in 1975; in China, the lowest rates of population increase are in the core areas of Shanghai and Beijing.

China operates a residence permit system (called *hukou*) to control the movement of rural inhabitants. It also operates a policy of rural industrialization providing local jobs and promoting local self-sufficiency. As elsewhere, labour is displaced from the farms as more efficient techniques are employed; so new rural jobs are needed. In Jiangsu Province, near Shanghai, 10 000 000 farmers left the land between 1978 and 1985, leaving 15 000 000 still on the land. However, Zhu Tong-hua of the Chinese Research Institute for Small Towns said in 1985 that he expected that Jiangsu's farms could be farmed efficiently by about 4 000 000 farmers.

What are we to do with the remaining 11 000 000 [he asked]. They have to improve their standard of living, but they mustn't suddenly flood into the already overpopulated cities. We have to attract them

As farming methods become more efficient, displaced farmers must find new forms of employment. These Chinese turn their hands to "carp farming."

to the small towns. That way, the peasants will leave the land but remain in the countryside, while at the same time increasing their income and helping to consolidate the rural economy.

These goals have been successfully pursued, as can be seen in the fact that there is now some industry in evey small town in Jiangsu, and the province's industrial output now surpasses its rich agricultural output.

Import Substitution and Export Promotion

A third very important choice facing newly industrializing countries is whether to opt for a policy of import substitution or one of export promotion. Import substitution creates industries that substitute domestic production for imports. Export promotion encourages industries whose chief purpose is to produce goods for international rather than domestic sale.

In both cases, the initial development of industry requires the availability of investment capital. The capital may come from surpluses generated by the primary sectors of the economy. It may also come from foreign loans or direct foreign investment. Different countries use different combinations of these sources. Japan used domestically generated surpluses in its initial phase of industrialization, avoiding foreign loans or multinational investment to protect its national independence. Brazil, on the other hand, has used loans and multinational investment extensively to gain quick access to money to support its rapid development.

Whatever the source of investment funds, many countries have chosen to use them to develop import-substituting industries as their first

The economies of all countries may be classified into three sectors: primary, secondary and tertiary. Primary activities are those of farming, fishing, forestry and mining, where the product is obtained directly from the environment. Secondary activities are those such as manufacturing and construction, where the primary raw materials are processed into something else before they are considered useful. Tertiary activities are services such as education, health care, finance and transportation.

phase of industrialization. Generally, these industries use low levels of technology, large supplies of labour and locally available raw materials. Such industries produce textiles, clothing, footwear, processed foods, furniture and household goods. They provide a basis for further industrial growth by introducing industrial techniques, labour and management training, and by encouraging local entrepreneurship. The industrializing countries usually try to protect their import-substituting industries by tariff barriers, to reduce or eliminate competiton. However, many import substitution industries enjoy a certain measure of "natural" protection from competition because they use local raw materials, have plentiful labour and need not pay for international transportation. If the protective tariff is set high enough foreign competition is virtually eliminated. There is a risk in this: domestic production may not be as efficient and low-cost as it could be. The contrast between Ghana and the Ivory Coast illustrates the point: Ghana set very high import tariffs to protect its domestic industries; the Ivory Coast pursued a relatively low tariff policy. Both countries effectively reduced their reliance on imported consumer goods (Ghana from 25% of all imports in 1972 to 18% of all imports in 1982; Ivory Coast from 49% to 26% during the same period). But through the 1970s and the early 1980s, Ghana's industrial output fell at an average rate of 2.4% per year, while the Ivory Coast's industrial output rose at an average rate of 8.6% per year.

Import-substituting industries are likely to grow fairly quickly if they are efficiently run. They generate extra wealth by providing jobs and by expanding their markets gradually to replace imports. As the first phase of import substitution is completed, growth slows to a rate equal to the growth of the domestic market alone. The maintenance of a high industrial gowth rate then necessitates choosing either to move to second phase import substitution in the capital and durable goods sectors or to export promotion in the consumable goods sectors already in place.

Capital goods are those that are used to help make other products. Examples include steel mills, printing presses and computers.

The capital and durable goods sectors of an economy are different from the consumable goods sector. They rely much more on the intensive use of expensive equipment and usually must produce large quantities of goods to be efficient. Examples are petrochemicals, steel, automobiles and large domestic appliances such as refrigerators. The cost of initiating second phase import substitution is high, and the quantities required for efficient operation are often too great for many small countries to absorb. In order to share the cost and widen the market, some groups of small countries have tried to combine their domestic production capacities and markets into larger free-trade areas somewhat like the European Common Market.

Nevertheless, second phase import substitution has been adopted as an industrial development policy in many countries. India and China are two countries that have followed the path of second phase import substitution. India is now one of the top ten industrialized countries in the world, on a total product basis rather than on a per capita basis. It manufactures a very wide range of goods, including such consumer durables as cars and such capital equipment as power stations. It still protects its industries with high tariffs and import quotas. There are few imported cars or films in India, but Indian cars and Indian movies are common.

China is following a similar path. Between 1978 and 1985 it spent over US$10 billion of its US$17 billion international monetary reserves to buy capital technology and assistance from the more industrially developed nations in order to develop its own capital goods and consumer durables industries. In 1986 it announced plans for a joint venture with the West German firm of Volkswagen to construct an auto plant near Shanghai to manufacture Santana sedans for the Chinese and export markets. The case of the French refrigerator factory illustrates more specifically the Chinese desire to manufacture their own second phase goods. In 1984, the Chinese bought a bankrupt French refrigerator factory. They sent 100 technicians to Lorraine to dismantle, number and pack every single piece of equipment in the factory. The factory was then totally reassembled in the port of Tianjin, near Beijing, and opened for production in 1985.

Second phase import substitution can also suffer from the disadvantages of protection noted earlier in relation to first phase industries. The lack of competition resulting from tariffs, quotas or import prohibitions enables inefficiency and high-cost production to occur. In Argentina high tariffs on caustic soda imposed at the request of a potential domestic producer made the thriving soap-export industry collapse, since the domestic product was much more expensive than imported soda. These higher costs and inefficiencies have caused some countries to turn to export promotion for industrial growth, among them Brazil, Japan, South Korea, Singapore, Mexico and Taiwan. In such cases, exporting industries must compete on the world market in both quality and price, and inefficient producers do not survive.

World Bank data indicate that countries favouring export promotion have generally fared better in industrial growth than those favouring import substitution. From 1970 to the mid-1980s, average annual industrial growth rates were 13.6% for South Korea, 8.9% for Singapore, 8.2% for Brazil and 7.2% for Mexico, compared with 4.3% for India, 4.2% for Uruguay and 0.6% for Chile. There are risks, however, in a policy of export promotion. Exports are vulnerable to the uncertainties of international markets. The chief world market is the USA, and when the US economy is growing, its people buy lots of imports from abroad; but during times of recession its people buy fewer goods from abroad.

Both India and China have very large populations and are thus able to support second phase import substitution much more easily than many smaller countries can.

The refrigerator factory was opened in Lorraine in an attempt to remedy the high rate of unemployment there.

The freedom of individual countries to protect their domestic markets is restricted by the possibilities of international retaliation. A country trying to protect its home market in one sector may find its exports in another sector jeopardized by other countries retaliating by erecting their own protective barriers. Because of the importance of international trade to the economic health of most countries, there is a General Agreement on Tariffs and Trade (GATT) which aims to keep trade channels as open as possible.

The USA is by far the world's largest market, and many countries not only gear their production almost solely for the US market but also depend upon success there for their survival. Talk of protectionism in the USA sends shivers through much of the world.

The industrial health of the exporting countries is thus closely tied to the state of the American market. There is additional risk in the increasing tendency of developed markets, chiefly the USA, to turn to protection to save their own industries. We will look at this topic again later in this chapter when we discuss problems facing industrialized countries.

Basic Needs and Megaprojects

A fourth choice facing newly industrializing countries lies in the area of basic needs and megaprojects. Basic needs industries are those that serve the needs of the local population for jobs, housing, clothing, domestic wares and so on. They usually form a component of integrated development strategies rather than stand alone. Megaprojects are giant projects such as hydro-electric dams, railway construction, international airports and so on.

There are arguments about the costs and benefits of both approaches. The benefits of a basic needs strategy are obvious. The local people obtain the goods and training that are basic to their existence. China's industrial development followed this strategy after it broke with the USSR, which was sponsoring a megaprojects approach in the early 1950s. Small-scale production was encouraged in every commune: jobs were created, housing built, clothing produced, training acquired, education and literacy improved and people's basic material and economic needs satisfied. The present government of China continues the basic needs approach. In the village of Fenghuang in central China, for example, 80% of the labour force is no longer engaged in farming, but works in a variety of small-scale industrial operations. As Han Bingqing, manager of the Fenghuang Industrial Combine, said in 1985, "In the past, the big items for us were bicycles, sewing machines, and watches. Now these are just middle goods. Our big goods are washing machines, motorcycles, refrigerators, and tape recorders." The chief benefit of a basic needs approach is the development of a productive, independent, literate and employed population. It is a benefit incapable of measurement in monetary terms, and one which more and more countries seek. The costs to be set against these benefits are those of industrial dispersion as well as of possible inefficiency.

The costs are essentially those of slower growth and higher prices.

The benefits of megaprojects are chiefly infrastructural. Energy projects, railways, major airports, steel mills, petrochemical factories, universities and the like meet the needs of the nation as a whole. Continuing the successful operation of megaprojects, however, requires a fairly large population base. Brazil and Egypt have had success with their giant energy projects, while China is planning a similar move with the Three Gorges Dam on the Yangtse river. Some smaller countries have proceeded with such megaprojects while having neither the population

Fig. 4-5
Income distribution curves for Brazil, showing progressively unequal distributions, 1960, 1970, 1980

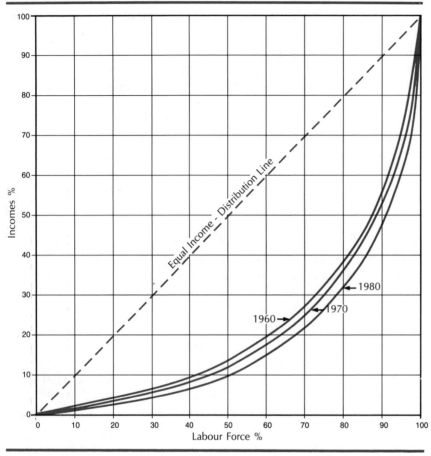

Source: World Bank, *World Development Reports*, 1981 and 1985

base nor the necessary infrastructure to support them, and the resulting facilities now stand underused or idle. Large airports in Tanzania and Somalia stand almost empty, while a cement factory in Mali, built to produce 50 000 t of cement a year, produced only 5 t in 1984. Another problem with megaprojects is that jobs are often provided for the few rather than the many. Income distribution throughout the society tends to become more unequal. In Brazil, for example, the increasing inequity of incomes since 1960 may be seen in Fig. 4-5. So while Brazil as a nation has become richer, the wealth has not been equally shared. The government claims that eventually the benefits of industrialization will "trickle down."

The choice between basic needs and megaprojects as industrial development strategies is therefore between a strategy in which everyone benefits a little immediately and improvements come slowly and another by which some people benefit greatly immediately and others benefit later. The length of the delay depends upon the overall speed of growth and the way benefits are distributed through society.

DISCUSSION AND RESEARCH

14. Multinationals are one of the prime agents in the spread of industry to developing countries. They are often criticized for paying lower wages to local labour than to their own domestic labour. What are the reasons for this criticism? What likely would happen if they paid local labour at the same rates as their domestic labour?

15. India has generally followed industrial development strategies of market planning, agglomeration and megaprojects. China has pursued central planning, dispersion and basic needs development. Both countries are industrializing successfully. What other factors would you look for to decide which set of strategies may be most appropriate for a newly industrializing country?

16. You have just assumed total power in a mostly agricultural country of 20 000 000 people. The capital city of 4 000 000 people is growing rapidly as people move from the countryside in search of work; but work is not available. It is predicted by an outside agency that your country's population will double within the next 24 years; illiteracy is high; health care is low. Your country's main products are fruit and minerals, both for export, and basic foodstuffs and cottage industry products, both for the home market. Your country is also heavily in debt as a result of import purchases by your predecessor. You want your country to become more developed and your people to have higher living standards. First, define what social and economic goals you wish to achieve; in effect, this means define what you consider to be "more developed." Then organize and justify a development strategy for your country.

A Theory of Industrial Development

The choice between the various development alternatives we have discussed is influenced fundamentally by the type of political system governing a country. The theory to be presented here seeks to provide a generalized development model based upon a market viewpoint. It is difficult to present a similar model from a central-planning viewpoint, for although Karl Marx did postulate a generalized organizational sequence from feudalism through bourgeois capitalism and socialism to communism, centrally planned models vary according to the wishes of the different governments in determining what best meets the needs of their countries. The USSR and China have developed entirely different and successful models under different central plans. It is misleading to generalize about the forces at work in developing centrally planned economies. Each has its own priorities and requires individual analysis.

Walter Rostow, in *Stages of Economic Growth*, identifies five stages of development, applicable to all societies but viewed from a market perspective.

The Traditional Society

In Rostow's view, the essence of a traditional society is that its people have little collective ability to raise their economic productivity because they lack the technical and scientific knowledge to do so. Traditional societies have to devote a high proportion of their resources to farming. Rising out of the agricultural system is a rigid hierarchical social structure, with political power concentrated in the hands of the landowners. Upward mobility is slight; family and inheritance are highly valued. Rostow includes the whole pre-Newtonian world in this stage of growth. Examples are medieval Europe, Shogunate Japan, nineteenth century Russia, dynastic China, and any other society today with the characteristics just noted.

Rostow argues that Karl Marx's definitions of feudalism are similar to his own definitions of traditional societies.

Preconditions for Takeoff

According to Rostow, it takes time to alter a traditional society. Old beliefs and the security of traditional ways are difficult to challenge. Frequently the viewpoints of powerful and established people cannot be altered without a revolution. Except in Western Europe, where the transition occurred more or less spontaneously, the preconditions for takeoff have often been spurred by the intrusions of a more economically developed society. The entry of Commodore Perry's ships into Tokyo harbour in 1853 is a good example of such an intrusion. Rostow also notes that Peter the Great's (1682–1725) conviction that Russia needed to modernize helped to set the stage for the preconditions for takeoff in Russia long before takeoff actually occurred.

The industrial development of North America and Australia is seen by Rostow as having been inherited at the preconditions for takeoff stage through emigration from Western Europe.

Signs of the preconditions for takeoff are a growing acceptance of technology, a rapidly increasing population, the growth of education, the rise of banks, the building of transport and communications systems, the development of effective centralized government, the shifting of spending from those who prefer to act in their own interests to those who give priority to the public interest, and the growing efficiency of farming. Farming changes are crucial; the diminishing numbers of farmers must be able to feed the swelling urban populations, and prevent unemployment in the towns by demanding industrial products. If farmers do not get good prices for their products, the industrialization process is slowed and the society suffers from unemployment as well as hunger.

Takeoff

Takeoff occurs when the bulk of society has come to accept and favour the idea of change. Change itself becomes steady and self-sustaining rather than erratic. Increasing returns from higher productivity are ploughed back into additional modernization and expansion. Output per person increases enormously, and real wages rise. The country as a whole benefits greatly from advances in a few leading industries. For example, in Britain the textile industry led the takeoff phase; in the USA, Canada, France, Germany and Russia it was the railways, and in Sweden, the exploitation of raw materials. After takeoff, Rostow notes, such leading industries are usually replaced by domestic consumer goods industries such as cars, food processing, electrical appliances and electronics.

Another characteristic of takeoff is the widespread diffusion of literacy, which usually results from compulsory education. Mass circulation newspapers then become established. According to Rostow, democracy becomes the preferred system of government, choice in the political arena accompanying consumer choice in the market place. Health care improves and life expectancy increases.

Rostow notes that leading industries vary greatly from country to country and from time to time; but they are all characterized by an ability to induce a chain of industrial expansion in other sectors. A growing economy always has leading industries, even after the takeoff stage.

India displays many characteristics of a society in takeoff. This scene from Bombay shows some of the products of India's growing industrial sector: cars and films.

John Molyneux

Drive to Maturity

The drive to maturity is a long period of sustained change. Technology gradually spreads throughout all areas of economic activity. Society adapts to the changes and growing service activities create universal educational and medical facilities. Since people are better off individually in material ways, travel and a variety of recreational activities become common. Democracy becomes firmly established, and governments begin to appropriate and apportion ever-larger parts of the national wealth. As the old ways gradually die, people begin to feel free in their choice of beliefs. The society gradually comes to assume that it can do almost anything it wants.

The five-year plans of various countries are seen by Rostow as the means to achieve takeoff, the drive to maturity and the age of high mass consumption.

The Age of High Mass Consumption

During the age of high mass consumption, Rostow believes that the leading sectors shift more toward services, especially those of finance, information and government. Material production continues to grow through the application of such refined inputs as automation. Social welfare becomes a higher value and people talk of the quality of life rather than of the standard of living. There is a broad range of choices, not only for the individual but also for the whole society. Should the society increase its leisure? Explore space? Develop the ocean beds? Clean up the environment after the drive to maturity?

DISCUSSION AND RESEARCH

17. Using the criteria presented by Rostow, research the history of Canada and attempt, with approximate dates and examples that match the criteria, to ascertain how well Canada fits the stages of growth model.

Problems Facing Industrialized Countries

While some countries vigorously pursue a policy of industrialization, others hold back. They see some of the problems the industrialized countries face. As the President of Zaire said in 1972:

> We have certain advantages in being underequipped. We have to be proud that we have never made errors such as those which are regretted by some countries considered as completely developed. Therefore, we refuse to follow blindly the trend of developed countries which want production at any price. We do not believe that peace and happiness are derived from the number of cars in the garage, the TV antennas on the roof, or the volume of noise in one's ears. . . . How does it help to have innumerable factories if their chimneys spread poisonous products over us all day and night? We do not want these destructive industries which kill the fish in our rivers, depriving honest people of the pleasure of fishing or drinking clean water . . . We desire only that when scientists will have transformed the world into an artificial one, that in Zaire an authentic nature will remain.

Subsequent data from the *World Development Report 1985* indicate that during the preceding decade industrial production in Zaire actually declined, as it did in Argentina, Bolivia, El Salvador, Ghana, Jamaica, Kuwait, Liberia, Libya, Madagascar, Nicaragua, Sierra Leone, Uganda, the UK and Zambia. Elsewhere things were different. During the same decade, industrial growth rates averaging more than 10% per year were experienced by Cameroon, Congo, Egypt, Jordan, Niger, South Korea, North Yemen and Paraguay.

The president of Zaire pinpointed several of the disadvantages of industrialization, which we will now look at in more detail.

Pollution

Pollution is the term applied to the production of waste materials in

Atmospheric pollution clouds the sky and corrodes the landscape near Bogota, Colombia.

John Molyneux

quantities greater than the environment can handle. The environment has always had its own "cleaning cycles"; dirty water is purified through the natural water cycle and dirty air is cleansed in the oxygen cycle. As industry has grown, however, the natural cleaning cycles have become overloaded in many heavily industrialized parts of the world.

In the past, there have been several pollution disasters. One of the worst incidents was probably the lethal smog of London, England, in 1952, when a mixture of fog and industrial pollutants killed hundreds. After that, London banned the use of coal in domestic fireplaces and worked to control factory emissions. By the mid-1970s the cleaner air made it possible for London to receive twice as many hours of sunshine per year as it had in the early 1950s.

Another disaster occurred in Japan in the 1960s, when a factory near the fishing village of Minimata put unwanted mercury wastes directly into the sea. No one thought much about this until several fishermen became seriously ill. Some were blinded, while others suffered severe nervous disorders. Gradually the disease was traced to the large numbers of mercury-contaminated fish taken from local waters.

In 1984 at Bhopal, India, another disaster killed many hundreds of people when a local factory error released poisonous gases into the atmosphere.

The use of coal was not banned at a single stroke because most homes had no alternative source of heat.

Most dangerous atmospheric pollution occurs under high pressure conditions, i.e., when the atmosphere is calmest rather than when the factories are busiest. Normally the motion of the atmosphere disperses pollutants until they are so diluted as to be of little danger. When the air is calm the downward drift of air under high pressure conditions actually pins pollutants close to ground level. Pollution counts are always highest when atmospheric pressure is high. Acid rain is different in that it occurs in low pressure conditions, and its effects are so widespread precisely because the atmosphere disperses the pollutants.

The giant Kennecott operation near Bingham, Utah, is the USA's largest open-pit copper mine. Applying technology in the pursuit of raw materials can reshape the earth's surface.

Acid rain is a less dramatic but more common problem. It is caused chiefly by burning coal and oil and smelting non-ferrous ores, both of which release sulphur and nitrogen oxides into the atmosphere. Acid rain kills fish, weakens and kills vegetation and, in West Germany, is the suspected cause of up to 2000 infant deaths a year. In North America, data published in *bridges* in 1986 2 indicates that while the USA produces about seven times as much as waste acid gas as Canada, Canada produces more per person. Also, most Canadian sources are metal smelters, while most US sources are coal-burning electricity-generating stations. Canada has undertaken to cut its sulphur emissions in half by 1994; meanwhile it maintains some political pressure on the US to act more firmly against the coal-burning electrical utilities. One of the largest US electrical utilities, the federally owned Tennessee Valley Authority, has decided to reduce its sulphur emissions by 60%. To pay for this it has raised consumer rates by about 10%.

Environmental pollution has indeed become a serious problem in industrialized countries, and most industries are now under considerable public pressure and facing growing amounts of government legislation to restrict the quantities of waste they produce. Unfortunately, the environment is international in its scope while government legislation is restricted by national boundaries, and few governments are yet willing to risk forcing their countries' industries into an internationally uncompetitive situation by making them pay for pollution controls.

Marilyn MacKenzie

Butchart Gardens, north of Victoria, BC, were planted to mask former quarrying operations. Do you think the environment and the scale of the Kennecott mine would permit its restoration?

Environmental Aesthetics

The quarrying, dumping, blasting and emission of toxic fumes that often accompany industrialization generally make the environment unattractive. The landscape near Sudbury, Ontario, became notorious in the late 1960s when the early lunar astronauts practised there. The rocky surface, laid bare by smelter gases that had destroyed the natural vegetation, was the closest thing to the moon's surface that could be found on earth. Sudbury cut down its toxic smelter emissions and dilutes its remaining emissions by spreading them over a wider area.

It is possible to improve the appearance and surroundings of industrial operations. Factories can be landscaped, tree screens planted and the barren land resulting from strip mining can be resodded and planted over. Butchart Gardens near Victoria in British Columbia is an excellent example of what can be done to mask former unsightly quarrying operations. The grassed and treed Buffalo Pound in Estevan, Saskatchewan, is another example of an imaginative use of a former quarrying site.

Resource Depletion

The problem of identifying resources is aggravated by the need to define the level of mineral content in an ore that would qualify it as a resource. For example, in 1750 the amount of copper required in an ore to make it worth mining (and therefore a resource) was 13%. Today it is about 0.25%.

The world is finite, and most of the resources we use are not renewable. This leads many people to argue that the West should reduce its use of resources and leave some for other places and future generations. While it is true that most of the earth's resources are finite, there are some other things to consider.

One thing that is often misunderstood is the meaning of the term *known reserves*. "Known reserves" does not refer to reserves that are known, but reserves that can be profitably developed at existing prices. As a result, the known reserves of most resources cover periods of only 30–40 years into the future. Generally, industries do not spend time or effort searching for or developing resources not likely to be needed for another 30–40 years. Moreover, resources are only important to an industry if they can be developed at current prices. Usually, it costs more to develop the deeper parts of a mine or the remoter areas of a forest. Industries prefer to avoid these more expensive resources and use the cheapest first. The more expensive resources, although they are known about, do not count as part of the known reserves until the market price of the product can cover the cost of their development. It is therefore difficult to inventory resources, since we cannot judge now just when a resource will become worth developing. Nor do we know what substitutes may be developed for a particular resource. That too depends on a balance of price and input costs.

Disease

Silicosis (black lung disease) affects thousands of coalminers in Western Europe and North America and is one of the most widespread industrial diseases.

Some kinds of industry can be dangerous to workers and can cause such diseases as asbestosis and silicosis. These are serious lung disorders caused by air contaminated with asbestos or silica particles. Because of the cancer risk associated with inhaling asbestos particles, the USA in 1986 announced its wish to eliminate entirely imports of asbestos from Canada. Canada has itself greatly reduced its use of asbestos. Most industrial health hazards are linked to contaminants in the air, although it can also be very dangerous to work near highly radioactive substances, or around acids, pesticides and other toxic substances. The risks posed by industrial hazards such as these can be lessened by protective clothing and caution; but accidents occur. Also, ignorance of the risks has been a severe problem for workers, and many now suffer through the lack of proper advice and care in the past.

Industry-related health risks are not restricted to plant workers. They may also endanger the health of the surrounding community. Japan, for example, has 85 000 recognized victims of environmental pollution, with diseases ranging from bronchitis to metal poisoning. Brazil found that in industrial Cubatao, on the south coast, as many as 12 children out of every 10 000 were being born without brains, while 44% of the local population suffered from various lung diseases. In Canada, several hundred Indians in northwestern Ontario have been poisoned by mercury, a by-product of paper manufacturing that was released into local rivers and retained in the fish. Throughout North America concern over toxic emissions from road vehicles has brought a more rigorous system of pollution controls.

The Loss of Jobs to Developing Countries

Many developing nations offer relatively cheap labour as well as government policies favouring industrialization, and many companies have taken advantage of these facts. However, these new operations can cause problems for the workers in the original home plants. The home plant may be shut down, creating unemployment. In the USA there has been a persistent problem of unemployment created by multinationals shifting their operations to other countries. In the latter half of the 1960s the American Federation of Labor claimed there was a net loss by the USA of some 700 000 jobs by this process. The trend continued throughout the 1970s. General Electric and RCA cut their US payrolls by 39 000 jobs but added 49 000 jobs elsewhere in the world. By the mid-1980s it was estimated that the USA was losing about 500 000 manufacturing jobs yearly to the newly industrializing countries of southeast Asia and Latin America. Because of lower wage rates in the developing countries, manufactures can be much cheaper than US-made goods. At the end of 1985 the average hourly wage rate in manufacturing in the USA was $12.82, in Japan it was $6.42, in Taiwan $1.90, Mexico $1.68, South Korea $1.32 and Brazil $1.20 (all figures in US$). Japan's multinationals pursue a similar philosophy, investing abroad even more widely than US multinationals.

In the face of lower priced competition, the industries of many developed countries ask for protection by tariffs or quotas. Higher tariffs have not generally been successful because the imports from developing countries are cheap enough that they can still enter the market at lower prices than goods produced in the developed country. Accordingly, quotas are increasingly popular as the protective device. To some extent quotas have worked to protect jobs and even to create them. Japanese car imports to North America became so restricted by quotas that Japanese car firms built factories in North America to maintain access to the market. Japan, however, has a labour shortage, and generally does

The costs of unemployment are varied. They include the loss of income by the unemployed, and the resulting loss of income by those who provided goods and services to them. As well there are the numerous personal costs of enforced idleness, such as demoralization and loss of initiative. There are also the costs of support by the rest of society, and the social tensions produced by an increasingly desperate workforce. In some of the older industrialized parts of England in the mid-1980s, unemployment affected as much as 50% of the workforce.

A textile factory near Shillod in central India. Establishing industry in rural areas is an important part of development plans in many countries.

John Molyneux

In 1985, when Canada removed its quotas on imported low-priced footwear, the price of shoes fell by about 15%. The Canadian shoe industry meanwhile lost about 10 000 jobs.

not mind the loss of jobs. The situation is different for many other countries.

Developed world protection not only has the effect of maintaining jobs there but also of denying them to the unemployed of the developing countries. In addition, it also has the effect of denying low-priced goods to consumers in the developed world, not all of whom are individually wealthy. Protectionism in Canada is illustrated in the following article.

Industry backs call for garment import quota

By ROBERT GIBBENS
Globe and Mail Reporter

MONTREAL —
The federal Textile and Clothing Board's call for emergency global quotas on garment imports has been welcomed by the clothing industry, but companies say the proposed ceiling is too generous.

The board made the recommendation in a report on import quotas released by Regional Industrial Ex-

pansion Minister Sinclair Stevens.

The Canadian Textiles Institute, the industry's main lobby group, and individual garment manufacturing companies say the textile board's call for a two-year freeze on imports of foreign-made garments at around the 1984 level of 237 million units is still too high.

At that level, they said, more cuts may occur in domestic output, more factories may close and more jobs disappear.

From late 1976 until the end of 1979, Canada applied worldwide

clothing import quotas under the terms of the safeguard clause of the General Agreement on Tariffs and Trade — a move designed to provide breathing space for domestic producers to adjust to a higher level of imports by raising their productivity.

Bilateral restraint agreements with about 20 exporting countries followed and, in 1982, were renewed until the end of 1985. Imports, however, have increased in the past two years.

Imports rose from 166 million units in 1982 to 202 million in 1983, 237 million in 1984 and may rise to more than 250 million by the end of 1985 — because of expected surges in August and September.

The domestic industry believes it should be allowed to recover some market share and that the 1983 level of imports should be the basis for the maximum global quota.

The federal textile board estimated in its report that 24,000 jobs have been lost in the textile and clothing industries since 1981 — a drop of 13 per cent. Of those, it said, 15,000 disappeared because of the surge in imports in the past two years.

The textile institute's president, Eric Barry, complained that the federal board's recommendations have been in the Cabinet's hands for more than two weeks and contended that swift action is essential if more deterioration in the domestic industry is to be avoided.

The Globe and Mail, Toronto, 1985 7 20

DISCUSSION AND RESEARCH

18. Who gains and who loses from a policy of protection on the part of an industrially developed country?

Anti-Growth

In the industrialized world, especially in North America and Western Europe, there has been much debate over the desirability of continued growth. One of the most persuasive contributions to this discussion was a computer study called *The Limits to Growth*, published by the Club of Rome in 1972. Although its message has been somewhat modified since then, it remains a potent expression of the concerns many have about continued economic growth. It forecast doom before the year 2100 if growth continued at the present rate, and recommended certain policies to limit growth to avoid disaster. Restricted growth has accordingly become the watchword for many people, with the aim of creating a "conserver society."

Others regard those who would limit growth as shortsighted pessimists who accept too easily the results of the 1972 study which (they say) falsely limited inputs. They argue that continued growth is not only possible but desirable. They claim that resources exist in plenty, that new resources will be made available by developing technology and that the world's people still lack sufficient material wealth. The first of the following articles offers a sympathetic account of the Club of Rome's report. The second gives a freewheeling critique of the same.

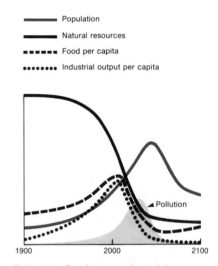

——— Population

━━━ Natural resources

■■■■ Food per capita

••••••• Industrial output per capita

Projection for disaster adapted from computer-output chart in *The Limits to Growth*.

The worst is yet to be?

The furnaces of Pittsburgh are cold; the assembly lines of Detroit are still. In Los Angeles, a few gaunt survivors of a plague desperately till freeway center strips, backyards and outlying fields, hoping to raise a subsistence crop. London's offices are dark, its docks deserted. In the farm lands of the Ukraine, abandoned tractors litter the fields: there is no fuel for them. The waters of the Rhine, Nile and Yellow rivers reek with pollutants.

Fantastic? No, only grim inevitability if society continues its present dedication to growth and "progress". At least that is the vision conjured by an elaborate study entitled *The Limits to Growth* [prepared by Dennis Meadows for the Club of Rome].

Meadows, 29, had studied the new field of "systems dynamics." His mentor was M.I.T. Professor Jay Forrester, the brilliant developer of a computer model that could simulate the major ecological forces at work in the world today. Forrester's model begins with the recognition that all these factors are interlocked. Human population cannot grow without food for sustenance. Since just about all the globe's best land is already under cultivation, farm production can rise only through use of tractors, fertilizers, pesticides — all products of industry. But more industrial output not only demands a heavier drain on natural resources that are scarce even now; it also creates more pollution. And pollution ultimately interferes with the growth of both population and food.

. . .

The question Meadows had to answer was: How long can population and industrialization continue to grow on this finite planet? Unlike the doomsday ecologists who predict that man will drown in pollution or starve because of overpopulation, Meadows's system concludes that the depletion of nonrenewable resources will probably cause the end of the civilization enjoyed by today's contented consumer.

End in Collapse

The sequence goes this way: As industrialization grows, it voraciously consumes enormous amounts of resources. Resources become scarcer, forcing more and more capital to be spent on procuring raw materials, which leaves less and less money for investment in new plants and facilities. At this stage, which might be about 2020, the computer's curves begin to converge and cross (*see chart*). Population outstrips food and industrial supplies. Investment in new equipment falls behind the rate of obsolescence, and the industrial base begins to collapse, carrying along with it the service and agricultural activities that have become dependent on industrial products (like medical equipment and fertilizers). Because of the lack of health services and food, the world's population dwindles rapidly.

In an attempt to find a way out of this basic dilemma, Meadows postulated other scenarios. He assumed that there are still huge, undiscovered reserves of natural resources, say, under the oceans. Testing that possibility, Meadows' computer shows that industrialization will accelerate — and the resulting runaway pollution will overwhelm the biosphere. Might not new technological devices control pollution? Sure, says the computer, but then population would soar and outstrip the ability of land to produce food. Every advance in technology consumes scarce natural resources, throws off more pollutants and often has unwanted social side effects, like creating huge and unmanageable unemployment. What if pollution was abated, the birthrate halved and food production doubled? The readouts are no less glum. There would still be some pollution from every farm and factory, and cumulatively it would still trigger catastrophe. After running thousands of such hypotheses through the computer, Meadows sums up his conclusion tersely: "All growth projections end in collapse."

The Meadows team offers a possible cure for man's dilemma — an all-out effort to end exponential growth, starting by 1975. Population should be stabilized by equalizing the birth and death rates. To halt industrial growth, investment in new, non-polluting plants must not exceed the retirement of old facilities. A series of fundamental shifts in behavioral patterns must take place. Instead of yearning for material goods, people must learn to prefer services, like education or recreation. All possible resources must be recycled, including the composting of organic garbage. Products like automobiles and TV sets must be designed to last long and to be repaired easily.

A little more time

Even if there are no improvements in existing technology, the world is not likely to be threatened with a physical shortage of raw materials until about AD 100 000 000

This may be the time to finish off the dying cult of extreme ecodoom. Professor Wilfred Beckerman has long made thoughtful people his debtors by writing into the Club of Rome's equations his admirable product called Beckermonium, named after his grandfather who failed to discover it in the nineteenth century. Ever since his grandfather failed to discover it in about 1856, the world has had no supplies of Beckermonium at all, which on the Club of Rome's equations should have made the world come to a halt some time soon after 1857: especially as, even in 1974, the things we have not yet discovered are far more important and numerous than the things we have so far discovered. Anyone can play the Beckermonium game by defining it as something unknown in their grandfather's day but found to exist since.

This is probably the best quick way of understanding the flaw in the extreme econonsense; but, as some people do not see it yet, it is good now to have a whole book from Mr. Beckerman on the subject [*In Defence of Economic Growth*. By Wilfred Beckerman. Cape, £3.95.] full of admirably numerate facts. This article will pinch some of the best of these facts without further attribution, and spice them with his and our own comments. A continuing demolition job on the cult is important, because its wrong — if well-meaning — views have been

responsible for a number of deaths. These include malaria victims in Ceylon after the banning of DDT; burned children after the wrongly-based anti-phosphates campaign against detergents had destroyed fireproofing in some clothing, and pneumonic victims in brownouts caused by conservationist opposition to power stations.

A prolific mile

The prophets have assumed four limiting factors on the world's economic growth, in ascending order of respectability: they say the world will run out of raw materials, will suffer ever-increasing pollution, will have too large a population, and too little food.

On raw materials, the Club of Rome reached its equations by assuming that actual reserves of any material cannot be more than two to five times "known reserves", with nil elasticity of supply and substitution after that. It then asked the computer what would happen if demand for precisely these things went on expanding exponentially. The computer replied, naturally, that everything would then break down.

This mode of argument could always have proved that world production of most things stopped long ago, because "known reserves" of most materials all through history have been only a few decades' worth of demand. This is because, if reserves of any material represent more than that, it is not worth looking for more of that material for a while. At present, "known reserves" of most metals are historically rather high — about a hundred years' supply — but random samples suggest that the natural occurrence of most metals in the top

mile of the earth's crust is about a million times as great as present known reserves, so we could probably extract one hundred million years' supply of metals from that top mile by existing technology. Towards the end, it would be a bit uncomfortable to mine to the depth of one mile at every point on the earth's crust, but by AD 100 000 000 we may be able to think up something.

Even without mining, sea water is now known to contain about a billion years' supply of sodium chloride and magnesium, 100m years' supply of sulphur, borax and potassium chloride, more than 1m years' supply of molybdenum, uranium, tin and cobalt. Most of these are materials with a rather high elasticity of substitution. Those who say we should be worried by AD 100 000 000 also seem to assume that, in the rather long period between now and then, there will be no advances in recycling, in producing substitute materials, or in production techniques. In practice, there are going to be huge technical advances in all of these over a very short period ahead. Scientists already nearly know how to mine manganese nodules from the seabed (according to a World Bank report, a mining rate of 400m tons a year should be possible for a literally unlimited period of time at production costs "a fraction of current costs"): technical improvements in the past few years will allow low-grade porphyry copper to last for 600 or 700 years at present rates of use; a large part of the earth's land mass has not been explored for any minerals in any detail; new mining techniques (such as softening rock through chemical or vibrational action, and the use of induction heating and hydraulic jets) are on the point of breakthrough.

. . .

In listing ''pollution'' as its second cause of coming breakdown, the Club of Rome supposed the most ''optimistic'' possible assumption was that the ratio of pollution to output might be reduced by one quarter over the next hundred years. Actually, smoke pollution per unit of industrial output in London had then already been reduced by 85 per cent in the fifteen years after 1953, and in the United States during the present decade all air pollution is expected to fall to about one-tenth of what it was. Some ecologists say that today's technologies are steadily more pollutant and dangerous than yesterday's. But usually the opposite turns out to be true. Recorded accidents in Britain's industry in 1900 were six times those in Britain's much larger industry in 1970; ecologists who complain that the carbon monoxide concentration around Oxford Street may reach about 20 ppm (parts per million) for about two minutes a day at peak travel times (compared with 50 ppm all day long in many factories) should note London's 1847 report on drainage and sewerage that ''the space bounded by Oxford Street, Portland Place, New Road, Tottenham Court Road, is one vast cesspool'', which makes it unsurprising that 20 000 people then still died from typhus in England every year. If a Club of Rome had rightly forecast Britain's present quantum of travel, industry and urban workforce exponentially forward from 1850, it would have proved that this plague-ridden, industrially maimed nation must long since have disappeared beneath several hundred feet of horse manure.

The third reason for supposed eco-doom is the growth of population. The breakthrough in reducing infant mortality rates all over the world after the late 1940s (itself, surely, a good thing) did by the early 1960s seem to threaten such a population explosion. It then brought its natural antidote of breakthroughs in both birth control technology (the pill, etc) and often in birth control attitudes (permission of abortion, etc). Now the World Bank reports that ''of the 66 countries for which accurate [fertility] data are available, as many as 56 show a decline''. This includes poorer countries. The real problem is that in the next twenty years doctors may break through into conquering some of the great debilitating diseases, allowing us to keep many more old people alive, just as we started to keep many more children alive in the twenty years after the 1940s: that is the real problem we should now be humanely debating.

The world's food problem has nothing to do with physical limits on food production. Even if there were no new discoveries in food-growing technology from now on, and we continued to cultivate only the very small proportion of the earth's surface now used as farmland, a raising of all other countries' efficiency of cultivation to that of the Netherlands would already suffice to feed 60 billion people (today's world population is 3.7 billion). Those who say that more intensive cultivation always ruins the soil should note that the land in Holland has been farmed with increasing intensity for 2 000 years. Some big improvements in food-growing technology are almost certain during our children's lifetime. . . .

If the rate of growth of rice yields in India and Pakistan in 1965–71 were

continued for a century, all of mankind would indeed die, because the surface of the earth would be covered with rice to a depth of three feet. But this should not obscure the world's two real agricultural problems. First, about 60 per cent of the world's workers still labour on farms; with modern techniques, every country will soon be able to feed itself with under 10 per cent of its workers there; this rather imminent threat of technological unemployment for half the world's workers is a major turning point in history. Secondly, the flock away from agriculture to the towns will be handled least well in the poorest countries, from which the biggest flight from the land is still to come.

Crusades that are needed

Extreme environmentalism is now on the wane. Mr. Beckerman quotes reports that sales of the main ecological newspaper have already fallen by 80 per cent from their peak. He is sternly critical of those who drove or leaped on the bandwagon: the middle classes who interpreted environmentalism to mean that other people should not disturb their peace and solitude, radical youth eager to condemn materialism, the newspapers and clergymen and academics who told what some must eventually have known to be untruths because this inflated their importance, the alarmingly innumerate scientists. Yet there was a real passion for doing good among very many of those who interested themselves in these issues. Those who prefer to stick to facts rather than fancies should consider why they fail to attract this potential force for doing good to the crusades that are needed — such as the devising and financing of performance contracts for all who will bring re-employment opportunities, modern urban management systems, and nutrition programmes (of which transport, not cultivation, will be the key) to the world's growing urban poor. Such things, however, need action, not just nice spine-chilling calls for inaction.

DISCUSSION AND RESEARCH

19. Do you as a consumer feel exploited by industrialists? If so, how could the situation be remedied?

20. What arguments could the leader of a developing country use to persuade an anti-growth adviser that growth is desirable?

21. If an anti-growth philosophy was universally adopted, what values would have to be given up by (a) the developed nations, and (b) the developing nations?

22. To what extent does economic development depend on people's knowledge of their environment?

23 How is the environment changed by industrial growth?

Deindustrialization

Deindustrialization is the opposite of industrialization. It is the process of diminishing rather than increasing industry. It is one step toward what is sometimes called the post-industrial society.

The United Kingdom, which was the first nation to become industrialized, may also become the first nation to deindustrialize. The *World Development Report 1985* notes that the UK has experienced in the last decade declining industrial production at an average annual rate of 0.3%, making it the only industrial country to decline. Some industrial countries, however, had very slow rates of industrial growth compared to rates elsewhere in the world. Sweden had an average annual industrial growth rate of only 0.2%, West Germany 1.6% and Italy 1.9%. Even Japan's average annual industrial growth rate fell from a high of 13.5% in the 1960s to 5.5% in the 1970s and early 1980s. All other industrial countries, without exception, showed similar slow-downs in their rates of growth (i.e., Italy 6.2% to 1.9%, Canada 5.2% to 0.9%, the USA 2.8% to 1.2% and West Germany 4.9% to 1.6%).

Reasons for the slow-down of industrial growth in the industrialized countries include higher oil prices from 1973 to 1985 and massive inflation and recession in the late 1970s and early 1980s. They also reflect the slow but persistent restructuring of the industrialized economies to a greater service orientation as the share of world industrial production taken by the newly industrializing countries increases. Throughout the 1970s and early 1980s, the average annual growth rate of the service

Jobs in the service sector have always existed in every country. What has been happening through the process of economic development has been that the service sector has consistently taken an increasing share of total job creation. It now takes significantly more than the primary and secondary sectors combined in a growing number of countries. Some people have popularized this process as a "Third Wave" or a "Megatrend" but it is not new.

sector exceeded that of the manufacturing sector in the UK, Austria, Canada, Netherlands, Belgium, France, the USA, West Germany, Norway and Sweden.

During the 1960s, the growth of manufacturing was faster than the growth of services in these countries. It remains to be seen how quickly and smoothly the industry/service balance will change. The slow-down of industrial growth in the industrialized countries has its offsetting counterpart in the speed-up of industrial growth in countries such as Burma, India, Honduras, Philippines, Morocco, Colombia and Uruguay, all of which had faster industrial growth after 1970 than before, and none of which is an already industrialized country.

There is a growing awareness in the already industrialized countries that the products of their older and usually more labour-intensive industries, such as textiles, shipbuilding and steel, cannot compete with the lower labour-cost products of the newly industrializing countries. The industrialized countries have a range of options in these circumstances. One is to let their own labour-intensive industries die, and attempt to replace lost industries with newer high-technology ones. Another option is to protect their uncompetitive industries by tariffs and quotas, protecting the jobs of their own workers (at the expense of jobs in the newly industrializing countries). Yet another option is to improve productivity to make uncompetitive industries competitive again. A further option is to let the newly industrializing countries have the cheaper end of the market, reserving for themselves the expensive market. Examples of these options are numerous. The following clipping illustrates the situation.

Although India ranks among the world's top ten countries in total industrial capacity, about 70% of its people still work in the primary sector. It is a moot point whether its total capacity permits it to be called an industrialized country; certainly the majority of its people do not have a significantly industrialized lifestyle.

ROBOTICS

Technology as co-worker

How quickly things change. Alvin Toffler's 1980 bestseller, *The Third Wave*, makes no mention of industrial robots. When Toffler was constructing his post-industrial vision of tomorrow, the notion that robots held the promise of salvation was improbable, simply the stuff of science-fiction.

It's no wonder then that back in 1980 Tim Pryor was having problems explaining what he did for a living. To keep from boring non-technical friends he described his company's highly complex visual inspection systems as "optical do-jiggies." These days, his business is as focused as the equipment he produces. When you meet the president of Diffracto Ltd. of Windsor, Ontario, his business card says "Robotics" — and everybody understands.

In less than three years, the robot has become at once the most familiar and most feared aspect of technological change in North America. They look vaguely human with their articulated arms and grippers, but there any similarity ends. They don't get grouchy, bored, sick or hung-over. They are a potent symbol of technology in its new role as co-worker in industry and business.

Robots are the tip of the iceberg of a whole new grab-bag of technologies and inter-related manufacturing processes now available to Ontario companies. Computer-aided design, computer-aided manufacturing (CAD/CAM) and robotics all promise to improve productivity and control manufacturing quality better than ever before.

Speaking to the second annual CAD/CAM and Robotics conference in Toronto last spring, Roy Phillips, president of the Canadian Manufacturers' Association remarked: "CAD/CAM and robotics can have a more profound impact on productivity, labor markets, working conditions and the quality of life in Canada than any other technological development since the introduction of the computer 31 years ago in Canada.''

The dynamics of technological change require three dependent components. They are the vendor, the buyer, and the skilled worker. All three have a vested interest in change; all three are more active in Ontario than many people recognize.

In October, Chrysler Canada's new mini-van, a cross between a car and a van, started rolling off a state-of-the-art assembly line in Windsor, Ontario, at a rate of 57 cars per hour. It's the latest word in what one U.S. trade journal describes as the most advanced auto-manufacturing plant in North America. More than half of the company's robots are installed here. So hopeful is Chrysler of its new assembly line that officials estimate 90 per cent of the new autos will be ''dealer-ready'' with no defects. That's at least as good as the standards set by the Japanese.

Across town, 63 engineers and scientists at Diffracto are putting the finishing touches on what could be a breakthrough in robotics technology.

Diffracto is out to develop a three-dimensional color vision system for robots. ''We're going after the Holy Grail of robotics,'' says Pryor.

''Most vision systems today can see only in two dimensions, and in gray images. That's like seeing with one eye closed and being color-blind.'' If Diffracto can develop a truly commercial robot-eye vision system, it will be at the forefront of a new generation of technology.

Like many other businessmen trying to market applied technology, Pryor represents a new breed of science entrepreneur, all trying to carve a market niche for themselves in Ontario and around the world.

In 1982, according to a Canadian Manufacturers' Association survey, only 5.7 per cent of large Canadian companies were using industrial robots. And barely 1.3 per cent of small- and medium-sized firms could boast of having steel-collared workers. Ontario manufacturers have been especially slow to adopt this new technology. There are over 300 industrial robots in Ontario today, mostly working in the auto industry. In Japan, there are 18,000 sophisticated robots working away on factory floors. The National Research Council estimates that, by 1987, Canadian manufacturers — mostly in Ontario — must invest upwards of $42 million in robots if they want to stay competitive with the rest of the world. The story is more encouraging with CAD/CAM. Evans Research Corp. forecasts national CAD/CAM sales rising to $300 million in the same period — up from $57 million in 1982. . . .

As yet, Don MacLeod, president of Savage Shoes Ltd. in Cambridge, can't see much use for robots in the footwear business, but computer-aided design is another thing. In 1978, Savage and four other shoe manufacturers bought a $140,000-CAD system and installed it at Conestoga College in Kitchener. The reason it's at the community college is ''to keep it on neutral ground,'' says MacLeod. Although the shoe industry is fiercely competitive, he and his partners realized that no one company could buy a shoe design system and make it pay. But collectively, spreading the costs would allow them all to achieve the required economies of scale.

On a first-come, first-served basis, each company can transmit data about the sizes and styles of a particular line of footwear over the telephone directly into the CAD system. It's up to the computer to figure out the possible leather patterns that go with up to 300 size and width combinations, then draw a pattern that can be used by the leather cutters back at the plant.

''What used to take at least three weeks now takes one day,'' says MacLeod. Achieving this kind of productivity increase is vital to Ontario's footwear industry. Since the late 1960s, Ontario's hold on the Canadian market here has declined from over 60 per cent to 38 per cent, as a result of low-cost imported goods. MacLeod sees this technology as one way, perhaps the only way, to salvage the industry and get back market share. ''If we're going to have a future at all, we'll have to have the latest state-of-the-art technology to survive.'' . . .

The changing industrial relationships caused by high tech are complex. Companies such as Diffracto are selling revolution, a new way of seeing and doing things. Savage Shoes is buying survival. There are few management precedents for this kind of transaction.

Reprinted from ''Ontech - Ontario Takes Up the Technology Challenge,'' by permission from the Government of Ontario, 1984

Fig. 4-6
Distribution of employment in the Canadian labour force, by major category, in percentages, 1881-1981

Employment	Category	1881	1901	1921	1941	1951	1961	1971	1981
Primary	Agriculture Fishing Forestry Mining	51.2	44.3	36.6	29.3	20.7	16.8	8.4	5.0
Secondary	Manufacturing Construction	29.4	27.8	26.5	26.3	32.6	31.7	26.8	29.0
Tertiary	Services	19.4	27.9	36.9	44.4	46.9	51.3	64.8	66.0

Source: Urquhart and Buckley, *Historical Statistics of Canada; Canada Year Book*, 1968 and 1973; and World Bank, *World Development Report*, 1985.

Fig. 4-7
Rural-urban distribution of Canada's population, in percentages, 1881-1981

	1881	1891	1901	1911	1921	1931	1941	1951	1961	1971	1981
Rural	74.3	68.2	65.2	58.3	54.7	50.3	49.1	37.1	28.9	23.9	24.5
Urban	25.7	31.8	34.8	41.7	45.3	49.7	50.9	62.9	71.1	76.1	75.5

Source: Urquhart and Buckley, *Historical Statistics of Canada; Canada Year Book*, 1968, 1976-77, 1981.

STATISTICAL ANALYSIS

24. Construct a compound line graph to illustrate the changing pattern of employment in the Canadian labour force using the data in Fig. 4-6.

25. Construct a compound line graph to illustrate the changing pattern of rural-urban occupancy in Canada, using the data in Fig. 4-7.

26. On a 3-cycle semi-log graph (see Appendix 4) plot the primary data from Fig. 4-6 and the rural data from Fig. 4-7. What do you notice about the nature and rate of change of both lines? What explanations can you suggest for the changes? What is likely to happen in the future?

27. On the same graph used for assignment 26, but with an additional scale for billions of dollars, plot a line for the data in Fig. 4-8 on page 168. How do you explain the slope of this line in view of your answers to assignments 24, 25 and 26? What do you think it means in practical day-to-day terms?

Fig. 4-8
Canada's GNP in current dollars, 1926-85

Year	GNP	Year	GNP
1926	5 146 000 000	1956	32 058 000 000
1927	5 561 000 000	1957	33 513 000 000
1928	6 050 000 000	1958	34 777 000 000
1929	6 139 000 000	1959	36 846 000 000
1930	5 720 000 000	1960	38 359 000 000
1931	4 693 000 000	1961	39 646 000 000
1932	3 814 000 000	1962	42 927 000 000
1933	3 492 000 000	1963	45 978 000 000
1934	3 969 000 000	1964	50 280 000 000
1935	4 301 000 000	1965	55 364 000 000
1936	4 634 000 000	1966	61 828 000 000
1937	5 241 000 000	1967	66 409 000 000
1938	5 272 000 000	1968	72 586 000 000
1939	5 621 000 000	1969	79 815 000 000
1940	6 713 000 000	1970	85 610 000 000
1941	8 282 000 000	1971	93 402 000 000
1942	10 265 000 000	1972	103 407 000 000
1943	11 053 000 000	1973	112 584 000 000
1944	11 848 000 000	1974	144 616 000 000
1945	11 863 000 000	1975	165 445 000 000
1946	11 885 000 000	1976	190 027 000 000
1947	13 473 000 000	1977	207 714 000 000
1948	15 509 000 000	1978	229 698 000 000
1949	16 800 000 000	1979	261 961 000 000
1950	18 491 000 000	1980	289 859 000 000
1951	21 640 000 000	1981	339 797 000 000
1952	24 588 000 000	1982	358 302 000 000
1953	25 833 000 000	1983	390 340 000 000
1954	25 918 000 000	1984	420 819 000 000
1955	28 528 000 000	1985	479 446 000 000

Source: *Canada Year Book,* 1922-77; *Canada's Business Climate,* Toronto-Dominion
   Bank, 1978-85; Statistics Canada.

Employment Patterns and Rates of Industrial Change

Indicators are statistics that can be used as the basis for drawing inferences about other aspects of society. For example, Paraguay has an annual rate of population growth of 3.7%. That is a statistic. It is also an indicator, since it can be used as the basis for drawing inferences about other aspects of the society. It is usually possible to "read into" most data a whole series of related items. Clearly, however, the more you know ahead of time, the more you will be able to draw valid and worthwhile inferences. What inferences can you draw from an annual population growth rate of 3.7%?

Where industrialization exists, its rate of change varies dramatically from time to time and place to place. The societies that first began the process of industrialization now are generally accustomed to change. Others are experiencing a variety of social and political upheavals. In this section we will try to develop a global view of the role of industrialization in the socio-economic changes occurring throughout the world.

There is no single index that can be used to measure either the amount or the rate of change in the world. However, we do have indicators which we can use to interpret change. Assignments 24 to 27 involve some of these possible indicators, namely employment categories, rural-urban ratios and GNP. The statistics show the degree and rate of change in a particular sector, and their relationship to other types of change. A fall in the rural percentage of the total population suggests more than just population change. The correlations of this fall indicate that the society changed from an agriculture-forestry-mining base to an industry-service base, and that it became much wealthier in the process. The figures also suggest, by extension and interpretation, that literacy increased and health care improved. The statistics, again by extension and interpretation, suggest rising living standards, improved economic efficiency, changed social structures and greater individual freedom. Indicators may be used in this way — with care — to make inferences in other areas.

Good indicators correlate well, though not perfectly, with other possible indicators, and they thus permit fairly good, though not perfect, interpretation. In assignment 26 we saw how well the rural component of total population correlates with the proportion of the labour force in primary activity in Canada. This was a dynamic correlation, because it was shown to exist over time though both data sets changed. The strength of this dynamic correlation permits us to assume that a significant correlation can also be established for a single moment of time. For instance, a rural percentage of 50 suggests that primary employment also will fall into a certain range and that other associated variables will show expected correlations. We can test this assumption by establishing the strength of the worldwide correlation between rural percentages and primary employment.

STATISTICAL ANALYSIS

28. Using the data for rural percentages (Column Y of Appendix 3) and primary activity (Column Z_1), *either* (i) calculate a correlation coefficient, using the grouped data technique described in Appendix 4, *or* (ii) construct a scattergraph to illustrate the extent of the relationship.

    a. In either case, comment on the relationship established.

    b. Do you think the percentage of the labour force engaged in primary activity is a useful indicator of the stage of economic growth? Why or why not?

Countries that have not yet undergone much change often are found to concentrate on primary economic activities, chiefly farming and fishing. If a high percentage of the population is employed in the primary sector then it is likely that society's technology will be relatively simple and its way of life — from a Western viewpoint — materially poor. A high percentage of people in primary activities indicates that people still do most of the work needed to grow food themselves; machinery, chemical fertilizers and other modern aids will be scarce and yields will generally be low in relation to the work done. In many such societies, hunger is a common condition, and starvation may be frequent. Children tend to share their parents' expectations about life. Change is so slow that it is hardly noticeable within the span of a single lifetime.

By contrast, a high proportion of the labour force in the secondary sector indicates a society that will produce goods in large quantities. As a result, its material standard of living should rise fairly rapidly. The primary sector shrinks as workers move to the growing secondary category. Farming output per unit of labour input increases dramatically, making surplus labour available for the secondary sector. As long as this surplus is being created by improved farming yields, wages in the secondary sector tend to remain low, keeping factory labour cheaper than labour-saving equipment. Under these conditions there generally is some urban poverty. A high proportion of labour input per unit of output almost guarantees low wages, especially where the product must be sold cheaply to be sold at all.

A large percentage of the labour force in the tertiary sector indicates a service-oriented society. The quantity of goods a society has depends upon the way it reached the tertiary phase. It is possible for a country to bypass the secondary phase, and enter the tertiary phase with wealth derived from a primary source. Such a country will have few, if any,

It is the official policy of some major US unions that workers in countries exporting to the USA should be paid wages equal to American workers. What are your views of this policy?

Marilyn Mackenzie

A society whose population works largely in the primary sector is likely to rely mostly on low technology and to be materially poor. This Mexican farmer still uses an ox-drawn plough.

The question sometimes arises as to whether jobs in the service sector are as "good" as jobs in the primary and secondary sectors. What do you think this means?

factories. Examples of countries that have passed directly from the primary phase to the tertiary phase include several OPEC members as well as some countries dependent upon tourism. More often, however, a country in the tertiary phase has gone through the secondary phase. Its factories will be efficient, often highly automated and highly productive per unit of labour input. Wages are usually correspondingly high. Because of the high labour productivity in the secondary sector, most people are employed in one or other of the various service occupations, such as health care, education, finance, communications and government. This describes a post-industrial society, gaining its living mostly by doing things for other people, rather than by making things for other people.

STATISTICAL ANALYSIS

29. In accordance with the idea of using labour force categories as an indicator of change, construct a map showing the degree of change achieved by different countries around the world. Use the data in Columns Z_3 and Z_1 in the following manner: first, calculate the ratio of tertiary to primary; for example, Canada's ratio is 66:5, reducible to

13.2:1. Second, group the countries as indicated below, and draw a graded shading map showing them. Third, make up a title.

Ratios: 10.0 and over   very bright orange

5.00–9.99	bright orange
1.00–4.99	medium orange
below 1.00	pale orange

a. Compare your map with those available for assignments 7 and 8 in Chapter 2, and assignment 6 in Chapter 3; comment on the relationships.

b. Are there any unexpected plots? What explanations can you suggest for these anomalies?

c. Which country has the greatest degree of change still to come, assuming it follows the pattern?

d. Suggest some of the associated pressures that may occur in those parts of the world still facing the greatest changes, assuming they follow the pattern.

30. The map in assignment 29 has the disadvantage that it does not take into account all three employment categories. To do this we may use a triangular graph such as that shown in Appendix 4. To avoid cluttering the graph, plot only the following countries:

Algeria	China	Greece	Ivory Coast	Portugal
Angola	Czechoslovakia	Hungary	Jamaica	Sweden
Australia	France	India	Japan	UK
Brazil	West Germany	Israel	Mexico	USA
Canada	Ghana	Italy	Poland	USSR

a. What groupings can you identify in the plotted distribution?

b. Insert an arrow on the graph to indicate the main direction of change.

c. Suggest explanations for any major anomalies.

d. What socio-economic changes and pressures might occur in the future in those countries you identify as near the start of the process of change, assuming change actually occurs?

DISCUSSION AND RESEARCH

31. What kinds of societies suffer the greatest stress from change? What sorts of stress are likely to occur? What can be done to minimize them?

CASE STUDY

SOUTH KOREA: Industrialization

South Korea, officially the Republic of Korea, is in the midst of industrialization. The process is relatively recent and has been deliberately sponsored by the government.

Until the end of the nineteenth century, the entire Korean peninsula was an independent country ruled by an isolationist dynasty and having no formal contact with any country but China. It remained aloof when Japan embarked on the process of industrialization under Emperor Meiji in the 1870s. However, in 1910 Japan invaded Korea and made the entire peninsula a colony. During the Japanese colonial period (1910–1945), the southern part of the Korean peninsula was developed agriculturally to supply food to Japan. Industrial growth was generally suppressed in typical colonial fashion by the Japanese, who wished to reserve the Korean market for their own manufactured exports. Only during the preparations for World War II did the Japanese begin to develop an industrial base in Korea, and then mostly in the northern end of the peninsula, where the major mineral deposits and better hydro-electric sites occurred.

In the colonial period, Korean industry was operated by and for the Japanese. They brought in machinery, entrepreneurs and skilled labour. Korean participation was limited until World War II when Japanese labour was drawn back to Japan and many Koreans were provided with manufacturing jobs in Japan itself.

When World War II ended, Korea was divided in two approximately along the line of the 38th parallel. South Korea was left with most of the population, the bulk of the agricultural land and some light industry, while North Korea contained most of the heavy industry and almost all the electric generating capacity. The economy naturally suffered tremendous disruption. Its trade pattern with the Japanese empire was in shreds, its internal balance was upset and the Japanese managerial class had gone. In what is now South Korea, manufacturing production in 1945 was less than 20% of its prewar level.

It is therefore a tribute to the people of South Korea that they were able in 1945 to produce at least something from all sectors of the economy. By 1948 the country was producing a wide range of simple manufactured products, such as bicycles, shoes, textiles and water pumps, mostly for their domestic market.

This early growth was brought to an abrupt halt in 1950 by an invasion from North Korea. The ensuing Korean War (1950–1953) diverted potential growth resources to defence, and halted development. In 1955 with the war over a fresh start was needed. The USA was an important source of assistance, but industrial strategy was developed by the South Korean government. The strategy was very simple: produce goods domestically for the Korean market to reduce the need for imports (a strategy of import substitution). This produced some industrial growth, but did little to improve the general standard of living. Political turmoil characterized the period 1953–60, and little industrial growth occurred.

The Korean Army took control in 1961, and in 1963 General Park was made president. Under his leadership, a new export-led growth strategy was implemented. By 1965 the taxation system was revised to foster exports, the foreign exchange rate stabilized, monetary reforms to encourage saving and investment were in place and the country was open to foreign capital. The year 1965 is widely regarded as the turning point for South Korea. The rate of industrial growth more than doubled almost immediately as a result of the export drive. The proportion of manufacturing output that was exported, which had been zero in 1955 and only 6% in 1965, jumped to 25% by 1975, 35% by 1980 and about 45% by 1985.

All other economic indicators showed similar growth patterns. Real wages grew, national wealth became more widely distributed, employment growth rates grew faster than population growth rates, industry diversified and domestic consumption grew. The country as a whole became more wealthy and South Korea began to describe itself as an economic power. The government continues to base its industrial strategy on policies set down in the mid-1960s, although the government now takes a less active role and allows market forces to act more freely.

The chief industrial sectors being pushed by the government include cars, ships, steel, machinery, textiles and electronics. The car target for 1991 is 4 000 000 vehicles, ranking South Korea third in the world behind the USA and Japan. The steel target for 1991 is for South Korea to become similarly prominent as the world's third largest steel exporter. It is also that by 1991 machinery make up at least 20% of all exports. In textiles, the target is to become the world's chief exporter, but South Koreans recognize that their country will decline in relative textile importance as more newly industrializing countries begin to compete more effectively. In electronics there is much hope for growth, but also an awareness that the international market is already highly competitive.

How has South Korea done it? How, since 1965, has the country changed from a marginally subsistent agricultural economy to one of Asia's leading industrial powers?

The reasons are varied and, although we will look at them one by one, that is not meant to indicate any order of priority.

Direct Foreign Investment (DFI)

DFI includes capital, technology and management. It is often provided by multinational companies or smaller international firms. Korea's DFI relationship with Japan ended in 1945. There was no DFI between 1945 and 1962. The trade liberalization that began after the change in government in 1960–61 included a variety of incentives to foreign investors, such as a guaranteed period of five years without payment of any Korean income tax and guarantees allowing the repatriation of principal and profit. Subsequent planning changes have not only maintained the initial guarantees but added other benefits for foreign investors. For example, legislation controlling labour is more strict for Korean workers in foreign-owned firms than for those in purely Korean firms.

The inflow of DFI that began again in 1962 was initially very small, but grew rapidly, especially after 1965 when diplomatic relations were reestablished with Japan and Japanese investment re-entered Korea. Japan has become Korea's largest supplier of DFI, accounting for about 75% of all foreign investment. This has come primarily in the form of machinery and technology, taking advantage of 40% lower labour costs in South Korea. South Korea's steel industry was one of the first beneficiaries of Japanese DFI, and it has now grown to rival that of Japan itself. Shipbuilding is another DFI success story. However, as South Korea's industry has become more sophisticated, the Japanese have begun to withhold the technological aspects of DFI in order to avoid competition with their own growth industries. A prime example is VCRs (Video-Cassette Recorders), where the Japanese refused to let South Koreans have access to the technology. The Koreans therefore took the Japanese machines apart to see how they worked and now market their own versions.

Technological Mastery

It is difficult for a nation to develop a powerful industrial base if its technological knowledge remains the property of foreigners. South Korea has obtained such knowledge through DFI, licensing agreements and direct purchase. People are sent abroad for education, training and work experience. Foreign technical journals are studied and foreign products taken apart and analyzed. Technical institutions have been established. Firms are encouraged to provide high school educations for their assembly line workers. Training is provided for workers to upgrade their skills. The result is a technologically sophisticated work force and an aggressively innovative managerial group.

Planning

The importance of government planning has already been noted. Korea has used a series of five-year plans, starting in 1962. The early plans set targets for the development of savings, the creation of DFI incentives, the beginnings of infrastructural growth and the establishment of basic industries such as steel, cement, chemicals and textiles. Subsequent plans sponsored the growth of shipbuilding, car and construction activities. The most recent plans aim at the development of world-scale electronics and computer industries.

Planning, although primarily industrial in purpose, has affected other aspects of Korean life. The government realized that social disruption would accompany any rapid widening of the gap between urban-industrial and rural-agricultural incomes,

A handpump outside the front door is a sign of technological progress in Chil Won Li, South Korea. The existence of several levels of technology side-by-side is common in transitional societies.

Unicef/E. Bowne

especially through the inevitable urban migration, resulting in problems with housing and jobs. Accordingly, agriculture was from the beginning included in the planning process in order to improve the productivity of agriculture and raise the quality of rural life. In particular, the second five-year plan (1967–71) introduced the Saemaul (New Community) Movement, which has effectively sponsored a variety of land reclamation, irrigation, afforestation and animal husbandry projects. It produced Suwan 264, a type of high-yielding rice that helped to make South Korea self-sufficient in rice production; the need for any food imports other than meat has been virtually eliminated and farm incomes have improved dramatically.

General Trading Companies (GTCs)

South Korea's growth has been aided by the creation of GTCs. The largest ones are Daewoo, Hyosung, Hyundai, Lucky, Samwha and Samsung. Daewoo is fairly typical of these GTCs. Founded in 1967 as a small textile manufacturer and trader, Daewoo moved rapidly into construction, finance, shipbuilding, machinery, energy and resource development, heavy construction equipment and electronics. It is now a 35-company group, and is South Korea's leading GTC in export sales.

While South Korea is busy chasing Japan, it is mindful of being pursued itself by other more newly industrializing countries such as Malaysia. The process of industrial diffusion continues.

In this poor rural area of Thailand, industrial diffusion means organized basket- and dress-making and market gardening.

Unicef / Melanc

Conclusion

Industrial growth is undoubtedly a controversial topic. Many countries are now experiencing the benefits of industrialization, and other nations want to share in these advantages. Comparisons of industrial expansion with population growth and food production show a high level of industrialization generally correlates well with low rates of population growth and high levels of food production. Does this mean that industry holds the key to the future well-being of many overpopulated or hungry countries?

On the other hand, many people worry about the problems caused by industrial growth. They point to the pollution of the natural environment and the depletion of resources. If we share this viewpoint, we may feel that a large part of the world's population may have to seek other solutions to the problems of hunger and material poverty.

Arguments rage over the consumption of resources. Energy resources in particular, essential to industrial prosperity, are a major concern. If energy can be abundantly produced, we may assume that the necessary technology also will facilitate the continued growth of industry. But if energy really is scarce, as some maintain, then the prospects for industrial expansion are indeed dim. In the next chapter we will take a closer look at the energy situation.

5 ENERGY

Introduction

Every act, every movement, even every thought requires energy. People need energy for everything: to eat, dress and house themselves, to make things, to travel, and, generally, to make life more comfortable. All sources of energy exist in the environment in one form or another. Therefore, all types of energy production have some environmental impact.

As the world's population increases, so will its need for energy. And as people's general aspirations for more food, improved diets and readier access to the products of industrialization increase, the more energy will be required to realize these aspirations.

Significant increases in energy production are possible only by applying technology, but though a great variety of energy technologies exist, they are neither evenly implemented nor universally accepted. Some technological changes are resisted because they are believed to be either economically impractical or socially and politically undesirable.

The melting of the polar ice caps would raise sea levels, flooding millions of hectares of coastal lowlands, including much valuable farmland, and rendering millions of people homeless.

Much confusion surrounds energy issues. Will the world run out of energy within a few decades? Is energy virtually unlimited? Will thermal wastes gradually melt the polar ice caps? Should the developed countries now reduce their use of energy and change their lifestyles? Will the developing countries have enough energy to meet their needs?

Confusion arises because there are several different answers to each of these questions. Experts have conflicting views on the energy situation, and no consensus has yet been possible regarding either what to believe or what to do.

It is generally agreed that energy is one of the major concerns of our time. Its continued availability is of vital interest to farmers and industrialists alike all over the world. To act wisely and discover our own answers to the many questions involved in the issue, we need to learn as much about energy as we can.

Doug Sneyd

"It's called Energy Crisis."

Reprinted by permission of *Toronto Star* Syndicate.

In this chapter we will study the world's main sources of energy, as well as its chief energy consumers. In addition, possible future sources will be discussed. Finally, we will look more closely at nuclear energy, one of the major sources of both hope and concern regarding the world's current energy situation.

Total Energy Production

Every country produces energy. Since the sun is the world's primary energy source, the amount of energy generated by a nation will depend to a large extent on its ability to convert solar energy to other useful forms. People have always depended upon the sun for energy, and they have gradually learned how to extract solar energy from a variety of sources.

The first form of transformed solar energy used by human beings came to us without the need to learn about it first. Food energy is largely solar energy converted by photosynthesis into a form that people and animals can use (see Appendix 1). Human and animal labour are basic products of solar energy. All nations depend on food for basic energy, although some obtain it more successfully than others. An examination of Column I in Appendix 3 indicates the national differences in obtaining energy from food. The average daily amount of food energy actually taken in by individuals in different countries ranges from a high of 16 540 kJ (Belgium) to a low of 7 262 kJ (Ethiopia), a ratio of 2.3 to 1. This is a very large variation for something as essential as food. The range in the amounts of food energy actually required by an individual each day is much narrower. These figures are given in Column N, and are calculated by the FAO on the basis of the climatic conditions, body size and age compositions of national populations. Actual food energy required for daily survival ranges from a high of 11 382 kJ (Finland) to a low of 9 072 (Burma, Indonesia, Vietnam), a ratio of only 1.25 to 1.

The range of food energy consumed overlaps the required range at both ends. Some countries produce and consume more food energy than they need, while others produce and consume much less.

One reason for the greater efficiency with which some societies convert solar energy into food is that they use energy to help them. Highly productive societies use large quantities of additional energy in the form of fertilizers, tractor and truck fuels, artificial heating, irrigation and drainage pumps, grain dryers, herbicides and pesticides. There's also the energy required to manufacture the machinery they use. As an example of how much the application of additional energy can raise farming productivity, note that in the 1940s, with limited energy inputs, the

Photosynthesis is the process by which the chlorophyll in plants uses the energy in sunlight to transform carbon dioxide and water into carbohydrates and oxygen. All life ultimately depends upon this process.

The solar oven at Mont Louis in southern France.

All plant matter, including timber, is the direct product of photosynthesis.

The removal of the normally thin woodland cover in semi-arid areas, such as the Sahel, has posed particular problems: the supply of moisture from plants to the atmosphere has been reduced, and so the climate has become even drier. Moreover, the unprotected soil has had its finer clay grains blown away by the wind, leaving behind the coarser sand grains. Thus the soil has become more sandy and therefore less fertile, reducing the prospects of successful reforestation. The process called *desertification* has set in.

average Ontario farmer could produce enough food for 15 people. By the 1980s, with additional energy inputs, the same farmer could feed 80 people.

Fire, or the burning of plant matter, is another simple form of solar energy conversion. The discovery of fire was a major step in technological development. Today many societies still depend upon wood as a fuel, and some areas with rapidly increasing populations are in danger of severe deforestation. The World Bank estimates that about 1.5 billion people in the developing world depend almost exclusively on firewood for domestic heating and cooking. In India, as much as 25% of all non-food energy consumed comes from firewood, while for most countries in west and central Africa the proportion is as high as 90%.

It is common in many developing countries to see people doing little else in a day but collect firewood. Studies show that, in Tanzania, it requires the equivalent of up to 300 person-days a year to meet the firewood needs of a family of five. A report in *African Business* 1983 10 warns that the forests of Niger will be gone by the year 2006 unless conservation measures are undertaken or alternative sources of energy can be used.

Flowing or falling water is another example of converted solar energy used by societies at all levels of technical development. Waterwheels and mills are simple methods of tapping the energy of the solar-powered water cycle. At a higher technical level, hydroelectric generating stations serve the same purpose, but more productively.

Another important step toward advanced technology occurred when societies learned to extract the solar energy stored in fossil form as coal and oil. Much of the world's coal was formed from the compacted remains of ancient forests. It is commonly found now as layers (strata) within rock from the Carboniferous period, which occurred about 250 million years ago. The burning of coal represents the use of fossilized solar energy millions of years old. The same is true of oil and natural gas, except that the conversion to gas and oil from solar energy is slightly less direct (sun→plants→marine life →oil and gas, rather than sun→plants→coal).

The ability to extract stored solar energy from fossil fuels and apply

Fuels obtained from fossilized material are called *fossil fuels*. The chief ones are coal, petroleum and natural gas.

Soviet physicists at Akademgorodok, Siberia, continue their experiments in nuclear fusion.

Paul Almasy

this newly released energy to machinery enabled some countries to develop as industrial powers. Societies that used fossil energy (initially coal) were greatly changed. In this period of change, called the Industrial Revolution, these countries also learned to produce food energy with greater efficiency. They also developed new attitudes: they began to feel that the physical environment was filled with opportunities and challenges that could be met and overcome through the use of newer and better technologies. The application of technology and the increased ability to generate energy taught some societies that people were to some extent capable of manipulating their environment.

Developments in energy production have allowed people to use their environment in new and different ways. Today, in some parts of the world, many people are able to choose from a much wider range of foods, jobs, residential locations and leisure activities than before, although this is not the case everywhere. The technology of energy conversion has contributed greatly to freeing people from the bondage of insufficient food production. The latest developments in this area are now under way. The splitting of the atom has led to an energy industry now based on nuclear fission, with the possibility of nuclear fusion in the future. If the intensive research into fusion technology proves successful, people will have access to an energy source similar to the sun's, whose radiance is the sign of an ongoing fusion reaction.

Nuclear fission means the splitting of atoms; *fusion* means the combining of atoms. Each is a form of atomic power.

STATISTICAL ANALYSIS

1. As a symbol of the level to which solar energy conversion technology has developed, we will use per capita electricity generation as shown in Column P of Appendix 3. We want to see how it correlates with the ability to grow food as indicated in Column I of Appendix 3. Use the *rank correlation technique*, explained in Appendix 4, for the sample of countries marked with an asterisk (*) in Appendix 3.

   a. Calculate the value of ρ (rho).

   b. Suggest explanations for the degree of correlation between the two variables exhibited by the value of ρ.

2. Using the data in Fig. 5-1, construct a map of the world with proportional circles (see Appendix 4) to show the percentage regional distribution of energy production.

Fig. 5-1

Energy production by major region, all forms of energy in tonnes of coal equivalent (tce)

Tonnes of coal equivalent (tce) is a measure used to make comparisons possible among different energy sources. Values are obtained by converting the energy content of such different sources as coal, oil, hydro-electricity and other fuels to the amount of coal needed to produce the same amount of energy.

Major Region	Production	
	Total tce	*Percentage*
Africa	499 797 000	5.5
Asia (excl. Middle East & USSR)	1 051 108 000	11.6
Europe	1 266 584 000	13.9
Middle East	1 208 629 000	13.2
North & Central America	2 597 808 000	28.6
Oceania	127 962 000	1.4
South America	341 372 000	3.8
USSR	2 001 267 000	22.0
World Total	**9 094 527 000**	**100.0**

Source: *Yearbook of World Energy Statistics*, 1981; *UN Statistical Yearbook*, 1982-3.

Fig. 5-2

The world's major coal-producing countries

Country	t
USA	592 967 000
USSR	507 671 000
China	433 966 000
Poland	142 722 000
West Germany	126 981 000
UK	106 258 000
South Africa	103 617 000
India	88 900 000
East Germany	80 863 000
Australia	75 055 000
Czechoslovakia	63 220 000
North Korea	42 000 000
Canada	33 002 000
France	21 070 000
Romania	17 704 000
Spain	17 006 000
Japan	16 759 000
South Korea	13 139 000
World Total	**2 615 302 000**

Source: *Yearbook of World Energy Statistics*, 1981;
UN Statistical Yearbook, 1982-3.

The main sources of energy differ from region to region. The Middle East, for instance, produces a great deal of oil but very little coal or hydroelectricity, whereas Europe produces large quantities of coal and hydroelectricity but relatively little oil. Production data for the major energy sources are given in Figs. 5-2 through 5-5.

Fig. 5-3
The world's major oil-producing countries
(*OPEC member)

Country	tce
USSR	885 487 000
Saudi Arabia*	714 107 000
USA	613 304 000
Mexico	167 803 000
Venezuela*	162 235 000
China	147 174 000
UK	128 266 000
Indonesia*	114 375 000
United Arab Emirates*	105 956 000
Nigeria*	103 513 000
Iran*	94 839 000
Canada	91 497 000
Kuwait*	82 154 000
Libya*	80 145 000
Iraq*	65 418 000
Algeria*	57 477 000
Egypt	47 255 000
Argentina	37 126 000
Norway	34 173 000
Australia	28 945 000
Qatar*	28 356 000
Oman	23 700 000
India	21 701 000
Malaysia	19 847 000
Romania	16 866 000
World Total	**4 055 830 000**

Source: *Yearbook of World Energy Statistics*, 1981;
UN Statistical Yearbook, 1982-3.

Fig. 5-4
The world's major hydroelectricity-producing countries

Country	mkW·h
USA	272 674
Canada	263 164
USSR	186 744
Brazil	130 680
Norway	92 693
Japan	90 567
France	72 600
China	65 550
India	49 155
Italy	45 700
UK	37 969
Sweden	37 802
Switzerland	36 097
Austria	30 831
Yugoslavia	25 118
Mexico	24 618
North Korea	23 000
Spain	22 909
West Germany	21 400
New Zealand	19 483
World Total	**1 783 772**

Source: *Yearbook of World Energy Statistics*, 1981.

Fig. 5-5
The world's major natural gas-producing countries

Country	tce
USA	713 483 000
USSR	551 548 000
Canada	93 712 000
Netherlands	90 893 000
Romania	52 137 000
UK	46 889 000
Norway	36 096 000
Mexico	32 255 000
West Germany	23 200 000
Algeria	22 288 000
Indonesia	22 288 000
Venezuela	19 486 000
Italy	18 297 000
China	16 944 000
World Total	**1 902 535 000**

Source: *Yearbook of World Energy Statistics*, 1981;
UN Statistical Yearbook, 1982-3.

STATISTICAL ANALYSIS

3. Looking at Figs. 5-2 through 5-5, would you say that the generation of power depends more on technological expertise or on geographical location? Give reasons for your answer.

4. The world uses coal, oil, natural gas and hydroelectricity in approximately equal quantities. The USA, which ranks first in production of three of the four major energy types, is probably the world's top producer of energy. Calculate which other countries are among the world's top ten total energy producers.

5. Fig. 5-6 is a graded shading map showing the geographical distribution of electricity production.

   a. What real similarities and differences does this map show compared with those for population increase (Chapter 2), food production (Chapter 3), and industrialization (Chapter 4)?

b. What explanations can you suggest for the variations in energy production around the world?

Fig. 5-6
Variations in per capita electricity production throughout the world

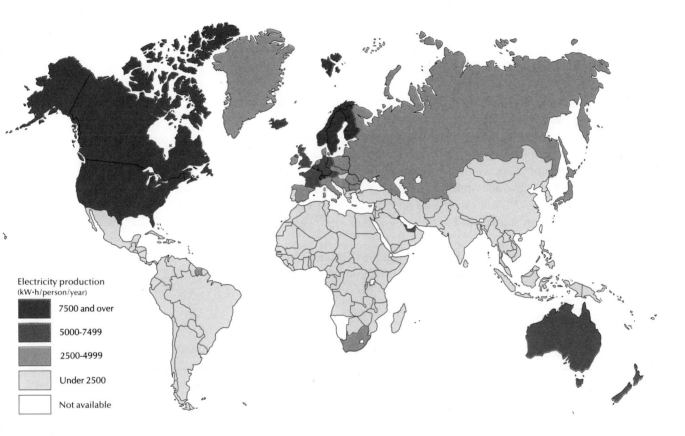

Electricity production
(kW·h/person/year)

7500 and over

5000-7499

2500-4999

Under 2500

Not available

Total Energy Consumption

Every country uses energy, even if it is mainly in the food its people consume. This basic energy is used in the business of daily living: walking, playing and, most of all, working.

Most societies now also use additional forms of energy for other purposes: some to pump irrigation water and provide light and heat for their people; others to drive machinery and move people and goods from place to place. As a society's technical abilities increase and it becomes aware that many of its economic aspirations can be met, that society usually also increases the demands on its energy-producing capacity. The growth of industry and trade cause a society to attempt to maximize its use of available energy sources and to seek new and more efficient methods to generate energy.

Electricity is the product of some of the most efficient methods of energy generation. Its large-scale production requires a high level of

The ability to increase power output is largely a function of technology and invention. Kettles had boiled for centuries before the early industrialists thought to harness the steam to drive machinery. Who knows what unexpected sources of power await us in the future?

Fig. 5-7
Energy consumption by major region, all forms of energy in tonnes of coal equivalent (tce)

Major Region	Consumption		
	Total (tce)	*Percentage of world total*	*kg / person*
Africa	205 296 000	2.4	411
Asia (excl. Middle East & USSR)	1 415 751 000	16.8	561
Europe	2 083 585 000	24.5	4 296
Middle East	138 460 000	1.6	1 371
North & Central America	2 770 922 000	32.6	7 369
Oceania	103 082 000	1.2	4 443
South America	240 394 000	2.8	977
USSR	1 535 941 000	18.1	5 731
World Total	**8 493 431 000**	**100.0**	

Source: *Yearbook of Energy Statistics, 1981; UN Statistical Yearbook, 1982-3.*

technological achievement and may therefore be used to represent the energy level of any particular country. Electricity has been used more and more widely over the last 100 years, a trend which will probably continue for many years to come. It is clean at its point of use, although this is not necessarily true at its point of generation. It is also immediately effective and versatile. With these attractions the demand for electricity has often outstripped the available supply from hydroelectric generating stations. Consequently, coal, oil, gas and, increasingly, uranium have all been used to generate greater quantities of electricity. About half the coal annually produced in the world is used for generating electricity. This is called *thermal electricity* to distinguish it from hydroelectricity. More thermal electricity is now produced than hydroelectricity, and it may continue to be more important than hydroelectricity as long as the demand for electricity surpasses the capacity of even the big new hydro projects. Fig. 5-7 lists some data on world energy consumption.

Thermal electricity, produced by the burning of coal or oil, is one of the major sources of atmospheric pollution.

STATISTICAL ANALYSIS

6. Using the data in Fig. 5-7 construct a map of the world with proportional circles (see Appendix 4) to show the percentage regional distribution of energy consumption.

    a. What significant differences do you notice between the production map available from assignment 2 and the consumption map you have just drawn?

    b. How do you explain these differences?

7. From the data in the Totals columns of Figs. 5-1 and 5-7 calculate consumption to production ratios. For example, the USSR's ratio is 1:1.3, indicating that it is more than self-sufficient in energy. Which is the least self-sufficient region? The most self-sufficient? How do per capita consumption figures affect your observations about self-sufficiency?

8. Classify the world into regions of energy surplus, energy balance and energy deficit. Suggest possible solutions to a deficit situation.

9. List what you anticipate to be the world's major energy flows given the information in Figs. 5-1 and 5-7. Construct a map to show these flows and indicate which are major and which are minor.

    World energy flows are mostly in oil. Indeed, half of the world's total trade is in oil and half the world's total shipping tonnage consists of oil tankers. Oil tankers are the largest ships afloat and they are the products of the world's most advanced shipbuilding technology. Japan and Europe, with their dependence on the world's major energy flows, are also among the world's largest shipbuilders.

The Organization of Petroleum Exporting Countries (OPEC) has demonstrated that energy deficient regions cannot rely on either the cheapness or the security of trade with the surplus regions. Beginning in 1973, OPEC has made the deficit areas very much aware of the extent of their dependence on oil.

The 13 members of OPEC are Algeria, Ecuador, Gabon, Indonesia, Iran, Iraq, Kuwait, Libya, Nigeria, Qatar, Saudi Arabia, United Arab Emirates (Abu Dhabi, Ajman, Dubai, Fujairah, Ras al Khaimah, Sharjah, Umm al Qaiwain) and Venezuela.

Oil tankers are the largest ships afloat. This is a supertanker of 190 000 t; some are over twice as large.

OPEC and the World Oil Market

OPEC has been a part of the world energy scene since 1960, when a small group of oil-exporting countries (Iran, Iraq, Saudi Arabia and Venezuela) banded together to try to remedy the price squeeze being put on them by the world's major oil companies.

They were aggrieved by the low royalty rates they were obtaining from the oil companies and by the large amounts of money that foreign governments were raising by taxing oil products. Within a few years they had successfully doubled their royalties, which rose from about (all figures in US$) $3/m^3$ (about $0.50/bbl) to about $6/m^3$ (about $1/bbl). The selling price of oil in the economically developed countries still remained low at about $11/m^3$ (about $1.75/bbl). Much of the economic growth that occurred in the developed countries during the 1950s and 1960s was enabled by these low oil prices and was, therefore, at the expense of the oil-exporting countries.

The developed world's thirst for oil to fuel its economic growth gave a new intensity to the search for oil in other parts of the world. Several nations which found oil subsequently joined OPEC, which expanded to 13 members. As newly oil-rich countries joined OPEC, new oil exploration companies entered the search for additional oil supplies. While the oil-producing nations were increasingly cooperating to get a better deal for themselves, the oil companies faced increasing competition among themselves for access to the oil supply.

The stage was set for higher oil prices. From 1970–1973 various OPEC nations obtained higher royalty rates from the oil companies. What finally allowed OPEC to take charge of the world oil market was the Arab-Israeli war of late 1973. At that time the OPEC nations, led by the Arab countries, accounted for 55% of the world's total oil exports. Motivated by political and economic considerations, OPEC cut off all supplies to nations supporting Israel, notably the USA and the Netherlands, and set quotas for all other nations. OPEC's actions caused extremely rapid rises in oil prices. Within months, oil prices jumped from $11/m^3$ ($1.75/bbl) to $70/m^3$ ($11/bbl), followed by regular price rises for the next several years. By 1981 the price had reached $220/m^3$ ($35/bbl).

Middle East oil has by far the lowest production costs of any oil in the world. This, together with the region's huge reserves, guarantees that the Middle East will always be an important factor in the world oil scene.

OPEC ministers used to meet monthly in Vienna to decide the following month's oil prices.

Just as the developed world had underestimated the political and economic consequences of forcing low prices on the oil-exporting countries throughout the 1960s, so OPEC underestimated the impact on the developed world of enforced high prices in the 1970s. The initial impact was severe, and the developed world's official reaction finally was to reduce its reliance on oil fuels.

Energy conservation became official policy. Building codes were altered to require better insulation against heat loss in new buildings. Owners of existing buildings were encouraged to improve their insulation. On the highways, lower speed limits were introduced, and higher average distances per fuel unit were required of car manufacturers. New sources of oil were vigorously and successfully sought in non-OPEC areas such as Mexico, the North Sea, the Arctic and off-shore areas. There was a great expansion of the work to obtain oil from such vast deposits as the Alberta Tar Sands and the Colorado Oil Shales. At the same time, work began on the development of alternative fuels which could change the· distribution of energy sources in the total energy supply.

North American car manufacturers generally met the new legal requirement for greater average distances per fuel unit by including an increasing number of small cars in their product mix, and by reducing the sizes of their larger models.

These policies succeeded, but only in exchange for higher prices and slower economic growth. Nevertheless, the demand for oil dropped drastically. By 1978 the developed world's reliance on OPEC oil was significantly reduced.

OPEC's initial reaction to the cessation of demand growth in 1978 was to raise the price of oil. Upward pressure on prices was increased by the outbreak of war between Iran and Iraq, two of OPEC's major producers, each wanting extra revenue to finance its war. The price, therefore, rose from $81/m³ ($13/bbl) in 1978 to $120/m³ ($19/bbl) in 1979, $200/m³ ($32/bbl) in 1980 and $220/m³ ($35/bbl) in 1981. However, such price increases could not be sustained; in fact, OPEC faced serious problems. Competition from non-OPEC suppliers such as Mexico, Norway and the UK cut severely into OPEC's share of the world market. There was a glut of oil on the world market, and OPEC members disagreed among themselves about how to handle the situation. By 1985, prices had dropped to about $165/m³ ($26/bbl) and by 1986 prices were hovering around $60–65/m³ ($10/bbl).

The Middle East, with its huge supplies of cheap oil, will always be able to undercut production costs elsewhere. However, the known existence of alternative oil sources such as the tar sands and the oil shales will also always limit prices the Middle East may wish to charge.

The existence of OPEC has had considerable impact. OPEC countries experienced some fairly rapid economic changes, and the accompanying social changes have created some difficult pressures, especially for the Islamic members. In the parts of the developing world without oil, life was made harder for millions by the increased costs of imported oil and such oil products as fertilizer and pesticides. Many developing nations are now heavily in debt, which will hinder their development for years. The developed world became extremely conscious of the need to conserve demand and secure supplies. And although the profound

Off-shore drilling in Canada's Beaufort Sea is both expensive and environmentally hazardous, and is economically justified only when oil prices are high. Even a small oil spill in the fragile arctic ecology could be both environmentally and economically disastrous.

changes in the oil market led the developed world into prolonged inflation and unemployment, they may also have hastened the transition to the postindustrial era.

DISCUSSION AND RESEARCH

10. If you were an OPEC minister, what arguments could you present to justify a high price for oil?

11. Within OPEC there are many different views regarding price policy and the rate of oil extraction. Research and explain these views.

12. How would you justify calls for a reduced rate of growth in total energy consumption?

13. What values are appealed to by calls for greater national energy independence?

14. Under what conditions are the Alberta Tar Sands and the Colorado Oil Shales likely to be brought into full production?

15. What are the likely effects of a rise in the price of energy? What if the price of oil alone goes up in relation to the prices of other energy sources? What if oil becomes significantly cheaper than other energy sources?

16. Trade in energy is mostly in oil. What are the benefits gained by both sides of the trade? What are the disadvantages to both sides?

17. **a.** Who gained from increasing oil prices during the period 1973 to 1985? Who lost? Consider both short- and long-term changes.

    b. Who is gaining from falling oil prices after 1985? Who is losing?

18. North America has only about 6% of the world's population, but uses about 35% of the world's energy.

    a. What is the implied criticism in this statement?

    b. How would you answer the criticism? Do you accept the criticism? Give reasons for your answer.

Toronto's brightly lit skyline is a sign of plentiful and relatively inexpensive electricity.

Ontario Hydro

Future Energy Sources

There has been much talk in recent years of an energy crisis. In the developed countries, some people think that energy is too heavily relied on to maintain a very high standard of living. Others see no problem; and there are those who want even greater energy production. Those in the first group often argue that the world should adopt what is called a "soft" energy policy; this would decentralize production into a multitude of small units, each using local energy sources that are as environmentally clean as possible and each serving a local community. Others, mostly among the second group, favour a "hard" energy policy, with energy production centralized at locations especially favourable to it, distributed to the population through pipelines and power grids.

What the developed world has today is for the most part a hard energy policy.

In the developing world there are concerns about the future availability of low-cost energy and the existence of the appropriate techniques to produce it. Energy-producing capabilities are the result of complex factors, such as universal education, scientific methodology, the availability of capital for development and effective market demand for production. As in other areas, we see here the need in a developing country for all aspects of a development program to be planned together; sectoral planning brings few rewards. In many developing countries, the factors favourable to energy production are lacking: illiteracy is high, capital is scarce and the population is generally too poor to create much market demand. In such cases, the lack of energy production capacity usually reinforces traditional lifestyles. In more developed countries, however, energy production capacity is determined by the lifestyles demanded, and its availability permits personal lifestyle choice.

Sectoral planning is planning for the development of a sector or part of the economy only. For example, planning for the reduction of birth rates is sectoral when no plans are made at the same time to improve old age security and deal with the other changes a reduction in birth rates will need and bring.

There is a difference between demand on the one hand and desire, want or need on the other. Demand means that the desire, want or need is supported by the willingness and ability to pay.

When considering the question of an energy crisis in the developed world, the issue of lifestyle is important. Put most simply, the choice for developed countries is between two approaches to life. One choice could be a high-energy lifestyle based on personal comfort and convenience, but stressful to the environment. A very different choice would be a low-energy lifestyle supporting a stable environment, though possibly with fewer comforts and conveniences.

The likelihood and pace of future energy developments, therefore, depend on people's beliefs and, ultimately, upon their values. Meanwhile, in the developing world people face a different choice: to remain on a low-energy lifestyle or attempt to produce or purchase a higher energy future.

If people throughout the world decide to demand greater energy development, the following possibilities exist.

Both the World Bank and the International Energy Agency expect the future rate of demand from the developing countries to exceed that from the developed countries. They expect total world demand to continue to grow at about 3–4% per year.

Conventional Oil and Gas

Production can be maintained or increased in existing oil and gas fields by employing more efficient but also more costly extraction techniques. New fields also may be opened up. When an oil field is first tapped the oil is usually under pressure to escape. Drilling tends to produce "gushers" whose natural pressure must be controlled. As production continues, the natural pressure lessens and the rate of oil flow diminishes. Simple pumping, called *primary extraction*, is introduced to maintain the desired rate of flow; as the pressure drops, more powerful pumps are needed. Production costs rise. Under natural pressure, an oil field may yield 10% of its contents; with primary extraction pumping, another 10% or so may be extracted. But 80% still lies underground.

If a well "gushes" these days it is regarded as a problem, because it denotes poor drilling control techniques. In the early days, a "gusher" was a reason for joy; oil had been found. Nowadays, however, the dangers of fire and explosion are given greater attention. So is the cost of waste.

Some of the remaining 80% can be obtained by what are called *secondary extraction* methods. In secondary extraction, shafts are drilled to below the level of the oil and the rock is flooded with water pumped down under great pressure. Because oil floats on water, the oil is driven upwards by the water into the areas of rock near the base of the well, where it is available for pumping (see Fig. 5-8). Another 30% of the field's contents may be obtained in this manner. About half of North America's oil production currently comes by means of secondary extraction techniques.

Even after secondary extraction has been used about 50% of the field's original oil is still underground. Recovering some of this oil requires the use of special chemicals in the underground flooding process instead of water. The chief chemical used so far has been carbon dioxide, but oil companies are looking increasingly to special low-viscosity fluids. Such processes are generally called *tertiary extraction* or *enhanced oil recovery*. Tertiary processes cost more than lower level extraction techniques. Whether engaging in tertiary production is worthwhile depends upon the selling price of oil. If it is too low, the oil stays in the ground; it is known about but not counted as part of the known reserves because it is too expensive to obtain at current prices. If prices rise, however, tertiary recovery may become profitable. So known reserves increase without any need for new drilling. Because oil and gas production depend on a combination of technology and price, it is not yet known what limits there

Fig. 5-8
Secondary oil extraction

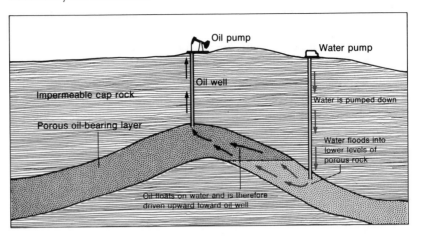

are to their recovery from existing fields. There is abundant oil in most existing North American fields, though many wells have been shut down. Recovery is simply too expensive at current prices, and it becomes more expensive as the amount of oil remaining in the field dwindles and becomes difficult to extract. It is unlikely, therefore, that all the oil will ever be taken from any field.

Even within existing fields all oil traps have not yet been discovered. Continued drilling still reveals new "pools" which can be brought into production when the price is right. More exploratory drilling occurs in the fields of Alberta and Saskatchewan, for instance, than in the Arctic. This is partly because the prairie basin has not yet been fully worked over, partly because drilling costs are much cheaper in the Prairies than in the North, and partly because the connection of a producing well to the existing pipeline system is much cheaper in the Prairies than it is in the Arctic.

Oil production can also be increased by developing new areas. Generally the lowest cost areas, where extraction is easiest, are opened first. During the 1970s oil exploration, stimulated by higher prices, increased tremendously. Several new fields were found, most notably off the east coasts of Mexico and China and in the North Sea. With falling prices in the 1980s oil exploration eased somewhat, but new finds were made, including off the coast of Brazil in 1985. The costs of exploration and development in new areas are often very high, and will not be incurred unless prices warrant the effort. For example, the cost of drilling an exploratory well on the Arctic mainland is about 20 times higher than in Alberta; on an Arctic island, about 40 times higher; and in Arctic off-shore waters as much as 150 times higher. Oil exploration in

Brazil went heavily into international debt during the 1970s, in part because of its reliance on expensive imported oil. It decided to aim for energy independence, pursuing its own oil sources at almost any cost. Canada's exploration efforts in the Beaufort Sea and off Newfoundland have a somewhat similar purpose.

remote "frontier areas" is hazardous and expensive, and supportable only by high oil prices.

In addition to higher exploration costs, there are extra, and perhaps decisive, costs incurred in gaining access to markets when oil is found. Pipelines are the most efficient means of transporting oil and gas to markets, but their capital costs are enormous. They also can present problems to environmentalists and to local groups whose use of the land may be disrupted. This is particularly true in Arctic areas, where pipelines cannot be buried and where both local people and wildlife rely directly upon the land to live. In addition, pipelines are worthwhile only if huge quantities of oil and gas are present to transmit and there is a matching demand in the consuming areas. The quantities of oil and gas in remote areas need to be much greater than in more accessible fields before pipelines are even considered. And the selling prices of oil and gas need to be high enough to cover all the costs.

Even with the help of advanced geological testing and growing knowledge of underground rock structures, oil companies never know whether oil is present underground until a well is drilled. About one well in ten strikes oil worth developing.

Non-Conventional Oil and Gas

Oil and gas will continue to be available, although at a higher cost, when all existing and frontier fields are economically exhausted. The fuels will come from sources that are now tapped in only a very limited way. These are the so-called non-conventional sources. For the most part non-conventional sources are tar sands, oil shales, heavy oils and coal, all of which can produce oil, but not in the conventional way.

The Alberta Tar Sands contain about 130 000 000 000 m^3 of oil. At Canada's mid-1980s rate of consumption of about 100 000 000 m^3 per year, the Alberta Tar Sands could provide oil to Canada for a long time, though at a higher price. The Orinoco Tar Sands in Venezuela are even larger, containing over 320 000 000 000 m^3 of oil, while the Oil Shales of Colorado and Wyoming contain about 350 000 000 000 m^3 of oil. For comparison, the Middle East contains about 75 000 000 000 m^3 of conventional oil, but has the lowest production costs of any oil in the world, and will continue to be important in world markets. Furthermore, most tar sands and oil shales are close to (or even at) the earth's surface. Although this oil may often be obtained by strip mining techniques, these methods create serious environmental consequences because they disrupt the soils, plants and natural drainage patterns.

Heavy oils, as at Cold Lake in Alberta, also offer potential sources of energy once the technology for simple extraction has been developed. The production of synthetic oil and gas from coal represents another large potential source of supply. Gas has been made from coal for about 200 years, although it now has been effectively replaced by natural gas.

Non-conventional oil does not flow like conventional oil. It requires processing before it can be obtained. The oil in tar sands, for example, has to be separated from tightly-packed gritty particles of sand. In its natural state it is virtually a solid rock, requiring mining rather than drilling or pumping.

At the Alberta Tar Sands near the Athabasca River, oil coats the grains of sand in the rock and can be extracted only by costly mining and processing operations.

Oil distillation from coal is not new either, but its technology is used today only in South Africa, which lacks its own oil but considers national energy independence as a higher priority than the high price of distillation.

Coal

Coal use is more stable than oil use because the major consumers are also the major producers and international trade is correspondingly small. The three largest producers and consumers are the USA, the USSR and China. Together they account for over half the world's production and consumption of coal. Because of the sharp rise in oil prices in the 1970s, coal production also rose sharply as many countries turned to it as a substitute for expensive oil. From 1973 to 1985, world coal production increased by 30%, and can be further increased using existing technology.

Fortunately, coal is plentiful. It represents about 85% of all known fossil fuel reserves on earth. At its World Energy Conference in Nairobi in 1981, the UN conservatively estimated the amount of recoverable coal in the world at 2 500 000 000 000 t. A few years earlier, in 1978, a Soviet physicist named Vladimir Kuzminov estimated the world's coal reserves at 8 400 000 000 000 t. These are huge amounts, sufficient to last for many hundreds of years. Unfortunately, coal also is dirty. It was partly for this reason that coal was replaced by oil as the world's major energy source, especially when oil was also cheaper. Now there is a renewed and growing demand for coal, and this is causing some problems.

There are four major problems associated with large-scale coal use. Two of these are connected with acid rain and the *greenhouse effect*, both of which result from pollutants released into the atmosphere by the burning of coal. The two other problems concern degrading the environment through strip mining and the human health hazards associated with underground mining.

Acid rain, also discussed in Chapter 4, is caused by the emission of sulphur dioxide and nitrous oxide from burning coal for thermal electricity generating stations and metal smelters. Large scale users can be fairly readily identified. It is possible to install "scrubbers" and other pollution control devices and to use more of the less-polluting low-sulphur coals. Both solutions, however, increase the immediate cost of use and reduce the current competitive price edge of coal. Moreover, these precautions can only reduce atmospheric pollution, not eliminate it.

Since 1850 the carbon dioxide in the air has increased by about 15%, largely through the burning of coal and the destruction of forest. This proportion continues to increase. The burning of all fossil fuels produces carbon dioxide, but for a given quantity of heat, coal produces 25% more carbon dioxide than oil and 75% more than natural gas. The use of forests for fuel also adds carbon dioxide to the atmosphere, and reduces the environment's ability to re-absorb it. All vegetation absorbs carbon dioxide, but forests (especially tropical forests) absorb more than other vegetation types. Their continuing destruction is a matter of serious environmental concern.

The ramifications of the greenhouse effect are not fully known. Some scientists think that an increased cloud cover will cause atmospheric cooling. Most scientists think that the atmosphere will become warmer. Those scientists who believe in a warming effect think that the

The sun's rays on their way to the earth's surface consist mostly of short-wave energy, and pass fairly easily through the carbon dioxide in the atmosphere. As the earth's surface is heated it radiates energy back into space. However, it does so mostly in the form of long-wave radiation, which cannot easily penetrate the carbon dioxide in the atmosphere. The lower layers of the atmosphere therefore accumulate heat. This accumulation of heat is called the *greenhouse effect*.

warming will be greatest in the polar regions, causing drastic changes in the world's wind systems and precipitation patterns.

At a conference sponsored by Environment Canada and the Canadian Science Writers' Association (reported in *bridges* 1986 2), scientists presented different views about the economic impact of the greenhouse effect on Canada. Some thought that a warmer climate would allow a northward expansion of Canada's agricultural areas and the support of a much larger population. This, however, would put additional pressures on water use, especially from the Great Lakes basin. Water levels would decline, posing problems to shipping and industrial effluent disposal. Others argued that lower lake levels would expose fresh land for farming and recreation and would lessen the risk of flooding. Another possibility is that, since carbon dioxide is a vital plant food, food production would increase. Increased warmth could also damage Canada's forests, because of the harmful effects caused by the increased number of weeds and insect pests. These are just some of the differing views about possible economic consequences of the greenhouse effect.

Strip-mining for coal is eight times more productive per hour of labour than underground mining. In North America, it occurs mostly in the western plains between Saskatchewan and New Mexico, where it competes with cattle ranching, wheat farming, wildlife management and recreation for land use. From its start in the late nineteenth century, strip mining tended to treat the land it used as land that was being withdrawn from other potential uses. However, increasing public pressure provoked by landscape destruction and degradation caused some mining companies in the 1950s and 1960s to begin programs of landscape renovation once they had taken out the coal. Starting in the 1970s, such programs were enforced by legislation. There is still much degraded land from former years in strip-mining areas; renovation has a long way to go.

Human health hazards linked to coal arise mostly in underground mining and are caused by the inhalation of coal dust. Improved mine ventilation and the use of protective breathing equipment help, but the problem continues to be serious. In the USA a federal program to compensate miners suffering from a variety of mine-related respiratory diseases costs over one billion dollars a year; it is financed by a tax on coal. Underground mining also poses some of the most serious risks to life among all industrial occupations. Fatal accidents in mining account for about 15% of all employment fatalities in Canada. The seriousness of the environmental and health problems associated with coal mining and use lead some people to argue against any great expansion in the use of coal, though it is a relatively cheap and plentiful energy source.

Hydroelectricity

In the developed world most of the productive hydroelectric sites close to major markets are already in use, and there is little prospect of making them more efficient. New developments are being forced into remoter locations, where the most productive sites are used first. Since it is not worth building expensive transmission lines unless quantities of electricity are large, remote projects, such as Churchill Falls and James Bay, are huge. Electricity is neither cheap nor easy to transport. The operations involved in developing hydroelectricity in remote areas are as complex as those used in the mining of frontier oil and gas. Moreover, because the areas of land needed for hydroelectric developments are so large, the jurisdictional disputes and land claims arising from local populations are significant additional cost factors or significant political restraints to development. As in all cases of development, these costs have to be weighed against the expected benefits. Once the necessary generating equipment is installed, hydroelectricity has two great advantages over oil, gas and coal: it is inexhaustible (in the sense that it is a renewable resource) and it is clean at its point of use.

In the developing countries, potential hydroelectric sites are still relatively plentiful. There may, however, be problems related to the flooding of valuable farmland by reservoirs, a problem especially severe in countries with food deficits. In tropical areas, there is also the increased risk of disease from water-breeding pests. Africa, for example, has developed only about 2% of its potential hydro power, despite such huge projects as Aswan, Kariba and Cabora Bassa. South America has developed only about 8%, despite the giant Itaipu project. On both these continents, large projects have been the norm, and more are planned.

In China, the policy of local self-reliance meant that for many years the effort went into a multitude of small local hydroelectric stations. The country gained about 100 000 small generating stations scattered among its largely rural population. Now Chinese policy is also turning to giant schemes. In mid-1986 the Chinese government signed contracts with Hydro-Québec and BC Hydro for developmental studies on what could become the world's largest hydroelectric plant. It is the Three Gorges project on the Yangtse. The USSR, which first sponsored a megaproject approach to industrial development in China in the early 1950s, itself has some of the world's largest hydroelectric plants, notably in south-central Siberia at Boguchany, Bratsk, Krasnoyarsk and Kuibyshev.

Even though it provides vast amounts of energy, hydroelectricity is still limited. Water will never disappear from the earth, although it may change form (as during an ice age). It will never be increased in quantity either. The only way to increase hydroelectric capacity is to use the same water many times over, either through a series of hydro dams along a river, or by pumped storage facilities, where the used water is recycled during off-peak hours back to a reservoir upstream from the dam so that it may be used again.

Nuclear Electricity

Nuclear electricity is generated by using nuclear fission instead of coal to produce heat. The heat boils water to produce steam to drive turbines.

Nuclear reactors are fueled by uranium. Two types of uranium occur together in nature, differing only according to their atomic units. Uranium-238 has a mass of 238 atomic units; it accounts for over 99% of all natural uranium. The remaining portion consists of uranium-235, but it is this small portion that is fissionable. When a neutron (a sub-atomic particle) hits an atom of uranium-235, the uranium atom splits (or fissions) and releases a huge amount of energy, as well as more neutrons. When these neutrons hit other atoms of uranium-235, these atoms also split, releasing more energy and more neutrons, and setting up a chain reaction. If uncontrolled, the chain reaction occurs very quickly, releasing its energy with explosive force. When a neutron hits an atom of uranium-238, it is absorbed and fission does not occur.

Despite the presence of neutrons, naturally occurring uranium does not, of course, explode. The neutrons are either absorbed by the 99% which is uranium-238 or they travel so quickly that they miss or pass right through the 1% which is uranium-235. Accordingly there are two

The uranium mine at Rabbit Lake, Saskatchewan.

methods of creating fission energy artificially. One increases the proportion of uranium-235 in the mix through a process called "enrichment." The other slows down the neutrons so they have a better chance of hitting an atom of uranium-235. Most countries using nuclear energy have opted for the first choice; Canada chose the second, using heavy water as a moderator to slow down the neutrons.

When controlled fission is obtained, a reactor generates electricity much as a thermal power station does with steam-driven turbines turning the generators. Because both coal and uranium are readily transportable, the characteristic geographical sites of both thermal and nuclear generating stations are similar. Since electricity is expensive to transport, user costs are kept as low as possible by locating generators as close as possible to major markets. Ideally, the stations are also located near plentiful supplies of fresh water, because the steam must be cooled back to water to be recycled. There is no chemical or radiation change in this water, but it is a source of waste heat. Ontario is experimentally using this waste heat to breed fish more quickly than in naturally colder waters.

Unlike coal-powered generating stations, nuclear stations are relatively clean. Nuclear stations do not emit pollutants. They do, however, sometimes provoke fears of radioactive discharge and waste disposal. We shall examine these concerns in more detail in the case study at the end of this chapter.

Many countries are coming to depend heavily on nuclear generated electricity as a major energy source (see Fig. 5-9). Although nearly 15% of all electricity produced worldwide comes from nuclear reactors, the proportion reaches as high as 65% in France and 55% in Belgium. Other leading nuclear countries include Finland (45% of all national electricity production), Sweden (40%), Switzerland (35%), Bulgaria (30%), Taiwan (30%) and West Germany (30%). Canada generates about 10% of its total electricity supply by nuclear means, although Ontario's figure is closer to 40%. Developing countries are also increasingly committed to nuclear energy projects, although the World Bank will provide no funding for the construction of nuclear electricity stations. Reactors are functioning in Argentina, Brazil, China, Cuba, India, Mexico, Pakistan, Philippines, South Korea and Taiwan, while Egypt plans to have its reactors operational by the early 1990s.

The nations of Eastern Europe are also heavily involved in the development of nuclear electricity. The USSR alone has 60 reactors at work. In all countries, however, there is hope that nuclear fission will eventually be replaced as an energy source by nuclear fusion, wherein energy is released by combining hydrogen atoms, as in the sun, instead of by splitting uranium atoms, which is how fission works. The advantages

In the mid-1980s, 34 countries had nuclear generating stations either operating or at some stage of construction. There were nearly 550 stations altogether, over 200 in Western Europe, 150 in North America, 100 in Eastern Europe and the USSR, 75 in Asia, and the rest scattered in South and Central America and Africa.

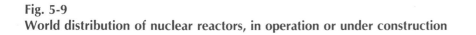

Fig. 5-9
World distribution of nuclear reactors, in operation or under construction

Number of nuclear
reactors per country

● 10 or more

• Less than 10

Data from *Nuclear News*, 1985 8.

of fusion over fission are its virtually limitless raw materials (essentially sea water for hydrogen or deuterium) and its absence of environmentally damaging waste products (inert helium). Technology is the key, and much intensive international work is going on, such as the co-operative effort between the USA and the USSR to generate very high magnetic fields.

DISCUSSION AND RESEARCH

19. Canada tries hard to sell nuclear reactors to other countries, chiefly those searching for rapid economic growth. Sales have been made to Argentina, South Korea, Romania, India and Turkey. "The developing countries need energy for development," say the proponents of such sales. "To refuse to share our abilities would be to support poverty and starvation." Opponents claim that such sales are unwise in view of the perceived risks of nuclear energy. Research the case for both sides.

Wood

Depending on the level of technology used, wood will produce energy in four different ways. It can be burned to produce heat directly. It can be processed into charcoal and then burned to produce heat directly. It can be burned to boil water to produce steam to drive turbines to generate electricity. And it can be processed into *methanol*, which can be substituted for gasoline. As the level of technology rises through these four possibilities, the level of actual use declines, so that methanol is the least used form of wood energy. One reason for the limited development of methanol is that gasoline is much cheaper. Brazil, however, has had great success with a somewhat similar fuel called ethanol, produced from sugar cane. As many as 80% of the new cars and trucks in Brazil now run on ethanol. The program began in 1975 as a result of OPEC's oil price hikes and the burden of debt Brazil began to acquire to pay for expensive imported oil. Though ethanol costs twice as much as oil, Brazil continues to support the program to avoid going further into international debt. In a land where increased food production is also an objective, critics question the loss of farmland to sugar cane destined for ethanol production.

The Science Council of Canada has estimated that if methanol were used to replace gasoline in cars then an area the size of Nova Scotia would be needed to grow trees to fuel 10 000 000 cars for a yearly average travel distance of 15 000 km.

The use of wood for electricity production is very limited. Wood lacks the thermal efficiency of coal and oil, although it has the advantage of being renewable. There are several small wood-burning electric generating stations in the USA. The world's largest project is in the Philippines, where the government has launched a rural electrification program using wood from trees known locally as "miracle trees." The trees, which mature sufficiently for cutting in four years, are planted around numerous small and scattered generating stations.

Charcoal production is increasing in many developing countries, and in wooded areas it is becoming a common sight to see smoke rising from many charcoal ovens. However, the preparation of charcoal uses more than half of the potential energy in the wood, and the developing world is becoming seriously short of wood. Paradoxically, it is this very shortage of wood that is causing the increased use of charcoal. Charcoal is much more compact and easy to carry than wood and, because many people in rural areas have to travel so far to find fuel, they prefer the convenience of charcoal. Charcoal use will likely increase until major reforestation schemes are implemented and people can again obtain local fuelwood supplies.

If you walk through almost any town or village in any developing country you will notice small cooking fires almost everywhere. The effect on atmospheric pollution is severe.

The direct use of wood for heat energy is widespread in the developing world. About 35% of the world's population relies directly on wood for cooking and heating. In Africa, this figure goes as high as 80%. Moreover, about 90% of all wood harvested in developing countries is used directly for fuel. The immediate problem of fuel supply is extremely serious, but so are the allied problems of deforestation, soil erosion, flooding and desertification. The World Bank estimates (*The Energy Transition in Developing Countries*, 1983) that 50 000 000 ha of trees need to be planted throughout the developing world before the year 2000 to supply enough firewood to meet the demand. Planting must be continued thereafter to provide for sustained use. Some countries, notably China, India, South Korea and the Philippines, have already made an effective start.

In North America many people are turning to the direct burning of wood as an alternative to oil for home heating. Altogether, about 10 000 000 homes have woodstoves. Unfortunately, the combined atmospheric pollutants are greater than from many industrial centres, and more and more jurisdictions are insisting on stringent emission controls for woodstoves.

Animal Dung

The use of dried and compacted animal dung for fuel is common in many developing countries. In India, almost 185 000 000 cows create as much as 15% of the nation's total energy. The manufacture and sale of cow dung "patties" is widespread.

When it is used as a fuel, however, the dung is not then available for much-needed fertilizer. The World Resources Institute in Washington issued a report in 1985 called *Tropical Forests: A Call for Action*. Because of the lack of readily available firewood, it says, communities in Africa, Asia and Latin America are burning an estimated 400 000 000 t of animal dung each year, representing an enormous loss to the fertility and productivity of their farmland. This loss is thought to have reduced grain harvests by more than 14 000 000 t/y, nearly double the food aid provided by the USA, Canada and Australia.

Of increasing importance is the use of dung to manufacture methane gas. In theory, the dung from one cow should produce enough methane to cook for one person without destroying the fertilizing quality of the dung. The production of methane (often called *biogas*) has begun in several countries, including India and South Korea, but the world leader is China. China's nearly 10 000 000 biogas processors produce energy equivalent to about 20 000 000 t of coal. These are effective, especially in the south, where climatic warmth aids the process. About half the raw material comes from farm animals, especially pigs, and the other half from human waste (called "nightsoil"). The residue of sludge is removed from the "digestors" twice a year to fertilize the fields for rice planting (spring) and wheat planting (fall). Biogas processors create no environmental problems; instead, they reduce the risks from diseases associated with untreated wastes, reduce the atmospheric pollution associated with burning dung, and counteract the problems of deforestation by providing an alternative fuel. At the same time they permit the use of the same dung as a fertilizer.

Garbage

It is estimated that the energy in about 6 t of garbage equals that in 1 m^3 (about 6.3 bbl) of oil. That energy is usually released by burning the garbage to boil water to produce steam, which then may be used to generate electricity or provide local heating. For example, Chicago and St. Louis have small garbage-burning electric generating stations, using about 1 000 t of garbage daily and saving the equivalent of 150 000 t of coal annually. Baltimore, Vancouver, Montréal and Québec City also burn garbage to produce steam heat.

The problem with the use of garbage to generate electricity is that it is such a mixture of things. However, over the last several years the technology of "mass burning" has been developed in Europe. Ferrous metals are removed by magnets and the remaining material is burned on continuously moving grates. Even so, one of the by-products of burning garbage is dioxin. Accordingly, Pollution Probe, an environmental group in Toronto, wants the Ontario government to cancel its plans to build 16 garbage-burning energy producing plants across the province.

Using garbage for energy disposes of material that otherwise poses a major problem. In all large urban areas vast amounts of garbage are produced daily, and disposal is increasingly difficult. Landfill sites are more and more difficult to use because no community wants to have garbage dumps near it. New York City, for example, must send all its daily 20 000 t of garbage to its existing landfill site on Staten Island. This site is already 10 storeys high and will be reaching 50 storeys by the year 2000 if no alternative solution is found. Look for further developments in the burning of garbage for energy. Such burning will add to the world's atmospheric pollution, but only in a relatively minor way compared with the pollution from fossil fuels. Also, the existence of unburned garbage is itself a serious environmental problem, especially given the highly toxic nature of much industrial waste.

India has about 70 000 biogas processors, of which about 50% are thought to be inoperative. They require more land than many Indian villages can spare; they require more water than is frequently available; they cost more than most villages can afford. They need human waste as well as cow dung, and there are cultural barriers against such a use for human waste. They benefit women more than men, for the main use of biogas is in cooking, and women play only a small role in decision-making in India. And they are widely held in rural areas to produce a less satisfactory heat for cooking than either firewood or cow dung.

Wind

The world's winds offer a great source of energy, but it is not easily tapped. The most persistent (and therefore most useful) winds occur over the oceans and at high altitudes, where obstructions are few, but where the need is least and the opportunities for tapping it minimal. Over land, winds are more erratic because of the numerous obstructions. They have, however, traditionally provided energy for centuries, chiefly through windmills and windpumps.

Modern research seeks the most efficient ways of using wind energy to produce electricity. Most existing plants are quite small, serving only local needs, often supplementing other, primary sources of electricity. Wind turbines already produce electricity for the Magdalen Islands in the Gulf of St. Lawrence and for Vancouver Island and Prince Edward Island. In California, the world's largest "wind farm" (with 5 000 turbines spread over 12 000 ha) is located in the Altamont Pass east of San Francisco. Wind turbines are also proposed for extensive use throughout much of Canada's Northland. Larger projects are being researched in North Carolina, Québec and Saskatchewan.

Wind-generated electricity is environmentally very clean. Its major disadvantages are noisiness and unreliability, due to the erratic nature of the wind. Also, too much wind can be as bad as too little. Most wind-powered generators need a minimal wind speed of 5 metres per second (5 m/s) to work; but they can be damaged if winds exceed 25 m/s. Accordingly, most existing plants have an automatic shut-off for when winds become dangerously strong. The possibilities for supplementary electricity production are high, however, and we can expect to see more wind-powered generators in the future.

One of an array of experimental wind turbines for generating electricity in northwestern Prince Edward Island.

Tidal Power

Only one large tidal power plant has been built, located at the mouth of the river Rance in northwest France. It works well, except for two disadvantages: there is a dead time of about an hour at high tide, and again 5–6 hours later at low tide. Since both high and low tides occur twice each day, there are at least four hours daily during which the plant produces no power. In addition, the times of high and low tides differ each day, coming later by about 50 minutes each 24 hours.

To be effective, tidal power plants need the tidal range (the difference in height between low tide and high tide) to be considerable. The Mediterranean Sea, for example, has virtually no tidal range, so tidal power is an impossibility. According to the UN, there are only

John Molyneux

The experimental tidal power plant at Annapolis Royal, Nova Scotia. It delivers electricity to the local grid to a maximum of 20 000 kW. Landowners upstream complain of increased flooding.

about 25 locations in the entire world where tidal power is a real possibility. These are chiefly in parts of the English Channel, the Irish Sea, the White Sea, the Barents Sea and the eastern coasts of North America and Australia. One major possibility is in the Bay of Fundy in Nova Scotia, where several feasibility studies have been done and a small pilot project built at Annapolis Royal.

The fact that tidal power is technically possible does not necessarily make it economically worthwhile. Costs have to be weighed against those of alternative energy sources, and consideration given to the constancy of output levels. Tidal power cannot yet meet these criteria, and these problems are expected to take a long time to solve.

Solar Power

The amount of solar energy that actually penetrates the atmosphere and reaches the earth's surface equals about 1000 times the world's total usage

The maximum level of solar energy available is about one kilowatt per square metre of ground (1 kW/m²), and then only for an hour or so around noon on cloudless days during high summer in the tropics. At other times and places, quantities are much less.

of all other energy sources. It is not, however, equally available at all times and in all places. Neither is it available in a very concentrated form. Nevertheless, within the tropics and other persistently warm and sunny places, solar energy has great potential. At Big Trout Lake in northern Ontario, which receives 85% as much sunshine as Florida per year, Ontario Hydro is experimenting with a 10 kW solar array (i.e., an array of solar panels) to meet local needs, which are currently served by generators that run on diesel fuel made costly by the remoteness of the area.

Solar energy may be used directly for such things as crop drying, or indirectly through such devices as solar collectors, photovoltaic cells and concentrating mirrors. In the sunny parts of the tropics, UNESCO estimates that electricity provided by simple photovoltaic cells could power water pumps able to irrigate up to 100 ha of farmland each. Larger amounts of electricity can be produced using mirrors to concentrate the sun's rays on a boiler in which steam is produced to drive turbines. There are, however, two major disadvantages: the mirrors take up a lot of space on the ground and require the most precise engineering. At Barstow in the Mojave Desert, an experimental site consisting of a black boiler (for heat absorption) is surrounded by mirrors covering 40 ha of land. It was built in 1981, and it works; but the electricity produced is more expensive than that from other conventional sources. Precise engineering enables the mirrors to swivel constantly to track the sun across the sky.

Other uses for solar energy range from cooking on small portable heaters (as shown in the photograph from Dakar) to storing summer-heated hot water in large underground caverns for winter use to heat buildings in Sweden. It is also possible that one day will see the building of huge solar collectors in space to beam the collected energy to earth by microwave.

Geothermal Power

Geothermal energy is derived from the heat of the earth's interior. Most commonly, it is available in or near volcanic regions where the underground molten rock is nearest to the earth's surface. Volcanic heat boils the natural ground water to produce steam, or water pumped down in pipes and recirculated to the surface as steam. The steam is used to drive turbines to generate electricity. Areas of volcanic activity are relatively localized on the earth's surface and developments are concentrated in only a few countries, chiefly the USA (California, Idaho), the Philippines, Italy, Japan, New Zealand and Iceland. Small amounts are also produced in El Salvador, Mexico, the USSR, China, Hungary, Indonesia, Kenya, Nicaragua, Turkey, Honduras and North Yemen.

A solar cooker developed at the University of Dakar in Senegal.

Ocean Water

Most of the earth's surface is water. The energy potential in this water is enormous. Excluding tidal power, this energy is now available in three different forms. There is energy potential in the movement of the waves, in the temperature differences between the upper and lower layers of water and in the chemical composition of the water. Experiments with wave converters to turn the movement of the waves into electricity are underway in the UK and Japan, but progress has been slow.

Experiments have also been undertaken by the USA and France to generate electricity from the temperature differences between the surface and deeper waters. In tropical areas, ocean surface temperatures are usually about 28–29°C, while a few hundred metres down temperatures may be only about 4°C. This difference can be used to make electricity. The technique uses a pipe to circulate ammonia from the ocean surface down to the colder waters and back to the surface again. The surface water heats the ammonia until it turns into gas, which is then driven down toward the colder water. On its way it passes through turbines, generating electricity. As it cools, the ammonia recondenses into a liquid, and returns to the surface, where the cycle begins again. The advantage of placing the turbines in the gaseous part of the cycle is that they are more efficiently turned by gaseous than by liquid ammonia. Such operations are called Ocean Thermal Energy Conversion units, and offer considerable prospects for the future although, at the moment, their electricity is too expensive.

Ocean water may also be used to produce hydrogen fuel through electrolysis. Water's two main constituents are hydrogen and oxygen. If hydrogen is extracted, oxygen is produced as a "waste." When hydrogen is subsequently burned as fuel, it re-combines with oxygen and produces water as a "waste." The cycle is both useful and simple. The problem is cost. The extraction of hydrogen from water requires large amounts of electricity, and is not worthwhile unless electricity is very cheap. Some people see the solution resting in a series of nuclear generating stations (which can produce electricity cheaply) distributed around the coasts, producing hydrogen from sea water. The reason for engaging in this massive use of one type of energy to produce another is that hydrogen offers certain advantages in transport and storage that electricity does not. Hydrogen may be the fuel of the future, but much research remains to be done in techniques of large scale production.

Hydrogen is the chief fuel used in the US space shuttles.

Deuterium, also called heavy hydrogen, offers great potential for future supplies of energy. It is available from water, and its energy capacity is huge. For example, 1 g of deuterium can yield 150 000 kW h of electricity, whereas 1 g of uranium-235 will yield 20 000 kW h, 1g of coal 0.0037 kW h, and 1 g of wood only 0.0018 kW h.

DISCUSSION AND RESEARCH

20. The United Nations expects the world's need for energy to increase at a rate of about 3%/y. This means that the amount produced should double every 25 years or so.

  a. Why do you think there is an increasing need for energy?

  b. What do you think will be some of the major problems in meeting this growing need?

21. What effects are oil price changes likely to have on the development of so-called "soft" energy sources such as solar, wind, wood, garbage and animal dung?

22. There are drawbacks to the production and use of all forms of energy. Some have been noted in the text. Research and suggest what others there may be.

23. Needing an energy source for a remote island in Canada's High Arctic, you can choose from among a woodstove, diesel generator, solar converter or wind-powered generator. Which would you choose, and why?

24. If you could design the perfect source of energy, what characteristics should it have?

The reactor face of the Bruce "A" Generating Station in Ontario. Only the first fueling can be done by hand; thereafter, radioactivity requires the use of this fueling machine.

Ontario Hydro

CASE STUDY
Nuclear Energy

It would be appropriate and, to some, sufficient to say that nuclear energy is under a cloud. Rarely does an issue evoke such strong responses. For ex- ample, consider the accompanying statements on nuclear energy.

Nuclear power poses risks not shared by any other energy technology. These risks threaten the very fabric of our civilization, as well as the continued viability of our democratic institutions and our legal system. Such risks far outweigh any benefits to be expected.

Nuclear power is an energy option. It can supply electricity. However, 85% of our energy needs are non-electrical, and we are not short of electricity. . . . There is little market for nuclear electricity. Nuclear power programs in many countries, including the USA and China, are at a standstill.

Nuclear power currently supplies about 1.3% of Canada's delivered energy. Obviously, whether we push it or not, nuclear power will not make a big difference in the overall energy picture for at least the next 50 years. Even in Ontario, if all the nuclear plants were shut down tomorrow, there would be no shortage of energy or electricity. The need for nuclear power in Canada is a total myth.

In addition, Canada is the world's largest exporter of uranium, for which there are exactly two uses: bombs, and nuclear reactors. These two uses are not mutually exclusive. Uranium used to generate electricity can subsequently be used to make bombs, by extraction of the plutonium stored in the spent fuel.

Even if nuclear war is somehow avoided, and electricity does replace oil at some future time, nuclear power cannot play a major role without the large-scale use of plutonium. The advent of a plutonium economy, as it is called, may well mean the end of democracy, because of the extraordinary security problems which will arise. If plutonium becomes a common fuel for nuclear generating plants, thousands of ordinary workers will become security risks. Their private lives will have to be investigated — family, friends, political leanings, past associations, and so on. And if a genuine threat of nuclear terrorism rears its ugly head, who is to say that torture will not be authorized to track down the terrorists before it is too late?

Excerpted from a talk to the Canadian Bar Association by Gordon Edwards, 1981 3.

The need of the world for energy sources is unequivocal. The provision of shelter, of food, of other basic material needs to free literally billions of today's world from hunger and want, all depend on energy. The provision of a just and sustainable society has a definite correlation with the availability of energy. Demand for energy by lesser-developed and developing countries is burgeoning. It is no wonder — when about 27% of the people of the world live on much less than the average world per capita consumption of two kilowatt-years per year (equivalent to continuously burning twenty 100-watt light bulbs). A considerable number of this group exist at one-tenth or less of this figure (0.2 kWyr/yr per capita). However, 22% of the world use 2–7 kWyr/yr per person. The remaining 6% (including Canada) enjoy per capita energy use of 7–12 kWyr/yr. The sources of energy are from nuclear power, coal, oil and other fossil resources, hydroelectric power, biomass and developing alternatives such as solar [power]. Amplifying the energy available to the large fraction of the world's population who are well below the average level will call for a large increase in the world's supply. This is needed even with the postulate of significant per capita reduction for the energy-rich portion of the world. Supplying energy in order to reach such distributive justice must lead to utilization of every possible energy source, including nuclear energy.

Les Shemilt, writing in *Signs of the Times*, published by the United Church of Canada in 1981.

I have long been amazed by the stormy demonstrations of thousands, by the speeches of well-known and un-known politicians, by all kinds of campaigns in Western countries di-rectly against the construction of nu-clear power plants. It is very difficult to explain to a layman that a nuclear reactor is not a nuclear bomb, that coal and oil-fired power plants pre-sent a far greater danger to the en-vironment, to public health, than a nuclear plant. The development of nuclear energy is one of the necessary pre-requisites for retaining the eco-nomic and political independence of every country, both highly developed and developing. If the economies of these countries continue to depend to a more or less significant part on the supply of fuel from other countries then the West will live under the con-stant threat of having these supplies embargoed. This will result in hu-miliating economic dependence. Problems concerning the develop-ment of nuclear energy in the alter-natives of economic development must be solved without baseless emotions and prejudices. It is not merely a question of the so-called "quality of life." The issue is far more important — economic and political indepen-dence, preservation of freedom for our children and grandchildren.

Andre Sakharov, Nobel Peace Prize winner and Russian dissident, quoted in the Montréal Medal Address at the 62nd Canadian Chemical Conference in Vancouver 1979 6 6.

What's happening in the nuclear in-dustry is being called a disaster. . . . The trouble is, it's the wrong disaster. No one will learn anything from it except investors. What's needed from the nuclear industry is an actual ca-tastrophe — such as it almost gave us at Three Mile Island . . . If there had been a meltdown instead of just talk of one, an event would have oc-curred that the whole world is waiting for. We don't need a nuclear war. We do need a nuclear accident — and a nice big one. Soon.

There is room for argument on how big the accident needs to be. Some people think that a city the size of Los Angeles or Edinburgh has to go be-fore a majority of the race will really get concerned about nuclear peril. Me, I'm more hopeful. I think Three Mile Island would have done nicely. Be-cause of the plant's location and be-cause of the prevailing wind patterns, probably no more than a hundred peo-ple would have died from initial con-tact with the radioactive steam. The rest would have had time to flee . . . and be exiled from their part of Penn-sylvania for at least a decade or two. If we had those exiles — noisy, bitter, but alive; nearly every one an ardent convert to nuclear disarmament; one or two dying now and then from the delayed effects of radiation sickness (so as to keep the media interested) — we would not now be having a debate about a nuclear freeze; we would be having the freeze it-self. . . . The world would be far safer than it is.

Noel Perrin, Professor of English at Dartmouth College, quoted in *Energy Alert* Fall 1983.

These quotations address themes of overwhelming importance. Topics such as survival, nuclear war, democracy, political and economic independence and the quality of life now and in the future are major issues. That the authors of the quotations think these matters rest on whether we continue to develop nuclear energy is an indication of the strength of opinion about nuclear energy.

Let us look more closely at these opinions. People often either support or reject nuclear energy for one or more of the following reasons.

It costs less/It costs more

Both claims are true and justifiable. Costs of all types of energy production vary enormously from one part of the world to another, and what may be true in one area is not necessarily true elsewhere. Costs also vary over time, and for different energy sources. For example, from 1980 to 1985 the world price of oil dropped by almost half; for uranium it was exactly halved; but the price of coal actually increased by about one-third.

The cost of energy production from any type

of fuel is determined by more than the price of fuel. It is determined also by the cost of plant construction and maintenance and by the accounting techniques used to pass expenses along to consumers. For example, a choice must be made between including a portion of the cost in the consumer price during planning and construction or delaying such inclusion until after the plant is operating. Factors leading to national differences in the costs of energy production vary from country to country. Therefore, the relative costliness of any means of energy production varies according to a host of such factors.

France, for example, claims that its cost for nuclear electricity (1984–85 prices, all in US$) is about 3 cents per kW·h, compared with 6 cents for electricity from coal and 10 cents for electricity from oil. Japan claims a similar price advantage for nuclear electricity: 5 cents/kW·h compared with 6 cents/kW·h from coal and 7.5 cents/kW·h from oil. Ontario Hydro cites figures of 2 cents/kW·h for nuclear electricity and 3 cents/kW·h for electricity from coal. In each location hydroelectricity is acknowledged to be even cheaper than nuclear electricity (Ontario Hydro, for example, quotes 0.6 cents/kW·h for hydroelectricity). However, the commercial hydro sites available in these places were fully developed long ago. Moreover, none of them have cheap and easy access to coal and oil. Conditions are different in some other countries, such as the USA.

The USA has large reserves of coal and generates about half its electricity from that source. Construction costs for nuclear plants have risen very rapidly since the early 1970s and now are at least twice as high as construction costs for coal-fired stations. Nuclear fuel continues to have a significant price advantage over coal, even in the USA, but because of the greatly increased construction costs, the cost of electricity production from nuclear sources is at least as high, if not higher, than the cost of electricity from coal. Both are at about 5 cents/kW·h.

The reasons for the rapidly escalating cost of nuclear electricity in the USA are unique to that country, and cause much of the confusion that surrounds the nuclear energy issue. In the early 1970s the OPEC oil crisis profoundly affected American thinking about energy. "Energy self-sufficiency" became a catch-phrase describing a goal to be achieved by conservation, exploration for new sources and a rapid expansion of the nuclear energy program. Throughout the decade, nuclear electricity was slated to grow from about 2% of all electricity produced to about 12%. Most electric utilities enthusiastically supported this plan, to their eventual regret. Many projects were hastily conceived, planned and built and, frequently, put into production without full controls. The problem of haste was compounded by the variety of nuclear plants constructed. Each was in effect a custom-built reactor. Accordingly, costs rose. By the late 1970s construction costs for nuclear stations surpassed those for coal-fired stations, and the offsetting advantage of cheaper nuclear fuel was lost. At the same time, the Three Mile Island accident occurred (see page 218 for further discussion) through a combination of mechanical breakdown and human error. As a consequence, the US nuclear industry faced a greatly expanded list of government-required safety measures, which further raised costs. Perhaps more importantly, the prospect of more nuclear plants met with greatly increased public fear and hostility, which also raised costs through the need to engage in hearings and litigation. The nuclear industry came to a virtual standstill. Most electric utilities cancelled or abandoned their nuclear construction projects.

The situation is different in Canada, particularly in Ontario. Nuclear fuel is plentiful, whether natural uranium, thorium or plutonium. Canadian reactors are almost entirely standardized on the CANDU design, which differs from any in the USA. With only slight modifications, the CANDU reactors can operate on any of the plentiful nuclear fuels. Design standardization has helped to keep costs down. Standardization also makes it easier to make adjustments so that malfunctions in any reactor can be corrected in others and a uniform set of safety practices can be developed for all reactors. Canadian reactors have a much higher operating efficiency than American ones, producing far more electricity per unit of cost.

The proven ability of Canadian reactors to maintain high levels of operating efficiency is a major factor in keeping nuclear electricity costs lower than the costs of alternatives.

It is environmentally clean/It pollutes

Proponents of nuclear electricity claim that it is a non-polluting form of energy. They point to the lack of toxic emissions such as those produced by the burning of hydrocarbons (coal, oil, gas). Nitrous oxides and carbon dioxide given off by burning hydrocarbons cause acid rain and enhance the greenhouse effect. Supporters also assert that the very small amounts of waste produced by nuclear reactors are not an environmental problem. Opponents of nuclear energy agree in their serious concerns over the environmental damage caused by coal-fired electricity generation, but argue that the possibility of radiation-releasing accidents and the highly toxic radioactivity of nuclear waste products pose environmental problems that cannot be ignored. Let us look at these issues more closely under the next two points.

It is safe/It is dangerous

Concerns about the relative safety or danger of nuclear power plants focus on two different but related issues. These are: How safe is nuclear power production on a day-to-day basis? And, given the magnitude of a possible nuclear catastrophe, can nuclear energy ever be safe enough?

Radiation is an inescapable fact of our lives, and always has been. Most of it comes as part of the spectrum of electromagnetic radiation given off by the sun, of which heat and light form only a small portion. It also exists as radio and television waves, radar, microwaves, infrared and ultraviolet radiation, and so on. A portion of it at the highest frequency end of the electromagnetic spectrum is what is called *ionizing radiation*. Ionizing radiation is that part of the electromagnetic spectrum which electrically charges particles (called ions) in the substances it hits. There are several types of ionizing radiation: X-rays, gamma rays, cosmic rays, alpha and beta particles and neutrons. Only materials emitting ionizing radiation are said to be radioactive.

Different types of ionizing radiation have different characteristics. For example, X-rays are extremely high frequency waves with great penetrating power; gamma rays are similar to X-rays. Cosmic rays are actually microparticles bombarding the earth from outer space and from which we are largely but not entirely protected by the atmosphere. Alpha particles are relatively large and easily stopped by even a sheet of paper, but are dangerous if inhaled or swallowed. Beta particles are much smaller than alpha particles; they can penetrate the top layers of skin, although they can be stopped by aluminum foil or a few millimetres of wood. Neutrons are even more penetrating, but cannot pass through water or concrete.

We measure ionizing radiation in *grays* or *sieverts*. These units replaced *rads* and *rem* on the basis of 1 gray = 100 rads, and 1 sievert (Sv) = 100 rem. One gray represents the absorption of one joule of energy per kilogram of irradiated tissue. One sievert measures the amount of biological damage caused to the tissue by a gray of radiation. Not all types of ionizing radiation cause the same amount of biological damage per gray. For example, one gray of alpha particles is more damaging than one gray of beta particles or gamma rays. By reason of its biological relationship, the sievert is more commonly used as a radiation measure, although quantities are usually so small that the common practice is to use millisieverts (mSv).

The chief source of ionizing radiation is the solar system itself. Cosmic rays constantly bombard the earth and, although the atmosphere offers good protection, it is an imperfect shield. Small quantities of radiation penetrate to the earth's surface, with less reaching lowland than highland areas. Quantities range from about 0.3 mSv/y at sea level to about 0.5 mSv/y in highland areas, and over 0.8 mSv/y in mountainous areas (e.g., Buenos Aires 0.3 mSv, Frederiction 0.35 mSv, Calgary 0.45 mSv, Denver 0.55 mSv, Mexico City 0.6 mSv, Quito 0.65 mSv — all measurements are per year). The higher the altitude, the thinner the atmosphere and, therefore, the greater is a person's exposure to cosmic radiation. For example, a transcontinental or trans-oceanic flight in a jetliner increases radiation by about 0.05 mSv per flight. Similarly, living or working in a 50-storey building, or visiting an equally high tower, increases radiation exposure by about 15–20% per hour.

Another major source of radiation is the earth, which has a radioactive core and many radioactive rocks in its crust. Quantities of radiation vary from place to place, depending upon major rock type. Granitic areas generally produce about 0.3 mSv/y of radiation, while sandy areas produce only about 0.2 mSv/y and clay areas 0.1 mSv/y. Since most building material is a product of one or more of these major rock types, people are also exposed to radiation in and from buildings. The average brick home produces about 0.1 mSv/y of radiation, while New York's Grand Central Station, built of and located on granite, produces more radiation than any nuclear power station is permitted to. The air inside all buildings also is radioactive because of the radon gas it contains. In general, quantities vary from about 0.02 mSv/y to about 0.2 mSv/y, and are always higher in buildings with poor ventilation, since the radon gas seeps into the buildings from the ground below and accumulates inside unless ventilation is good. People can reduce their exposure to radon gas by getting outdoors more and by opening the windows as much as possible. It is one of the ironic penalties of the drive for energy conservation that many people have improved the insulation

of their buildings and thereby increased the likelihood of accumulating radon gas.

Other sources of radiation include luminous clocks and watches, which may add another 0.01–0.03 mSv/y. TV or video screens may add a further 0.005 mSv/y. The need for people to have medical X-rays increases their exposure to radiation by about 0.1–1.0 mSv/y, depending upon the part of the body X-rayed. Some medical X-rays provide the body with more ionizing radiation than all other sources put together. Nuclear weapons testing fall-out adds 0.04 mSv/y to everyone's radiation exposure. Worried? The human body produces about 0.25 mSv/y of radiation.

Nuclear generating stations in North America are limited by law to a maximum radiation emission of 0.05 mSv/y. In practice the radiation emissions are lower. At the gates of the Pickering nuclear plant near Toronto, measured emissions are about 0.01 mSv/y.

Most nuclear power stations contain many built-in safeguards to lessen the risk of radiation leaks in the event of an accident. The worst nuclear accident in North American history occurred in 1979 at Three Mile Island, near Harrisburg, Pennsylvania. According to official government data, most of the harmful radiation was contained by the built-in safeguards, and average radiation over an 80 km radius outside the plant did not exceed 0.015 mSv/y. A subsequent presidential commission declared that the affected area would likely produce only one additional case of cancer due to the accident. This figure is disputed by many local residents, over 2 000 of whom have filed lawsuits against Consolidated Edison, the owner of the reactor. The residents claim there have been abnormalities in crops grown since the accident, that cancer deaths have risen above the normal level and that there has been an increase in cancer among farm animals.

In 1957 there was a more serious accident at Windscale in northwest England, when a reactor caught fire and leaked about 1 000 times more

USSR Embassy Press Office/Ottawa

The control room switchboard of Unit Four in the Leningrad nuclear power plant.

radioactive material than the reactor at Three Mile Island. There was a much more serious accident in 1986 at Chernobyl, near Kiev in the USSR. That reactor exploded and burned, largely through a series of human errors going back to the construction and design stages. The Chernobyl accident released about one million times as much radioactivity as Three Mile Island. About 30–35 plant workers and firefighters died within three months of the accident, either immediately as a result of the explosion and fire, or later from severe radiation damage. Around Chernobyl, about 100 000 people had to be evacuated and rehoused elsewhere. These people will probably be monitored for signs of cancer for the rest of their lives. Existing water supplies were taken out of use, and new wells were drilled up to 100 km away. Elsewhere, radioactive rain

fell on crops in Western Europe and for weeks the sale of milk and fresh vegetables was restricted. In England, farmers were prevented from selling sheep for slaughter. Reactions to the Chernobyl disaster were mixed. On one side were views such as those expressed by the West German newspaper *Handelsblatt*: "Opponents of nuclear energy have a new beacon of light. It is Chernobyl, and in terms of publicity it is already 1 000 times more effective than Three Mile Island." In Brazil the *Folha de Sao Paulo* commented that "The myth of the complete safety of nuclear reactors has collapsed." On the other side, the Israeli newspaper *Yediot Achronot* noted that "Humanity will not give up nuclear energy just because the Soviet Union . . . did not take the necessary precautions to avoid accidents." In France *Le Point* stated that "The Soviet Union has lost all credibility in dealing with the peaceful uses of nuclear energy." The *Indian Express* asserted that "The debate must result in greater international co-operation to prevent or at least minimize such disasters." Meanwhile, Sweden is phasing out its plans for the expansion of its nuclear industry, while Japan plans to expand its nuclear program to account for 60% of the nation's electricity by 1994.

In Canada and the USA, debate focuses largely on whether a similar disaster is possible in North America. Opponents point to the similarities among all nuclear reactors; they use uranium as a fuel and certain special alloys to construct the water (cooling) tubes. Supporters point to basic design differences between Chernobyl and North American reactors, noting that Chernobyl (like Windscale) used graphite as a moderator, while all North American reactors use water as a moderator. Graphite (a form of carbon) is more dangerous because it burns, and water does not. They add that, unlike Chernobyl, North American reactors are housed in extremely thick and strong containment buildings, which cannot be penetrated by even the direct impact of a jumbo jet.

The chance of death from nuclear reactor accidents in North America has been estimated to be about 1 in 300 000 000, compared with about 1 in 4 000 from a car accident, 1 in 25 000 from a fire, 1 in 100 000 from air travel, and 1 in 2 000 000 from lightning. Smoking and obesity are also more significant risks than radiation exposure. An instantaneous radiation dose of 10 000 mSv is needed for immediate death. An instantaneous dose of 1 000 mSv may cause serious nausea, but not immediate death, although there would be a 1 in 100 chance of developing cancer later. Compared with these mega-doses, present doses of "background" radiation are small. They nevertheless increase the chance of cancer by about 1 in 50 000. In other words, the probability of getting cancer is much greater from general radiation than from nuclear accidents. Note, however, that this is true only because nuclear accidents are rare. When they do occur, survivors stand a much greater risk of cancer.

Waste disposal is not a problem/Waste disposal is a problem

Proponents of nuclear energy argue that the quantities of waste produced by a reactor are small enough to be safely contained on-site for many years and that, in the future, either the waste may be re-used in a new fuel cycle or the technology of waste disposal will become so secure that waste disposal will become a minor problem. Opponents argue that waste is so radioactive that it will present a hazard for generations to come and that there will be a continuing and serious risk of water or ground contamination.

A nuclear reactor produces about 100 t of used fuel bundles each year, of which 0.3% is plutonium. The used fuel is extremely hot, each bundle giving off more heat than an electric stove with all four burners on HIGH. It is also extremely radioactive, to the extent that a person could receive a lethal dose within 30 seconds. All used fuel fresh from a reactor is handled by remote control from behind extensive shielding. At first it is stored in deep tanks filled with water, where it loses both its heat and its radioactivity. Within 10 years, as much as 99.9% of the original radioactivity has decayed. It is a general characteristic of radioactive materials that if they emit high levels of radiation they decay (or lose their radioactivity) quickly, but that if they emit only low levels of radiation they retain their radioactivity for long periods of time. The unit of time used to measure the decay of radioactive materials is the half-life, which is the time it takes to lose half its radioactivity.

Plutonium (0.3% of the used fuel) has a half-life of 24 000 years, but emits only low-level radiation. Nevertheless, its presence in the used nuclear fuel bundles is a hazard. Current plans for waste plutonium are of two types. The first, suitable for the CANDU type of reactor, is to recover the plutonium from the used fuel, mix it with fresh uranium and use the mixture to generate more electricity. Waste plutonium can also be mixed with thorium to generate additional electricity. The second plan is to bury it inside sealed containers deep underground in geologically stable areas such as the Canadian Shield. Scientists are experimenting in New Mexico and Sweden to ascertain the best sorts of sealed containers and the most appropriate types of geological formation for long-term storage of nuclear wastes. Canada is pursuing its own experiments at Lac du Bonnet, Manitoba.

The need for long-term burial of nuclear wastes is not yet considered urgent by the nuclear industry, since a reactor produces only about 100 t of waste a year, and existing on-site storage is adequate for many more years. Nevertheless, the nuclear industry needs to be able to guarantee that buried waste products will not contaminate the environment. Its record with on-site storage in deep-water tanks has so far been good, but the industry is aware of the different problems associated with deep burial, especially given the long half-life of plutonium and the risks of contamination of ground water in the future.

The world needs more electricity/The world has enough electricity

This issue is related to the question of industrial growth dealt with in Chapter 4. It relates also to the growth of population discussed in Chapter 2. The matter is one that lends itself to different interpretations, dependent upon a country's collective wishes in terms of overall economic development. In Ontario alone, for example, there are many who argue that the province already has enough electricity generating capacity to meet existing peak load demands, and this is true (peak load in 1985 was 20.5 mkW on December 18, up from the previous record in 1984 of 18 mkW; total capacity permits delivery of about 25 mkW). Others argue that these demands are met only if all generators are working, including those mothballed for

being too expensive or damaging to the atmosphere. In any event, they continue, it is unrealistic to expect all generators to be available for use at all times, since they all need routine maintenance and suffer from periodic problems. They add that, unless generating capacity is increased, Ontario will lose its attractions as a province for industrial investment and growth. What do you think?

It could lead to peace/It could lead to war

These are assertions based on belief rather than factual analysis, and neither peace nor war would conclusively prove the truth of either assertion. Proponents of nuclear energy claim the greater availability of energy will lead to higher living standards and the removal of dangerous dissatisfactions arising out of hunger, poverty and unemployment. Opponents assert that the spread of nuclear energy makes increasingly available a dangerous technology that could be devastating. They point to the risks of terrorism, and the fact that most nations with the capacity to make nuclear weapons also have large nuclear electricity programs. Supporters reply that terrorists have achieved publicity without nuclear technology, that China has nuclear weapons without a strong nuclear energy program, that Canada, Japan, West Germany and Spain all have large nuclear energy programs without having developed the capacity to make nuclear weapons, that the enrichment of uranium ore needed to make weapons runs about 90% compared with 1–3% for nuclear reactors, and that enrichment is a very expensive and technologically advanced process, beyond the capacity of most countries. There is no solution to the dilemma thus posed. Nevertheless, certain questions should be asked:

- What alternative energy souces are available? Are they sufficient to meet present demand? Will they be sufficient to meet future demand?

– What alternative energy sources are available? Should present demand be determined by their availability? Should future demand be restricted by their availability?

– How will the cancellation of nuclear power programs prevent the construction of nuclear weapons? How will the expansion of nuclear power programs aid the construction of nuclear weapons?

– In what ways are nuclear power stations similar to nuclear weapons? In what ways are they different?

– Do weapons delivery systems depend upon the existence of nuclear power plants?

Ontario Hydro

The Bruce nuclear complex in southern Ontario. The rectangular buildings in the fore- and background contain four reactors. Heavy water is manufactured at the site between them. The squared reactor shells are considered more psychologically acceptable than dome or funnel shapes.

Conclusion

The pattern of world energy production is not identical with that of world consumption. Some regions, such as Europe and Asia, experience energy deficits and need to draw upon the surpluses of other areas, such as the Middle East. A growing trend in the world is to aim for greater self-sufficiency in the deficit regions, leading them to decrease waste while developing new energy sources. Meanwhile, the major surplus region, the Middle East, is attempting to preserve its share of the world energy market while also opting to use more of its own supplies for economic development. Must the developed world become a "conserver" society, or will its technological skills permit it to tap new sources of energy? Must the surplus regions continue to support economic growth elsewhere by exporting fuels, or will they succeed in seizing some of the potential for industrial development themselves? While such questions may be difficult to answer, one thing at least is certain: changes in energy production patterns will affect the lifestyles of people around the world. Energy production is one of many factors influencing the quality of life in a nation. In the next chapter we will discuss this complex topic, quality of life.

6 QUALITY OF LIFE

Introduction

Quality of life is a difficult concept to define. It includes such diverse considerations as numbers of people, adequate food and good health, opportunities to pursue different cultural, political and economic aspirations as well as intellectual and spiritual goals, in all cases with regard for a mutually supportive relationship between people and their environments (see Appendix 1). The factors that yield a particular quality of life are unique to each society, and reflect, among other things, its values and technological opportunities. Within a single society, however, different features and opportunities are usually unevenly distributed, so that the quality of life varies. Quality of life thus has a relationship with population trends, resources use, applications of technology, environmental equilibrium and the aspirations of people.

It is equally difficult to specify the features regarded as important to an acceptable or desirable quality of life. Different human beings give priority to different sets of factors. To some people the quantity and quality of food are significant factors affecting the quality of life. To others a desirable quality of life may mean good job opportunities, access to green spaces, women's rights, universal educational opportunities and diverse leisure possibilities.

Bomac Batten Limited.

An apartment building in
Shanghai, China.

A Berber tent in the Atlas
Mountains of Morocco.

A house in Montego Bay,
Jamaica.

A street scene in Aurangabad,
India.

Marilyn MacKenzie

Marilyn MacKenzie

John Molyneux

Marilyn MacKenzie

Greenlanders paddle their kayaks past a glacier.

DISCUSSION AND RESEARCH

1. The photographs illustrate different levels of material existence. How do you think different levels of material existence affect the quality of life?

2. The quality of life available varies substantially throughout the world. To what extent do you suppose the variations are caused by technological differences?

3. Select any single materially developing society. It could have a national, ethnic or religious base. For the society you select, research the non-material qualities that offer support to the people.

4. Make a list of the things that affect the quality of your life: rank ten items (objects, values, opportunities, etc.) in order from the most to the least important. Do other people agree with your list? Does it matter if they do not agree? Why?

In this chapter we will examine the quality of life as it relates to economic development and environmental concerns. The chapter ends with a case study on the role of women in development.

Quality of Life and Economic Development

Any discussion of the factors making up a desirable quality of life centres largely on the subject of choice. Choice is necessitated by the limited nature of our lives, whether material, intellectual or spiritual. We cannot have everything we want, nor fulfil all our dreams; so we choose among those things we most desire and which are available to us.

Societies also must choose. Generally the number of choices available to a society varies with its spiritual and material wealth. Some societies have more resources and can make more decisions regarding their use. Priorities are established; each society determines what it wants to accomplish, and then acts according to these priorities. Should it clear rats from its granaries, for instance, or use its resources to raise the level of literacy? What should be done about a factory that will go out of business if it has to pay for pollution control? It should be noted in this regard that no society is single-minded in its pursuit of a single means to accomplish its goals, or wholly agreed in its definition of its goals. Conflict over social goals and the means to achieve them generates much of the tension within any and all societies.

A society's ability to achieve its priorities depends upon its character and its ability to implement these goals. Some factors are essential for survival and are thus desired by all people. Without them, people will die, or exist in abject poverty. These essential minimum qualities for human life are called basic needs. The provision of basic needs is one of the chief goals of economic development, although there are many different strategies for achieving this goal.

The American Declaration of Independence notes that people have certain "unalienable rights," including "life, liberty, and the pursuit of happiness." In Africa, there is a saying, "Human rights begin with breakfast."

Adequate Food as a Basic Need

Food, of course, is the most basic need. In all countries it is the poor, especially women and children, who get the least food. Data from the World Bank (*Staff Occasional Paper No. 23*, 1978) suggests that in Latin America, for example, the wealthiest 10% of the population consumes 25% more food than it needs, while the poorest 10% consumes almost 30% less than it needs. Similar data are also shown for Africa, Asia and

A study in Bangladesh in 1983 reported that males under 15 had 16% more to eat than females under 15, that males between 15 and 45 got 29% more to eat than females between 15 and 45, and that males over 45 got 61% more to eat than females in the same age range.

the Middle East. The World Bank also notes that while Brazil as a whole consumes more than enough food (105% of its requirements) as many as 35% of its people do not get enough to eat. Data published in *Scope 1986 5* indicated that at least 40% of Canadian children aged 11–14 have at least one medical problem caused by malnutrition, while as many as 1 500 000 children across the country suffer from malnutrition problems related to poverty.

There are proportionately fewer hungry and malnourished poor people in relatively wealthy countries. Libya is about four times wealthier than Brazil on a per capita basis, and only about 5% of its population is reported to lack enough food to eat. Canada and the USA also have hungry people, as the networks of food banks and other charitable organizations attest.

This means that improvements in food availability must be connected to the eradication of poverty through economic development. The problems of economic development appear to be twofold. One problem is to raise the overall per capita wealth of a country. The other is to ensure a more equitable distribution of wealth within a country. National wealth is shared unevenly in all countries, but more unevenly in some than others.

	Percentage of national income received by		Ratio of Richest 20% to Poorest 20%
	Richest 20%	Poorest 20%	
Brazil	67	2	33.5:1
Peru	61	2	30.5:1
Kenya	60	3	20.0:1
Mexico	58	3	19.3:1
Venezuela	54	3	18.0:1
Tanzania	50	6	8.3:1
Canada	40	5	8.0:1
USA	40	5	8.0:1
India	50	7	7.1:1
Sri Lanka	43	7	6.1:1
UK	39	7	5.6:1
Sweden	37	7	5.3:1
Hungary	36	7	5.1:1
Malawi	51	10	5.1:1
Denmark	37	8	4.6:1
Japan	41	9	4.6:1

(Based on data in *World Development Report 1985*)

The income inequalities are greatest among some of the developing countries. On the other hand, some developing countries have a more equitable distribution of income. However, although these countries have been relatively successful in eradicating relative poverty among the poorest sectors of their populations, the problem of small overall national incomes remains.

The countries with the smallest per capita national incomes often face the highest rates of population increase. In these cases, any gains in overall wealth are shared (unequally) by an ever-increasing number of people. At an international conference in Zimbabwe in 1984, for example, the FAO noted that projections to the year 2000 for Africa forecast an average annual population growth rate of 3.4%, but an annual average increase in food production of only 2.6%. From 1974 to 1984, total food production in Africa actually fell by 10%, partly because government policies favoured urban rather than rural dwellers (see Chapter 3) and partly because of prolonged drought. Population grew by about 40% in the same decade.

What can be done? Most authorities now seek ways of eliminating poverty using an integrated basic needs approach to development, examined later in this section. The World Bank insists that "the only practical hope of reducing absolute poverty is to assist the poor to become more productive."

Increasing the productivity of the world's poorest and hungriest people involves improved food production, better health care, more education, greater overall wealth creation, more equitable income distribution, improved housing, cleaner water supplies, better sanitation, reformed landholding systems and the restructuring of many beliefs and attitudes.

Various reports suggest that no particular type of political system in a developing country is any better at producing these improvements in the quality of life. Successes have been achieved by centrally-planned nations such as China and Cuba, by partly socialist countries such as Yugoslavia, mixed economies such as Sri Lanka and full market economies such as Taiwan and South Korea. The important factor seems to be the political will to succeed rather than the type of political organization.

Sri Lanka's record on life expectancy, literacy, and fertility reduction, in relation to its low income level, is widely regarded as one of the best in the world.

For many African countries, the undernourished percentage of their populations clearly increased, and poverty became even more widespread. Zaire's percentage rose from 34 to 44, Niger's from 36 to 47, Mali's from 38 to 49, and Chad's from 34 to 54.

STATISTICAL ANALYSIS

5. Using the data in Columns R and S of Appendix 3, construct a scatter-graph as shown in Appendix 4. Scale the vertical axis to show food production indices (Column R) and the horizontal axis to show population growth indices (Column S). Draw in an *equal change line* (a line that joins all points that represent the same degree of change on one axis

as they do on the other, i.e., 0 and 0, 100 and 100, 200 and 200, etc). Mark in the world indices of 160 (food) and 155 (population) by means of a distinctive symbol. Use contrasting symbols to indicate the continents to which the different countries belong.

a. What does the space below the equal change line mean? What does it say about the quality of life in any country in this space? Which continents have most countries in this space? Can you identify the country that has made the least progress in improving its overall quality of life as measured by food availability?

b. What does the space above the line mean? Which continents are best represented here? Which individual country has made the most progress in improving its quality of life as measured by food availability?

6. Using the data in Column T of Appendix 3 (per capita food production), draw a graded shading map to show four classes as follows:

126 and over	bright orange
101–125	pale orange
76–100	pale black
75 and under	dark black

a. What do you think the class divisions signify?

b. Why are two colours used?

c. In which parts of the world are the countries that have an index of 100 or lower located?

d. Suggest some solutions to their problems.

Literacy as a Basic Need

In its simplest definition, literacy is the ability to read and write. For the purposes of improving the quality of life, however, its wider definition as "basic education" is more useful. The wider definition includes the development of various communication, living and economic skills. Simple literacy data can serve as a marker for basic education.

The number of illiterate people in the world is very much the same as the numbers of poor and hungry people. As with food, women are worse off than men. Of all illiterate people, 60% are women, and in some societies the figure is nearer 80%. Data from the Ministry of Education in North Yemen reveal that only about 15% of primary school children are girls; in the early 1960s only 3% were girls. In societies where illiteracy for the total population is high, frequently almost the entire female population is illiterate. This situation results in personal deprivation, and retards the prospects for improvements in food production, health care and population growth rates. A society's desire for more food is seriously hindered if women, who are often largely responsible

Unicef/Ray Witlin

Literacy is a basic need for societies as well as individuals. The women of Challapata, Bolivia, will be able to take a broader role in their families and community when they can read and write.

for food production, cannot read and write and are not receptive to new ideas. The impact of female education on population growth is more measurable. A 1983 report on Kenya (*Kenya: Population and Development*, World Bank) noted that the average ideal size for a family decreases as the woman's education increases, from 8.7 children for women with no education to 5.7 for women with Grade 11 or higher.

Improvements in literacy can do a great deal to eradicate poverty, but many developing countries are reluctant to increase the share of their already scarce incomes spent on education. This is especially true since changes due to education are less immediate and visible than the results of similar expenditures on roads or irrigation projects. UNESCO noted in 1980 that developing countries as a whole were spending only about 4.5% of their national incomes on education, whereas the developed countries spent 6%. Another difficulty is that some developing countries see mass education as a step toward revolution or as a form of Western imperialism. A further problem has been to define the purposes of education. During the 1960s and 1970s, education was regarded as human

The educational process is lengthy, requires much hard work and does not provide an easily measured pay-off. All we know is that the correlation between an educated workforce and high productivity is significant.

Interestingly, Cuba has stated publicly that the main reason for its literacy program is the conservation of its revolution.

Although literacy is a basic need, some of its effects can be controversial. Teaching Spanish to these Indian children in the Chiapas highlands of Mexico will make it easier for them to interact with the general population, but may dilute their culture.

capital development; that is, the investment in creating a more literate population was similar to any other sort of capital investment because it would eventually generate increased economic growth. However, this approach was criticized for treating people as a technical resource and ignoring their individuality. Other approaches were suggested, such as using mass education to assist people to become more open to the idea of change. In 1979 for instance, John Kenneth Galbraith emphasized the importance of breaking the existing "accommodation to poverty." The chief problem of this approach was that it tended to divide societies between traditionalists and modernists. More recently, at the 18th World Conference of the Society for International Development held in Rome 1985 7, educational "disconnection" was discussed. Some individuals could be "disconnected" from the normal educational mainstream to pursue special educational needs (e.g., apprenticeships, alternative schools, adult literacy programs, etc.).

Despite the problems, many countries push ahead with their literacy programs, particularly the enrolment of children in primary school. Although rapid population growth means that the real number of illiterate people in the world is increasing, the proportion of the population that is illiterate is decreasing. UNESCO forecasts the decline will go from 29% illiteracy in 1980 to 25% illiteracy in 1990, despite an absolute increase in the number of illiterate people in the same period from 814 000 000 to 884 000 000.

The following article from the *UNESCO Courier* illustrates one person's view of the impact of education.

Look closely at these figures. There are clearly two different definitions of illiteracy being used by UNESCO in its publication of these figures. The definition used for the relative figures is different from that used for the absolute figures. How do we know?

"I was made to work like a plough"

by Yusufu Selemani

I had missed the opportunity for schooling during my childhood because the nearest school was forty-three miles [70 kilometres] away. When I grew up I felt very bitter about that. Those were hard times. But now educational facilities have been brought closer to the people — to the village and work-place. And so I was only too happy to take advantage of this great opportunity for learning right here at my factory.

When I was first employed at this factory, I used to face burdensome problems because of my illiteracy. Whenever I was asked to carry a bag of coffee, my supervisor had to accompany me to the store to make sure that I deposited a bag of coffee of a particular grade in the appropriate storage places. Now that I have become literate, I can do this job all by myself without being physically escorted by my supervisor. How can you as an adult and father of children tolerate being treated like a child — "go there, take this, bring that" — all under close physical supervision? But now I can even detect mistakes made in the storage exercise and point them out to the supervisor.

I can now read all the letters I receive from my relatives and friends and I am able to reply to them. I can without anyone's help send money home. Previously I had to beg and implore someone to help me write letters for me to my wife and send her some money whenever she went home. In that process, all my secrets were exposed. It is also possible that the person who writes letters for you to your wife can write a lot of rubbish and you don't know about it.

Literacy has opened our eyes and it has done us such a lot of good that I now believe that if anyone refuses to become literate he should be dismissed from his job. I now realize that when I was illiterate I was made to work like a plough being dragged by a cow and that was a humiliating experience.

The benefits of literacy are innumerable. Now that I have become literate I feel that before I was carrying a small lantern but now a pressure lamp has been brought to me. I can now see much better. I can now hold a pen and sign my own name instead of using a fingerprint.

As a result of literacy I now understand the whys and wherefores of things and because I understand I can now maintain my own self-respect. If I see a signpost which says ''Don't Pass,'' I stop and thereby preserve my self-respect. If I don't obey the instructions I will lose my self-respect. People realize that yesterday and the day before this man used to get his letters written but now he can write them himself.

Literacy has broadened my mind. For example, through literacy primers I have now learned the best methods of growing maize on my little plot of land.

Before, the word education used to terrify me. When you heard that someone had an education you were led to believe that it was something very difficult and inaccessible. Previously it never occurred to me that the so-called educated man must have started from scratch too — that is, by acquiring the basic literacy skills first. Instead, you thought that this man was *born* with education. It was a baffling phenomenon. Education had the aura of some kind of magic. But now I know that anyone can learn and anyone can get an education. I realize that education is a thing that is taught to you and education is development.

Ndugu Yusufu Selemani is a worker at the Tanganyika Coffee Curing Company Limited, Moshi (Tanzania). He is thirty-eight years old and has been working at the factory since 1967. He is married and has five children. He started to learn to read and write in 1975.

UNESCO Courier 1980 6

STATISTICAL ANALYSIS

7. Using any appropriate technique, such as correlative mapping, scatter-graph, or statistical correlation, describe and explain the extent and nature of the correlation between literacy rates and the satisfaction of food needs for the countries of the world, using information in Columns W and O of Appendix 3.

DISCUSSION AND RESEARCH

8. In what ways do you think improvements in literacy can help to eradicate poverty?

9. What do you think are the barriers to improvements in literacy, besides those mentioned in the text?

Good Health as a Basic Need

Good health is partly a matter of adequate food and proper nutrition, and partly a matter of correct sanitation and a disease-minimized environment. All of these correlate highly with basic literacy. Although much has been done in these areas already, poor health remains a serious problem.

Although good health is of universal concern, there are differences in both the nature and extent of concern among the countries of the world. The most common measure of a nation's health is its average life expectancy. Compare the following selection of life expectancies given in Column G of Appendix 3:

Australia	74.3 years	Angola	41.1 years
Austria	72.6 years	Bolivia	48.7 years
Canada	73.9 years	Chad	32.0 years
East Germany	71.6 years	India	45.6 years

However, note Sri Lanka at 69 and China at 67. These are the only two countries among the lowest 25 per capita GNPs in the world with life expectancies of over 60.

A major component of the relatively short life expectancies in developing countries is the very high rate of infant mortality, i.e., the death rate for infants under one year old. In the developing world, infant mortality rates are often more than ten times higher than in the developed world. In some developing countries (e.g., Burkina Faso, Sierra Leone), one baby in five dies before the first birthday. The child death rate (children aged from one to five) in developing countries is also about ten times as high as in developed countries. Throughout much of Africa, for example, about half of all deaths occur among children under five. Even for those who survive past the age of five, average life expectancies are still about 5–10 years shorter than in developed countries. Within their shorter lives the people of the developing world in general suffer more frequently from a wide variety of diseases.

Compare these infant mortality rates: Malawi 169/1000, Benin 152/1000, Bangladesh 135/1000, New Zealand 12/1000, Finland 8/1000, Japan 7/1000.

Some typical child death rates are: Mali 33/1000, Niger 31/1000, Sudan 21/1000, Tanzania 19/1000, Italy 1/1000, West Germany 1/1000.

The factors that cause short life expectancies, high infant and child mortality rates, and adult diseases are numerous and varied. They are aggravated by population growth, overcrowding, lack of education, poor nutrition, insanitary environments and all the other characteristics of general and extreme poverty.

The most widespread diseases are connected with poor sanitation, such as cholera, typhoid, polio and the various intestinal parasitic diseases. Another group of common diseases comes from inhaling bacteria and viruses in dirty and dusty overcrowded conditions. These airborne diseases include tuberculosis, pneumonia, diphtheria, bronchitis, measles and chicken pox.

Helminths are the various types of parasitic worms. It is estimated that over a billion people in the developing world are afflicted by them.

The vector-borne diseases are the third major group, including malaria, sleeping sickness, Chagas's disease, bilharzia and river blindness. These diseases are transmitted by various vectors (or carriers), such as mosquitoes, flies and snails, and are restricted to certain geographical environments. In this respect they are less strongly associated with extreme poverty. Nevertheless, they affect millions.

Vector-borne diseases are easier to deal with in the sense that insecticide spraying does not require people to change their lifestyles. They are also more difficult to deal with in that insecticides are expensive and many vectors have developed immunity to them.

Women launder clothing while vultures scavenge along the banks of the Rio Pamplonita in Colombia. One of the community's most serious health problems, intestinal infection, comes from drinking impure water from the river.

Unicef Photo

Third World Needs Good Pumps

Four-fifths of diseases in the Third World are linked to dirty water or lack of sanitation, says the *New Scientist* in a report on the International Drinking Water Supply and Sanitation Decade of the 80s.

Among them are river blindness, schistosomiasis, malaria and diarrhea, which alone kills about 20,000 children every day.

Three out of five people in the Third World have no easy access to clean water. In rural areas this figure drops to one in three. Women and children often spend most of their day collecting water. In hilly areas of Kenya, women spend nine-tenths of their time on this task.

The problem can be solved for many by making underground water resources more easily accessible by handpumps. UNICEF and the World Bank are both striving to find a design for a hand-pump that is cheap and easy to maintain.

Improvements in sanitation will be harder to achieve. Only one in four people in the Third World has access to any kind of sanitation. In some areas, ignorance and taboos make it difficult to introduce new customs.

Engineers are slowly acknowledging that Western-type sewage treatment cannot be adapted for use in many parts of the Third World.

To achieve a marked improvement by the end of the decade, every day half a million people would have to be provided with better sanitation. The costs for such a project are estimated at $300 to $600 billion over ten years. Currently about $6 to $7 billion are spent yearly.

Legacy, Vol. II, No. 4, 1983, published by the Ontario Ministry of the Environment.

Many of the health problems of developing countries can be treated with current techniques. Sanitation diseases can be countered by good hygiene, better waste disposal, improved water supplies and immunization. Breast feeding can reduce early childhood malnutrition and help protect against many infectious diseases. Airborne diseases can be countered by better ventilation of homes, wider spacing of buildings, a cleaner environment and immunization. All these techniques, however, incur a cost and require an awareness of causation that does not always exist.

Nevertheless infant and child mortality rates are falling. Within the developing world infant mortality rates fell from an average of about 145/1000 in 1965 to about 80/1000 in 1985, but varied greatly in range, as the following statistics indicate:

	Infant deaths/1000			Infant deaths/1000	
	1965	1985		1965	1985
Cuba	54	20	Pakistan	150	119
Costa Rica	74	20	Saudi Arabia	164	101
Sri Lanka	63	37	Sierra Leone	230	198
North Korea	64	32	Somalia	166	142

Similarly, average life expectancies in the developing world increased from about 45 years to about 55 years in the period 1960–1985, but ranged in specific countries from Guinea (32 to 37) and Somalia (34 to 39) to China (41 to 67) and Jamaica (63 to 73). Over the same period, the average infant mortality rate in the developed world fell from 29/1000 to less than 10/1000, and the average life expectancy increased from about 70 years to about 75 years.

The implementation of widespread primary health care in developing countries is largely responsible for these improvements. First efforts to improve health care were generally modelled on programs in developed countries. This tended to produce a number of big-city hospitals serving the urban population. Most developing countries are now shifting their emphasis to primary health care in the countryside, although it is still common for up to 80% of health expenditures to go to treating the 20% of the population who live in the cities. However, primary health care is getting greater attention and funding from many of the developing world's governments. The aim of primary health care is to provide a package of non-physician-related activities such as prenatal care, immunization, midwifery, first aid, nutrition and health education, better food storage, improved sanitation and safer water supplies. China uses thousands of "barefoot doctors" across the countryside. Gambia, mean-

Primary health care, adopted as official policy by the World Health Organization at an international conference in Alma Ata in the USSR in 1978, is partly a sort of preventive medicine designed to create a lifestyle which reduces the risk of becoming sick. It is also partly a defence against much sickness treatable by people with some medical training but who are not physicians. It is a logical policy because there are not enough doctors to care for people who become sick (and become sick repeatedly if their lifestyle does not change).

while, provides local health care workers for all villages with populations over 400; it has immunized about 75% of its children against the most common diseases and pump wells for clean water are installed in almost half its 2 000 villages.

Fig. 6-1
Incidence of river blindness in part of West Africa

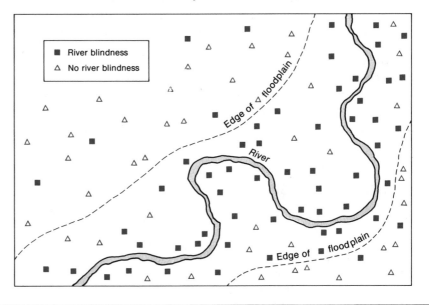

Slow victory over river blindness

By Claude Begin

OUAGADOUGOU, Upper Volta (Reuter) — The common sight of elderly blind men being gently led through the dusty streets of half deserted African villages by young children with swollen limbs should soon become only a bad memory.

For West Africa is winning a decade-old war on river blindness, a disease which has heaped human and economic hardship on millions of people for centuries, according to the World Health Organization (WHO).

Onchocerciasis, more commonly known as river blindness, is a parasitic disease the clinical manifestations of which range from itching, rashes and thickening of the skin to eye lesions leading to total blindness.

Parts of the Near East as well as Central and South America are affected. But the savana area of the Volta basin in West Africa is among the worst onchocerciasis zones in the world.

There are about 100,000 blind victims spread over seven West African nations and an estimated 1 million more, including young children, are suffering from the earlier stages of the debilitating disease.

But now, thanks to a privately financed, WHO-led international campaign, river blindness is being dramatically wiped out, according to Adeline Mate, at the campaign headquarters here.

The crippling disease is transmitted by small black flies which, unlike mosquitoes, breed in fast-flowing water such as waterfalls or dams.

"The black fly transmits a tiny thread-like worm into the body of the victim. These worms multiply under the skin and start reproducing millions of minute parasites which circulate in the body and eventually penetrate the eye," explained Mate.

The link between living near rivers and the risk of onchocerciasis has long been recognized by local people, many of whom have moved from fertile lands to settle in less hospitable, often arid areas, adding economic hardship to human misery.

In 1968 it was decided to take large-scale action against the black fly in order to reopen fertile land to human settlement.

Helicopters and other aircraft poured thousands of tons of insecticide on 11,000 miles [17 500 kilometres] of river.

"It has been a dramatic success and we have eliminated the fly in 80 per cent of our program area, which covered a total of 300,000 square miles [750 000 square kilometres]," Mate said.

WHO reports show that six years after the start of its operations there is a marked decrease in the disease in all the villages treated.

"And the incidence is nil among children under five in most countries while no child under 10 suffers from river blindness in Mali," Mate said.

The success is such that in parts of Upper Volta many people have returned to their riverside dwellings.

The picture is not all rosy, however. There have been several cases of reinvasions in previously fly-free areas, mostly during the rainy seasons.

"We suspect the flies are to be found beyond the original program area, which will have to be extended," Mate said.

And a drug has yet to be discovered to kill the parasite, or at least make it infertile, in the human body.

The program will have to continue for another decade because the parasite has a 20-year lifespan. Only then will the scientists deem it a complete success.

The Toronto Star 1983 6 26

STATISTICAL ANALYSIS

10. Fig. 6-1 is a map showing the locations of settlements in a part of West Africa in which "river blindness" (onchocerciasis) used to be common. Ascertain the ϕ (phi) coefficient of relationship (see Appendix 4) between the incidence of river blindness and the location of settlements on the floodplain of the river. It was the use of such correlative techniques that led to partial control of the simulium fly, which breeds along the water's edges and is responsible for transmitting river blindness.

11. From Column U of Appendix 3, select the 20 countries with the lowest per capita GNP (Gross National Product), excluding Western Sahara, for which data are unavailable. Set up a table with seven columns, and enter the names of the 20 selected countries in the first column in any order. Enter their appropriate per capita GNP data in the second column. In the third column, enter their appropriate life expectancies from Column G of Appendix 3. Use the fourth column to rank the GNP data from 1 (highest) to 20 (lowest). In the fifth column, rank the life expectancy data similarly from 1 to 20. In the sixth column, calculate the difference in rank by subtracting the life expectancy rank from the GNP rank, and head the sixth column "Net excess of life expectancy rank." Some of your answers in the sixth column will probably have negative values. In the seventh column, rank the information in the sixth column from the largest positive number to the largest negative number.

   a. The low GNP data may be taken as an indicator of poverty; the life expectancies as an indicator of health care. What do your calculations in the sixth column tell you about the relationship?

   b. Why do you suppose some countries are doing a much better job of health care than others, even though they may be poorer?

c. Do you think that literacy would be a better basis than GNP for effective health care? Give reasons.

Other Factors

Within any given society it is unlikely that there will be a general coincidence of individual priorities. Some people will want one thing, others another. The differing priorities will tend to be least, however, among people near the survival level. Most of these people will tend to give top priority to their basic needs. As societies secure sufficient food and good health, people see more opportunities, and can make more choices. Attention can be given to a larger variety of desirable life qualities.

Within most societies, wealth tends to be distributed in a more or less hierarchical manner in which the wealthy groups and the poor also tend to have different concerns about the quality of life. The wealthy may want to ban insecticides in order to preserve wildlife; the poor, however, may fear that this will cause food prices to rise. Every society is beset by many such conflicting drives. Even societies operating close to survival level will, because of the largely hierarchical nature of most societies, have differing opinions about many goals and policies.

It is difficult to rank the desired qualities of life. Priorities are established depending on individual tastes. In general, people rank courses of action according to the degree of personal satisfaction they hope to gain measured against the effort needed to succeed. People consider long- and short-term satisfaction and past experience. If the enjoyment is worth the effort, the activity will be accorded a high priority. For example, people will fight and die for political freedom if they value it highly enough. An evening at a theatre may give much satisfaction, too, but people rarely risk their lives for theatre tickets.

Quality of life thus means different things to different people at different levels of development. Most people see the aim of the development process as the provision to all people of as wide a range of choices about their lifestyle as possible, including spiritual and intellectual values as well as material characteristics. Development is, therefore, of people and for people; and the vehicle is raising the quality of life.

A *hierarchy* is a group of people or things arranged in a graduated series. A good example is the army, in which people are put into grades from private to general. Hierarchies also exist in business and in most social organizations. Generally the group at the top receives a larger portion of the group's total rewards. For example, the upper 5% of a society usually receives more than 5% of that society's income.

DISCUSSION AND RESEARCH

12. Many people value certain qualities of life so highly that they refer to them as "rights."

   a. What do they mean by this?

    b. Can "rights" exist?

    c. What happens when different "rights" clash, as for example, the "rights" to jobs and clean water?

13. Is democracy a "right" or a "privilege of achievement"?

14. What do you think the centres of power are in a country? Does the level of development make any difference to the number and type of power centres?

If the rewards are greater than the effort, the activity will gain a high priority.

USSR Embassy Press Office/Ottawa

Development Strategies

Characteristics of Poverty

Poverty is generally hard to define but easy to recognize, partly because it exists in two forms: absolute poverty and relative poverty.

"Absolute poverty" describes a quality of life characterized to an extreme degree by malnutrition, hunger, illiteracy and disease. People living in absolute poverty are at the very margin of survival and are concerned with the provision of basic needs. They are vulnerable to the slightest problem in their environment. Such vulnerability understandably tends to make people cautious and averse to risk. To many of these people the notion of development is a highly risky venture into the unknown, often proposed by a government they distrust or by outsiders they do not know. It involves departures from known techniques and requires a trust many are unprepared to give, since their lives may be at stake.

A drought can kill people living in absolute poverty; they have neither reserves nor alternatives.

Even though the old and tried methods may not have yielded much, they have permitted the survival of those in a position to decide about future courses of actions. To attempt change risks changing their chances of survival for the worse.

"Relative poverty" describes a quality of life below the standards accepted by a particular society. What constitutes poverty varies from country to country. Poverty defined by the Canadian government is different from poverty as defined in Peru. In each case, however, the people living in relative poverty may feel as poor in relation to their society as do those living in absolute poverty in another country. To this extent, relative poverty is a state of mind, although no less real in its characteristics. Relatively poor people, even in a wealthy country, tend to live in more crowded conditions, to have less education and more sickness, to spend larger proportions of their incomes on food and housing, and to eat less nutritious food.

The differences in fact between absolute and relative poverty are more of degree than type. In both cases, their problems can be addressed by development.

Development Strategies to Raise the Quality of Life

There is considerable argument about the most appropriate development strategies to use, ranging from free market operation to centrally controlled planning. Both can point to successes and failures. There is also argument about what is called "bottom up" or "top down" development. Bottom up development stresses that development should be aimed at the grass roots level and expand upward. The advocates of top down theory feel that unless the powerful are involved in development, change will not occur.

Neither view is linked exclusively with free market or centrally planned systems. It is quite possible to have bottom up or top down development in either system. In fact, the likelihood is that both systems will operate more on a top down basis simply because governments tend to be centralized. However, central governments may choose to decentralize much decision-making, and free market systems may add elements of central planning.

International development of whatever philosophy and of whatever approach has had a long history, broadly divisible into colonial and post-colonial eras.

The Colonial Period

Colonial development dates back to the empires of the ancient world, and it always had the well-being of the colonizing country at heart. Nevertheless, its effects on the subject nation were probably never entirely negative. Some people contend the colonial powers provided the essential infrastructure for development: road and rail networks, basic educational and health facilities, administrative organizaton and international linkages.

Critics of colonialism claim that these alleged benefits were provided accidentally as by-products of the need to satisfy the colonizing country rather than to benefit the colony directly. They also point out a number of other problems in the colonial legacy that collectively hinder subsequent development.

For example, the road and rail links were built to connect producing areas with ports, not different internal parts of the country important to the local inhabitants.

One problem has been the lack of national pride. Nationalism exists, but nationalism born through repression and anger that sometimes has not replaced the group and tribal loyalties that are traditionally the focus of such feelings. This is aggravated by imposed colonial boundaries that contain within them groups of people of different languages, traditions and cultures. These often continue into the post-colonial period and render nation-building extraordinarily difficult. Related to this is the continued existence of national armies, taken over by the new rulers at independence and often used as guarantors of personal power rather than as a national defence force.

The rationale of many military dictatorships in the developing world has been (and still is) that the army provides the only coherently organized group in the country.

Another problem of colonized people is the loss of their independence and freedom. Colonials lose their ability to control their destinies, to determine their political and economic future. During the colonial era they lost their apprenticeship in the modernizing world, for it was then that the imperial powers were developing their industries and general wealth. Colonial policies insulated the colonies from these developments. Colonizing countries often practised policies of deliberate neglect and discouraged local initiatives and local industry. Colonies were regarded merely as providers of raw materials and markets for manufactured goods. Even simple and basic items such as matches and candles were often prohibited to local manufacture. Because of the importance given to raw materials, many colonies were forced into single-product export economies, leaving them exposed to the vagaries of world markets and lacking economic depth and variety. For example, Gambia was forced to rely on exporting peanuts, Ghana cocoa, Kenya coffee, Tanzania sisal, Zambia copper and Zimbabwe tobacco. In essence, colonies were forced to produce what they did not consume and consume what they did not produce.

These trade patterns also limited individual countries to developing institutional links with their colonizing country rather than each other, leaving them relatively isolated at independence. Furthermore, these trade patterns were largely controlled by the imperial powers, who set the prices and took the profits. This left little capital in the colonies, a condition which further hindered development after independence.

Colonial administration was usually centralized in the major cities. Thus it was the cities that benefited from medical care, piped water, better sanitation and housing, more schools and so on, creating a widening gap in the quality of life between urban and rural areas. This gap still exists, and has been a persistent development problem in a number of ways.

The Post-Colonial Period

Colonialism gradually ebbed from the globe in the 1950s and 1960s, and a variety of development efforts took its place. Foremost among these have been the plans of the newly independent nations, assisted by the international community, chiefly the United Nations and its various agencies. Also important have been the efforts of individual nations, such as the USA, the UK, France and Canada. Additional help has come from a number of non-governmental organizations (NGOs) such as Oxfam, the Red Cross and various church groups.

Some development efforts from the international community have concentrated on the provision of infrastructure, others on farm and industrial programs and still others on the needs of specific target groups. The thrust of development is gradually moving away from providing export markets for the industrially developed nations toward raising the material quality of life in the developing nations.

Raising the quality of life of the people in developing nations and

The great gap in the perceived quality of life between urban and rural areas has attracted millions of rural dwellers into the cities. The cities cannot cope, and now pose major problems throughout the developing world.

providing them with more opportunities is at the heart of what is now called *basic needs development*. This is not a particular strategy, nor does it arise out of a particular political philosophy. It is instead a statement of the purpose of development and provides a cohesive organizational framework. Its aims are to create integrated development in food production, health care, education, housing and so on. A further aim is to encourage people to feel productive, to develop their initiative and self-reliance and to expand their choices.

The value of the basic needs concept lies in its integrative approach. It forces simultaneous development on a number of fronts. For example, sanitation and hygiene depend on education, which in turn depends upon good health; all are linked to good nutrition. Action in one sector without corresponding action in another may actually be counterproductive, as when water is supplied without drainage thus attracting insects that spread disease. An integrated basic needs approach avoids both costly duplication and counterproductive waste.

Nevertheless, many are opposed to basic needs development. They most commonly object to the program's paternalism. People are provided (often by outsiders) with services over which they often have no control and which may be unrelated to their actual wants. Critics feel that a better way is to raise the incomes of the poor and then let them decide how to spend their money. Another objection is that basic needs development uses money that might otherwise be invested in overall economic growth. Industrialization is seen by many as the route to wealth and power. People in middle-income countries fear that developed nations will reduce aid to them in order to provide more aid to meet the basic needs of lower-income countries. Many industrialists in developing countries also fear that a basic needs approach will restrict their growth by reducing the amount of money available for investment. Because this would also reduce their ability to compete in the developed world's markets, they view any pressure from the developed nations to institute basic needs policies as a disguised form of protectionism. Others feel that basic needs development is so all-encompassing and dependent upon assistance from the developed countries that it could endanger their newly won independence. Still others see it as irrelevant in view of their existing projects of job creation, rural development and so on.

Objections to paternalism are rooted in the belief that individual people should decide for themselves what their own needs are. These objections are countered by those who claim that people should be encouraged to participate in the decisions about their needs. These claims are discounted by still others who say that needs are personal and not subject to group decision.

Quality of Life and Levels of Development: Three Examples

The world has never been uniform nor is it uniform now. Great differences exist from one part to another and, because of the highly uneven nature of development, the differences may be greater now than in the past. Nevertheless, most people divide the world conceptually into only a few parts. Some classify it into a rich and industrialized North and a poor and largely agricultural South; others use a political division into the West, the Communist bloc, and the Non-Aligned nations; still others see an economic basis for classifying the world broadly into the market-oriented First World, the centrally-planned Second World, and the developing nations of the Third World. All recognize, however, that the world is really much more complex than the use of these simple labels indicates.

The use of examples is a bit like the use of labels; but the real world is too complex to portray it completely. Examples must therefore represent much more than they are themselves. With this precaution in mind, we will use three examples to illustrate the quality of life at three different levels of development: Colombia from the Third World, the USSR from the Second World, and the USA from the First World.

Third World Development: Colombia

Colombia stands at the high end of what the World Bank classified in 1985 as the lower middle-income countries of the world. It is in many ways characteristic of Third World countries.

Colombia has an area of 1 138 914 km², a population of about 29 000 000, with a density of just over 25 people/km². Its people are, on the whole, relatively well fed, consuming about 107% of the food they need, although there are slight protein deficiencies in their diet. Average daily protein intake is 48 g against a recommended per capita norm of 56 g/d. The distribution of food is by no means even throughout society, although specific data are not available. Per capita GNP is about US$1 380/y, compared with a world average per capita GNP of about US$2 470: this figure ranks Colombia approximately equal with Tunisia, and Turkey. Colombia's total GNP is only about the same as that of Kuwait, which has a population only one-fifteenth the size of Colombia's. The projected rate of population growth to the year 2000, at 1.8%/y, is about the same as the world average, having come down from 2.6%/y in the 1960s and 1.9%/y in the 1970s. Nevertheless, Colombia's total population is predicted to increase to nearly 37 million by the year 2000, and to 60 000 000 by the year 2010. Meanwhile, population is increasing more slowly than food output, largely because Colombia emphasizes integrated rural development projects.

Life expectancy of the average Colombian increased from about 55 years in 1965 to about 63 years in 1985, and the literacy rate is now over 80%. Infant mortality has been cut from about 80/1000 (1965) to 53/1000 (1985), while the child death rate in the same period was reduced from 8/1000 to 3/1000. There is one nurse for every 800 people, and one doctor for every 1 700 people; and about 50% of its teenagers are enrolled in secondary school. Annual per capita energy consumption is about 800 kg coal equivalent, although per capita electricity production, at about 900 kW·h, is relatively low, as can be seen in Column P of Appendix 3.

These statistics tell of considerable success in raising the quality of life above that often associated with the Third World. Comparisons with other countries in the Third World show that Colombia is performing better than some in some areas and worse in others. Its life expectancy, for example, is significantly higher than Bolivia's although markedly lower than Cuba's.

Part of the reason for Colombia's success has been its integrated rural development policies. Started in 1970 with a few pilot projects, the integrated rural development program initially emphasized agricultural technologies to help small farmers increase output without making major changes in their routines. The goal was to improve their food supplies and reduce their overall poverty. By the mid-1970s the number of pilot projects increased to twenty. At the same time, the Colombian government incorporated the idea of integrated rural development into its national development policy. Since then attention has been paid to the needs of existing commercial farmers for improved access to new technology and of small subsistence farmers for access to both credit and agricultural education as well as technology. For the most part, the Institute of Colombian Agriculture (ICA) assists small farmers to develop their existing knowledge of multi-cropping rather than introduce radical changes. In addition, ICA emphasizes diet and nutrition education, health services and literacy training. The extent of local community involvement in the program can be seen from the fact that the central agency for co-ordinating the rural development program has never had more than 95 employees.

Signs of Colombia's increasing
material prosperity. Above, new
housing for the Colombian middle
class in Bogota. Below, highrises
in downtown Bogota reflect
Colombia's growing commercial
sector.

The integrated rural development program has increased agricultural production. However, there is agreement more work is needed on the educational and health components. Nevertheless, because the program has raised the basic quality of life for many people in the rural areas, its emphasis is now shifting to increased food production. New target areas (the program is not yet in effect throughout the entire country) are chosen more for their agricultural potential than their poverty. Education and health programs of these areas are being addressed by the extension of existing institutions.

Colombia's industrial output is increasing at about 2–3%/y, only slightly more quickly than population. This means that the availability of industrial products to people is expanding only relatively slowly. For example, only one person in ten has a radio, one in 17 a TV, and one in 60 a car. Part of the reason for the limited availability of such goods is that much of Colombia's industrial production is concentrated on basic items. Processed food, fertilizers and textiles account for about 60% of total production, compared with about 30% in Canada, 35% in Brazil, 45% in India, and 75% in Pakistan). Another reason could be cultural: David Morawetz, in a World Bank research publication (*Why the Emperor's New Clothes Are Not Made in Colombia*, 1981) reported many Colombians who were interviewed made it clear they do not highly value material wealth. As one person said, "Colombia is a country of mañana, a country of fiestas. . . . We like to have a good time while we work. . . . I wouldn't like to live under the sort of discipline and policing the Americans have even if it would make us richer."

Second World Development: The USSR

The communist world includes both developed and developing countries. The developed part is known as the Second World. It includes Eastern Europe and the USSR and operates in an economic collective called the Council for Mutual Economic Assistance (COMECON). Its economic system is centrally planned.

The USSR is not atypical of Second World countries. It is a vast land, more than twice the size of Canada. Its population of about 275 000 000 ranks it third behind China and India. The land is rich in natural resources, with the USSR ranking fourth in the world in terms of total wealth as indicated by GNP and equivalent USSR data (after the USA, Japan and West Germany). However, its per capita figure of US$2 600 ranks it 44th, approximately equal with Argentina, Chile, Poland, Portugal, Romania, South Africa and Uruguay.

The total quantity of food available to the population is sufficient, but meat is scarce and lacking in variety. The government has encouraged farmers to increase meat production by feeding part of the grain harvest to livestock, although this has led to some shortages of wheat. The USSR thus often purchases large supplies of wheat on world markets.

There are serious housing shortages in the major Soviet cities, and people often have to share small rooms and kitchens. For example, about 1 000 000 of Moscow's population of 8 000 000 live in shared-family accommodation. On the other hand, despite the scarcity of housing, government subsidies make the available accommodation relatively inexpensive.

Soviet industrial output is largely geared to capital goods and military needs. Although there has been a persistent effort through a series of five-year plans to increase the supply of consumer goods, their availability is erratic. The USSR does not release data, but reports from visiting Western journalists indicate a growing availability of goods encumbered by a number of problems in manufacture and distribution.

One significant problem is a shortage of computers. The Ninth Five-Year Plan published in 1971 endorsed the idea of creating a vast computer network across the entire USSR, linking organizations at every level of economic activity and ensuring the efficiency of the central planning principle. This has not yet happened. It is estimated that only about 35% of even the largest enterprises, and virtually none of the smaller enterprises, had computers by 1985.

Despite both the excellent educational and medical services (literacy almost 100%; proportion of teenagers enrolled in secondary school 97%; 1 doctor for every 270 people; 1 nurse for every 100 people; infant mortality probably about 10–15/1000, although current data are not available), concern is being expressed about life expectancy, especially for men. Women tend to live longer than men, but the difference is now wider in the USSR than elsewhere. Soviet men now have an average life expectancy of 62 years, down from 70 years in 1970. For Soviet women the figure is 76 years, up from 74 years. The Paris-based National Institute of Demographic Studies accounts for the decline in Soviet male life expectancies by citing a deteriorating standard of living, alcoholism, industrial accidents, tobacco addiction, and armament expenditures cutting into health services.

Political freedom is another concern to some Soviet citizens. In law it exists for all, but in practice there are many for whom it does not. There is, for example, only one official political party, and social, political and economic advancement often depend upon party membership. Travel into other political jurisdictions is severely restricted and sometimes impossible. Nationalist minorities such as Latvians, Kazakhs and Ukrainians are forced, as parts of the USSR, to conform to Russian-directed policies. Political dissent is discouraged and many so-called "dissidents" find themselves in prisons, psychiatric wards or exile.

In 1985 the new Soviet leader, Mikhail Gorbachev, ruled that liquor stores should be open for only a couple of hours a day in order to reduce the time lost on the job to alcoholism.

Only a minority of Soviet citizens actually belong to the Communist Party.

USSR Embassy Press Office/Ottawa

Reindeer are a major source of meat in the USSR's vast northeastern region. Mikhail Rakhtul, a holder of the Order of Lenin, leads a reindeer-breeding team.

In 1986 a document addressed *To The Citizens of the Soviet Union* was made available to *The Guardian* newspaper in England and NBC TV in the USA by some senior officials in Moscow. It stated that "The Soviet Union lags 10–15 years behind the capitalist countries in its economic development, and this lag is growing. The USSR is now on the path to becoming one of the underdeveloped nations." It added that the Soviet people's standard of living is one of the lowest in the industrialized world and that food shortages are causing a rising infant mortality rate. The report went on to say that "the eternal hunt for the most basic goods and small everyday things leaves people neither the time nor physical strength to satisfy their spiritual and cultural needs, and is killing their human dignity." The document called for reforms, arguing against the "abuse of power and other chronic diseases natural to a party permanently in power" and recommending the creation of "different political organizations, all with the aim of building a socialist society" that would be in the best interests of the workers, farmers and intelligentsia. The document concluded with an appeal to the Soviet public to discuss the issues and to write to the press and TV about its proposals.

First World Development: The USA

The First World consists chiefly of the countries of North America, Western Europe, Japan and Australasia, all operating independently under a system of market planning, but all members of the Organization for Economic Co-operation and Development (OECD). The USA is not particularly typical of the group, but it is by far the most dominant, and its lifestyle influence, spread by film and TV, is pervasive.

The USA is a large, well-populated, rich and powerful nation. It is the world's chief producer of food and industrial goods, and the world's chief market for the products of other countries. Both socially and economically, its people generally live well. Its total GNP is the highest in the world, and its per capita GNP (US$12 820) ranks 9th.

Life expectancy in the USA is about 75 years (79 for women, 72 for men); infant mortality is 11/1000; there is one doctor for every 520 people and one nurse for every 140 people; and the people generally have access to ample food of great variety. Literacy is almost 100%; 97% of its teenagers are enrolled in secondary school, and the proportion of them going on to higher education is the highest in the world (58%, compared with 39% in Canada, 30% in Japan and 21% in the USSR). Per capita energy consumption is extremely high at about 10 000 kg/y coal equivalent (compared with about 7 500 kg/y in the USSR).

Its people have a large measure of political freedom. They may choose among political parties and are free to travel as they wish. Minority groups are to some degree encouraged to join the mainstream on the melting-pot principle, but have not been forced to. There has recently been an awareness that other cultures have something to offer, and educational systems are increasingly offering foreign language classes (especially Spanish).

On the other hand, in November of 1986 Californians passed a law making English the state's "official language," an act aimed at blocking the funding of Spanish-language services to a rapidly growing Hispanic population.

Nevertheless, the USA has its problems. One is racial prejudice. This is reflected in a number of ways, such as in the shortage of blacks in high-paying jobs or the reluctance of many whites to live in areas populated by even small numbers of blacks. Black ghettos are a feature of the geography of nearly all large US cities. Blacks also represent a disproportionately high number of those below the official poverty line. In the mid-1980s the US had about 33 000 000 people living below the official poverty line; 28% were blacks (35% of all blacks), although blacks make up only about 11% of the total population. Immigration from Latin America is adding another layer to the existing social hierarchy; since around 1960 Hispanics have become the largest component of the normal immigration flow, and now make up about 6% of the total population. As many as 28% of them, however, live below the official poverty line.

Another major concern to many is the violence of much US life. Approximately 200 000 handguns are sold in the USA each year, and almost 10 000 people are killed by them. Individual poverty is also a problem, characterizing most urban slums and occurring in rural pockets such as parts of West Virginia. However, whereas in 1960 the proportion of the total population living below the official poverty line was 22%, it had fallen by the mid-1980s to 14%.

Despite these problems, the people as a whole enjoy a standard of living and a quality of life that are the envy of much of the rest of the world. The situation is well illustrated by the activities along the border with Mexico, where the US has built a huge fence to keep illegal Mexican migrants out, patrolling it on a 24-hour basis with helicopters and ground squads with night-vision binoculars and guard dogs. As many Mexicans say, "All you do in the US is work hard and earn a lot of money; all we do in Mexico is work hard." The quality of life in the USA is a lure to many.

Immigration into the USA far exceeds that into any other country in the world.

Christmas in Idaho. The average American family enjoys an enviable standard of living.

K.C. Bell

A Development Game

In trying to forecast the future, experts often use games theory to see how a situation may be resolved. It is possible for us to study development opportunities in a simple form by means of a game. Salient problems may be reduced to symbols in a model (see Fig. 6-2), and the game rules applied.

Fig. 6-2
The survival model

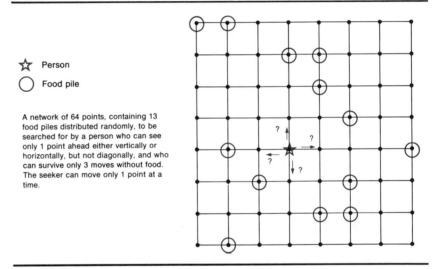

☆   Person

◯   Food pile

A network of 64 points, containing 13 food piles distributed randomly, to be searched for by a person who can see only 1 point ahead either vertically or horizontally, but not diagonally, and who can survive only 3 moves without food. The seeker can move only 1 point at a time.

In the survival model the network of lines represents a society's environment. The food piles represent the chances of survival. There are three main components of the game:

- the number of food piles, or survival chances, available to the society, randomly distributed in the environment;
- the length of time the seeker is able to survive without finding a food pile, namely three moves;
- the distance the seeker can see ahead, namely one point at a time.

As you examine the environment from outside it is fairly obvious which points the seeker should follow, but to the seeker, who can see only one point ahead, the right path is obscure.

At the simplest level, the seeker (society) wanders along, finding food piles by chance. Perhaps the seeker follows the same pattern over and over as the annual harvest renews the food piles, and survives. The seeker who fails to discover a successful pattern fails to survive.

As the seeker (society) becomes more aware of the environment's patterns, three new ways of improving the survival situation become apparent. First, the number of food piles (the material wealth of the society) can be increased, which means that supplies are more readily available. Second, the seeker can be allowed to survive more than three moves. This may mean that the society gains improved storage capacities or health services. Third, the seeker can be allowed to see more than one point ahead. In other words, education and other information services available to society are improved.

The development game undoubtedly has limitations, but it stresses the importance of wealth creation, the need for buffer stocks and the significance of improved health and education levels.

Gatherers and hunters, and then farmers?

One of the longstanding beliefs in much of the academic community has been that a bounteous environment inhibits human effort, that people in fact need a challenge.

Satellites provide excellent information about the environment; most countries use the information, even if they lack satellites of their own.

STATISTICAL ANALYSIS

15. Set up the survival model as a game between two sides. One side distributes the food piles (fewer than 13 to make the game harder, more to make it easier) in a pattern unknown to the other side. The seeker can start anywhere, and is permitted to know what, if anything, lies at the adjacent vertical and horizontal points only. After a one point move in any vertical or horizontal direction the seeker is again permitted to know what lies at the adjacent vertical and horizontal points. The seeker is allowed three unsuccessful moves before failing to survive. Variations of the game should be tried, using:

  — more or fewer food piles;
  — longer or shorter survival periods;
  — the ability to see farther ahead than one point.

a. Which of these variables is in practice the one most likely to influence the outcome of the game?

b. In order to guarantee survival in real life do you suppose it would be better for a society to put its development effort into more wealth creation, more capital accumulation and storage, or improved education?

c. Does the game say anything about economic growth versus basic needs development?

Danish diners enjoy the traditional "long table."

The Danish Tourist Board

DISCUSSION AND RESEARCH

16. To what extent do you think the quality of life in North America depends upon the amount of aid which it provides to the developing world?

17. It has been said that the world is like "four people and four apples." What do you suppose this means? How would you respond?

18. Is there a "geography of happiness"? Explain your answer.

Environment and the Quality of Life

People have always depended on their environment as a provider of resources. In their quest for a better quality of life, people have also changed their environments, a fact which has offered both positive and negative consequences for the quality of life.

Initially, gatherers and hunters tended to deplete certain favoured plant and animal species, but the environment was generally rich and the impact small. Migration soon produced access to fresh supplies. Later the discovery of farming had more massive effects. Certain species of plants were favoured, while unwanted ones were called weeds and discarded. Forests were cleared to create new farmland; irrigation systems disturbed existing water patterns; terraced hillsides changed the face of the landscape. The domestication of certain animals guaranteed their survival, while other animals that competed with or preyed on the domesticated ones were hunted and destroyed.

The growth of trade renewed pressure on the forests, since timber was needed for ships. The forests of the eastern Mediterranean, the centre of early Western civilization, had virtually disappeared 2000 years ago. A thousand years ago, the demands of migrating farmers almost destroyed the forests of Western Europe. Five hundred years ago, building the navies of Spain, Portugal, France and England required the virtual destruction of what was left.

Industrialization began about 200 years ago, and accelerated human impact on the environment. At the same time, populations began to increase rapidly and, in industrialized areas at least, expectations relating to the quality of life began to rise. The environment was, therefore, forced to provide more resources than ever before and to deal with the increasing quantities of waste products generated.

So great has been the impact of industrialization that we need to examine environmental concerns relating to the quality of life in two groups: the non-industrial and the industrial.

Some Non-Industrial Environmental Concerns

Over the world as a whole, degradation of non-industrial environments is a massive problem and its effects on the quality of life are severe.

Over two thousand years ago, while ancient Greek philosophers bemoaned the deforestation of the hillside by grazing goats, the Chinese had virtually completed the removal of their eastern forests for new farmland.

Even as recently as the 1950s, big game was hunted in East Africa partly because it was thought to pose a threat to domesticated animals. Game animals were believed to carry the tsetse fly.

In Ivory Coast the destruction of the coastal forests by new farmers was so severe that the government had to prohibit further expansion and designate the remaining forest a National Park. Meanwhile, in many cities, shanty towns are forced to occupy unused hillsides, stripping them of vegetation cover and heightening the risk of soil erosion and landslides.

Deforestation can be a serious environmental problem. Unless conservation measures are taken, the topsoil on this Guatemalan mountainside will erode, making significant reforestation difficult.

The deterioration of natural systems (see Appendix 1) in some developing countries is partly a symptom and partly a cause of the low quality of life endured by millions. People are forced by survival needs to destroy the very resources that give them life.

Burdened by rapid population growth, people clear and plant land unsuited for farming. They clear plots in the rain forest by slash and burn methods, exposing the infertile soils to erosion. They cause erosion by ploughing and cropping hillsides too steep for farming. They dig and plant in areas too dry for farming, causing dustbowls, and move increased numbers of livestock into areas already grazed to the limit, causing overgrazing and destruction of vegetation cover. In cities, the poor build illegal and unserviced shanty towns, then have to live in all the diseases of overcrowded insanitary conditions.

The degradation of the environment causes the life-support base to be further eroded, lowering even more a quality of life already sinking under the combined pressures of disease, malnutrition and population growth.

There are four main areas of concern. Let us look briefly at them.

John Molyneux

Deforestation

Throughout the developed world the total area of forest has stabilized and even increased as a result of public pressure and tree-planting programs. It is in the developing world, containing over half the world's forests, that the problem is acute. The present forest area in the developing world is about 1 200 000 000 ha, but it is being consumed at an increasing rate (about 20 000 000 ha/y in the mid-1980s). The increasing rate, coupled with increasing populations, means that existing forests will be gone by the year 2025 unless reforestation and conservation practices are introduced. It will have mostly disappeared for fuel, for new farmland and for building material.

The developing world also contains about 75% of the world's population and about 95% of the world's farmers.

Deforestation also causes other environmental damage. Soil erosion becomes more common, leading to increased silting of river beds (hindering navigation) and reservoirs (restricting their capacity to hold irrigation waters). Flooding also increases as the water-retaining capacity of hillside forests and soils is reduced. Dry weather stream flow is reduced for the same reason and dustbowls are created. In wider terms, the oxygen-producing cycle of the earth is endangered.

As a result of deforestation in the Himalayas, floods now affect 8 000 000 ha more of northern India than before deforestation.

Trees, like all plants, take in carbon dioxide and free oxygen, keeping the carbon as part of their structure.

Just as the developed countries gradually realized the benefits of forest conservation, so are some developing countries. Governments are taking the lead, especially in getting fast-growing trees planted in rural areas. South Korea has established a village woodlot program to supply firewood; the Philippines provides seedlings and advice throughout the countryside; Kenya has developed a home-garden program for quick-growing thorn and eucalyptus for firewood. The impact of these initiatives is so far small, but they are a beginning.

Desertification

Desertification is the process by which productive land is turned into a desert. The first modern example was the North America dustbowl of the 1930s. It has not, however, been the last. The most recent is now occurring in the lands along the southern edge of the Sahara Desert. The situation there is aggravated by the normal tendency of the persistent northeast trade winds to blow sand southward.

These lands are known collectively as the Sahel. Sahel is from an Arabic word meaning "border zone."

Under severe pressure from increasing human and animal populations, the Sahelian countries have suffered a degradation of their environment that has led to persistent and widespread famine. UNESCO estimates that about 20% of the total land mass of Africa is undergoing desertification, with around 80 000 000 people directly affected by the accompanying food and fuel shortages.

Contamination of Water Supplies

In non-industrial areas, water supplies may be contaminated by insect pests, human and animal wastes and agricultural chemicals.

Insect contaminants may be in the water, such as those that thrive in the bilharzia snails and whose impact is spreading in the tropics as irrigation systems are extended. Other contaminants may be only associated with water through breeding needs, living on the surface or along humid banks and biting those who live or work nearby. Mosquitoes and simulium flies are examples.

The impact of these vector-borne diseases is considerable. Bilharzia is spreading in nearly all the water-based cultures (i.e., cultures reliant on widespread irrigation) of hot lands. It exists in China, Egypt, Africa, South America, the Middle East and Indo-China. Malaria is even more widespread in the tropics, where it aggravates malnutrition by driving people through fear of malaria from the more fertile river lands. The bite of the simulium fly causes blindness, making people avoid fertile alluvial areas, although in West Africa the fly has been brought under control.

Contamination of water supplies by human and animal wastes is an even larger problem in the developing world. It leads to a number of parasitic diseases as well as to cholera, typhoid and polio. These diseases have a significant impact on the quality of life for those who have them.

Contamination of water by agricultural chemicals is much more a problem of the developed countries. Fertilizers and pesticides eventually drain into rivers and lakes. Fish are the first victims, but all eaters of contaminated fish — birds, wildlife and people — are affected. The problem is much more serious in Western Europe than in North America, because the quantities of chemicals used per hectare of cropland are much greater there. Per hectare use of fertilizer on cropland in Canada, for example, is only 432 t, and in the USA only 1 116 t. In Western Europe, however, Belgium uses 4 990 t, Ireland 6 182 t, Netherlands 7 888 t and Switzerland 4 476 t. Other Western European figures are similarly high. The Rhine is often described as the most polluted river

Successful control of the simulium fly has taken place mostly in the valley of the Volta, largely with Canadian aid. However, since the dangerous helminths can survive in the human body for up to 14 years, and since any bite of a human carrier by a simulium fly can start the cycle again, there is a clear need for continued action for many more years.

The period 1981–90 was declared by the UN to be "Drinking Water Supply and Sanitation Decade."

Shoe

Copyright: Jefferson Communications Inc. (1984); Distributed by TMS; Reprinted with permission Toronto Star Syndicate.

in the world; however, its pollutants extend far beyond agricultural chemicals.

Destruction of Cropland

Where the developing world is concerned over soil erosion and desertification, a similar concern exists in the developed world over the destruction of cropland. The USA is said to be losing topsoil through soil erosion at the rate of about 100 000 000 t/y. It is also losing productive farming areas at the rate of about 500 000 ha/y, land which is being lost to new roads, urban expansion, subdivisions and so on. Canada experiences proportionately similar rates of loss.

Erosion is a natural process; it is usually balanced by deposition elsewhere. Soil eroded from higher land is usually deposited in river lowlands or deltas.

Most soil erosion is a product of ignorance or laziness. Farmers who cause it plough with the slope instead of across it or leave fields fallow without a cover crop. Monoculture gradually exhausts the soil and growing open crops without a filler crop exposes the soil between the rows. The problem is a quiet but persistent one, and not all farmers have learned the techniques for dealing with it.

The chief solution to monoculture is crop rotation.

Some Industrial Environmental Concerns

Environmental concerns related to industry are numerous, varied and severe. Some of these were covered in Chapter 4. Let us look here more closely at industrial pollutants.

The range of environmental pollutants produced by industry is large and includes such items as inadequately tested drugs (e.g., thalidomide), improperly dumped poisons (e.g., mercury, dioxin), and incompletely processed residues (e.g., sulphur, nitrogen oxides). No place is safe from these pollutants unless control measures are installed.

Pollutants are those materials that either by quantity (e.g., carbon dioxide) or by quality (e.g., dioxin) cannot be handled by the natural cleaning action of the various environmental cycles.

Control is slow in coming. Some countries see the costs of control as uneconomic in terms of the demand for more production. Brazil, for example, has been called the "World's Worst Polluter" by the United Nations, but Brazil is desperate for industrial growth and modernization. The USSR is reported to be "first" among Europe's polluters because of its desire for industrial production. Similar situations exist in India and south and southwest Asia. North America also experiences serious industrial pollution, but because of public pressure has begun to install pollution controls. For example, it restricts the use of leaded gasoline. There are also legal requirements to reduce polluting emissions. But problems remain, partly because of the size and variety of North American industry, partly because of the difficulties in monitoring such a massive operation and partly because not all governments are yet convinced by public pressure to act, especially as scientists often disagree over the evidence. For example, in 1986 US scientists were arguing over the

Air pollution hangs over Delhi, India. In many places, the desire for economic growth is so great that environmental and health threats remain unaddressed.

effects of acid rain, some (such as Hubert Vogelmann of the University of Vermont) saying that acid rain killed trees, others (such as William Brown of the Hudson Institute) saying that it has never been shown to be the principal cause of any of the environmental problems of which it is accused.

From among the great variety of industrial pollutants, let us look more closely at one: dioxin.

Dioxin is regarded by many as one of the most serious environmental hazards produced by industry. It is produced by the burning of almost anything, and is thus created by many electricity generating plants as well as by all industrial operations that use burning for any purpose whatsoever. It is also produced by incinerators, woodstoves, coal fires, outdoor barbecues, camp fires, forest fires and cigarette smoking.

Dioxin is a compound of hydrogen, oxygen, carbon and chlorine. It is the presence of chlorine in the compound that makes it a dioxin. There are as many as 75 different types of dioxin, and about 135 associated compounds called furans. The many different types of dioxins and furans vary greatly in toxicity; the most deadly is considered to be second only to plutonium and 10 000 times more lethal than DDT. Theoretically, it would take only 1/200th of a drop of this particular dioxin to kill a person, compared with as much as 400 drops of arsenic.

The seriousness of the dioxin problem is still a matter of scientific debate. Its effects on people have been documented as a result of accidents and other chance exposures to the chemical. In 1949 an accident at a chemical plant in West Virginia exposed 200 workers to dioxin; they suffered headaches and nausea, but there were no recorded long-term effects. During the Vietnam War many soldiers were exposed to the dioxin contained in the defoliant Agent Orange. They suffered a variety of health problems and in 1984 were collectively awarded US$250 000 000 as compensation. In 1976 an explosion at a chemical plant in the Italian town of Seveso exposed 35 000 people to dioxin; they suffered nausea and skin rashes and, although many birds, rabbits, chickens and plants died soon after the accident, no people died and no long-term effects have shown up in the population. In the early 1980s people in the area of the Love Canal in Niagara Falls, New York, were evacuated because dioxins were leaking from previously dumped industrial wastes; the buildings of the community were subsequently destroyed.

The evidence of dioxin's effects on human beings is not clear. As a result, many scientists assert that dioxin is not really the hazard some people think. On the other hand, there are those who claim that any hazard is too great.

DISCUSSION AND RESEARCH

19. Select two: cholera, typhoid, malaria, dysentery, river blindness (onchocerciasis), bilharzia (schistosomiasis), sleeping sickness (trypanosomiasis). Research their causes and symptoms and describe their direct and indirect effects on the quality of life.

20. Which forms of pollution are easiest to deal with? Which are the most difficult? Why?

21. Does development mean replacing one set of environmental problems with another set?

22. Which world has the worst pollution: the developed or the developing? (What does worst mean: worst in quantity, worst in type, worst in its effects, worst to deal with?)

23. What do you think of the concept of risk? Is some risk acceptable? Or only some types of risk? Or no risk at all?

Assessing the Quality of Life

The problems of assessing the varying qualities of life around the world are enormous because quality is more difficult to judge than quantity. How, for example, do you compare the value of a forest with a seascape? Or the ability to hear a live concert performance with the ability to hear the cry of the loon on a northern lake?

We will, nevertheless, try an assessment. There are two ways in which it may be approached: we can select many criteria and apply them to a few sample countries; or we can use a single representative criterion and apply it to all countries. Neither method will give us a total picture, but the alternative of applying many criteria to all countries is difficult without the use of a computer.

We will use both methods, to make the map produced in assignment 25 more meaningful. The criteria to be used are listed in Fig. 6-3. Since we can use only items for which measurable data are available, we must omit religious freedom or minority rights, efficiency, the moral climate and so on. These factors can influence the quality of life considerably, but we cannot assess them numerically.

STATISTICAL ANALYSIS

24. Use the technique of *percentage deviation from the mean*, as explained in Appendix 4.

    a. For each group of data, for the different criteria given in Fig. 6-3 calculate the group mean (i.e., the mean of data group A, then the mean of data group B, etc).

    b. Calculate the percentage deviation of each datum from its appropriate group mean.

    c. Decide whether deviations above or below the group mean add to (+) or subtract from (−) the quality of life. Insert appropriate + or − signs to all your calculated percentage deviations. Thus, if R represents road deaths per million people, then the fewer the better, so a deviation of 41 below the mean would be a plus (+41). If, however, W represents average weekly dollar wages, then the more the better, and a deviation of 41 below the mean would be a negative quality (−41). Use your judgment in this part of the exercise.

Fig. 6-3
Quality of life data (Note: not all countries publish sufficient data for inclusion)

Country	A	B	C	D	E	F	G	H	I	J	K	L	M	N	O
Australia	2.0	74.3	13 448	5	107	6 906	1 754	100	559	48.9	1 112	464	11 080	1.9	10.9
Bolivia	5.6	48.7	8 761	49	16	283	23	63	2 117	1.6	547	9	600	11.2	1.4
Canada	2.5	73.9	14 104	5	139	15 515	2 396	99	548	68.6	1 149	428	11 400	2.5	14.8
Ecuador	33.2	60.7	8 786	43	67	341	79	76	1 622	3.3	318	8	1 180	6.7	2.7
France	100.7	74.2	14 200	8	404	5 235	1 998	99	580	45.9	927	343	12 190	1.0	19.4
Greece	76.3	71.9	15 242	36	101	2 408	392	84	423	28.9	350	90	4 420	0.8	3.3
Israel	197.8	73.9	12 789	6	854	332	343	88	371	29.3	253	107	5 160	1.8	6.0
Italy	187.6	72.8	15 301	10	356	3 257	1 386	94	345	33.7	243	310	6 960	1.6	6.4
Jamaica	219.2	64.7	10 794	19	35	1 047	118	96	2 845	6.0	383	42	1 180	1.5	1.0
Japan	323.8	76.1	12 109	10	234	4 957	3 163	99	779	46.0	688	203	10 080	1.0	17.6
Kenya	34.6	49.1	8 631	77	11	99	2	47	11 835	2.1	33	7	420		0.2
Pakistan	124.2	51.3	9 660	52	7	190	48	21	3 481	0.4	71	3	350		
Portugal	109.5	68.7	13 423	25	54	1 515	119	71	544	13.8	162	119	2 520	2.1	9.7
Saudi Arabia	5.2	53.1	12 134	59	2 891	966	1 709	25	1 642	5.3	295	17	12 600		
Sweden	18.5	75.5	13 259	5	432	11 569	2 229	99	506	79.6	847	345	14 870	1.2	19.4
Thailand	102.5	56.2	9 664	74	33	316	155	79	7 215	1.1	125	6	770	12.7	4.5
UK	229.7	70.8	13 923	2	272	5 043	1 515	99	654	47.7	963	256	9 110	1.4	8.9
USA	25.5	73.0	15 338	2	79	10 251	3 063	100	524	78.8	2 110	520	12 820	9.4	12.3
USSR	12.3	69.0	14 234	15		4 837	1 066	100	340	8.9	504		2 600		
Venezuela	21.0	67.4	11 126	17	427	2 166	279	77	888	5.8	405	93	4 220	12.8	4.6
West Germany	246.8	73.0	14 855	4	713	5 980	3 869	99	452	46.4	383	377	13 450	1.2	21.7

Criterion	Unit
A Population density	people/km^2
B Life expectancy	years
C Food adequacy	kJ/person/d
D Food production efficiency	percentage of population in farming
E Trading wealth	international reserves US$/person
F Electricity generation	kW·h/person
G Material wealth	gross manufactured output US$/person
H Education	percentage of population literate
I Health	people/physician
J Communication ability	telephones/100 people
K News availability	radio receivers/1 000 people
L Ease of travel	cars/1 000 people
M Total goods and services	GNP/person
N Crime	murders/100 000 people
O Dissatisfaction levels	suicides/100 000 people

Source: *UNESCO Statistical Yearbook, 1983.*

d. Add the deviations across the columns, so all deviations for one country are accumulated in an empty column on the right. Do not forget to subtract negative values.

e. Rank the countries from highest to lowest according to their accumulated totals.

f. Evaluate the results.

g. In which areas could the quality of life in Canada be improved in relation to the other sample countries?

25. Using the GNP/person data in Column U of Appendix 3 as representative of the choices available in a country — and therefore indirectly as a measure of the quality of life — draw a graded shading world map showing four classes as follows:

$	colour
6 000 and over	bright gold
4 000–5 999	gold
2 000–3 999	pale gold
under 2 000	very pale yellow

a. How does this map compare with the population maps you drew in Chapter 2? What conclusions are possible?

b. How good are the GNP/person data as a means of measuring quality of life? Could you select a country to live in solely on the basis of GNP/person?

CASE STUDY
Women and Development

In almost all societies the people having the lowest quality of life relative to others in the same society are women. The extent of the gap varies from society to society, being generally smallest in the more developed countries and largest in the developing countries. Even in the more developed countries of North America, the status of women is still a matter of widespread concern; a quality of life gap between men and women exists in North America despite progress towards equality.

The situation is somewhat different in the USSR and China, where communism has long pursued equal treatment of the sexes and where shortages of labour (in the USSR) and skilled labour (in China) have also encouraged the employment of women in a wide variety of non-traditional jobs. However, even in these countries a gap remains between the qualities of life for men and women.

The situation in the Third World differs markedly in degree from those in either the First or Second Worlds. Women in many of these societies tend to be more or less confined to traditional domestic roles, defined and imposed by the patriarchal nature of the societies.

In most countries of the world, baby boys are greatly preferred to baby girls, although the degree of preference varies. Boys are perceived to offer status, a greater potential for work and potential security in old age. Thus in most countries, especially the developing ones, social attitudes tend to foster a warm reaction to the birth of a boy, but lukewarm or even hostile reactions to the birth of a girl. Even before they can be conscious of it, therefore, girls occupy a low status position in male-dominated societies. The effects of these social attitudes vary from country to country. In rural

Marilyn MacKenzie

Women in China are encouraged to pursue a wide variety of nontraditional jobs.

China, for example, the official government birth control program until 1986 strongly recommended only one child per family, driving many people secretly to kill or abandon first-born baby girls in the hope of having a boy later. The *China Youth News* admitted in 1982 that deaths of baby girls were so common that in many rural areas over 60% of the children were boys. In 1986 official government policy was altered to create less pressure on parents in rural areas to have only one child.

The situation is somewhat similar in India, where there is a fairly widespread practice of aborting female fetuses once they have been identified through amniocentesis. The Indian Health Minister has defended the practice of amniocentesis, but attacked those who abuse it. "Such abortions," he told the Indian Parliament in 1982, "arise not due to any particular loophole in the existing law . . . , but are essentially due to social prejudice about a female child." Instead of changing the law, he suggested, India should "change society and its outlook . . . to raise the status of women."

In other countries, as for example throughout Latin America, the Arab world and much of Africa, where birth control policies exist they are neither so rigorous as in China nor so sophisticated as in parts of India. The tendency seems to be that parents continue to have children of both sexes until they are satisfied with the number of boys. Accordingly, birth rates in these countries are much higher than the world average, and many women are almost entirely confined to child-bearing.

The low status of women does not end with adulthood. Most poor women, and that is most of the women in the world, suffer from more malnutrition than poor men do because they eat less than their share of the family food, providing more for their husbands and sons, whose diets remain inadequate too. Dietary surveys in rural Bangladesh, for example, have indicated that males consume more than females in all age categories; the greatest discrepancies occur among those aged 45 and over, where males consume 60% more than females. Assertions that men need to eat more than women because of their greater average body weight have

Women in Western Samoa do their lessons. Learning to read and write is perhaps the most important single step women in developing countries can take to increase their influence and involvement in their communities.

Unicef Photo

been challenged by Dr. Epstein, a British anthropologist, who claims the smaller average body weight of women could be a result of many generations of lower food intake.

Poor women also suffer far more from illiteracy than do poor men, although it is a major problem in both groups. The numerous development programs of the last few decades, including those associated with the United Nations Decade For Women (1975–85), have hardly touched most of the world's women. Although the law in most countries gives girls and boys equal access to education and literacy programs, boys are usually preferred for a variety of cultural reasons. The number of illiterate females far exceeds the number of illiterate males. Where culture requires segregation of the sexes outside the home, girls have difficulty obtaining an education: women teachers are scarce, girls' schools are rare and, if boarding is needed, parents prefer to pay for boys rather than girls to go to school. Thus enrolment figures for girls are usually far below those for boys. For example, UNESCO data show that in the Middle East enrolment percentages for males are: ages 6–11, 80%; ages 12–17, 60%; ages 18–23, 25%. Comparable figures for females are 60%, 40%, and 10%. The pattern is similar in other parts of the developing world, but not in the First or Second Worlds, where male-female enrolment figures are practically equal. South Asia's figures for the same age ranges are: males — 75%, 35% and 10%; females — 50%, 20% and 5%. Girls are less likely than boys to be enrolled in elementary schools and have a proportionately even smaller chance of continuing their education through adolescence and early adulthood. In elementary school, the enrolment of girls is approximately 65–75% that of boys, but in college the enrolment of girls is only about 40–50% that of boys.

Quite apart from the effect that lack of schooling has on the job aspirations of many women, there is also a far-reaching and direct negative effect on their children. Numerous studies show that education assists mothers in raising children. A World Bank study of 29 developing nations showed that each additional year of schooling for girls meant on average 9/1000 fewer infant and child deaths. Improved female literacy has also been shown to improve overall life expectancies (both male and female). In addition, continued education delays marriage for women, reducing the opportunities for early pregnancy while enabling them to become more knowledgeable about and accepting of the use of contraceptives.

One of the better known examples of successful development involving women is the AMUL (Anand Milk Union Limited) Dairy Cooperative in India, where women have traditionally gained income from caring for dairy animals and selling milk. AMUL has enabled women to sell as a cooperative, eliminating middlemen and generating higher incomes for themselves. This frees them from their traditional dependence on moneylenders. They can now afford veterinary care for their animals. Family planning has become more popular. Better food is available and more children are attending school. As the younger women become better educated, they begin to take a greater share in the management of the cooperative. As a result, education for girls is becoming more highly valued in the community. The World Bank is sponsoring similar development models for women in other Indian states, chiefly Rajasthan, Karnataka and Madhya Pradesh.

Nevertheless, despite successes, the situation for hundreds of millions of women throughout the developing world remains desperately poor. Typically, women bear the children, raise the family, grow the food, collect the firewood, cook the meals and participate little in the monetary economy. From the standpoint of much national planning and most national statistics, women are "invisible." And although women in developed countries do not earn money from their domestic work either, they participate in the monetary economy of their individual countries, through paid employment outside the home, to a much greater

Marilyn MacKenzie

Indian schoolgirls. Around the world, increased educational opportunities raise the quality of life and broaden the range of choices women can make about their lives.

extent than do women in developing countries. Data indicate that the participation rate of women in the monetary economies of developed countries is generally at least 50%, whereas in many developing countries it is about 5%.

The invisibility of most women in the monetary economies of most developing countries does not prevent the majority of them from characteristically working a double-day. In addition to their child-rearing and home-making functions, they must also work outside the home, either as unpaid agricultural labourers or at other tasks, such as making baskets and rugs to sell. In most developed countries too, the women who work in paid employment outside the home usually also do the housework and cooking. As a result, women in all countries consistently tend to work at least two or three hours per day longer than most men.

Women make up 70% of the agricultural labour force in many developing countries. Their work often determines how much food is available to the family, since they are commonly responsible for growing subsistence crops, caring for small animals and tending garden plots for consumption or for sale at local markets. In addition, women frequently weed, harvest and store field crops. In some places they form the majority of the plantation workers. Yet new agricultural methods are usually taught to men. Cooperatives and other forms of self-help are usually dominated by men, and women find it difficult to obtain credit on their own. Agricultural research has focused heavily on cash crops, controlled by men, and not on the subsistence crops grown by women.

Despite their need of paid employment, nearly all women in the developing world and many women in the developed world cannot compete with men for new jobs in the modern sector. Relatively low levels of skill, little training and continuing domestic responsibilities combine to keep women in the area of intermittent work and low wages. When women find work in industry, they have tended to be concentrated in low-wage, labour-intensive jobs in textiles, clothing and footwear. Because much of their labour is not valued in money terms, or because they work only intermittently for money, they miss out on many of the social security or employment benefits that may exist.

The World Bank notes that whereas women and girls worldwide constitute half the total population, a third of the paid labour force and perhaps an estimated two-thirds of all the hours worked, they receive only one-tenth of the world's income and own only 1% of the world's property.

While women clearly need the help of dedicated development efforts, it is a paradox that current development trends have frequently worsened the quality of life for women. Drawn by the prospect of finding work in towns, cities, mines, plantations or even other countries, many husbands leave their wives with sole responsibility for sustaining their families. More and more young women and, to a lesser extent the widowed or divorced, are also moving to cities and towns to look for work. These trends have produced a phenomenal increase in the number of female heads of households. An estimated 35% of all households in developing countries are now in the sole care of women, a figure similar to those of many developed countries. Regardless of how these households come into being, they share a common characteristic: they are poorer than male-headed households, with fewer income-earning adults, less access to land and almost no prospect of an escape from poverty.

Since the start of the International Decade For Women in 1975, policy makers have become increasingly aware of the differing impacts that development programs have on men and women and of the need to pay special attention to women's problems in the development process. This awareness is particularly important in that many development programs aim directly at problems of general poverty, and women make up a disproportionately large number of the world's absolute poor. The new sensitivity toward women in development takes two forms: first, many programs aim specifically to raise the status and well-being of women. Second, programs that were regarded as neutral but whose impact may have actually been detrimental to women are being re-evaluated to ensure that women either benefit, or at least suffer no harm, from them. The widespread provision of day-care facilities is a high priority, whether to free girls and women for education or to provide them with opportunities for full-time work.

Despite the growing awareness among development program planners of the need to raise the status of women in society, and thereby their quality of life, there is nevertheless a long way to go. Perhaps the chief obstacle is the distance to be travelled in changing the overall views of many societies toward the role of women. We have already noted the male-dominated views of China and India, but similar views regarding the status of women exist in many countries, most notably those of South America, Africa and the Middle East. In these areas, women are regarded as the significantly less privileged half of the population, and such views are often accepted by many women themselves.

Unicef/Ray Witlin

With more women working, most societies face some new problems associated with child care. This group of childcare workers in Ecuador is practising role-playing to help them care for daycare children.

It is, however, the purpose of development programs to produce change, and herein lies one of the hurdles. While most societies in the developing world are happy to see economic development, they have reservations about the social changes that inevitably accompany it. When these changes affect the roles of women, who are at the heart of the traditional family structure, the changes may be seen as totally undesirable. The transformation of women's roles may be seen as an erosion of the

Unicef/Beyer

The world-wide acceptance of change for women is uneven, and can produce some unfamiliar images. These Yemeni women are training to work outside the home as secretaries, but may do so only in traditional costume.

foundations of traditional cultures. And when modernization is seen as synonymous with Westernization there is often a cultural reaction against modernization, justified by the claim that Westernization is destroying traditional values. Such views lead to a denial by traditional as well as developed societies of women's rights on the grounds that society and its values must be maintained. This situation is most noticeable in the Islamic countries, where a powerful religious and social funda-

mentalist movement has developed which openly avows its intention to deny women the rights that come with modernization and to maintain their role in its full traditional setting. In Iran, for example, where women claim an equal role in the overthrow of the modernizing Shah, many are now outraged by the steps taken subsequently under the Khomeini regime to restore their traditional and subservient status. They list among these steps the legalization of polygamy, the barring of women from certain professions, the unilateral right of men to declare divorce and the reintroduction of temporary marriages, which they see as little better than prostitution. Certainly the views of society are going to prove more of a barrier to women than the needs of the economy, especially in the short run. In the long run, however, it is the needs of the economy that must be addressed; social change will not occur unless the economy changes. Economic change provides the opportunity for social change, and though social change may be resisted, history demonstrates that it cannot be denied.

The status of women is, therefore, unlikely to improve unless economic development occurs, but even with economic development there are likely to be severe problems.

Korean mid-wife Koo Chin Myong and an expectant mother. The training and equipping of mid-wives make an important contribution to improving the status of women in developing countries.

Unicef/Joseph Brettenback

Conclusion

As we have seen, quality of life is an elusive concept, open to many different interpretations. An individual's lifestyle is made up of a number of features and this life is said to be "rich" if it holds a variety of interesting experiences. In this chapter we have found that some societies offer a much wider range of possible experiences than do others. The reasons for this may be rooted in some of the matters discussed in preceding chapters, or they may arise elsewhere. For example, the degree of crowding or amount of open space available can affect a person's quality of life significantly, but not always predictably; some like open spaces and others abhor them, while some like crowds and others do not. Equally, industrialization may be perceived as a benefit by some and a danger by others. At the same time, quality of life is profoundly influenced by factors that are difficult to describe specifically, among them political climate, moral attitudes, intellectual freedom and religious tolerance.

Because quality of life involves so many different elements, it is only partly a geographical concern. Undoubtedly, however, its variations from place to place create one of the most marked and persistent geographical effects of all: migration. The mass movement of human beings over the earth is largely the result of people's desire to find a better quality of life. Accordingly, in the next chapter we examine migrations.

7 MIGRATIONS

Introduction

If you are interested in the origins of humanity, read the book *Origins* by Richard Leakey.

Migrations are often a result of population growth trends in certain parts of the world; often they also reflect the different cultural, political or economic goals of people in different areas. And in a sense they represent humanity's attempts to produce more evenness or balance in its use of the world's resources.

Migrations have been a common feature of human history. From their origins, possibly in eastern Africa, people have spread over the surface of the globe in increasing numbers. Earlier migrants usually tried to hold on to the best areas of land they had settled, and there was often bitter conflict as later migrants tried to move in. History is full of examples of conflict arising from migration. The settled Chinese attempted to keep out the migrating peoples of central Asia by means of the Great Wall. The Goths overran the Roman Empire and eventually sacked Rome itself. The Spanish, Portuguese, French and British colonisers of the Americas dispossessed the indigenous peoples. Every race and nation can produce similar examples.

Migrants are people who move to take residence in another place. They may be divided into *emigrants*, who move out, and *immigrants*, who move in.

Why do people migrate? Where do they come from? Where do they go? We will attempt to answer these questions in the first three sections of the chapter. In later sections we will examine the benefits and problems of migration, including a discussion of urbanization. Completing the chapter is a case study of labour migration in the Middle East.

The following items provide a general idea of some of the main issues in migration today.

America's Latin Future

El Paso, Texas, is on the border, where you can quickly escape the Third World and hide in the First. Every day for several decades thousands of Mexicans have been doing just that. They are transforming the U.S. from a basically Anglo-Saxon country into one in which Hispanics will be the largest ethnic group.

The border between the U.S. and Mexico is a long stretch of desert with pairs of mirror-image cities: San Diego and Tijuana; Douglas and Agua Prieta; El Paso and Ciudad Juárez. In those cities poor Mexicans, Salvadorans, Guatemalans, Costa Ricans, Hondu-rans, and Nicaraguans crowd together — all without entry visas. The international border passes through the middle of the Rio Grande River, which has become little more than a brook as a thirsty U.S. has drained it upstream. On the north side stretches high barbed wire that is regularly cut at night and repaired the next morning. Those who wade across the river from Mexico and jump onto the opposite bank are in the U.S. The police arrest some 20,000 each month and send them back. The others, illegal aliens, are estimated at between two and twelve million.

If this continues and if the fertility rate of the Hispanic ethnic group remains at its present level, the U.S. will be a predominantly Latin nation within fifteen years. Of its 280 million inhabitants, 35 million will be of Mexican, Puerto Rican, Central American, or Caribbean ancestry. More than 29 million will be "Anglo"; more than 25 million will be great-great grandchildren of Germans; more than 33 million, descendants of African slaves.

Will they assimilate as the Italians, Irish, and Poles have done? Few believe that such a process will be without trauma. More likely, the Southern states will become culturally Latin, with a new language, new institutions, new foods, and new work relationships.

El Paso is a city with industry, commerce, and agriculture. Ciudad Juárez, its Mexican twin less than a mile away, is a Third World encampment swollen to a million inhabitants, where many go hungry and children die of disease on the scale of India. An El Paso worker without documents earns two or three dollars an hour — half the minimum union wage. But those few dollars, recrossing the Rio Grande, have become very valuable since Mexico's devaluation of the peso. In 1975 a dollar was worth five pesos; today it is worth 150.

The Border Patrol guards against clandestine immigration. Alan Eliason, who is responsible for about 340 miles [550 kilometres] of the border, reports, "In the past ten months we have arrested 846,721 illegal immigrants, but all we can do is take them back to the border. The law does not give us the right to search workplaces, and the Constitution prohibits our asking for documents. If Washington wants results it should legislate clear laws and double the personnel."

The law Eliason calls for was proposed in Congress but shipwrecked by the most heterogeneous of lobbies. It was opposed by large landowners and by industrial associations, who would have lost their half-price labor, and by Hispanic political groups, who believed they would be singled out by the color of their skin or by their speech. President Reagan visited some border cities last summer in search of votes, and now suggests that "illegals" living in the U.S. for at least seven years be given resident status, ending a semi-clandestine existence for five or six million people.

A tug-of-war exists over these issues. Immigrant defense organizations are asking for an increase in visa quotas (20,000 a year are now available to Mexicans with certain professions). Unionizing efforts are increasing, and election campaigns are carrying Mexican-American mayors and council members into office. The battle has intensified since a Supreme Court decision recognized the right of children of "illegals" to go to American schools.

Irma Herrera, a lawyer and founder of the Mexican American Defense League, says, "Unlike other immigrants, we have crossed only a border — not an ocean. And we were on these lands before they were. So there is no reason why we should lose our ethnicity — especially our language. By 1990 in California, Texas, and Arizona, black, Asian, and Hispanic minorities will be a majority."

From *Panorama* (Milan), reprinted in *World Press Review* 1984 2

There are two views on illegal immigrants: Tough and compassionate.

The question for other Canadians is why should anyone care about illegal immigrants.

After all, nobody asked these people to come here. They are breaking the laws of this country. These are hard times. Most likely these illegal immigrants are taking jobs away from Canadian citizens and immigrants who have come here the hard way, legally.

So if illegal immigrants are suffering, they have no one to blame but themselves. If they don't like it here, they can always go back where they came from.

This could be called the tough line on illegal immigrants and I have heard many people in the past weeks express these harsh sentiments.

But those who work with the illegal immigrants, the young lawyers who fight their cases and the social workers who try to help them, have a different view.

They say that when people come here illegally it's usually for a pretty good reason. They have family here, brothers and sisters and uncles and aunts, but under Canada's tough immigration laws they don't qualify to enter themselves.

They are over 21 and they don't

have a letter from a Canadian firm offering them a job. And they don't have enough money to claim they are going to start a business of their own and employ other people.

Often they come from South American countries where their politics endanger their lives. Many are former students who stay on after their courses have been completed because they have no hope of a job back home. And many come from countries mired in poverty. Even the menial jobs that illegal immigrants have to take here seem like bonanzas. They work hard, save money and send it back to their families.

So there are two conflicting ways to consider illegal immigrants, and the government itself seems to swing uneasily between them. Sometimes the government treats illegals as law-breakers who should be caught and thrown out of the country. At other times, the government seems full of compassion and relaxes its rules.

Canada has never had a consistent policy for dealing with people who come here without official permission.

Our policy isn't based on how much people need Canada. Our policy is based on how much we need them. We even call the government that deals with immigrants, the ministry of "employment and immigration."

Unless people have a solid job offer or can show they have enough money and experience to start a business here and employ people, they have to be part of a nuclear family to get into Canada.

An immigrant can bring over his fiancee or his wife and her dependent children and he can even adopt an orphan under the age of 13. And he can also bring in unmarried children

under the age of 21 or parents or grandparents over the age of 60 along with dependants.

They are also allowed to bring over ''unmarried, orphaned brothers, sisters, nephews, nieces or grandchildren under 18.''

In many cultures, the word family includes many more people than are defined by these tight, narrow categories. And the Canadian Bar Association, among others, has asked the government to expand its categories so that families can be reunited. But so far, the government has not acted.

Exceptions are occasionally made, of course. But by and large, our immigration policy is restrictive.

In 1984, the government expects that between 90,000 and 95,000 immigrants will come to Canada legally. This is less than we were doing 100 years ago. In 1884, Canada took in 103,824 immigrants.

David Lewis Stein, *The Toronto Star* 1984 1 22

Too Many Doctors

''With 5,000 doctors unemployed, the British Prime Minister is determined to 'do something' to curb or even reduce the growing number of colored doctors in the National Health Service,'' reports Batuk Gathani in the conservative *Hindu* of Madras [Sept. 7]. ''The British Medical Assn. at its annual meeting in June passed a resolution calling for control on the number of overseas doctors entering Britain and on the length of time they stay.''

Nearly a third of the doctors working for the National Health Service were born overseas. ''A majority of

them are doing the least popular jobs in less attractive British hospitals.'' The Overseas Doctors Assn. in the U.K., which represents 20,000 non-British doctors — half from India and Pakistan — feels that 90 per cent of its members should go home after training. ''The association seems resigned to the new controls and the growing specter of racism in the profession.''

On the other side of the problem, John Worrall writes from Nairobi for the Gemini News Service of London [Sept. 2] that the Geneva-based Intergovernmental Committee for Migration (ICM) is urging the return from Europe and the U.S. of professionals who are badly needed in their own countries. It is trying to reverse the ''brain drain'' by finding professionals jobs at home and paying their airfares. The ICM has reintegrated 3,000 professionals into Latin America and now is working in Africa. It brings people home only to fill specific vacancies to avoid increasing Third World employment problems.

World Press Review 1983 11

10 Poles in Day 4 of hunger strike to free their families

Ten men who want their wives and children freed from Poland are in the fourth day of a hunger strike outside the Polish Consulate in Etobicoke.

The men, most of whom fled the country after martial law was imposed last year, have vowed to continue their protest until all their family members have been given exit visas.

Jerzy Smierzchalski, 28, who wants

to be reunited with his wife, Iwona, and son, Thomas, 3, said they will try to survive on water until they achieve their dream.

"We want to get 23 people out," Smierzchalski said. "That's 10 wives and 13 kids."

Smierzchalski, a Solidarity leader, fled a Polish registered ship in Greece in January, 1982 and received government sponsorship to live in Canada six months later.

He said he jumped ship because he was afraid to return to Poland after the Soviets took control of the government. "I was chief of Solidarity on my ship," he said. "I was afraid back in Poland I'd face some kind of punishment."

Smierzchalski said he's made repeated attempts to get permission for his wife and son to leave, but so far has been turned down.

He said he warned the consulate in August that if something wasn't done he'd go on a hunger strike.

Cal Millar, *The Toronto Star*, 1983 11 10

DISCUSSION AND RESEARCH

1. What different reasons for migrating can you suggest?
2. What are some of the problems connected with migration?
3. If you were to migrate, what would motivate you most? Why?
4. What would you expect to be the likeliest problems when people of different cultural groups come into contact through migration? In what ways could such problems be reduced or solved?

Why Do People Migrate?

Most people have some affection for their place of birth, feelings of local allegiance, regional loyalty or national pride. These may be expressed with different degrees of intensity. Some people close their minds to other people and places; others seek to travel and to meet other people with different backgrounds.

Migration is therefore most likely to appeal to the more mobile and open-minded people in a society. Even so, migration requires that ties be broken and problems be solved. Friends and relatives must often be left behind and established social and economic positions given up.

The Paz Castellano and Gomez families share a tent in Teupasenti. As Mennonites, their religion forbids them to take sides in the Nicaraguan war, so they have fled to Honduras.

Refugees from the war in Afghanistan attend a clinic in Peshawar, Pakistan.

Prospective migrants must think of the pros and cons of migration. They must compare their known quality of life with the quality of life they expect to achieve in a new location. This involves such considerations as job opportunities, wages, standards of living, the provision of social services and a host of allied factors. They must weigh perceived advantages against expected disadvantages, such as the need to learn a new language or to adjust to a different set of cultural values.

Some migrants are able to make such choices unhindered by external pressures. Refugees, on the other hand, are forced to migrate. They may need to escape political, military, religious, social or economic oppression. Examples of forced migrations include: Chileans from Chile (1975), Chinese from Vietnam (1975 to the present), Jews from Germany (1930s), Ethiopians from Ethiopia (1980s), Africans from South Africa into the "homelands" (1980s), US blacks to Canada (nineteenth cen-

The UN has a special agency to help refugees. It is called the UN High Commission for Refugees. Estimates in the mid-1980s indicate there are up to 15 million refugees in the world, over half in Africa alone. Many refugees spend years in camps while awaiting acceptance by some country as immigrants.

tury), US southern blacks to the north (nineteenth and twentieth centuries) and Asians from Uganda (1960s–70s). The following articles provide some views of recent situations.

600,000 refugees from drought, strife seek help in Sudan

By Michael McDowell

The telexes tell the story — famine victims arriving at the Canadian doctor's primitive clinic at the rate of more than 100 a day, dying babies, starving children with bloated stomachs, crippled adults.

The cables to Toronto ask for medical supplies, nursing and administrative help as swiftly as money allows — to save a small number of the more than 600,000 casualties of Ethiopia's drought and civil war who have fled into eastern Sudan.

The doctor, 33-year-old specialist Elliot Kravitz, writes that Wad el-Helieu refugee camp, his base, is home to 954 people, 200 of them children under 15.

"Mostly they are Tigre drought victims but possibly there will be more Eritrean war victims soon . . . Urgent request to send administrator for two to three months . . . Too busy to get a complete picture of all refugees . . . Drilling deep borehole delayed by basalt layers," he writes.

Dr. Kravitz, who left for Sudan a month ago, is part of a fledgling Canadian project trying to make a tiny dent in the health problems caused by famine that affects an estimated 150 million people — one third of the people of Africa.

In his camp, the most common cause of death among children is measles. The major killers among adults are tuberculosis and kala-azar, a disease caused by a parasite.

Dr. Kravitz was sent there by Canadian Physicians for African Refugees, an organization set up eight months ago by Toronto general practitioner Mark Doidge, its president.

"There are five million famine refugees in Africa and they are not getting a fraction of the attention the boat people got in Canada. I began writing letters to the United Nations and the Government of Sudan asking if they would be interested in a Canadian medical contingent going there and they said yes," he said in a recent interview.

Dr. Doidge, 28, recruited medical specialists familiar with emergencies and people with managerial expertise for the organization's board — including the director of a major Canadian drug company.

To date, CPAR has raised $20,000 — a tenth of its target — mainly through mailings to doctors.

"Elliot Kravitz has worked with boat people in Thailand and among the poor in India. He left his job at Mount Sinai emergency at a few weeks' notice to go to Sudan," Dr. Doidge said.

"We got three boxes of medicine to him recently which is a logistical feat. We have to send him more and want additional medical personnel to help children under 5 and lactating mothers particularly.

"The refugees at the camp are just holding their own, 'water-wise.' It's frightening. There are three million people hit by the drought and famine in Ethiopia alone.''

Dr. Doidge will visit Wad el-Helieu later this month.

The organization, which is seeking support from the Canadian International Development Agency, needs more money and ultimately hopes to send three doctors, two nurses and a manager to work with Dr. Kravitz.

''We urgently need money now. People have been generous and the work is of immediate relevance to the children and adults of Sudan. This is a good example of how Canadians can act on their reputation for international concern,'' Dr. Doidge said.

The Globe and Mail, Toronto, 1984 2 17

LONDON — The telegram they delivered to Apartment 23 on Tchaikovsky Street, Leningrad, read simply: ''Home on Friday. Had a cold. Feeling fine now. Love Oleg.''

Irina Chulkov read the message and sat down. ''I didn't know whether to cry or go to dance in the street with excitement. Then I went calm and cold inside. I knew this is how I must be if we were to survive.''

For this message from her husband, Oleg Chulkov, fourth officer on the Soviet cargo ship Mekhanik Evgrafov, was in their own private code. Very simply, it said: ''The way is clear. We escape this weekend.''

Within two days Oleg's ship would be in port. Two more days and it would leave Leningrad again, but this time it would be sailing him to freedom in Britain. And Irina would be with him.

That telegram meant that 10 years of dreaming, two years of planning, and months of difficult and dangerous

preparation to construct a sort of ocean-going ''wooden horse,'' were over. Now Oleg's madcap scheme was to be tested.

And certain imprisonment and possible death awaited the Chulkovs if he had got it wrong: ''Betraying the Motherland'' is the crime the state levels at recaptured Russian runaways. Fifteen years' hard labor is lenient: Oleg's position of trust could make him eligible for a sentence of death.

What would make any young couple take such a risk? ''For our love for each other. And for freedom,'' says Irina in her perfect but accented English.

Irina Chulkov was Irina Shumovich, daughter of a successful engineer and regional official, when she first thought of fleeing. ''I was 14 maybe. Learning at a specialist school where English is a priority. I loved English and North American literature. Even the books they would allow us showed bits of a life that was so different.

''Then I started to see films. I was fascinated by the rooms people lived in. Such colors. Such size. So much space.

''In France they broke pieces of those long white loaves and dipped them in their coffee. So carelessly. Sometimes they didn't even finish the bread. Oh, to be so rich as to be able to waste a little.

''But it was more than that. It was the whole world. The music, and the museums. The different cities. The people. Once my friend — she was Jewish so they let her go — sent me a card from Rome. She was going off to see Vienna and then Florence.

''I cried for days. To see Rome! And Vienna. In one lifetime! I think

I knew then I must leave Russia. But how?''

Oleg's own dream of escape had begun when he was 10. His mother, an English teacher, had been sent to Britain on a course. ''Two months. She was told not to praise England when she came home. But she was a woman. She loved clothes, shops, she couldn't hide her wonder.

''That's why I joined the merchant navy. As a cadet I was taken to Sweden and Holland and Italy and Greece. We could walk for an hour or two on the shore with two seniors to watch us.

''I saw so much to open my eyes. I knew I must escape one day from a ship — and that Irina would have to be with me.''

His mad and perilous scheme was to smuggle Irina to the West in his cabin. And in that 10-foot-by-8-foot cubicle there was only one hiding place — in the 15-inch-high slot beneath his bunk.

Most of the space was already taken up by two pull-out stowage drawers. Oleg planned to cut the drawers, and create a 6-foot-long, 12-inch high ''coffin'' for Irina.

The work was done in Leningrad during the two-day layover at the end of two successive trips. Oleg had volunteered to stand night watch — and Irina came aboard to ''keep him company.''

Cargo loading of the Mekhanik Evgrafov went on all night. And around midnight, when the noise was loudest and fewest non-workers were about, Irina would take a saunter to the door of the gangway leading to the deck and signal Oleg to begin cutting.

It took four nights to cut the wood

and then nail on the false backs of the drawers. And hours of patient clearing up of every speck of sawdust and the surreptitious dropping of the debris from the bridge into Leningrad Harbor.

Even then, it was to be three desperately dragging months of waiting before Oleg sent the famous "Had a cold. Feeling better" telegram which was their private signal that the escape would be made the coming weekend.

At midnight, after a carefully neutral farewell, Oleg leaves. And Irina agrees "to see him to his ship." They walk down to the tram stop, and she is nursing their only luggage: a bag containing a change of clothes, her wedding and childhood photos and the pick of her Western music cassettes.

"It was very, very cold. And I am shivering. Not fear. Excitement. As we come to the gangplank, I look at Oleg. I know if things go wrong we may never see each other again.

"But he is so calm and cool. And I think that even if they catch us and end our lives, it is better to try than to go on living in the Soviet Union."

Getting Irina concealed was simple. Visitors have to deposit their passports with the seaman on duty at the gangplank.

At midnight Oleg, as watch officer, simply told the guard to go and get changed to go ashore; retrieved the passport and casually remarked to the returning seaman, "Oh, you've missed Irina. She just left. Maybe you'll see her on the tram."

Based on Oleg's knowledge of the ship's routine and likely visits to his cabin by crewmen or the cleaning lady, this is how Irina would spend her ordeal:

From 1 a.m. to 7 a.m. she could cuddle behind him in his bunk. At 7 a.m., after a snack, she must go into the hole, to remain there until 12:30. From 12:30 to 3 p.m., when Oleg was officially resting before watch, she could hide in his curtained-off shower to stretch her legs.

Then from 3 p.m. to 1 a.m., apart from a brief respite at Oleg's dinner time of 8 p.m., she would remain hidden in her "coffin."

The first hideous snag came when Irina first slid into the hole. They had measured incorrectly. She was supposed to have room to move a little. Instead, once she had wriggled into place with the "roof" 3 inches above her face, she found it impossible to turn over.

She must spend 16 hours a day immobile on her back in total darkness with only a blanket between her and the steel deck.

Irina remembers only fragments of the voyage to Hull. Like the dreadful minutes when the cleaning woman made Oleg's bed, banging and thumping the mattress 6 inches from her face.

Like the heart-stopping night when a seaman burst into the cabin in the middle of the night — Oleg, as navigation officer was wanted on the bridge: He held her rigid under the blankets as he casually swung his feet to the deck.

For a day and a half they weathered a North Sea gale, Irina shudders as she remembers the sickness that overwhelmed her. It was so rough she couldn't even take her "exercise" in the shower alcove — every lurch flung her back into the cabin.

But most of the trip is just a nightmare memory of those hours beneath the bunk. "You have to know I am

terrified of the dark. Always I sleep with a small light. To be lying like this for so long . . . for me it was like being dead."

Life came back the moment Oleg lifted the trapdoor beneath his mattress, beckoned her up into the light and with his mouth against her ear breathed: "We are tied up to the shore. England. A few more hours . . . "

Getting ashore was almost ridiculously easy. At 20 minutes before 4 a.m., Oleg told the seaman guarding the gangplank: "Your relief will be up at 4 o'clock. I'm not sleepy. You might as well turn in now."

As soon as the man had gone, Irina scuttled across deck and hid between two garbage cans.

She waited for a signal from Oleg. Together they crept down the half-raised gangplank (all Soviet ships cut themselves off from contact with the shore at night).

Oleg jumped the 6 feet to the quay. And Irina dropped into his arms.

Then hand in hand Oleg and Irina Chulkov ran through a thin drizzle down the quayside of Hull.

They were spotted by British customs officers and spent four nights in jail while their requests for asylum were processed.

In Hull jail, they had separate cells. Solitary.

"I cried all night," said Irina. "I thought they had made up their minds to hand us back. Or maybe just Oleg. 'Why can't we be together our last night?' I asked. 'We are husband and wife.' 'Madame, this is Britain,' they said. 'We don't allow that sort of thing in prison.' "

They spent three more nights in a Manchester detention centre being debriefed by men from London. "Very nice. One spoke Russian." And then, on Oct. 11, 1983, at 6 p.m., they were handed aliens' documents and told, "You are free to go."

They spent their first night of total freedom pretending to be someone else. They registered at a small hotel near Euston Station as Swedes, named Svensen.

"We were afraid of the KGB," says Oleg. "I knew that at first the captain of my ship thought I had fallen overboard. They sent down divers at the Hull docks to look for me.

"But by now they would have checked in Leningrad. Found that Irina was also missing. And they would have searched my cabin and found the hole where she had been hiding. So they would be looking for us."

Gordon Thomas, *The Toronto Star* 1984 1 22

There are other reasons for migration. First, governments often sponsor internal colonization projects. Such projects account for the migration of Soviet citizens into Siberia, Brazilians into Amazonia, Chinese into Manchuria and Xinjiang, and northern Ethiopians into southern Ethiopia, among others. Migrants may be offered free or cheap land, be pressured by advertising, be denied job permits or food rations, or forcibly removed in trains or trucks by police or army personnel. Second, countries may want relatively cheap labour for work their own nationals are

A pioneer family in Choré, Paraguay. Paraguay's people and economy have benefited from the opening up of 26 000 km² to 400 000 settlers.

Unicef/David Mangurian

In 1985, Ontario farmers brought in 3 171 temporary migrant workers from the West Indies, up from 2 876 in 1984.

There are more Japanese in Brazil than anywhere else outside Japan.

either unwilling to do, because the work is arduous and low-paid, or unable to do because they are lacking in skills or in numbers. This type of migration includes the movement of West Indians into Ontario's fruit and tobacco farms, Mexicans into California's vegetable fields, Filipinos into Saudi Arabian oilfields and Indian doctors into British hospitals. Third, people move to escape relatively overcrowded conditions. Thus Britons migrate to Australia, urban dwellers to the countryside, and Japanese to Brazil. Fourth, people leave cold countries for warm ones; so many retired Canadians go to Florida or Arizona. Fifth, and very specifically, people may want a country to call their own, as Jews do Israel.

STATISTICAL ANALYSIS

5. Fig. 7-1 gives information on the number of immigrants arriving each year since 1901 in both Canada and the USA. Answer the following questions for either Canada or the USA (or both):

   a. Calculate the ratio of lowest year : highest year.

   b. Find and suggest reasons for this great variation in the annual level of immigration.

   c. Plot the actual data since 1901 as a normal line graph.

   d. Calculate a 10-year moving average as shown in Appendix 4; then plot the moving average data as a normal line graph starting in 1910.

   e. What do you notice about the long-term immigration trends? Can you explain them in terms of your answer to part **b** of this assignment alone?

6. Many thousands of people leave Bangladesh each year in search of work. Mostly they go to other Moslem countries, especially in the Middle East, but also to Algeria, Malaysia and Nigeria. They range from doctors to unskilled labourers. Most send part of their earnings back to Bangladesh. This money is called *migrants' remittances*, and is an important source of foreign currency to many developing countries besides Bangladesh. In 1982, it was estimated that Bangladesh received about $500 000 000 in migrants' remittances, equivalent to about 25% of all export earnings. Fig. 7-2 gives the main details of the destinations and types of migrant workers from Bangladesh, along with an indication of their remittances.

   a. Who gains and who loses from such an arrangement?

   b. Excluding "Others," which destination appears to offer the highest paying jobs overall?

   c. Which appears to offer the lowest paying jobs?

Fig. 7-1
Immigration to Canada and the USA since 1901

Year	Canada	USA	Year	Canada	USA
1901	55 747	487 918	1943	8 504	23 725
1902	89 102	648 743	1944	12 801	28 551
1903	138 660	857 046	1945	22 722	38 119
1904	131 252	812 870	1946	71 719	108 721
1905	141 465	1 026 499	1947	64 127	147 292
1906	211 653	1 100 735	1948	125 414	170 570
1907	272 409	1 285 349	1949	95 217	188 317
1908	143 326	782 870	1950	73 912	249 187
1909	173 694	751 786	1951	194 391	205 717
1910	286 839	1 041 570	1952	164 498	265 520
1911	331 288	878 587	1953	168 868	170 434
1912	375 756	838 172	1954	154 227	208 177
1913	400 870	1 197 892	1955	109 946	237 790
1914	150 484	1 218 480	1956	164 857	321 625
1915	36 665	326 700	1957	282 164	326 867
1916	55 914	298 826	1958	124 851	253 265
1917	72 910	295 403	1959	106 928	260 686
1918	41 845	110 618	1960	104 111	265 398
1919	107 698	141 132	1961	71 689	271 344
1920	138 824	430 001	1962	74 586	283 763
1921	91 728	805 228	1963	93 151	306 260
1922	64 224	309 556	1964	112 606	292 248
1923	133 729	522 919	1965	146 758	296 697
1924	124 164	706 896	1966	194 743	323 040
1925	84 907	294 314	1967	222 876	361 972
1926	135 982	304 488	1968	183 974	454 448
1927	158 886	335 175	1969	161 531	358 579
1928	166 783	307 255	1970	147 713	373 326
1929	164 993	279 678	1971	121 900	370 478
1930	104 806	241 700	1972	122 006	384 685
1931	27 530	97 139	1973	184 200	400 063
1932	20 591	35 576	1974	218 465	394 861
1933	14 382	23 068	1975	187 881	386 194
1934	12 476	29 470	1976	149 429	398 613
1935	11 277	34 956	1977	114 914	462 315
1936	11 643	36 329	1978	86 313	601 442
1937	15 101	50 244	1979	112 096	460 348
1938	17 244	67 895	1980	143 117	530 639
1939	16 994	82 998	1981	121 618	
1940	11 324	70 756	1982	121 147	
1941	9 329	51 776	1983	88 846	
1942	7 576	28 781			

Source: Urquhart & Buckley, *Historical Statistics of Canada; Historical Statistics of the US*, Bicentennial Edition; *Canadian Statistical Review*, 1984; *Statistical Abstract of the United States*, 1984.

Fig. 7-2
Migrant workers from Bangladesh, and their remittances

Destination	Professional and Technical Workers	Skilled Workers	Unskilled Workers	Total Workers	Remittances
Bahrain	0.27	1.00	1.96	3.23	1.00
Iran	1.69	1.09	5.19	7.97	6.00
Iraq	1.01	4.44	0.62	6.07	10.00
Kuwait	0.30	2.24	6.96	9.50	8.00
Libya	3.59	2.66	3.89	10.14	11.00
Oman	1.30	6.43	4.45	12.18	2.00
Qatar	0.40	2.05	3.07	5.52	10.00
Saudi Arabia	1.65	4.01	7.68	13.34	24.00
United Arab Emirates	3.92	14.90	12.98	31.80	12.00
Others (non-Middle East)	0.23	0.01	0.01	0.25	16.00
Totals	**14.36**	**38.83**	**46.81**	**100.00**	**100.00**

Source: World Bank *Staff Working Paper No. 454*, 1981 4.

Note: All figures are percentages

DISCUSSION AND RESEARCH

7. Why do you suppose people migrate to Canada in particular?

8. What sorts of people migrate?

9. Fewer people migrate than may wish to. What prevents them?

Where Do Migrants Come From?

Origins

Early members of the human race are thought to have originated in the plains of East Africa and pulsed outwards into Eurasia in waves as periodic phases of overpopulation and starvation occurred. People may have reached the Americas either by a land-bridge connecting Siberia with Alaska or by a sea-link connecting southeast Asia and the Pacific Islands with South America. Through time, most of the earth's habitable surface came to be occupied.

There is much speculation about the origins of humanity. While the earliest people seem to have originated in East Africa, there is evidence of other early humans in China and Indonesia.

European Empires

The creation of the European overseas empires, beginning in the fifteenth century and continuing into the mid-twentieth century, provided a strong incentive for migrants. Settlers were actively sought to populate the "new" lands, which were, of course, already occupied by other peoples. As early as 1634, for example, William Penn opened a migration office in England to attract people to the colonies in North America. Even earlier, in 1608, Samuel de Champlain founded Québec City, established the seigneurial system in New France and persuaded landowners to bring over colonists from France itself.

European empires, especially those of Britain, France, Portugal, Spain and Holland, were also responsible for the mass movements of many non-European peoples. In many parts of the tropics populations were small and labour scarce. Europeans, in their desire to acquire labour for their plantations and mines, took people from areas where labour seemed more than adequate to meet European needs (e.g., India and West Africa) and moved them to areas where the Europeans wanted them for work. Africans were shipped in slavery to work in sugar, coffee, cotton and tobacco plantations throughout the southern parts of the USA, the Caribbean and the eastern coast of South America. Similarly, Indians were shipped as indentured labour, only a notch above slavery, to work for the British throughout their colonies in the Indian and Pacific

Gandhi began his political career as an Indian in South Africa.

ocean basins. Large Indian populations are now found in such places as South Africa, East Africa, Malaysia and Fiji. Chinese, too, were often seized ("shanghaied") to work on railway gangs and ocean clippers, resulting in the dispersal of many Chinese to major seaports around the world.

The enforced movement of non-Europeans was small compared with the voluntary emigration of millions of Europeans. The empires founded by European countries were especially useful during their phase of rapid population growth, and were made possible by the concurrent phase of industrialization. The colonized lands provided a release for the growing population pressures in Europe; the growing populations at the same time provided recruits for the colonizing armies. And the industrial revolution provided the power to quell opposition, opening the way for a virtually continuous wave of settlers that was seen as legitimizing the territorial

An East Indian, Chinese and European railway construction gang near Nanaimo, BC, circa 1890.

claims of the colonizing countries. Europeans migrated in millions during the nineteenth and early twentieth centuries until now there are about as many people of European origin outside Europe as remain in Europe. Few areas of the world were untouched by European influence (see Fig. 7-3). Even today, the influence of the European heritage is widespread, despite the fact that European countries have generally dissolved their empires and reduced colonization (see Fig. 7-4).

While Europeans still emigrate, there is now also a drift of people of European origin back to Europe. This drift comes mostly from those areas of the world newly independent, where Europeans find themselves not only in a cultural minority, but also where they have become politically weak and generally unwelcome. Examples have included the return of many Dutch from Indonesia, Portuguese from Angola and British from Zimbabwe. European populations have not, however, disappeared entirely from former colonial possessions. A 1983 publication (*Accelerated Development in Sub-Saharan Africa*, World Bank) reported that many

European countries are no longer experiencing rapid population growth, being all in at least Phase 4 of the demographic transition.

The Dutch were not alone when they returned from Indonesia; there were also many thousands of Indonesians. Among them were the Moluccans, who had fought for the Dutch in the Royal Netherlands East Indies Army. The Moluccans wanted independence from Indonesia, and hoped the Netherlands could arrange it. They were disappointed and resorted to acts of terrorism, including hijacking trains and holding the passengers hostage. They now live in closed-off groups in three different Dutch towns.

Fig. 7-3
Approximate extent of European influence in 1900

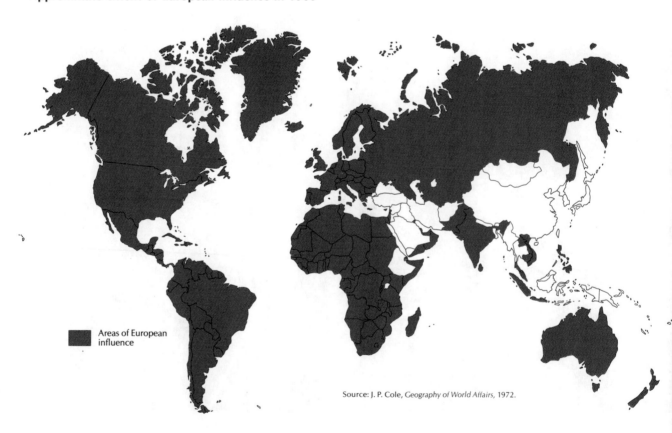

Areas of European influence

Source: J. P. Cole, *Geography of World Affairs*, 1972.

Fig. 7-4
Approximate extent of European influence in the 1980s

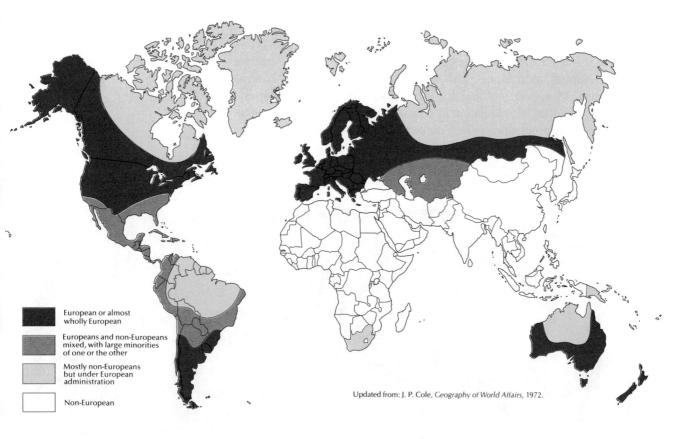

European or almost wholly European

Europeans and non-Europeans mixed, with large minorities of one or the other

Mostly non-Europeans but under European administration

Non-European

Updated from: J. P. Cole, *Geography of World Affairs*, 1972.

countries still rely heavily on European people for much of their managerial and skilled labour (e.g., Zambia 62%, Kenya 48%, Botswana 42%, Tanzania 31%). On the other hand, such reliance is diminishing with local development and is as low as 18% in Malawi and 13% in Nigeria.

The Non-European World

With the onset of death control in the non-European areas of the world, the same population pressures have built up there as developed in nineteenth-century Europe. This has led to heightened pressure for urban-industrial jobs and migration. An additional factor encouraging migration today is the availability of information. In the past, information about prospective destinations was usually sketchy and often coloured by travellers' tales. Now this is less likely to be the case; information is more detailed and its sources are more varied and authoritative. Moreover, the mass media have done much to spread information.

Migration is an increasingly limited option. Rural-urban migration in the developing world is limited by the inability of most cities to cope with growing numbers of inhabitants. Emigration to new countries is less easy than it was for nineteenth-century Europeans. Developing countries have no empires to colonize, and most prospective countries control immigration. Moreover, cultural and educational backgrounds often increase the difficulties of assimilation in countries that still take immigrants.

Despite the problems involved in migration, the number of migrants is growing around the world. Today, the major sources of migrants are southeast Asia, the Caribbean, the Indian subcontinent and Latin America.

Heritage Language Day celebrates multiculturalism in Halifax, Nova Scotia.

Fig. 7-5
Countries or country groups in which at least two students in the City of Toronto school system (Grade 9) were born

Country of Origin	Students	Country of Origin	Students
Portugal	543	Ireland	7
Caribbean	299	Spain	7
Vietnam	289	Angola	7
China	166	Tanzania	7
Hong Kong	149	South Africa	6
Guyana	97	Guatemala	6
United Kingdom	91	Peru	6
USA	83	USSR	6
India	80	Japan	6
Italy	66	Romania	5
Greece	65	Israel	5
Ecuador	58	Lebanon	5
Philippines	41	Uganda	4
South Korea	37	Malta	4
Lao PDR	33	Uruguay	4
Poland	27	Mexico	3
Pakistan	22	El Salvador	3
France	20	Finland	3
Kampuchea	18	Hungary	3
West Germany	17	Monaco	3
Yugoslavia	15	Switzerland	3
Australia	14	Turkey	3
Taiwan	14	Malaysia	3
Argentina	13	Netherlands	2
Colombia	12	Iran	2
Chile	11	Bangladesh	2
Burma	10	Ethiopia	2
Brazil	9	Mauritius	2
Cyprus	7	Nigeria	2
Czechoslovakia	7		

Source: *Grade Nine Student Survey*, Toronto Board of Education, 1982.

STATISTICAL ANALYSIS

10. Toronto is a major recipient of international migrants. The ethnic composition of its school system reflects the sources of migration. Fig. 7-5 presents data on this ethnic composition for the almost 40% of all Grade 9 students there who were born outside Canada.

a. On a world map, shade each country that is listed as a source of migrants to Toronto.

b. Select the 20 chief countries or country groups that are sources of student-migrants, and obtain the square roots of the student-migrant totals. For example, Portugal ranks first with a total of 543, and the square root of 543 is 23.3. Use the answers as the radii in millimetres to plot located proportional circles on a world map (such as the one in Appendix 2).

c. For all countries listed as supplying migrants to Toronto, calculate the number of students each has in Toronto per million of domestic population (see Column A of Appendix 3 for domestic populations). For example, Italy is listed as having a domestic population of 56 505 000, and the students in Toronto who were born in Italy number 66. This means that for every million people living in Italy there are 1.17 Italian-born students in Toronto in Grade 9 (66/56.5 = 1.17). Similarly, Portugal, with a population of 10 082 000, is represented by 53.87 Portuguese-born students in Toronto per million of domestic population. Large countries tend to supply more immigrants than do smaller countries, other things being equal. What, therefore, are we attempting to find out by performing these calculations?

d. Rank the 20 highest answers from **c** from highest to lowest. Does this list correspond with the 20 chief countries listed in **b**? If it does not, what explanations can you suggest?

e Toronto's immigrant Grade 9 students represent on average about six per million of total world population. Your answers to **c** ranged both above and below this world average. Such deviations from an average which may be used as a predictor are called *positive residuals* where the deviation is above the average and *negative residuals* where the deviation is below the average. Thus Greece, with a domestic population of 10 072 000, could be expected, if it conforms with the world average, to be represented in the Toronto school system by about 60 Grade 9 students. In fact it is represented by 65 Grade 9 students, creating a small positive residual. On the other hand, India, with a domestic population of 762 507 000, could be expected to have 4 575 Grade 9 students in Toronto, but in fact has only 80, creating a large negative residual. On a world map, shade all the countries with positive residuals red and those with negative residuals blue. What does this map suggest about the areas of origin of Toronto's immigrant Grade 9 students?

Where Do Migrants Go?

The W.G. Hunt homestead in Lloydminster, Alberta, circa 1910, presents an image of Canada's not-so-distant past.

Provided they can do so, migrants go wherever they believe the quality of life will be better. Over the last two centuries this has generally meant a movement to Australia and New Zealand, South and East Africa, and South and North America. Most of the emigrants have been European, but more recently there have been growing numbers of people from south and east Asia.

The movement of people has become more restrictive over the years. In the early phases of European migration, it was customary for migrants to crush the resistance of indigenous peoples by force of arms, backed by domestic industrial power. Native peoples all over the world had their lands taken from them. In the ensuing clash of cultures, the Europeans always eventually won. The Europeans expanded not only because they wanted to, but also because they were prepared to use force.

However, by settling in large numbers in the "new" lands when they did, the Europeans have effectively taken control of the world's migration opportunities. Australia, for example, excluded Chinese and Indian migrants until 1972; the countries of North America set quotas and entry qualifications. There are now no open lands available to international migrants. Migration today is much more controlled than in the past.

Most descendants of original European settlers have changed their attitudes as they have developed. It is no longer considered acceptable to crush different ethnic groups militarily or to transport slaves and indentured labour around the globe. The changed attitudes encompass some concern about Native rights and a growing recognition of the ethnocentrism of the past. Migration has become somewhat easier for non-Europeans in the past few years, although many restrictions still exist. Canadian immigration policy discriminated against non-Europeans until 1962, when a point system was established. This system made no reference to national origin, but considered such factors as age, education and job skills. The result was a dramatic change in the ethnic composition of the people admitted into Canada. In 1960, almost 80% of Canadian immigrants were European; by 1972 this proportion had dropped to only half that amount. Asian immigration rose from just under 5% to nearly 20%, and Caribbean immigration from 1% to 8%. The point system is still in effect, tied to an annual quota related to the estimated needs of the job market. The USA, still the world's chief destination for migrants, annually allows 170 000 people from the eastern hemisphere and 130 000 from the western hemisphere to immigrate. Only 20 000 from any single country, plus as many relatives as desired, are allowed. The ethnic composition of the USA's immigrant population also has changed greatly over the last few years. The chief sources now are Mexico, the Caribbean, Central America and southeast Asia. Prior to the 1960s, most immigrants were from Europe or Canada.

Different countries set different limits on their immigration policies. New Zealand will not admit anyone over 45 years old (unless they happen to be a dependent parent), nor anyone with more than four children. Switzerland allows only 20 500 new residents a year and Britain permits entry only to Commonwealth citizens with at least one parent born in Britain, except for foreign doctors, dentists and nurses. The Bahamas

Disease was an invisible ally of the Europeans, killing and disabling many Native peoples. However, while tuberculosis and influenza acted for the Europeans, malaria and sleeping sickness acted against them.

The new lands were never really "open," of course; they were used by someone, but armed force negated traditional use.

The Mexican quota, for example, is filled rapidly every year, while the German quota is never filled. Some people believe the USA should let other countries use these unfilled quotas, but there is much opposition to the idea.

One exit tax in the USSR requires emigrants to pay a sum equivalent to the cost of their entire public education. Few can afford it. Defection, if possible, is easier and cheaper. During 1985, over 100 Soviet citizens defected at the airport in Gander, Newfoundland.

It takes time for industrial workers to realize that new jobs are in the service sector. It takes more time for them to re-train. Meanwhile, there is a surplus of unemployed industrial labour.

will not issue a work permit to anyone wanting a job that a Bahamian might do instead.

Some countries have barriers to prevent people from leaving. The Berlin Wall is designed to stop people leaving East Berlin for the West, while Soviet exit taxes are legal barriers intended to discourage emigration. In nations restricting emigration, the only legal migration opportunity may be to go to another part of the same country. Indeed, internal migration is usually officially sponsored. Thus, Soviet citizens are attracted into Siberia by higher wages; Chinese find it easy to obtain work permits and land if they migrate to Xinjiang, Xizang (Tibet) or Manchuria.

Europe is now experiencing the problems associated with the later phases of the demographic transition model and the process of deindustrialization. Populations are virtually static and aging; industrial labour is relatively plentiful. European countries are now seeking to reverse earlier labour policies with respect to the several million "guest workers" deliberately recruited during the period of economic growth in the 1950s, 1960s and early 1970s from a number of countries in southern Europe, northern Africa and the Caribbean. The situation in France is discussed in the following article.

PARIS — The wheel of fortune has come full circle for immigrant workers in France.

The automobile firms that sent recruiting teams to north and west Africa in the 1960s and '70s are now bartering with union and government over how much they should pay Arab and African workers to return home for good.

Official policy now is to pay the workers for being laid off, pick up moving expenses and air tickets, and give more money to help them set up in their home countries — mainly the three north African Arab states of Morocco, Algeria and Tunisia and the black African states of Senegal and Mali.

Workers from numerous other countries, particularly Portugal, are also involved. Renault, as an exam-ple, employs 17,000 foreign workers (17 per cent of the total work force) who come from 70 countries.

Volunteers choosing the payoff will have their working and residence papers confiscated and will be barred from returning to work in France — a country that has become a second home for them. About 70 per cent of the immigrants have been in France for at least 10 years.

The immigrants are of two minds — torn between a lump sum and the practical problems associated with going home. These include, in some cases, relearning their native language; finding French schools for their children; and adapting to agricultural rather than industrial jobs.

The French government has said it will help immigrants start up small businesses, farms or shops. Sene-galese are being trained to go into the tourist industry back home, but Algerians are wary of returning to a country where unemployment is 30 per cent or more.

Akka Ghazi, a 36-year-old Moroccan who has become a prominent union leader among the immigrants, recalled how workers used to be recruited.

"Citroen sent teams, including doctors, to the Atlas Mountain region of Morocco and to the south of the country looking for able-bodied men, preferably illiterate," Ghazi said. "They were put on assembly lines and in the foundries. Nothing much was done to improve their skills or education. Now these men are being blamed for unemployment and unsafe streets."

Alan Tillier, *The Toronto Star*, 1984 4 8

DISCUSSION AND RESEARCH

11. What do you think may be some of the different values held by the various groups involved in the migration pattern within Europe today?

12. European guest workers were rarely offered citizenship. Do you think it would have been better if the countries of northern Europe had offered citizenship to their guest workers? What would be the advantages and disadvantages?

13. If demographic evolution and rate of industrialization are out of phase, as they have been in both northern and southern Europe, should migration be the solution; or should adjustments be made in demography and industrialization?

Workers in a permafrost mine in Pevek, Siberia. The USSR encourages migration to Siberia by offering higher wages.

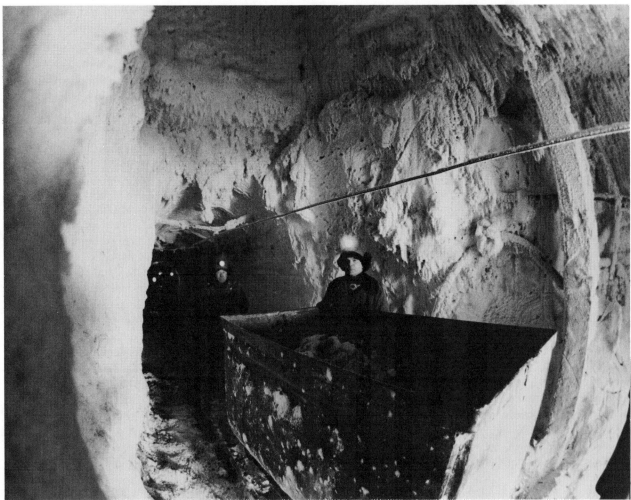

USSR Embassy Press Office/Ottawa

Benefits and Problems of Migration

Benefits

Migration does not occur unless there are benefits. If the benefits are not real the movement rapidly disappears. If the benefits are not long-lasting the migration trend may even be reversed; an example is the movement of West Indians from England back to the Caribbean, which started in the early 1970s. In the 1950s England had recruiting offices in the Caribbean; now there are offices in the UK for West Indians who want to return to the Caribbean.

The benefits of immigration to the receiving country are varied. One benefit can be a larger labour force in situations where the economic demand for labour is growing at a faster rate than the domestic population. By increasing the labour force, immigration helps the growth of the domestic market by increasing the size of the total wage packet and the purchasing power of the domestic market. This, in turn, helps industry to increase economies of scale. This means that the average cost of production per unit tends to fall as more and more goods are made. A large firm can buy more cheaply in bulk. More importantly, the fixed costs can be spread out over more units of production. For example, it may cost $5 000 000 for dies to stamp out car bodies. This is a *fixed cost*, regardless of how many cars are produced. If 10 000 cars are produced, then each will cost $500 for the dies alone, but if 100 000 cars are produced then each will cost only $50 for the dies. Many industrial products must be produced in great quantity to become saleable at acceptable prices.

Immigration may bring other advantages, such as fresh ideas, increased size and, therefore, increased international prestige and the greater likelihood of more successful political, economic and cultural independence. Immigrants bring fresh ideas and enthusiasms, partly because they are often young, and partly because they have different lifestyles and perspectives. Receiving countries which take in immigrants educated elsewhere also save the cost of education. It is estimated, for example, that the USA annually saves about $5 000 000 000 in this way alone.

Source regions may benefit from emigration because they gain some

Fixed costs are those that must be paid regardless of the quantity produced. They include the cost of the factory, the land it is built on, the equipment, and the taxes that must be paid. Costs that vary with the quantity produced (e.g., raw material costs, labour costs) are called *variable costs*.

relief from overpopulation or other problems. They may also benefit from the money emigrants often send back to the old country. Data from the *World Development Report 1983* indicated that migrants' remittances worldwide totalled about $35 000 000 000, with the chief gainers being, in order, Yugoslavia, Italy, Portugal, Turkey, West Germany, Egypt and Pakistan. However, migrants' remittances can cause inflation if they are large and the source region's output of goods and services fails to match the increased availability of money.

Both the destinations and the source regions benefit from migration because the countries involved increase their contact and ties with people from other parts of the world.

Inflation means more money in circulation in proportion to the quantity of goods and services available for purchase. This makes prices rise.

Problems

While migration can bring many advantages, it also can cause many problems. Emigration often results in a loss of skills and enthusiasms that the source regions can ill afford. England suffers from the loss of doctors to North America. In turn, England admits doctors from Pakistan, but Pakistan can recruit doctors from nowhere else. Some developing countries are being drained of much of their skilled labour by the admissions policies of more developed nations. Because it is often difficult for developing nations to provide sufficient high-paying work for their skilled labour, there is a tendency for people with internationally marketable skills to migrate. The source countries pay for the training but get no return on subsequent service. This is one reason for such devices as the USSR's exit taxes, discussed earlier.

This "brain drain" has involved over a half million highly trained people over the last 20 years. Most authorities estimate the cost to developing nations of training these people far exceeds any sum they receive as foreign aid. The Jamaican Prime Minister claimed in 1981 that from 1977–80 Jamaica lost as much as 60% of its newly trained workers to jobs in the USA, Canada and Britain. It had cost an estimated $200 000 000 to train those people, a sum seven times the total aid received by Jamaica from the receiving countries during the same time period. These losses are increasingly regarded as one of the chief hindrances to economic development in the developing world. Much advanced training is available only in the First World, and there is little developing countries can do about citizens who do not return home after completing their training.

These countries may also lose the most active part of their labour force, especially the people aged 20 to 40. This is less serious if jobs are scarce or if some of the migrants eventually return with technical skills they have acquired in the host country. For this reason, Algeria has

This poses a basic and crucial dilemma: which are more important, the rights of the state or the rights of the individual?

For example, returning Filipinos who have learned high level welding skills in the oilfields of Saudi Arabia have nowhere in the Philippines to use those skills.

gladly seen its young people leave for work in France. The Philippines, however, cannot always use the skills of returning workers in its industrial sector. Egypt cannot afford to lose the remittances that cease when workers return from work in the oilfields of the Middle East. According to a newspaper report of 1986 7 17, lost remittances had reduced the effective per capita incomes of 90% of Egypt's rural population by half. On the other hand, East Germany decided in 1961 that it could no longer afford to lose labour at the rate it had in the 1950s, and put up a guarded wall between itself and West Berlin. In some countries it is difficult for labour to leave, notably the USSR and China. Some developing countries that are losing highly skilled labour are also restricting emigration by requiring students to sign a formal commitment to return, not allowing spouses to accompany workers, imposing high emigration taxes, making passports almost prohibitively expensive to obtain and so on.

Calls for restricting immigration are not uncommon in Canada when the economy slows down.

Receiving countries also face problems from immigration. If the economy is slow, the domestic population often resents the competition from immigrants for jobs. Immigrants may also be blamed for competition in the housing market, and for rising costs in health care and education.

A Sikh priest in Vancouver. A society can benefit from the skills and values its various immigrants bring, but only if it is prepared to celebrate rather than condemn cultural differences.

The Public Archives of Canada

Such sentiments tend to ignore the benefits immigrants bring.

Prejudice and discrimination are possible concerns. The host society may eventually contain a number of cultural groups. The host society can benefit from the variety of cultures represented if it accepts and values the different lifestyles introduced by the immigrants and if the immigrants seek to some extent to accept the lifestyle of the host country.

The failure of either or both to adjust to different beliefs and values inevitably produces tension. One culture may be dominant, but cultural domination is no guarantee of racial or cultural harmony. Minor cultural differences may be ignored or regarded as interesting, but major differences in values are always a cause of tension. An essential ingredient for harmony in multicultural situations appears to be mutual tolerance and respect.

DISCUSSION AND RESEARCH

14. Europeans have been the world's major migrants. What benefits have they brought to areas they have colonized and settled?

15. What problems have Europeans caused by their intrusion into the realms of different cultures?

16. What do you consider the most basic differences in values that could cause diverse cultures to exist in a state of mutual suspicion and hostility?

17. Give some examples of cultural traits that can be accepted by all groups as "interesting"?

18. Suggest some values that all cultures hold strongly.

Many immigrant groups seek to preserve their cultures and languages as they integrate into the mainstream of Canadian society. This class is studying Jewish history and Hebrew.

Ontario Archives

Urbanization

Year	Percentage of world population that is urban
1950	25.4
1960	33.0
1970	37.2
1980	41.5
1990	46.1 (est.)
2000	51.1 (est.)
(Source: UN)	

Characteristics

Migration patterns demonstrate two traits. One is dispersal, shown by the spread of migrants over wider and wider areas of the earth's surface. The other is agglomeration, visible when migrants gather together in areas that appear to offer them the maximum net benefit.

Urbanization is one of the products of the drive for agglomeration. People move to the cities in search of what they hope will be a better life than they believe they can obtain in the countryside. Movement from country to city is the chief type of migration in the world today. It involves millions in most parts of the developing world, although urbanization has now virtually ceased in the developed world.

STATISTICAL ANALYSIS

19. Using the data in Column V of Appendix 3, construct a graded shading map of the world to show the different degrees of urbanization. Use four classes, as follows:

highly urbanized	75% – 100%	very bright red
moderately urbanized	60% – 74%	bright red
slightly urbanized	40% – 59%	pale red
not urbanized	0% – 39%	very pale red

    Compare the map with others drawn for assignments in other chapters. How do the different maps compare?

20. Obtain a correlation coefficient (r) for the relationship that exists between the degree of urbanization (Column V) and the annual percentage population increase (Column H). Use the *standard deviation technique*, based on a sample, as shown in Appendix 4. Discuss the meaning of the value of r. You will probably find that the correlation is only moderately strong. There are reasons for this; what do you think they are?

As populations swell, marginal lands are brought into use. With only a machete or an axe, it can take a group a month to clear one hectare.

Causes

Urbanization is tied both to an increase in population and to a revolution in agricultural productivity. As the population of a region increases, the prime farming areas gradually get used up. New villages appear; marginal lands are brought into use; remoter areas are pioneered and settled. Eventually all the available land in the region is in use. The Indo-Gangetic Plain, lowland China, Guatemala and Java are examples of fully used areas. As population continues to increase in size, a land-hungry population surplus develops. Where possible, this surplus can be accommodated by migration to other regions still relatively empty.

Brazil, for example, is encouraging more and more of its growing population to settle in its less populated interior. It first built a new capital city at Brasilia, 1 000 km inland; then it began construction of a new road through the Amazon basin. Now it offers cheap land to farmers willing to settle in the interior. Indonesia would like more of its people to move into the relatively underpopulated areas of Sumatra, and so ease population pressures in Java. The USSR and China also want to move their people into the relatively empty areas of central Asia, although only partly for demographic reasons. In the past, Canada has

What other reasons could there be for the Soviets and Chinese wanting to populate the relatively empty areas of central Asia?

Canada has also moved many Inuit onto Arctic islands, and employs many of them as Canadian Rangers to help guard the northern areas.

used government sponsorship to tempt people into remoter areas such as the Peace River District, the Ontario–Québec Clay Belt, and the Lac St. Jean area.

If population pressures cannot be eased by migration to other areas, a country may face unemployment, poverty, declining living standards, overcrowding and disease. These problems may be somewhat alleviated by improvements in farming technology. Farming technology changed first in eighteenth century England, then throughout Europe, North America, Australia, New Zealand and Japan. At present, farming techniques are changing across southern Asia, Latin America and Africa. The immediate effect of this ongoing spread of improved agricultural technology is a reduction in the demand for farm labour.

These gangs were often called Luddites, after one of their leaders, Ned Ludd. Their main purpose was the destruction of machinery, which they felt deprived them of jobs.

The reduced demand for farm labour complicates the problem of rural overpopulation. When technology began to replace manual labour in eighteenth century England, gangs of dispossessed and frustrated farmworkers roamed the countryside. Similar unrest occurs today in some countries of southern Asia, Latin America and Africa.

Industrialization

The process of industrialization, as we saw in Chapter 4, is a corollary of changing agricultural technology. Industry provides jobs for not only the rural unemployed but also for the increasing population. Europe was fortunate when it went through the early phases of industrialization. There was little competition for its new technology; empires could be seized, and "surplus" people resettled there to act as suppliers of raw materials and buyers of manufactured goods. Countries that industrialized later could not do this as easily.

For many of the developing countries of the world, which lack enough opportunities for emigration, the cities and towns have become the chief destination of many rural unemployed. But there are insufficient factories and services; the demands being made on the cities and towns of the developing nations are in fact too great for them to handle. The same problems do not occur to this extent in more developed countries because they are already highly urbanized.

Most of the cities and towns of the developing world have existed since antiquity. They are therefore largely preindustrial settlements, having developed to supply religious, commercial, administrative, transportation and other urban services to the surrounding countryside. They seldom contain factories, although the number is increasing. Many argue it is better to leave them that way, and develop industry in the countryside; but agglomeration is a powerful drive, and the developing world's cities have become the major focus of many people's ambitions.

One sign of a pre-industrial society is the necessary closeness of markets to areas of production. This cauliflower vendor in Agra, India, pushes his produce to the marketplace.

John Molyneux

Central Places

Preindustrial towns tend to be fairly regularly distributed throughout farming areas. The spacing of the towns varies with the type of transportation most commonly used; people who walk require a closer spacing of towns than people using cars or buses. Spacing of the towns also is affected by general population density. The provision of any urban service requires a certain minimum number of people to make it worthwhile, such a minimum number being called the *service threshold*. Where the rural population density is low, service centres must be spread far apart to obtain a sufficient number of people (service threshold) within their urban field.

Thus the distribution of preindustrial towns and cities does not form an absolutely regular pattern. Working on the assumption that a regular pattern will be formed wherever possible, Christaller developed the *theory of central places*, in which he saw a pattern of towns and cities developing in response to the varied threshold requirements of different urban services. A bank requires a relatively low threshold population, so a small town may provide banking services. However, a university has a higher threshold requirement, so only a few towns will provide such a service. Christaller recognized the existence of a hierarchy of service towns, based on the provision of services with increasingly higher threshold requirements. One of his models is the *K3 Network*, in which towns are ideally arranged as shown in Fig. 7-6.

One of the major functions of pre-industrial towns is to serve as a market, and people generally need to be able to get to the market and home again in the same day.

For example, a McDonald's restaurant usually requires about 50 000 people as a threshold.

Fig. 7-6
The principle of Christaller's K3 Network, idealized

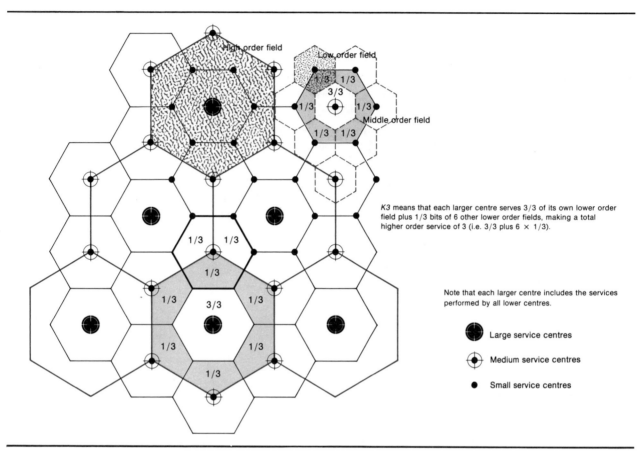

K3 means that each larger centre serves 3/3 of its own lower order field plus 1/3 bits of 6 other lower order fields, making a total higher order service of 3 (i.e. 3/3 plus 6 × 1/3).

Note that each larger centre includes the services performed by all lower centres.

⊕ Large service centres

⊕ Medium service centres

● Small service centres

Urban Hierarchies, Jobs and Migration

There are two trends regarding the location of industry. Industry may develop at points quite unrelated to the existing pattern of preindustrial towns, as at orebodies, or it may develop as part of the hierarchical pattern discussed above. Under a market system, the locations of industries are determined by their needs. Some needs are input-loaded, such as those for energy, raw materials and labour; others are output-loaded, such as that for good access to markets. This means that the location of any industry is largely determined by the particular type of industry and its individual needs.

For example, aluminum industries require access to energy, but clothing industries require access to markets.

Industries most influenced by the need for access to energy or raw materials will locate close to them to obtain the greatest net advantage. Such places may or may not coincide with existing locations of preindustrial towns. On the other hand, industries which are labour-intensive or market-oriented will locate in already existing towns where the labour and markets are. To obtain the widest access to labour and the maximum coverage of the market, thereby gaining maximum economies of scale, industries will locate in the largest service centres first. Only later will they expand into the smaller service centres. The degree to which this expansion has progressed becomes a measure of the degree to which industrialization has occurred. In the more developed countries industries will be found in even the smallest urban service centres. In developing countries, on the other hand, the filtering down process may not have progressed very far, and only the largest service centre may have any industry. Published information on this topic is rare, but Fig. 7-7, based on an article in *Economic Geography*, shows the extent to which manufacturing industry had penetrated some of the national urban networks in Africa by the late 1970s. For instance, all of Gambia's

Fig. 7-7
The percentage share of national manufacturing in some African capital cities

City	Percentage
Bathurst (Gambia)	100
Libreville (Gabon)	100
Monrovia (Liberia)	100
Bangui (Central African Republic)	100
Bukavi (Rwanda)	100
Dakar (Senegal)	81
Bujumbura (Burundi)	80
Freetown (Sierra Leone)	75
Blantyre (Malawi)	73
Abidjan (Ivory Coast)	63
Dar es Salaam (Tanzania)	63
Khartoum (Sudan)	60
Conakry (Guinea)	50
Donala (Cameroon)	50
Addis Ababa (Ethiopia)	47
Nairobi (Kenya)	42
Lagos (Nigeria)	35
Lusaka (Zambia)	35
Brazzaville (Congo)	33
Accra (Ghana)	30
Kinshasa (Zaire)	30
Kampala (Uganda)	28

Source: *Economic Geography*, Vol. 49, p. 11.

Fig. 7-8
Numbers of cities with populations of one million or more, 1950-2000 (projected)

City population	1950	1960	1970	1980	1990	2000
Developed countries						
5 000 000 or more	5	10	11	11	15	16
2 000 000 – 4 999 999	15	16	20	31	41	50
1 000 000 – 1 999 999	28	38	54	67	77	84
Developing countries						
5 000 000 or more	1	2	9	15	25	43
2 000 000 – 4 999 999	9	15	19	40	60	83
1 000 000 – 1 999 999	13	29	44	61	104	138

Source: United Nations, Population Division, *Trends and Prospects in the Population of Urban Agglomerations, 1950-2000*, 1975 11.

manufacturing was concentrated in Bathurst; there had been no expansion to any lower order centres. Uganda, on the other hand, displayed a much higher degree of industrial penetration down the urban hierarchy, with only 28% of its manufacturing located in Kampala.

Because industry and its accompanying jobs tend, in a market economy, to filter down the hierarchy of service centres from the largest to the smallest, job seekers tend to migrate up it. As the agricultural revolution occurs, people move to the towns for work. They may move first to the smaller local towns, but their ultimate destination will be those towns that provide the job opportunities. In many cases in the developing world, that means the very largest centres at the top of the hierarchy. The largest cities in the developing world have thus become the major destination of most rural-urban migrants.

STATISTICAL ANALYSIS

21. Using the data in Fig. 7-8 and an appropriate log scale from Appendix 4, construct a semi-log time-series graph to show the growing numbers of large cities throughout the world. Use red lines for the developing countries, and blue for the others. What conclusions do you draw?

22. One way of showing the hierarchical nature of urban networks is to apply the *rank-size rule* (see Appendix 4), which is based on simple observation and is, therefore, called an empirical rule. The rule states that the second city in a hierarchy will be approximately half the size of the first city, that the third city will be approximately one-third the size of the first city, and so on. We can best show the city rankings against size by drawing a log-log graph. Using the data in Fig. 7-9, and

Fig. 7-9
The thirty largest urban areas in each of four countries

Rank	Canada	Pop	India	Pop	USA	Pop	USSR	Pop
01	Toronto	2 883	Calcutta	9 166	New York	16 121	Moscow	8 302
02	Montréal	2 827	Bombay	8 227	Los Angeles	11 498	Leningrad	4 722
03	Vancouver	1 201	Delhi	5 714	Chicago	7 870	Kiev	2 297
04	Ottawa-Hull	753	Madras	4 277	Philadelphia	5 548	Tashkent	1 902
05	Edmonton	611	Bangalore	2 914	San Francisco	5 180	Baku	1 616
06	Winnipeg	591	Hyderabad	2 528	Detroit	4 618	Kharkov	1 503
07	Québec City	566	Ahmedabad	2 515	Boston	3 448	Gorky	1 373
08	Calgary	544	Kanpur	1 688	Houston	3 101	Minsk	1 370
09	Hamilton	542	Poona	1 685	Washington	3 061	Novosibirsk	1 357
10	St. Catharines	310	Nagpur	1 298	Dallas	2 975	Sverdlovsk	1 252
11	Kitchener	288	Lucknow	1 007	Cleveland	2 834	Kuybyshev	1 243
12	London	277	Jaipur	1 005	Miami	2 644	Dnepropetrovsk	1 114
13	Halifax	275	Coimbatore	917	St. Louis	2 356	Tbilisi	1 110
14	Windsor	245	Patna	916	Pittsburgh	2 264	Odessa	1 085
15	Victoria	232	Surat	913	Baltimore	2 174	Erevan	1 076
16	Regina	168	Madurai	904	Minneapolis	2 114	Chelyabinsk	1 066
17	Sudbury	152	Indore	827	Seattle	2 093	Omsk	1 061
18	St. John's	150	Varanasi	794	Atlanta	2 030	Donetsk	1 047
19	Saskatoon	144	Agra	770	San Diego	1 817	Perm	1 028
20	Oshawa	144	Japalpur	758	Cincinnati	1 660	Kazan	1 023
21	Chicoutimi-Jonquière	131	Vadodara	744	Denver	1 621	Ufa	1 023
22	Thunder Bay	122	Cochin	686	Milwaukee	1 570	Alma Ata	1 001
23	St. John	120	Dhanbad	677	Tampa	1 569	Rostov	966
24	Sherbrooke	105	Bhopal	672	Kansas City	1 327	Volgograd	956
25	Trois Rivières	99	Jamshedpur	670	Indianapolis	1 306	Saratov	881
26	Kingston	91	Ulhasnagar	648	Buffalo	1 243	Riga	858
27	Sydney	89	Allahabad	642	Portland, Ore	1 243	Krasnoyarsk	833
28	Brantford	83	Tiruchirapalli	608	New Orleans	1 187	Zaporozhye	824
29	Sault Ste. Marie	82	Ludhiana	606	Providence	1 096	Voronezh	820
30	Sarnia	81	Visakhapatnam	594	Columbus, Ohio	1 093	Lvov	699

Source: UN *Demographic Yearbook 1982.*
Note: Populations in thousands

appropriate log scales from Appendix 4, construct a log-log graph to show size (population) on the vertical axis, and rank on the horizontal axis. Use differently coloured dots for each separate data set, and join the dots with a line.

a. What do you notice about the hierarchical pattern?

b. How do the data fit the K3 theory?

	Population growth rate (%/y)	Urban growth rate (%/y)
Bangladesh	2.3	6.5
Mozambique	2.6	8.2
Lesotho	2.4	16.1
Zaire	2.6	7.5
Bolivia	2.7	6.9
Saudi Arabia	4.3	7.4
(**Source**: World Bank, 1983)		

The United Nations calculates that at the present rate of urbanization about half the world's population will live in urban areas by the year 2000. It also estimates that the total population of the world may then be over 6 000 000 000. By 2000, then, the world's cities may have the huge task of providing housing and jobs for over 3 000 000 000 people, while at the same time having spread over a fairly large part of the world's most productive farmland. The bulk of the increase will come (and is already coming) in the towns and cities of the developing world. An extreme example of the existing situation is given in the following article.

Rat caper Mexico's newest crime

MEXICO CITY — It would be difficult to imagine any new horrors to add to those already suffered by the inhabitants of Mexico City — the traffic, the dangerous driving, the poisonous air, the relentless din, the crime, the altitude, and the sheer size of this massive monument to urban mismanagement.

Yet a new horror is being visited on middle class car drivers in a particularly grotesque form of theft: The rat trap.

The thief waits by the roadside until he spots a car with an open window through which he tosses a frightened and angry live rat.

The driver unfailingly panics, skids to a halt, and bolts from the car together with his hysterical passengers. The thief then jumps in and roars off, presumably caging the rat for use on another day.

Not that a new rat would be difficult to obtain. Mexico City sets dreadful new records in contamination and abomination. It is an urban apocalypse now.

The definition is not rhetorical. Experts have seriously suggested that the toxic fumes rising constantly into the atmosphere, many from uncollected rubbish, could one day ignite.

The resulting conflagration could turn into a fire storm, gulping in oxygen to feed the flames, and suffocating perhaps hundreds of thousands of citizens.

In 1981, a municipal rubbish dump caught fire.

The flames and explosions continued for 10 days, adding 10 times to the already dangerous concentration of sulphur dioxide in the pitifully thin air. At 7,400 feet [2250 m] high, Mexico City never had much oxygen to start off with.

The city lies sprawled across its plateau a mile and a half up, surrounded by still higher mountains. The bowl acts as a trap for smoke and fumes, and an estimated 11,000 t of pollutants compete with the oxygen daily.

On most days a brownish-grey smog haze hangs over the city, and the snow-capped twin peaks of the volcanos, Popocatepetl and Ixtaccihautl, only 40 miles [65 km] away, are seen so rarely now that their visibility are occasions for comment in the newspapers.

The impact on the visitor accustomed to reasonable air is unpleasant and immediate. Within half an hour of arriving at the airport, I had a sore throat.

A city health officer has publicly reported that just breathing the air is equivalent to smoking 40 cigarettes a day. Add this to the newcomer's shortness of breath and a wildly pumping heart because of the altitude, and Mexico City becomes a malaise.

The oxygen is also shared by millions more people than the place can properly accommodate. The present population is estimated at 16 to 17 million, spilling over from the 590 square miles [1500 km²] of the federal district into the neighboring province.

This makes it the most populous conurbation in the world. By the year 2000, at the present rate of growth, there could be 35 million in Mexico City, although life may have come to a standstill before the millennium.

The city is literally killing its inhabitants. Thousands die annually from diseases directly caused by or related to the contamination and pollution.

Pollutants come from the area's 130,000 industries, many belching uncontrolled smoke, and the 2.7 million vehicles that circulate — ricochet would be a better word — in the metropolis, causing a rush hour that lasts all day.

Medical researchers have stated that as many as half the city's residents, usually the poorest, die of parasitical diseases.

About 40 per cent suffer from chronic bronchitis, and respiratory diseases are a major killer. Air pollution has been estimated at 100 times above the acceptable level, although other measurements indicate it is "only" 75 times over.

The mountains of garbage from households alone accumulate at the rate of 800 t a day, and are beyond the city's capacity for disposal.

The millions of poor who inhabit the slums which surround the city have no toilets or sewage systems, so they use any spare patch of ground they can find. Health authorities have suggested that 750 t of human excrement are deposited this way daily. The waste matter dries up and disperses as dust, which is then blown through the city, causing the parasitical ailments.

Mexico City must be the only place in the world where you can contract hepatitis just by breathing.

Peasants from impoverished rural communities reach the city at the rate of about 1,000 a day and are known as paracaidistas, or parachutists, a nickname deriving from their sudden appearance, as if dropped by night.

Their ramshackle slums are called *ciudades perditas*, lost cities. They have no names, are not on any maps, have no infrastructure or services, and contain millions of people, many of them Indians.

The worst are haphazard collections of hovels put together from corrugated tin, industrial cardboard, discarded plywood, and stolen building materials.

They occupy earth alleyways which turn into mud during the rains, and during the long dry season contribute to the dust and grit which can cut visibility downtown to a couple of blocks.

During daylight, these barrios are almost deserted. The men and women who are able to tolerate hours of queuing and travelling in jammed and dilapidated buses and (modern and efficient) electric trains to the city in search of work, have gone for the day.

At night nobody without an unavoidable reason to be there is foolish enough to set foot in the lost cities.

There are about 500 such places around Mexico City, but because of the austerity program which followed the devaluation crisis in 1982, work is even more difficult to find. Some social workers now say the influx has slowed and some might even be returning to villages.

The middle class, which only two years ago enjoyed an over-valued peso which brought it imported luxuries at reasonable prices, has been jolted by a devaluation raising [the cost of] these items six times.

Foreign travel is out of the question except for the rich. Even so, the first thing anyone buys as soon as it becomes possible, is a car.

These make up the final horror of Mexico City. Most drivers are single-occupant commuters, and 97 per cent of vehicles carry only a fifth of all travellers.

These commuters, Volkswagen "beetle" taxis, and broken-down buses emitting clouds of black diesel smoke, hurtle along main boulevards and choke side streets, sounding their horns incessantly, shouting insults, and playing music on their radios at earth-shattering volume.

Driving is fast, chaotic, aggressive and extremely dangerous. There is no lane discipline and vehicles shoot around each other like fairground bumper cars.

Triple parking is commonplace, and traffic police blow whistles furiously and fruitlessly, pausing only to take a mordida, "bite" or bribe, from some luckless driver who may — or equally may not — have infringed a regulation.

Drunken driving is a major hazard. In 1980, traffic accidents took 34,000 lives. For every 10,000 cars in the United States, statistics show, there are 3.19 deaths. In Mexico the figure is 56 deaths.

There are pleasant parts of Mexico City, of course — though beyond the means of anyone not rich. Sumptuous public buildings of the Spanish colonial period and afterwards, remain.

They stand as reminders that Mexico City was once regarded as the Paris of the Americas. Now they are often next door to modern buildings, abandoned half-way through construction, reminders of the economic present.

Only recently has Mexico acquired its first-ever town planner, who described his appointment as a good news–bad news joke. It was good to have his outline plan accepted in a 1979 nationwide competition; the bad news was that he now has the task of trying out his plans in the world's most unmanageable city.

It has become a new kind of monument; a terrible warning to developing countries about what happens to the capital with unplanned, rapid industrialization. For Mexico City it is too late.

Christopher Reed, *The Toronto Star* 1984 2 5

DISCUSSION AND RESEARCH

23. What actions can you suggest could be taken in rural areas to ease the growth problems of the cities?

24. What measures do you think could be taken within the cities to ease some of their accumulating problems?

25. The UN estimates that by 2000 there will be many cities with populations over 10 000 000, some with populations over 20 000 000, and a few (perhaps Calcutta; Mexico City; Sao Paulo) with populations over 30 000 000.

  a. What are the problems of great size?

  b. What are the advantages of great size?

  c. Is there an ideal size for a highest order (primate) city?

The Future

When discussing the future of urbanization, many people foresee the growth of super cities (megalopolises) and chains of formerly separate cities linked into single huge urban areas (conurbations). There are always pessimistic predictions of "concrete jungles" and polluted "human anthills." These forecasts are based on linear extrapolations of existing trends in rural-urban migration and may not necessarily prove to be correct. China and the USA provide examples of situations that may affect future patterns of urbanization, perhaps resolving some of the problems caused by inward migration.

China: 79% rural, 21% urban (*World Development Report 1985*)

China's population is still mostly rural; its towns and cities are essentially preindustrial, except for a few near the coast and along the major rivers. If normal migration patterns held true, China's rural population would now be migrating to the towns; but this is not happening on any large scale. Migration to the cities is banned by the government, and compensating rural development projects are designed to provide employment for people in the countryside.

The USA, on the other hand, has experienced massive migrations into its towns and cities. From 1950 to 1970, Greater New York City gained 2 000 000 additional inhabitants through inward migration. But the situation is changing. The problems of great size have caused many industries and businesses to leave the major cities. As a result, the rural population has been growing faster than the urban population since 1970. Dispersal has taken over from agglomeration.

To some extent the process may be likened to an expanding donut, with the hole representing the depopulated inner city areas, and new growth occurring around the edges. For example, Chicago lost 350 000 people from 1970 to 1980, but Greater Chicago grew by 100 000. Similarly, San Francisco lost 40 000, but Greater San Francisco gained over

100 000. But there has also been real movement completely away from the metropolitan areas. While New York City's population decreased by 800 000 people from 1970 to 1980, Greater New York's actually decreased by 900 000. Similarly, Boston lost 80 000, while Greater Boston lost 120 000. With a few exceptions located in the western and southwestern parts of the country (Los Angeles, San Diego, Dallas, Houston, Phoenix), US cities have begun to house fewer people. Most of the "Greater" cities of the north and east are also in decline and growth is occurring only in the west and south. Millions of people are on the move, and the centre of population in the US is shifting from the northeast to the southwest. Some of the reasons for this shift arise from crowding in the northeast; others are linked to the demand by industry and people for safer, warmer, sunnier, cheaper, quieter, cleaner places. Accordingly states such as Arizona, California, Florida, Georgia, Louisiana, Nevada, Oklahoma, Oregon, Tennessee, Texas, Utah and Wyoming are among the fastest growing areas in the USA. Rhode Island and New York State are in actual decline.

What will happen to people in the developing world, however, where they meet with inadequate job opportunities in the cities and can find no way of returning to rural self-sufficiency? There are growing millions who can neither feed themselves from the land nor find employment in the cities. To many, it appears that social and economic forces are out of balance and that political solutions must be found.

The centre of population is the point at which a country would balance if it were cut out and all people counted for equal weight. In the USA, the centre in 1800 was just outside Baltimore; in 1900 it was in Indiana; in 1950 it was in Illinois; by 1980 it was in Missouri. It has always shifted southwestward.

Tucson, Arizona. Populations of the "sunbelt" states are rising rapidly as the USA becomes a more decentralized and service-oriented society.

H. Armstrong Roberts/Miller Services

CASE STUDY

THE MIDDLE EAST: Migration of Labour

There are about 4 000 000 migrant workers employed outside their own countries in the Middle East. About half of them are from other Arab countries, but increasing numbers are from non-Arab countries such as India, Pakistan, Bangladesh, Sri Lanka, Burma, Indonesia, Malaysia and the Philippines.

The chief destination for most of these migrants is the oil-rich group of countries consisting of Bahrain, Iraq, Kuwait, Oman, Qatar, Saudi Arabia and the United Arab Emirates. Until 1973 the main economic activity of this group was exporting oil, and there was little internal economic development. However, the increases in oil price after 1973 removed a major development constraint. Money became available in large quantities, and this availability has since been maintained by borrowing on international markets if necessary. The governments of the oil group thus began looking for ways to raise the overall level of economic activity in their countries beyond that reached by oil exporting alone. There was a growing realization that, while they lasted, oil revenues should be used to finance the construction of a more durable economic base.

The group's decision to purchase economic development posed certain problems at the time and has created other problems since. Purchases of technology, equipment and managerial and entrepreneurial skills from the developed countries were relatively easy. But the purchase of labour was a greater problem.

All the oil-rich countries of the group have relatively small populations. The largest is Iraq with 15 500 000. However, Saudi Arabia has only 11 150 000, Kuwait 1 900 000, the United Arab Emirates 1 700 000, Oman 1 000 000, Bahrain 500 000 and Qatar 400 000. The available domestic labour supply is restricted by the small populations. The situation is made more difficult by the prevailing Islamic attitude against employing women in the paid workforce. It is further reduced by the characteristically high birth rates of the region, which create an exceptionally large proportion of very young and as yet unemployable children in the total population. It is reduced still more by the success of a rapidly growing educational system, which keeps greater numbers of young people out of the workforce, often until after university. For these reasons, the labour force actually available within the seven countries is quite small. Activity rates (the percentages of the total population actually employed in the labour force) are low by world standards, ranging from 18.4% in Qatar to 26.0% in Iraq, compared with a world average of 33.2%.

The scarcity of labour has to some extent been improved by importing labour from other countries into six of the seven countries under consideration. The exception is Iraq. Although Iraq has been at war with Iran through the 1980s, it has the largest population and the highest activity rate of the group. It therefore has less need of imported labour. Only about 5% of Iraq's labour force consists of imported migrant labour, compared with 41.7% in Oman, 51.8% in Saudi Arabia, 53.9% in Bahrain, 66.1% in Kuwait, 86.1% in Qatar and 90.3% in the United Arab Emirates. It is thus in this latter group of countries that the primary benefits and problems of labour importation are experienced.

Migrant labour has been the chief source of

John Molyneux

The influx of migrant workers into Kuwait required the building of many new housing developments like this one.

labour in the construction industry, helping to build roads, factories, schools, hospitals and houses. It is also a major factor in the service industries such as communications, teaching, medicine, trade and transportation. More workers are also being employed in the agricultural sector as domestic labour moves into the better-paying manufacturing and service sectors. The benefits of these developments to the receiving countries are clear, but there are also associated problems.

One is the sheer size of the influx of migrant

labour in relation to the domestic population. There are problems relating to the provision of adequate housing and health care for the immigrant labour, and additional problems connected with cultural and social adaptation. These problems exist even where immigrants form only a small part of the total population. In cases where the proportion of emigrants is as large as it is in some of the countries of the Middle East the problems assume importance. The domestic population fears being swamped by foreigners. This is compounded by anxieties which come from dislocation of traditional lifestyles brought about during rapid economic change. The result is social stress. Familiar ways of life disappear, values are challenged by new values and traditional identities are at risk.

Such problems were less severe in the 1970s, when most of the early migrants were from other Arab countries. In 1975 Egypt, Jordan and North Yemen supplied over half the labour migrating to the oil-rich group of countries. By the mid-1980s, however, these three countries supplied only one-third of the Middle East's migrant labour. Instead, more labour was coming from India and other non-Arab countries of south and east Asia, adding to the ethnic complexity of the workforce. It is projected that these trends will continue, partly because the original Arab suppliers of labour cannot continue to supply the demand for it, and partly because the mix of labour skills required by the oil-rich countries is changing as their economies develop.

Another problem with labour migration is that the worker usually sees the initial move as a prelude to moving the entire family. Though such moves are often illegal, they do occur. A study in Abu Dhabi (one of the United Arab Emirates) in the early 1980s indicated that as much as 35% of the entire population was illegally residing there. This is expected to increase as more immigrants come from farther afield, thus aggravating problems of housing, health care, education, minority rights, political representation and so on. There are occasional reports from the oil-rich countries that particular groups of illegal immigrants are being deported, but the drive for economic growth generally means that regulations must be relaxed for markets to be met.

Source countries also gain advantages as well as suffer disadvantages. We have already discussed the practice of migrants' remittances. Over the years, billions of dollars have been transferred in this way from the oil-rich countries to the labour exporting countries. The value of migrants' remittances to North Yemen has at least equalled and often exceeded the total amount of money earned by its regular export trade. For Egypt, the value of migrants' remittances has regularly been the equivalent of about 25% of its regular export earnings. These amounts are considerable and provide the labour exporting countries with tangible benefits. Another advantage gained by labour exporting countries lies in the reduction of their own domestic unemployment. This eases the burden on housing and medical facilities and permits the remaining domestic population, now additionally supported by migrants' remittances, to gain a greater individual share of national product and improve its standard of living.

The sending countries also suffer disadvantages. As the years have passed and the economies of the oil-rich countries developed, their demand for particular types of labour has changed. They no longer need the same numbers of unskilled workers, who led the first wave of migrants for the construction industries. They no longer need the unemployed from other countries. Now the oil-rich countries are looking for skilled labour, and for professional and managerial talent. The loss of more skilled labour from the labour exporting countries has led them to see their own domestic labour force being depleted qualitatively as well as quantitatively. They see the stunting of their own development by such losses. They also view the loss of skilled and managerial labour as the loss of the time and money it took to train them. And they are coming to see that migrants' remittances do not cover these costs. Since the labour exporting countries now retain more of their own unskilled and unemployed labour, they also face renewed problems of job creation and education that are only aggravated by the growing domestic shortages of managerial and professional people.

The picture is not simple. Some countries that export labour to the oil-rich nations nevertheless remain attractive to other foreign nationals, for whom they seem to offer more benefits than their own countries do. This produces, in effect, a secondary labour migration, a condition especially notable in Jordan and North Yemen. As people leave these countries for jobs in, say, Saudi Arabia, they leave labour vacancies which can be filled by workers from other countries, mainly Egypt, who move in to fill them. In this way, Egyptians unable to find work in one of the oil-rich countries still are able to find better-paying work than at home in Egypt. The picture is still further complicated by internal movements within the group of oil-rich countries. For example, Oman is an oil-rich country that attracts migrants from elsewhere; it also loses many of its own nationals to Saudi Arabia, which is perceived by many Omanis to offer even better opportunities than are available in Oman. A migration hierarchy is thus being established. It is driven by oil-funded development and affects the Arab peoples of the Middle East and, increasingly, the non-Arab peoples of south and east Asia. No one knows whether developing interracial friction will heighten the tensions in the Middle East or developing racial tolerance will lower them. Migration will continue, however, in the Middle East as it does, and always has, elsewhere.

Unicef / Joan Liftin

A grandmother comforts her grandchild in a Turkish migrant workers' tent camp. In Middle Eastern countries without large oil reserves, migrant workers remain largely agricultural and poorly paid.

Conclusion

From their origins, human beings have always migrated, and the earth's population has gradually spread over almost the entire land surface of the globe. In this process, many benefits and problems have developed. Opportunities for a new life have been created, new lands developed and natural resources discovered. Different races have come into contact and some mixing has occurred. However, migrations in some areas have also led to overcrowding, food scarcities and unemployment. Different ethnic and cultural groups have often clashed with one another.

As people have developed strong centralized governments, they have also sought to control the flow of immigrants. Increasingly, migration has been subjected to laws and regulations, and the flows now are more controlled than at any time in the past. Government action has in fact come to dominate much of what happens in the world. Governments generally try to act in the interests of their own countries, and so decisions about issues such as food supplies, natural resource use, birth control and migrations will be made according to these interests. In the next chapter, therefore, we will take a closer look at the political aspects of geography.

8 GEOPOLITICS

Introduction

Politics may be loosely defined as the process of decision-making by society as a whole, usually formalized at government level. Some political decisions are not directly related to geography — the minimum age for voting, for example. Other political decisions can be very much concerned with geography; these include decisions on trade, military alliances, migrations, foreign aid, industrial development, pollution control, land reform, population policies, energy development, resource use and territorial control. In some cases, geographical facts may cause political changes, such as the decision of the Swiss to restrict immigration because they believed the country had enough people already. In other cases, political facts may cause geographical changes, such as the decision of many countries to expand their oil exploration programs as a result of political uncertainties in the Middle East.

We see that geography can affect or be affected by politics. Geopolitics is the study of this two-way relationship between political beliefs and actions on one side and any of the usual concerns of geography on the other. This means that geopolitics is concerned with such matters as national population trends and policies, people's cultural, political and economic goals, the use of resources, the applications of technology to production, transportation, communication and national defence, and the equilibrium that exists between people and their physical environment.

As people look at their country, they develop political policies that are aimed at keeping the environmental characteristics they like, both physical and human, and changing those they do not. Politics may even be regarded as a means whereby a society organizes its environment — both physical and human — for preservation or change. Geopolitics is thus a key study in geography.

In this chapter geopolitics is discussed at the international level. In the first section we look at the differentiation of the world into different groups of countries, often referred to as "worlds." Following sections deal with relationships among these different groups. We then examine the concept of national power and attempt to assess the power of different countries. The next section examines the clashes that occur as a result of conflicting interests among countries, while the last section looks at

This is a good time to reconsider what are the "usual concerns of geography."

the opportunities for co-operation and peace. The chapter ends with a case study on South Africa, a country whose political beliefs have profound geographical effects.

Look first, however, at the following selection of articles. They give you some sense of the nature and extent of the relationships between politics and geography.

MADRID — Business leaders praise it, but unions are up in arms over Spain's drastic plan to revamp industry.

The new plan, passed last month by the year-old Socialist government in the Cortes, Spain's parliament, is called the law of industrial conversion.

It sets the standards for government aid to private and state industries that undertake to shut down or modernize and establish new plants based on advanced technology that will yield high profitability.

The president of the national business confederation, Carlos Ferrer Salat, called the law a positive instrument for Spain's reindustrialization.

But on Dec. 20, the day the law was approved, 1,000 workers of Altos Hornos del Mediterraneo, a steel plant near Valencia slated for shutdown, demonstrated and blocked the road to the plant. The town's trade unions called a general strike.

And the local organization of Prime Minister Felipe Gonzalez's Spanish Socialist Workers Party joined with the conservative opposition, the Communists and smaller local parties to protest plans to close the plant by this October, with the loss of 8,000 jobs.

Gonzalez is carrying out the liberal, capitalist revolution his rightist and centrist predecessors never accomplished. He is rationalizing capitalism through a tough industrial conversion policy aimed at eliminating factories — and jobs.

The Spanish economy was designed under the corporate state principle in the 1930s. Companies were established to create jobs, not to be productive. When firms failed, the government took them over. These state-owned albatrosses, especially in shipbuilding and steel, now run huge deficits.

State-subsidized private firms have grown fat and uncompetitive. And the policy hasn't protected workers. In the past seven years, Spain lost 780,000 jobs. Unemployment is running at a high 16-per-cent level.

The Socialists' policy is to drastically shrink, rebuild or close down government plants and use public incentives to get private firms to do the same.

It will provide subsidies and privileged credits to companies for modernization, pay compensation and unemployment insurance to displaced workers and help in workers' searches for new jobs. It has started with textiles and steel and will move to such industries as shipbuilding, fishing, shoes and electronic components.

Spain's workers say they understand the need for the conversion, in principle, but they promise to take to the streets if it means losing their livelihood. By next year, the process will cost 50,000 jobs. The government depends heavily on the Socialist UGT (General Union of Workers), to deflect the flak.

"We are in agreement with industrial conversion," UGT General-Secretary Nicolas Redondo said in an interview.

But the Communist Workers Commissions, which won 33.4 per cent to the UGT's 36.7 per cent in the last elections for local work-place committees, is delighted at the chance to win adherents by denouncing a policy it says favors the bosses over the workers.

Lucy Komisar, *The Toronto Star*, 1984 1 22

NAIROBI (AP) — President Daniel arap Moi has ordered all public institutions to stop buying electric and computerized typewriters, saying developing countries such as Kenya are not ready for them.

Such typewriters "do not reflect appropriate technology and must be discouraged at the moment," the official Kenya news agency yesterday quoted the 59-year-old leader as saying.

It said Mr. Moi disclosed the decree while touring private technical colleges in the East African country during the weekend, but did not elaborate on his reasons for ordering the ban.

The Globe and Mail, Toronto, 1983 10 18

NEW YORK (CP) — Sam Nujoma, head of the South-West Africa People's Organization, will visit Ottawa next week for talks with senior Government officials, it was announced yesterday.

Mr. Nujoma, whose organization has been fighting for the independence of Namibia (South-West Africa) from South Africa, will arrive on Monday and spend two additional days in the capital.

South Africa has been occupying Namibia, a former German colony under United Nations trusteeship, since 1920. South Africa ignored a 1966 UN resolution ordering it to withdraw, and in 1971 its occupation was declared illegal under international law.

South Africa has repeatedly invaded Angola in pursuit of SWAPO guerrillas. Earlier this week the two countries agreed to set up a joint commission to oversee the withdrawal of South African troops from Angola.

In London Mr. Nujoma said yesterday that SWAPO will press its struggle against South Africa despite the agreement on the troop withdrawal.

"The struggle will continue until Namibia is free," Mr. Nujoma told a news conference.

The Globe and Mail, Toronto, 1984 2 18

NEW DELHI — India has cleared the way for the rapid deportation of hundreds of thousands — possibly millions — of people it says have entered the country illegally since 1971.

And Prime Minister Indira Gandhi has given final approval for construc-tion of a $50 million barbed-wire fence to be built along India's 2,184-kilometre border with Bangladesh.

While the tough, new immigration policies will affect all of India, they will come into force immediately in Assam state, where strong feelings against immigration from neighboring Bangladesh led last spring to riots and massacres that reportedly killed more than 4,000 people.

India has already tightened border security on the 259-kilometre dividing line between Assam and Bangladesh.

Gandhi's government, responding to demands from the militant All-Assam Students' Union, has set up a new system of tribunals and authorized them to make the decisions on who has immigrated illegally.

A case against any suspect may be started by the government or by any two residents who file sworn statements with a tribunal. Decisions are to be made within six months after such a complaint is filed.

Under the law, an illegal migrant is any foreigner who entered India after March 25, 1971, without a valid passport or other travel document. That date marks the end of the second Indo-Pakistan war, which led to the creation of Bangladesh, formerly East Pakistan, as an independent state.

Bangladesh has denied there has been any significant infiltration of its citizens into Assam. Bangladeshi sources in New Delhi said construction of the fence would falsely imply that citizens of Bangladesh were so unsatisfied with their living conditions that they would illegally cross the border to enter Assam.

No official estimates are available from the Indian government on the extent of illegal immigration from Bangladesh or other neighbouring countries but the Bangladesh sources said it has amounted to fewer than 400,000 persons.

In Assam, unofficial estimates are that Muslims, mostly Bangladeshis, constitute more than 5 million of the state's 21 million people.

William J. Eaton, *The Los Angeles Times* 1983 10 18

During the past decade Third World military budgets have risen 400 per cent. . . . Almost 75 per cent of the arms transfers go to the developing continents. . . . They continue as part of foreign trade strategies of the U.S., the Soviet Union, France, Britain, and Germany. . . . Most Third World countries are spending more per capita on their militaries than on health and education. . . .

World Press Review 1984 5

Reprinted with permission, *Toronto Star Syndicate*.

DISCUSSION AND RESEARCH

1. What reasons could South Africa have for continuing to occupy Namibia?
2. What is the point of Macpherson's cartoon?
3. What do you suppose are the unstated reasons for the President of Kenya's ban on the use of electric typewriters and word processors in public institutions?
4. There are two views of Spain's drive to modernize its industry. What are the main points of both views? Which view do you suppose will prevail?
5. What are the benefits and problems of illegal migration?
6. How far is a state justified in taking measures to ensure the success of its policies?

The effects of geopolitical forces are often felt more immediately by the children in Third World countries. This pre-adolescent soldier fought in Uganda's National Resistance Army, which overthrew Uganda's previous government in 1986.

Unicef / Yann Gamblin

Different Worlds

WIZARD OF ID   **BY BRANT PARKER & JOHNNY HART**

By permission of Johnny Hart and News America Syndicate

The world is not uniform. There are great variations in rate of population growth, amount and quality of food intake, degree and type of industrialization, production and use of energy, quality of life and patterns of migration. Many of these variables exhibit fairly strong (although not perfect) correlations.

On the basis of these correlations it is possible to divide the countries of the world into different groups. The most fundamental division is into two: the more economically developed countries of the so-called "North" and the less economically developed countries of the so-called "South." This division was popularized by the publication in 1980 of the report of the Independent Commission on International Development Issues. The report profiled "two disparate sets of societies on the same planet," and considered the implications of their growing inequality to be "the greatest social challenge of our time." The commission reported that the nations of the "North" contain 25% of the world's population, but possess more than 90% of its manufacturing industry and receive more than 80% of its income. The commission also reported that nutrition, housing, education, health care, sanitation and life expectancy in the North are all "socioeconomic light-years ahead of the South's."

The differences between developed and developing countries are numerous. There is a wide choice of criteria we can use to determine whether any nation belongs to one group or the other. Money income, although important, is not necessarily the best criterion, however, for some of the world's money-rich nations are the developing oil-exporting countries. Key criteria tend to be infrastructural in nature, and include such elements as education, health, banking, and transportation and communication networks. Literacy is a useful criterion because it reflects the social penetration of the educational system, which is a major factor in a country's development potential.

This idea can be tested mathematically.

STATISTICAL ANALYSIS

7. First we must check to see how well literacy correlates with an important economic indicator of development. Let us use per capita energy consumption. The data in Column X of Appendix 3 are for per capita energy consumption of all types of fuel in terms of kilograms of coal equivalent. Standardization on coal equivalents makes it easier to compare the energy consumption levels of those societies that rely largely on hydro-electricity, oil or natural gas with those that rely largely on coal.

   a. Draw a scattergraph of the literacy data (Column W) and the energy consumption data (Column X). It is probably best to use a normal arithmetic scale for the literacy data and a log scale for the energy data. Insert a "line of best fit" and lightly shade a band along both sides of the line to include the majority of the nations.

   b. What do you infer from the graph as a whole?

   c. Which nations lie farthest from the line of best fit and outside your shaded band? Can you suggest or find any explanations for this lack of fit?

   d. What do you conclude regarding the value of literacy as a criterion for assessing development achievements?

8. Second, we shall see if variations in literacy can be used to explain variations in the per capita value of manufactured output (Column Q).

   a. Calculate the coefficient of determination (r^2) as shown in Appendix 4.

   b. Variations in literacy are not alone in causing variations in the per capita value of manufactured output. What other factors can you suggest?

9. Third, if you are satisfied that literacy is a useful criterion for separating the developed countries from the developing ones, draw a map showing the geographical distribution of the two groups (having first decided the dividing level of literacy).

   How does your map correlate with other maps drawn in earlier chapters (e.g., population, food, industry)? Does your map support a "North-South" model, and is it a helpful way of seeing the current world situation?

The basic division of the world into North and South has been frequently attacked as an oversimplification of reality. For one thing, the countries of the North are alike only in that they are more developed, and even then the type and level of development vary, as indicated in Chapter 6. Also the economic ideologies of group members range from capitalism to communism. These differences in development and ideology cause basic contrasts in the ways in which political decisions are made and carried out. Ideological differences between the capitalist countries and the communist ones have been one basis for classifying together the developed capitalist countries into what is called the "First World" while the developed communist countries are called the "Second World."

For a long time all the developing countries were collectively referred to as the "Third World." The concept of three worlds seems to have developed during the 1950s, the term itself being first used during the Bandung Conference of 77 Afro-Asian nations held in Indonesia in 1955. It probably evolved from political discussions starting in 1952 about the formation of a "third force" in the world, the other two forces being the Western and Communist worlds. The original Group of 77 that first got together as a coherent Third World political lobby at Bandung has since grown to well over a hundred members.

A coherent political lobby is a group organized to persuade others in government to pursue policies favourable to the group.

However, as time has passed, the Third World has seen its members quarrel and fight, become richer or poorer, and either remain neutral with respect to the First and Second Worlds or enter into alliances with one or the other. Third World differences in ideology, history, culture, resources and development are proving to be more powerful than the original bond forged by their common lack of development. The developing countries are no more unified than the developed ones.

Their differences tend to reflect the barriers created against outsiders by the common interests of sub-groups. For example, the Arab World is a sub-group, held together by common ethnic origins and, to some degree, by religious beliefs. Even so, its members vary from oil-rich to oil-poor, from democracies to dictatorships, from monarchies to republics. The Islamic World closely overlaps the Arab World, but not entirely and not to the exclusion of conflict. Iran (non-Arab) and Iraq (Arab) are both Islamic countries, but are in conflict.

Islam is split between two major sects, Sunni Moslems and Shi'ite Moslems, who are often mutually hostile.

Another important sub-group consists of oil exporting nations, some of which are Arab and some not, some in the Middle East and some not, but all of which are held together by a common economic concern.

Even so, some are densely populated, others are not, and they hold different opinions about strategies of oil development. Black Africa forms another common interest group, also internally divided by culture, ideology and history.

Yet another group consists of the newly industrializing countries, but their backgrounds and development strategies include such diverse examples as Brazil and South Korea. Moreover, the world's two most populated countries — China and India — are so unique that it is impossible to fit them neatly into any particular category.

Third World countries thus have an enormous range of interests and loyalties. Depending upon their particular circumstances, individual countries may belong to one or more sub-groups. For example, Nigeria belongs to the oil, Islamic and Black African groups; Indonesia belongs to the oil and Islamic groups; and Venezuela belongs to the oil and newly industrializing groups. It is clear that the Third World seldom speaks with a single voice.

In response to the complex differences existing within both the North and the South, the President of the World Bank (Tokyo, 1982) has identified eight discernible groups of countries. He names the eight "poles of special economic significance" as follows:

- Western Europe, characterized by a high level of international trade as well as by slowing growth;
- North America, characterized by high levels of output as well as by high levels of energy use;
- Japan, characterized by continuing high levels of output and exports;
- Eastern Europe, characterized by slow growth, shortages of consumer goods and restricted involvement in international trade;
- the Newly Industrializing Countries (NICs), including Brazil, Malaysia, Mexico, South Korea, Taiwan and about 15 others, characterized by rapid growth and a high level of exports, and gradually moving from labour-intensive industries into high-technology production;
- the oil-exporting countries of the Middle East, characterized by capital surpluses and shortages of labour, requiring massive labour importation to sustain economic development;
- the highly populated countries of non-industrial Asia, characterized by significant improvements in food production, leading many countries toward self-sufficiency, but still with much poverty;
- sub-Saharan Africa, characterized by declining or static development rates and by widespread poverty.

Despite the real complexity of the world, as noted in the eight-part schema above, its division into three worlds (First, Second and Third) is useful. It emphasizes the differences in ideology and economic management within the group of more developed countries. It highlights the common need for development within the developing countries, although it masks differences in the rates and strategies of development. It is a development model rather than a regional or interest-based model and provides a choice of alternative politically-based development strategies. It is the model we will use in the rest of the chapter, with the warning that, like all categorizations, it can be criticized for being oversimplified.

The map in Fig. 8-1 shows the geographical distribution of the three worlds. Remember that some countries, such as Argentina, Greece and Hong Kong, are on the borderline between the Third and First Worlds, while China, which sees itself as a developing country, is on the borderline between the Third and Second Worlds.

Fig. 8-1
The three worlds

DISCUSSION AND RESEARCH

10. What does China have in common with (a) the Second World, and (b) the Third World?

11. We have looked at three different attempts to classify the countries of the world: "North-South," Three Worlds, and eight groups of significance. What are the advantages and disadvantages of each method of classification?

12. The term "Third World" is sometimes criticized for suggesting a negative or inferior quality, as in "third rate," "third class," "third place," etc. What do you think?

Built in August, 1961, the Berlin Wall has ever since been a symbol of the strained relations between the First and Second Worlds.

Marilyn MacKenzie

First and Second World Relations

Although the First and Second Worlds both belong historically to European culture, they represent conflicting political and economic systems. Their differences are reflected in the ways in which the societies make decisions about the geographical development of their environments.

Such decisions must be made in all societies, whatever their organization. Population exists and its wants increase, yet resources are limited. How, then, are decisions to be made about what is produced, how much is produced, and how it is produced? How does a society decide on the balance between current consumption and saving (investment) for the future? Which products should be made within the country and which should be imported? Which energy sources to use? Where should industry be located? How many people should be let in or out? Who should get what in terms of income? These are some of the decisions having geographical consequences that must be made by all societies.

There are many types of political organization in the world, from dictatorship to representative democracy, all influenced by one or another social, religious or politico-economic principles.

Despite the variety of organizational systems in the world, we shall concentrate here on only two main types.

The completion of the phrase "To each according to . . . " is one of the major determinants of political philosophy. Should it be need? Or effort? Achievement? Social status? Inheritance? Political standing? Or . . . ?

The First World

Decisions about many aspects of the politico-economic systems of the First World tend to be made privately and individually in response to competition. Companies compete with one another to sell their products. Stores compete to sell their goods. Workers compete for the highest-paying jobs. Domestic firms compete with foreign firms. This book competes with other books that aim to serve the same market. It also competes with all other books in a school system because there is only so much money to spend on books. And the amount that can be spent on books competes with all the other things requiring educational funding, which compete with possible spending on health care, road building, new housing and so on. Everything, in fact, competes with everything else. It is always possible to see expenditures in one area as having taken away the same amount of spending from another area. The web of choice and decision-making is virtually unlimited. The method, sometimes even the place, in which competition works is called the market; for this reason First World systems are often termed market economies.

A similar competitiveness exists in the political process. Political parties compete at election time for votes, using all the techniques of persuasion they can muster. For example, if a society wishes to have incomes distributed more equitably, it will elect a government that promises to introduce social programmes. A society that wishes to maintain jobs in fields that are not competitive internationally will elect a government that creates high protectionist tariff barriers against imported

The cost of anything in terms of other things the money could have been spent on is called the *opportunity cost* of the thing bought. The opportunity cost of a school may be a length of new road or a jet fighter or a new hospital wing or any one of millions of other things the same amount of money could have been spent on.

Brenda Collins

In Canada, the co-operative movement has become an increasingly popular attempt to provide alternatives to all-out competition in marketing, housing and other areas.

goods, and will accordingly be prepared to pay higher prices for the domestic product.

The willingness to pay the price created by competition between supply and demand is the essence of this market. Low prices discourage production because producers cannot cover their costs; high prices encourage production by giving producers higher returns. Low prices drive out inefficient producers, allowing only the most efficient to survive, while high prices permit efficient producers to gain the greatest profits, allowing the inefficient merely to survive. In a market economy, however, prices are not determined solely by the suppliers. Consumers also have input. If prices are too high, few people will buy and prices will fall. If prices are too low, people will compete to bid the prices up in order to get what they want. Market prices thus tend to be a compromise between suppliers and consumers. If the price is fixed at anything other than the equilibrium price, there will be either not enough or too much produced. Such imbalances arise from a variety of sources, such as government price-fixing, quotas, regulations, and combinations of producers who restrict supply and keep prices up or of consumers who boycott goods and force prices down.

The impact of government on the operation of markets is considerable. Governments can use taxation and subsidies to raise or lower prices or to shift purchasing power from one sector of the population to another. They can establish regulatory agencies or develop and implement policies regarding health and safety, pollution control, quality standards and so on. Governments in all First World countries, play a large role in the operation of their markets. Their role is greatest in some of the mixed economies of Europe, where governments have appropriated the spending of about half the GNP. It is also significant in such countries as Japan and South Korea, where governments work with industry to prepare plans and production targets. The role of government in the market is generally least in North America and Australia, but is by no means absent.

Prices that balance supply and demand are called *equilibrium prices*. They are not necessarily stable; as supply or demand changes, so do equilibrium prices.

Selected central government appropriations of GNP:	
	%
Ireland	61
Netherlands	58
Belgium	57
Italy	50
Sweden	45
France	42
New Zealand	42
UK	42
West Germany	32
Australia	26
Canada	26
USA	25
Switzerland	19
Source: World Bank, 1985	

The Second World

The countries of the Second World generally have the same resources and wants as those of the First World, but they organize and meet them in a different way. Planning is governed by a prevailing philosophy of common ownership of the means of production and a universally equitable distribution of output. This was initially suggested by Karl Marx in his phrase, "From each according to his ability, to each according to his need," and underlined by Leonid Brezhnev on the 50th anniversary of the USSR, "All . . . enjoy equal rights, have equal duties, and bear equal responsibility for the country's destiny." Planning is directed by the central government, so Second World nations are often described as centrally-planned economies. Even where a great deal of decentralization has occurred, as in Hungary, local planners still proceed in conformity with the central government's beliefs. The fundamental beliefs are very similar in many ways to those of the First World: that every person has the right to good health, nutritious food, literacy, security, freedom and a rising standard of living. There is a central difference, however. Governments in the Second World believe that these rights are best achieved by strong centrally-planned and controlled economies that reduce the opportunities for wealth to be amassed by a few private individuals to the exclusion of many. From the point of view of these governments, the economic and political policies pursued by them better meet the needs of their citizens than would following policies like those of the First World market economies.

In the Second World the state, through its planning committees, determines what shall be produced, how much shall be produced, where it will be produced, how much it will cost, who shall be eligible to buy it and so on. The planning mechanism has been a series of five-year plans that began in the USSR in 1927. Each five-year plan has aimed at the overall development of the economy, with specific targets in the different plans. The first plan, for example, targeted agriculture, energy generation and heavy industry. The ninth five-year plan (1971–75) was directed at improving the standard of living. The twelfth five-year plan (1986–90) aims to achieve higher economic growth rates and greater personal prosperity. Once a five-year plan is drawn up, it goes before the annual Congress of the Communist Party for approval and subsequent monitoring.

Although governments in First World countries have taken over certain sectors of the market, many Second World governments are in the process of returning more decision-making to individuals. As a result, many farmers in the USSR have chosen to farm their own plots of land in addition to working on a state or collective farm, selecting for themselves what to grow. Farmers' markets now exist in most cities of the USSR. In Bulgaria families have the right to own and operate a plot of land as they please, provided they do it without hired labour. In China the pre-1978 philosophy of the "iron rice bowl" has been replaced with a limited system of personal profit-oriented incentives. Overall, the price mechanism is seen as a valid (but limited) guide for allocating resources and distributing rewards for effort.

However, Second World countries remain organized largely according to the central planning model. This affects both their internal

A report from Moscow in 1986 indicated that whereas the farmers' private plots occupied only 3% of Soviet farmland, they produced 30% of the food that was consumed in the USSR.

Mao Zedong's philosophy of the "iron rice bowl" was that everyone received a guaranteed annual income, regardless of other factors.

Novosti Press Agency

Farmers' markets represent one of the USSR's concessions to the attractions of a market economy. This Soviet farmer sells his melons in Tashkent, Uzbekistan.

It is a common view in the USSR that the USA is a single party state too: the USA is seen as having the Republican Democratic Party (i.e., the "Capitalist Party").

and their external operations. Imports and exports are regulated because the resources needed to pay for imports or produce exports have to come from the general economy. If the general economy is controlled, then imports and exports must also be controlled. Equally, people cannot travel freely, because that would cost money that might be more urgently needed for other things within the country.

In these ways, central planning shows a different attitude toward individual freedoms, which are generally regarded as less important than the common good. Central planning is regarded as sufficiently important for some forms of dissent to be seen as injurious to the common welfare of society. Elections are held and people are required to vote by law, but since the only candidates are from the Communist Party, the Communist Party is always re-elected, and voter turn-out is almost 100%.

DISCUSSION AND RESEARCH

13. Why do you think communist governments have found that central planning of all parts of the economy according to the perceived needs of the state is not practical?

14. Why do you think capitalist governments have found that individual planning of all parts of the economy according to the signals of the market is not practical?

15. In your opinion, what are the duties and rights of the state? What are the duties and rights of the individual? How do you think your answer would differ from that of a Soviet student?

Heartland Theory

In order to justify their different ideological bases, the First and Second Worlds compete with each other in many material and non-material ways. Improved lifestyles are one important way: the First World boasts the highest average material standards ever achieved by any society, along with the widest choice of available lifestyles. The Second World takes pride in the virtual absence of ethnic or sex discrimination, in its social welfare schemes, and in its freedom from poverty and oppression.

The two worlds also compete for influence in the rest of the world. The competition in this area is keenest between the leaders of the two worlds, the USA and the USSR. In the early twentieth century, Sir Halford J. Mackinder developed the "Heartland Theory," which he designed as a tool for explaining some aspects of geopolitical life. Mackinder felt that certain geographic realities could have a significant impact on European and world politics.

Mackinder's Heartland Theory is summarized in the following three statements. In each case the word "control" presupposes a combination of desire and ability. First, whoever controls Eastern Europe controls the *Heartland*. Second, whoever controls the Heartland also controls the *World Island*. Third, whoever controls the World Island ultimately controls the *World*. Eastern Europe contains good sources of industrial energy, chiefly coal and hydroelectricity, as well as fertile farmlands. Internal transportation is excellent. Control of the vast resources of Eastern Europe more or less guarantees control of sparsely populated Siberia, because Siberia, with deserts and mountains to the south and east and frozen seas to the north, is easily accessible only from Eastern Europe.

Mackinder theorized that once a country was securely based in Eastern Europe and Siberia it could gain access to the margins of the great land masses of Eurasia and Africa (the *Inner Crescent*) if it so desired. Heartland Theory predicted that a country seeking to penetrate the Inner Crescent would likely make its way first through Western Europe. This

Eastern Europe is loosely defined as the broad lowland area stretching from the Urals to Germany and from the Baltic/Arctic to the Carpathians/Black Sea. The *Heartland* is the area stretching from Germany into Siberia. The *World Island* is the whole of the Afro-Eurasian land mass.

Seen from Moscow, Western Europe is largely a collection of peninsulas at the western edge of the great Soviet land mass.

The USSR sees its East European allies, joined by the Warsaw Pact, as a defensive chain against a possible attack from Western Europe. Remember that it lost 20 000 000 people when it was invaded by Germany in World War II, and similarly large numbers in World War I and the Napoleonic invasions.

The Soviet view is that it was requested by the communist government in Afghanistan to help it in its struggle against rebels, and that such help has traditionally been a part of Soviet foreign policy arising out of its "Leninist internationalist" ideology.

path is geographically ideal because it provides excellent lowland transportation to ice-free open ocean ports. The theory asserted that the Heartland power would win any struggle between itself and maritime Europe, chiefly because of its superior internal transportation and resources. Once Western Europe had succumbed, and the Heartland power had gained access to the oceans, it could use its land and sea power to bring all the isolated power centres around the rim of Afro-Asia into its orbit. Thus the World Island of Afro-Eurasia would be under the control of the Heartland.

The Heartland power, because of its transportation system, could then extend its rule by pushing into the Outer Crescent (the Americas and Oceania). Mackinder believed that the countries of the Outer Crescent would be unable to resist penetrations from a central power; he forecast that the pressure would continue until the Heartland power eventually ruled the world.

A number of criticisms have been raised against Heartland Theory. Like all theories, for instance, it can be said to be a product of a particular time and situation. When Mackinder developed his theory he was watching the decline of an empire that had been spread and supported by the strength of the Royal Navy. As nations became able to collect larger and larger armies supported by increasingly destructive armaments, countries became less capable of dominating others by means of naval power. In turn, it has been objected that the growth of air power (especially long-range bombers and missiles) has made it unlikely that any one nation will be able to use even the largest armies to dominate the world.

Presented at the end of World War I, Heartland Theory is interesting as a geographically-based theory of world politics. While the theory has many limitations, it does provide one perspective on Soviet and American foreign policy. For example, the USSR expanded its control in Europe following WWII. It grouped its European satellites in a defensive alliance (the Warsaw Pact) and linked their economies closely with its own in COMECON (Council for Mutual Economic Assistance). The Soviets support communism in other European countries, particularly the warm water areas of Italy, France and Portugal.

Heartland Theory would consider the Soviet invasion of Afghanistan as a thrust into the Inner Crescent to open a route to the Middle East and Africa. Similarly it would view Soviet activities in Southeast Asia, Africa and Latin America to be consistent with the theory.

Both the USA and the USSR believe their alliances to be defensive, created to protect each of them against the possibility of aggression by the other. The Warsaw Pact is intended to protect the USSR from aggression from Western Europe, the source of periodic past invasions of Russia. The USSR also claims that the numerous military bases

Fig. 8-2
Member countries of alliances developed as part of the "containment" policy

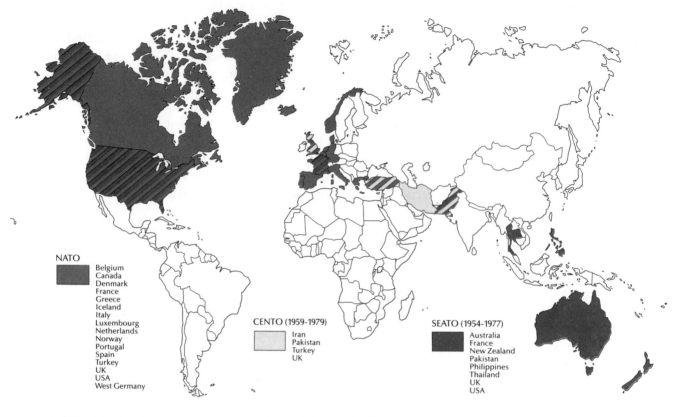

NATO

Belgium
Canada
Denmark
France
Greece
Iceland
Italy
Luxembourg
Netherlands
Norway
Portugal
Spain
Turkey
UK
USA
West Germany

CENTO (1959-1979)

Iran
Pakistan
Turkey
UK

SEATO (1954-1977)

Australia
France
New Zealand
Pakistan
Philippines
Thailand
UK
USA

Constructing a new aircraft carrier at Newport News, Virginia.

Fig. 8-3
Salient aspects of Heartland Theory and US "containment" policy

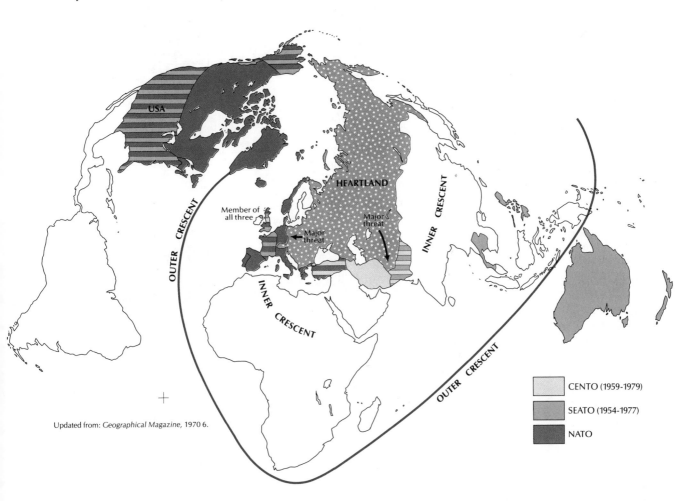

Updated from: *Geographical Magazine*, 1970 6.

provided to the USA by countries involved in what the USA claims are defensive alliances pose a threat to it. The USA, on the other hand, claims that aggression is more likely to come from the USSR. It sponsors a defensive alliance, NATO (North Atlantic Treaty Organization), because the US considers Western Europe as the first bulwark against the expansion of communism. Similar alliances within the Inner Crescent were SEATO (South East Asian Treaty Organization, 1954-1977) and CENTO (Central Treaty Organization, 1959-1979). Both were once parts of a general US policy of "containment" designed to prevent the spread of Soviet political and economic influence. Fig. 8-2 shows the members of these alliances; Fig. 8-3 shows the application of the con-

Fig. 8-4

Distances from Washington and Moscow of the capital cities of all countries with populations over 20 000 000

Country	Approximate distance from Washington (km)	Approximate distance from Moscow (km)
China (2)	10 400	5 400
India (1)	11 300	4 100
USSR (2)	7 200	—
USA (1)	—	7 200
Indonesia	15 500	8 700
Brazil (1)	6 400	10 500
Japan (1)	10 100	7 000
Bangladesh	12 200	5 200
Pakistan	11 200	3 900
Nigeria	8 100	5 800
Mexico	2 800	10 200
West Germany (1)	6 000	1 900
Vietnam (2)	12 500	6 300
Italy (1)	6 700	2 200
UK (1)	5 500	2 300
Philippines	12 800	7 700
France (1)	5 700	2 300
Thailand	13 300	6 500
Turkey (1)	8 100	1 700
Egypt	8 700	2 700
Iran	9 500	2 300
South Korea (1)	10 500	6 200
Burma	13 000	6 100
Spain (1)	5 600	3 200
Poland (2)	6 600	1 100
Zaire	9 800	6 600
Ethiopia (2)	10 600	4 800
South Africa (1)	12 700	8 500
Argentina (1)	7 900	12 500
Colombia	3 600	10 100
Canada (1)	1 200	6 700
Morocco	5 700	3 800
Yugoslavia (2)	7 000	1 600
Romania (2)	7 400	1 400
Algeria	6 300	3 100
Tanzania	11 900	6 600
Sudan	9 800	4 200
Peru	5 400	11 700
Kenya	11 300	6 000
North Korea (2)	10 300	6 000

1. = capitalist alignment   **2.** = communist alignment

No number = non-aligned

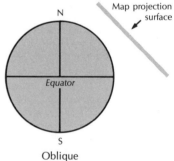

An *oblique* projection is one in which the plane of projection is neither polar nor equatorial, but somewhere in between. A *zenithal* projection is one in which the plane of projection is parallel to a tangent at the earth's surface at the centre of the projection. An *equidistant* projection is one in which distances are correct from the centre of the projection only. Oblique zenithal equidistant projections are widely used for all target maps, as on radar screens.

tainment policy visually. The containment policy can be interpreted from a Heartland Theory viewpoint. The US regards many Soviet policies as attempts either to destabilize its alliances or distract its attentions elsewhere. The USA responds to Soviet activities, as witnessed by the Cuban Missile episode of 1962, its invasion of Grenada, its intervention in Chile in the 1970s, and its ongoing support to the anti-communist rebels in Nicaragua through the 1980s.

STATISTICAL ANALYSIS

16. **a.** On a world outline map draw lines at 2 500 km and 5 000 km parallel to the borders of the USA and the USSR (remember that Alaska and Hawaii are part of the USA). Since this is a very difficult thing to do solely on a flat map, you should refer to a globe to do it properly.

    b. What contrasts strike you when you compare the two sets of lines?

    c. Which areas of the world are largely beyond the high intensity areas of influence of both the USA and the USSR?

    d. Which areas, if any, exhibit a marked degree of overlap?

17. Construct a scattergraph for the data in Fig. 8-4 and draw in an equal distance line. Name and colour the dots as indicated. How far does the graph support Mackinder's Heartland Theory?

Hemispheres of Influence

Heartland Theory is only one way of examining the geopolitics of international strategy. Another is to see how the world looks when a particular region is placed at the centre of a map. The maps used are based on *oblique zenithal equidistant* projections, which give an indication of the territories most easily falling within a nation's potential sphere of influence. Any areas not shown on a particular map (see Fig. 8-5) are literally on the other side of the world.

Sphere of influence denotes a territory over which a country claims or is acknowledged to have some political or economic rights but which it cannot or does not govern.

The USSR map shows that the Afro-Asian World Island is well within the USSR's sphere of influence. Compare it with the map of the USA's hemisphere, which includes only the northern parts of Afro-Eurasia and South America. The USA's hemisphere contains less land and far more ocean than that of the USSR and suggests the need for a large navy and extensive shipping links to other areas. The European hemisphere contains an even greater proportion of land than the USSR's.

Fig. 8-5
Selected hemispheres

The hemisphere of the USSR

The hemisphere of North America

The hemisphere of Europe

The hemisphere of China

Europe is the access point to more of the world's land than any other area.

The other maps in Fig. 8-5 illustrate various points: China is in a good position to assume an important world role; Australia is isolated from other Outer Crescent areas, and would seem to be vulnerable to any power controlling the World Island. The maps also show that South America is really only in the USA's sphere of influence (but note which European countries have the easiest access), and that Africa is most likely to be influenced by Europe and, possibly, the USSR. Where does the USA lie in Africa's world?

In this perspective can you see why the USA regarded the Cuban revolution as a threat? Soviet influence penetrated an area far outside its own immediate sphere of interest. The Distant Early Warning (DEW) line, the Strategic Air Command (SAC) bases at Goose Bay in Labrador and Thule in Greenland, and the entire North America Aerospace Defence (NORAD) organization were all established on the assumption that, if the Soviets ever attacked North America, they would do so over the Arctic. The USSR's installation of missiles in Cuba in 1962 was countered by an American blockade of all Soviet shipping to Cuba until the missiles were withdrawn. The Cuban crisis looked for a while as though it could have sparked a major military confrontation, and raised fears of nuclear war to their highest pitch yet. The USA thereafter gave more strategic attention to Latin America.

The USSR shipped missiles to Cuba by disguising them as ordinary freight and sending them on ordinary freighters. From the North American hemisphere map, can you suggest which Soviet port would have been used for the shipments, and which route the freighters would have taken? Can you also suggest, for airlines connecting the USSR and Cuba, where they would most likely need a refuelling station?

DISCUSSION AND RESEARCH

18. If you were the chief Soviet strategist, interested in testing the Heartland Theory, what areas would interest you? Why?

19. If you were in charge of American strategy how would you react to Heartland Theory?

20. The USSR alleges that NATO is the first line of potential US aggression; the US claims it is the first line of defence against possible USSR aggression. What evidence is there to justify both views?

21. At one time the maritime powers of Western Europe virtually ruled the world. Why do they not do so now?

22. Do you think the development of air power affects the current relevance of Heartland Theory? Why or why not?

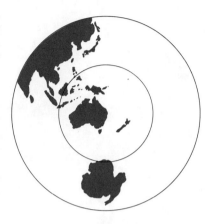

The hemisphere of Australia

The hemisphere of South America

The hemisphere of Africa

Missiles, Satellites and Nuclear War

Conflicting groups have always felt that whoever had the best weaponry had the best chance of making either a successful attack or a successful defence. Developments in technology have constantly resulted in improved weaponry, but until recent times, no weapons posed a planet-destroying threat as do those now available.

Missile technology, for example, has developed from its erratic beginnings in World War II to a situation where both the USA and the USSR have targeted missiles to all the major population and industrial centres in each other's countries, as well as those of the other's allies. Since missiles take only minutes to reach their targets, they represent a major threat.

Most missiles are ballistic in nature, which means that once launched they behave much like a thrown ball. They do not change course, and they come down at or near their target. This is their major weakness, since their tracks can be readily computed, and they can then be intercepted by other missiles. For this reason, both the USA and the USSR have anti-ballistic missile (ABM) missile defence systems.

Both countries have also developed missiles with multiple warheads (MIRVs — Multiple Inertial Re-entry Vehicles) in order to confuse the ABM missiles and minimize interception. They have developed large missile-carrying submarine fleets in order to have flexibility in launching sites and a retaliatory strike capability. And both have developed cruise missiles. Cruise missiles can fly low enough to elude radar; they are small, yet can carry a wide range of warheads; they can travel as far as most ballistic missiles; they can be programmed to change course and launched from submarines, ships, aircraft, land installations and even from the backs of trucks. They are, however, very slow by comparison with ICBMs (Intercontinental Ballistic Missiles), and their use as a first-strike weapon is unlikely. On the other hand, where stealth is the essence of aggression their use could be quite deadly.

Satellites add a further dimension to global strategy. For years, both the USA and the USSR have had numerous satellites surveying events on the earth's surface. Each has now developed attack or "killer" satellites that can destroy the other's satellites, and both are working on the development of satellites that could destroy ground installations with an intense beam of light called a "laser" (Light Amplification by Stimulated Emission of Radiation).

A new dimension to weaponry today is the ability to destroy the world with nuclear weapons. Arguments about nuclear weapons are strong and sincere for both supporters and opponents. Supporters argue that it is precisely because of the horrors of nuclear warfare and the certainty of retaliation that neither the US nor the USSR would ever be the first to use its nuclear arsenal. Both reasons have so far been effective deterrents to war. Opponents argue that the horrors are so great that nuclear weapons should be destroyed immediately and that, in any event, no more should be made since both sides have enough already to kill the other side many times over. Some opponents argue that the West should abolish its nuclear arsenal unilaterally because the USSR would never dare to use its nuclear weapons in the face of moral disapproval from other nations.

The horrors of nuclear war are well documented, as a result of the US's use of nuclear bombs against Hiroshima and Nagasaki in 1945. Present nuclear warheads are, however, hundreds of times more powerful, and their use would dwarf any destruction known before.

Disarmament

History is filled with examples of aggression. Ideas of disarmament are therefore often regarded as naive, particularly given today's lack of trust between the USA and the USSR. Nevertheless, each side regularly makes offers for disarmament and they meet periodically to discuss the topic.

Apart from humanity's general desire for peace, there are also serious economic reasons for concern over the mounting arms race. In the mid-1980s arms expenditures throughout the world totalled about $1 000 000 000 000/y. The FAO said that to provide adequate food to all the starving people in the world would cost about $20 000 000 000/y. The WHO budget for 1984 and 1985 together was $980 000 000. A half-day's military expenditures could finance the WHO's entire malaria

Bomarc missiles were the object of a Canada-US controversy over deploying nuclear weapons on Canadian soil. In 1971 Canada finished withdrawing its armed forces from their nuclear roles.

eradication program. Two hours' worth of military expenditure could eliminate river blindness.

Remember, opportunity costs are the alternatives lost. Money spent on one thing cannot also be spent on something else. The opportunities lost in this way are the *real costs* of whatever is actually bought.

The cost of military expenditure involves more than opportunity costs. The combined military organizations of the world require the direct and indirect services of about 50 000 000 people, who are thereby unavailable for other forms of production. They also consume large quantities of the world's mineral supplies each year, e.g., 11% of the copper, 8% of the lead, 6% each of the aluminum, nickel, silver, zinc and petroleum, and 5% each of the iron and tin. Various military purposes use about 500 000 km^2 of the world's land and commandeer about 25% of the world's spending for research and development. About 20% of the world's scientists and engineers are engaged in some form of military work.

Who does all the spending? The Stockholm International Peace Research Institute gives the data shown in Fig. 8-6. The data demonstrate that the military expenditures of Third World countries are rising rapidly. The Third World has also become the scene of many of the world's armed conflicts. In 1984 there were about 4 000 000 troops involved in about 35 different and ongoing military actions, only one of which (Northern Ireland) was outside the Third World.

The effects of militarization on lost development opportunities are obvious, but its effects on starvation, poverty, migrations and the general quality of life are also immediate and devastating.

Fig. 8-6
Percentages of total world arms expenditures

	1960	1970	1980
First and Second Worlds combined	95.5	92.8	83.9
Third World	4.5	7.2	16.1
Totals	**100.0**	**100.0**	**100.0**
Selected groups			
USA and USSR combined	62.6	58.7	48.0
Middle East	0.9	2.2	7.8
Africa	0.3	1.2	1.7
Latin America	1.3	1.3	1.8
Nuclear powers (USA, USSR, UK, France, China)	78.9	75.8	64.6
Main arms exporters (USA, USSR, UK, France)	73.3	65.8	55.8

Source: Stockholm International Peace Research Institute (SIPRI) *Yearbook*, 1981

In 1984 the Peace Petition Caravan converged on Ottawa from Newfoundland and BC bearing 450 000 signatures collected door-to-door. The petitions asked for an end to US Cruise missile testing in Canada, and for the transfer of funds from military to social programs.

The following article presents a view of the disarmament situation from China.

Stubborn Negotiators

Responding to an erratic arms dialogue

by Wan Guang

As the U.S.-U.S.S.R. conflict turns into a stalemate, many countries are rushing frantically to revise their foreign policies. There is considerable activity among foreign ministers reacting to the superpowers' resistance and dialogue, deadlock and activity, tension and peace.

Why have the U.S. and the U.S.S.R. reestablished negotiations but failed to make any progress? Why do they continue to accuse each other but still want to continue a dialogue? They do so because both countries are under pressure from world opinion to ease the tense international situation and to reduce the arms buildup, and because each superpower has its own need to negotiate.

From the Soviet perspective Mikhail Gorbachev, as a relatively new leader, needs to mend his country's internal affairs — especially the unstable economy. Gorbachev has said that only from a solid economic base "can the nation strengthen its international position and become a great and prosperous country, with the dignity it should have.'' Thus the U.S.S.R. wants a return to the détente of the 1970s.

On the American side, the Reagan government has its own difficulties. Domestic economic growth has slowed, and the American peace movement has expanded by leaps and bounds.

Nevertheless, President Reagan still wants to achieve arms superiority over the Soviet Union, as well as technological and economic control over the developed and developing countries. In his way he seeks to restore and strengthen global hegemony.

In the 1970s the Soviet Union was regarded as an equal to the U.S. in the balance of power. Gorbachev recently cited that balance as ''an important historical achievement.'' He said, ''We should not permit anyone to destroy what has been established by the Warsaw Treaty Organization and the North Atlantic Treaty Organization.''

Under these circumstances, the West sees the Geneva arms talks as ''the most difficult negotiations in the history of foreign affairs.'' Meanwhile, as the U.S. and the Soviet Union confront each other in a stalemate, they both strengthen their deployment of weapons. The Soviets make progress toward strengthening the Warsaw Treaty Organization, and they try to devise ways to weaken relations between the U.S. and her European allies. Similarly, the U.S. tries to strengthen its control over the NATO clique, and at the same time it schemes to drive a wedge between the U.S.S.R. and other European countries.

As usual, the Third World is the battlefield for the fierce struggle between the superpowers. Last May President Reagan stated that the U.S. must compete successfully in every part of the world — especially in Third World areas. The U.S. has begun an offensive in certain regions, while the U.S.S.R. does its best to protect the areas where it has military positions.

As America implements trade sanctions and a military threat against Nicaragua, the Soviets intensify their suppression of Afghanistan and support Vietnamese attacks against Cambodia. Such policies by both superpowers make it impossible to re-establish the tempo of the talks of the 1970s.

In an attempt to combat this situation, many countries are becoming more active in foreign affairs. They entreat Washington and Moscow to come to an arms reduction agreement to guard against harming other countries.

The superpower arms race is increasing the risk of war, but the ability to curb the superpowers and to protect peace also is increasing. More and more countries are taking their fate into their own hands.

From *OUTLOOK*, Beijing, reprinted in
World Press Review, 1985 10

Second and Third World Relations

Relationships between the Second and Third Worlds are mostly political and advisory in nature. The Second World's emphasis has always been to achieve internal self-sufficiency, and international trade has been restricted to necessary items only. The Second World has not established a large worldwide trading capacity. For example, the international trade of all of COMECON is about equal to that of West Germany. Data published by the World Bank in 1985 indicate that West Germany had a combined export-import trade worth about US$325 billion, while COMECON'S was worth about US$340 billion. About 18% of West Germany's trade is with the Third World; about 14% of COMECON's (and about 36% of US trade). Data also indicate that about 0.25% of total COMECON GNP is used in all forms of international material aid to the Third World, compared with about 1% of First World GNP.

The character of the political and advisory relationship between the Second and Third Worlds was defined by Leonid Brezhnev during a 1975 speech in Moscow:

> The line of our Party and state in international affairs is well known. It stems from the very nature of socialism and is wholly subordinated to the interests of the peaceful constructive labour of the Soviet people and our brothers in the socialist countries. Being a consistently class policy, it serves the cause of peace, freedom, and security of all peoples, the cause of their national independence and social progress, and meets the interests of the broadest masses throughout the world.

In conformity with this policy the USSR has regularly sent political and economic advisers to assist those in the Third World struggling to gain freedom, independence and social progress. Examples have included Angola, Burma, Chile, Cuba, Egypt, Ethiopia, Guatemala, Honduras, Malaysia, Nicaragua, Peru, Somalia and Thailand.

China is a special case. Attempts in the 1950s to assist the revolutionaries were eventually rebuffed by Mao Zedong, who regarded the Soviet urban and megaproject approach as inappropriate to China's needs.

Novosti Press Agency / I. Ryumkin

The Siberian town of Mirnyy. The Soviet government promotes settlement in its eastern provinces to strengthen its territorial claim to them.

Differences between the USSR and China have not eased. There has been fighting along parts of their 7 000 km common border through central Asia, and conditions are still tense in the area. Both countries are pushing for economic development throughout the areas near their common border. The USSR has encouraged the settlement of over 20 000 000 Soviet people along the line of the Trans-Siberian Railway, while China encourages its people to move to Manchuria and to Xinjiang and Xizang Autonomous Region (formerly Tibet). Recently the Soviets have improved Siberian transportation systems, notably the double-tracking of the Trans-Siberian Railway in the 1970s, and they continue to build up army camps and supply depots. In 1984 the USSR had 46 army divisions stationed along the Chinese frontier zone; in 1986 there were 55. The USSR also has SS-20 nuclear missiles deployed along the border.

A senior Chinese official, according to *The Toronto Star* 1986 1 20, has stated that the Chinese government views these Soviet actions, coupled with actual Soviet occupation of several thousand square kilometres of Chinese territory, as a serious threat to the security of China. The same official also stated that the USSR's increasing support of Vietnam poses similar threats, and that the Chinese government would like to see tensions reduced there first. The Soviet occupation of Afghanistan also troubles the Chinese.

Vietnam poses the same sort of strategic threat to China as Cuba does to the USA. Both represent the southern part of a potential pincer movement.

Canapress Photo Service/AP Photo

Geopolitics can create strange mixes. This joint exercise of the US and Egyptian airforces places (from the top) a US A-10 and F-16 (first and third planes) beside a Soviet-made MiG-21 and MiG-17 (second and fourth planes).

First and Third World Relations

A few of the more commonly expressed views on the varied and complex relationship between the First and Third Worlds are given in the following items.

Anatomy of inequality

The industrialized countries can criticize the countries of the South for not having shown sufficient perseverance and determination in their political and economic struggles. This shortcoming has made it easier for the North to dominate the South and has led to the present impasse. But since the days when many Third World countries achieved independence, the centres of responsibility have moved from London, Paris, Lisbon, etc. to Dakar, Kigali, Caracas, Bangkok, and so on.

For their part, the countries of the South can always point to the continuing deterioration in terms of trade, which is making them progressively poorer and the industrialized countries ever richer. Similarly, they can protest against the corrupt application of aid programmes which at present impoverish the receivers both materially and psychologically by developing an "assisted person" complex in them and making them bear the burden of heavy financial commitments.

From this three major conclusions emerge: the gap between the industrialized and the non-industrialized countries is growing bigger every year; all the remedies tried so far have failed; the need for a fundamental change in the nature of the relations between the industrialized and the non-industrialized countries is becoming increasingly urgent.

These relations are governed at present by an evolutionist, linear, diffusionist concept. Despite the obvious heterogeneity of our world, a "massification" ideology that is as tenacious as it is false would have us believe that every country and culture should behave in the same way and pursue the same goals, wherever on the earth's surface they may be situated. This is the basic idea of the theory of development, which presupposes the existence of a model society which supposedly possesses all the saving virtues and to the level of which the others must climb by the same ways and means which it employed and go through the same stages as those through which it passed. This model society is supposed to embody the future of all other societies. The vocabulary of this ideology reflects this pattern of events which is considered to be indispensable. Yesterday's "civilizing" mission becomes today's "aid" mission. Yesterday's "savage" becomes "undeveloped", and in the minds of those concerned the "colonized" complex is replaced by that of someone who is "aided".

It is clear that, for better or worse, the economies of both the non-industrialized and the industrialized countries are bound together, and that the growth of each should benefit the others.

The world is going through a crisis to which every expert is trying to apply his own diagnosis and his own treatment. Each of the protagonists, the North and the South, is praying for a change that is slow in coming.

It is therefore becoming imperative to find alternative solutions to the present development strategy. There has, of course, been no shortage of catch phrases, such as "basic needs", "self-centred development", "collective autonomy". But it is the entire conception and orientation of the ideologies underlying the idea of development which must be thoroughly revised, both by the North and by the South. It is no longer permissible to rely on day-to-day realism, which is often no more than a lack of new ideas.

UNESCO Courier 1984 1

Canada is committed to an Official Development Assistance (ODA) target of 0.6% of GNP by 1990 and 0.7% by 1995. These figures, while only 2-3% of total federal government spending, represent a substantial amount of money (approximately $2 billion in 1984). We need, therefore, to be sure we are clear on where ODA fits into our conception of our own economic and political wellbeing, our sense of moral responsibility and our overall foreign policy. There is a need to examine the objectives, policies and programs of Canada's cooperation with the Third World. In seeking the right balance in our programs abroad, we will have to decide the priorities we wish to attach to humanitarian objectives, to attaining commercial benefits, to sharing in the management and support of the global economy and the global environment and to achieving political stability and progress. Decisions will not be easy. Canadian funds for use abroad are limited.

Two sets of questions deserve special attention. The first relates to the role of Canadian official development assistance in Canadian foreign policy. How directly should ODA serve Canadian foreign policy interests? Should our bilateral aid be made more directly conditional upon the performance of recipient governments in such areas as economic management, respect for human rights and political likemindedness? What should be the nature of the linkage between our trade and aid programs? Should our practice of tying a large proportion of our bilateral assistance to procurement of Canadian goods and services be relaxed for the poorest countries, e.g. in Africa?

The second set of questions concerns priorities within the aid program. Does the focus of bilateral assistance remain valid in terms of sectoral concentration (agriculture, energy and human resource development), geographical distribution (some 42% to Asia, 42% to Africa and 16% to Latin America and the Caribbean), and target groups (80% of assistance to low income countries)? Can the critical role of women in food production and other development processes be better supported? What weight should ecosystem management in developing countries have in our policies? There are pros and cons to our channeling Canadian funds through multilateral agencies, such as the UN and the World Bank. Are Canadians satisfied with the current balance, approximately 60% bilateral and 40% multilateral?

Churches, provincial and municipal governments, private organizations, small businessmen and concerned Canadians from all walks of life have demonstrated both the desire and the capacity to help. The response to the crisis in Ethiopia has been most noteworthy, but there are many thousands of Canadians involved in humanitarian and economic and social development efforts elsewhere, often in ways the government could not duplicate even if it wished. How can the government assist Canadians best to help others? How much of the government's effort should be channelled through these Canadian non-governmental organizations (NGOs)? What changes would improve our program delivery?

Department of External Affairs, Canada, 1985

Let us now look more closely at aid and trade, which are perhaps the chief present components of the relationship.

Aid

Nearly 90% of the world's total aid is given by the First World to the Third World. The reasons range from a desire to win political friends, to increase domestic business and to relieve guilt over the First World's inequitable use of the world's resources and its colonial interventions of the past. First World propaganda is an integral part of the process, and so sources of aid are always identified.

There are also those in the First World who regard aid as a waste of time and money. They claim that aid makes the Third World dependent upon the First World and it would be better if it solved its own problems. These people deny any responsibility for Third World problems, claiming that in return for resources the First World has built railways, roads, towns and ports, and has introduced modern technology, medicine and education. They assert that the Third World's problems are the product of uncontrolled birth rates and an unwillingness to organize production efficiently. They also say that First World aid should go only to those Third World countries that have introduced birth control practices. Others go further, and say that no aid should be given at all. The following articles present views that are strongly held.

In the mid-1980s the USA made it clear that its aid should be directed towards those countries that made family planning and birth control part of their official policies.

The case for helping the poor

Remember you don't live here all alone. Your brothers are here too.

– Albert Schweitzer

We the North Atlantic Community of Nations represent 16% of the world's population but we control 65% of the world's wealth and 75% of the world's trade. An equitable distribution? — hardly. One which we should consider as lasting? — again, hardly. For as Pope Paul has pointed out in his encyclical *On the Development of People*: "Excessive economic, social, and cultural inequalities arouse tensions and conflicts and are a danger to peace".

Can this dichotomy between 'us' and 'them', the 'rich' and the 'poor', the 'haves' and the 'have nots' continue? As the hungry, the diseased, the illiterate watch us eating cake, how will they respond when we throw them some crumbs? How will they respond when they learn that we eat $4^1/_2$ pounds [2 kg] of food a day and then throw away enough to feed a family of six in India? How will they respond when they learn that the average dog in North America has a higher protein diet than millions of their children? How would you respond?

The problem in North America of course is that we're not aware of the problem; or more precisely we're (vaguely) aware that it exists but we're already tired of hearing about it. Prime Minister Pearson has said, "We are living on a powder-keg of anger and revolt. We are living in a world so small that the violence affects us all. We are confronted with the risk of international class war. The curious fact today is not that we do not know those things but that a great many people are bored with them and feel less and less obligation to do anything about them."

Extracted from *Oxfam of Canada* Sheet 1.01

The case against helping the poor

The less provident and able will multiply at the expense of the abler and more provident, bringing eventual ruin upon all.

by GARRETT HARDIN

If we divide the world crudely into rich nations and poor nations, two thirds of them are desperately poor, and only one third comparatively rich.

Metaphorically each rich nation can be seen as a lifeboat full of comparatively rich people. In the ocean outside each lifeboat swim the poor of the world, who would like to get in, or at least to share some of the wealth. What should the lifeboat passengers do?

We have several options: we may be tempted to try to live by the Christian ideal of being "our brother's keeper," or by the Marxist ideal of "to each according to his needs." Since the needs of all in the water are the same, and since they can all be seen as "our brothers," we could take them all into our boat making a total of 150 in a boat designed for 60. The boat swamps, everyone drowns. Complete justice, complete catastrophe.

Suppose we decide to preserve our small safety factor and admit no more to the lifeboat. Our survival is then possible, although we shall have to be constantly on guard against boarding parties.

The harsh ethics of the lifeboat become even harsher when we consider the reproductive differences between the rich nations and the poor nations. The people inside the lifeboats are doubling in numbers every 87 years, those swimming around outside are doubling, on the average, every 35 years, more than twice as fast as the rich. And since the world's resources are dwindling, the difference in prosperity between the rich and the poor can only increase.

As of 1973, the U.S. had a population of 210 million people, who were increasing by 0.8 per cent per year. Outside our lifeboat, let us imagine another 210 million people, (say the combined populations of Colombia, Ecuador, Venezuela, Morocco, Pakistan, Thailand and the Philippines) who are increasing at a rate of 3.3 percent per year. Put differently, the doubling time for this aggregate population is 21 years, compared to 87 years for the U.S.

Multiplying the rich and the poor

Now suppose the U.S. agreed to pool its resources with those seven countries, with everyone receiving an equal share. Initially the ratio of Americans to non-Americans in this model would be one-to-one. But consider what the ratio would be after 87 years, by which time the Americans would have doubled to a population of 420 million. By then, doubling every 21 years, the other group would have swollen to 354 billion. Each American would have to share the available resources with more than eight people.

The tragedy of the commons

The fundamental error of spaceship ethics, and the sharing it requires, is that it leads to what I call "the tragedy of the commons." Under a system of private property, the men who own property recognize their responsibility to care for it, for if they don't they will eventually suffer. A farmer, for instance, will allow no more cattle in a pasture than its carrying capacity justifies. If he overloads it, erosion sets in, weeds take over, and he loses the use of the pasture.

If a pasture becomes a commons open to all, the right of each to use it may not be matched by a corresponding responsibility to protect it. Asking everyone to use it with discretion will hardly do, for the considerate herdsman who refrains from overloading the commons suffers more than a selfish one who says his needs are greater. If everyone would restrain himself, all would be well; but it takes only one less than everyone to ruin a system of voluntary restraint. In a crowded world of less than perfect human beings, mutual ruin is inevitable if there are no controls. This is the tragedy of the commons.

Learning the hard way

What happens if some organizations or countries budget for accidents and others do not? If each country is solely responsible for its own well-being, poorly managed ones will suffer. But they can learn from experience. They may mend their ways, and learn to budget for infrequent but certain emergencies. For example, the weather varies from year to year, and periodic crop failures are certain. A wise and competent government saves out of the production of the good years in anticipation of bad years to come. Joseph taught this policy to Pharaoh in Egypt more than 2 000 years ago. Yet the great majority of the governments in the world today do not follow such a policy. They lack either the wisdom or the competence, or both. Should those nations that do manage to put something aside be forced to come to the rescue each time an emergency occurs among the poor nations?

Population control the crude way

On the average, poor countries undergo a 2.5 percent increase in population each year; rich countries, about 0.8 percent. Only rich countries have anything in the way of food reserves set aside, and even they do not have as much as they should. Poor countries have none. If poor countries received no food from the outside the rate of their population growth would be periodically checked by crop failures and famines. But if they can always draw on a world food bank in time of need, their population can continue to grow unchecked, and so will their "need" for aid. In the short run, a world food bank may diminish that need, but in the long run it actually increases the need without limit.

Besides, any system of "sharing" that amounts to foreign aid from the rich nations to the poor nations will carry the taint of charity, which will contribute little to the world peace so devoutly desired by those who support the idea of a world food bank.

Every one of the 15 million new lives added to India's population puts an additional burden on the environment, and increases the economic and social costs of crowding. However humanitarian our intent, every Indian life saved through medical or nutritional assistance from abroad diminishes the quality of life for those who remain and for subsequent generations. If rich countries make it possible, through foreign aid, for 600 million Indians to swell to 1.2 billion in a mere 28 years, as their current growth rate threatens, will future generations of Indians thank us for hastening the destruction of their environment? Will our good intentions be sufficient excuse for the consequences of our actions?

DISCUSSION AND RESEARCH

23. Would you argue with Garrett Hardin? Why or why not?

24. What are your ideas on the subject of "lifeboat ethics"?

25. Another idea that is sometimes suggested concerning aid is that of *triage*. In wars, the wounded used to be sorted into three groups: those who would likely survive whether they got medical help or not; those who would probably die with or without medical aid; and those who would die without medical help, but survive with it. Medical scarcities on battlefields were taken into account, so what was available was concentrated on the third group. The other two groups were left to survive or die without medical help. It is now sometimes suggested, in the light of world food scarcities and inadequate distribution facilities, that aid ought to be given only to those countries that are equivalent to the third group of battlefield wounded. What do you think?

First World aid is provided to the Third World through a variety of channels, some governmental and some non-governmental. Some aid goes directly from country to country (bilateral aid), while some goes to international agencies that distribute it to different countries according to need (multilateral aid).

The largest amounts of aid are provided by governments. Such aid is called Official Development Assistance (ODA); it is increasingly being disbursed multilaterally through various UN agencies such as the World Food Program, UNESCO, WHO and FAO. In the mid-1980s, ODA amounts were about US$30 billion per year from the 17 First World

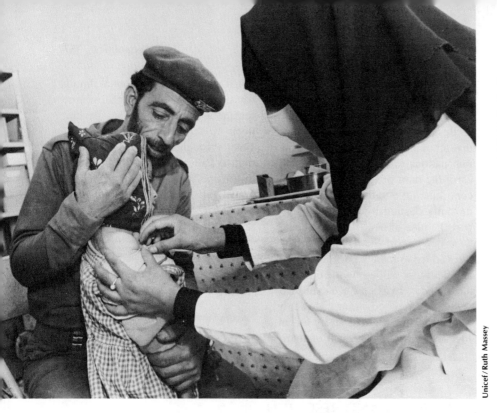

UN agencies disburse large amounts of ODA funds. Unicef (the United Nations Children's Fund) supports this mass immunization program in the Yemen Arab Republic.

Unicef/Ruth Massey

members of OECD, with the major contributing countries (in total amount of ODA) being the USA (31%), Japan (15%), France (13%), West Germany (10%), Canada (6%) and the UK (5%). On a per capita basis the countries rank as follows (data from World Bank, 1985):

		US$
1.	Norway	126.47
2.	Sweden	88.39
3.	Denmark	87.88
4.	Netherlands	87.44
5.	France	68.77
6.	Canada	60.42
7.	Australia	49.37
8.	West Germany	45.10
9.	Switzerland	44.06
10.	Belgium	41.50
11.	USA	36.45
12.	Finland	36.37
13.	Japan	35.83
14.	UK	25.54
15.	Austria	23.86
16.	Italy	19.56
17.	New Zealand	18.66

Fig. 8-7
Total Canadian Official Development Assistance (ODA), in Canadian dollars (percentages in brackets), 1970-85

	1970-71	1980-81	1981-82	1982-83	1983-84	1984-85
Multilateral aid[1]	83.21	508.87	545.59	594.52	674.53	690.84
	(21.7)	(41.1)	(38.6)	(37.6)	(39.2)	(34.5)
Bilateral aid[2]						
– to Governments	289.49	581.51	671.36	716.07	678.30	875.32
	(75.4)	(46.9)	(47.6)	(45.2)	(39.4)	(43.7)
– to NGOs[3]	11.01	148.79	195.27	272.23	368.77	435.10
	(2.9)	(12.0)	(13.8)	(17.2)	(21.4)	(21.8)
– Total	300.50	730.30	866.63	988.30	1047.07	1310.42
	(78.3)	(58.9)	(61.4)	(62.4)	(60.8)	(65.5)
TOTAL: All ODA aid	**383.71**	**1239.17**	**1412.22**	**1582.82**	**1721.60**	**2001.26**
	(100.0)	(100.0)	(100.0)	(100.0)	(100.0)	(100.0)
ODA as % of GNP	0.429	0.434	0.430	0.459	0.454	0.490

1. Multilateral aid is aid given by the government to a variety of different international agencies, such as the World Bank, the World Food Program, and various Commonwealth Development Programs, which may all use the aid where they deem it most appropriate.

2. Bilateral aid is aid given to a specific country. The sources of bilateral aid may be either the government or one or more of hundreds of Non-Governmental Organizations (NGOs) such as the Red Cross, Oxfam, CARE Canada, Canadian Council of Churches and Candian Labour Congress.

3. There are hundreds of Non-Governmental Organizations (NGOs) acting as collectors and distributors of aid throughout the world. They receive funds from governments as well as individuals, but distribute it only to the individuals and NGOs.

Source: *Annual Report,* CIDA, various years
Note: All figures are in millions of Canadian dollars

Canadian aid originates from many sources. Some aid organizations are private, such as Oxfam, CARE, Foster Parents Plan and the Red Cross, while others, such as the Canadian International Development Agency (CIDA), Canadian University Students Overseas (CUSO) and the Canadian Executive Service Overseas (CESO), are government sponsored. Private and public sources provide approximately equal funds. As an indication of where the aid in the form of money, technical assistance or food actually goes, the Official Development Assistance (ODA) appropriations are listed in Figs. 8-7, 8-8, and 8-9.

Fig. 8-8
Canadian bilateral aid disbursements, 1984-85

Anglophone Africa		Francophone Africa		Central America	
Angola	1.85	Algeria	5.84	Anguilla	0.07
Botswana	7.56	Benin	1.81	Antigua	1.41
Djibouti	0.32	Burkina Faso	11.21	Barbados	9.10
Egypt	10.73	Burundi	1.69	Belize	4.22
Ethiopia	47.00	Cameroon	33.36	Costa Rica	8.07
Ghana	45.97	Cape Verde	0.57	Cuba	0.06
Kenya	38.71	Central African Republic	0.49	Dominica	9.57
Lesotho	4.67	Chad	2.57	Dominican Republic	5.00
Liberia	0.36	Comoros	0.19	El Salvador	1.51
Malawi	4.31	Congo	1.17	Grenada	3.89
Mauritius	0.21	Equatorial Guinea	0.13	Guatemala	2.39
Mozambique	13.14	Gabon	0.87	Haiti	8.77
Namibia	0.15	Gambia	0.95	Honduras	20.45
Nigeria	1.70	Guinea	18.06	Jamaica	29.11
Seychelles	0.24	Guinea-Bissau	0.49	Mexico	1.78
Sierra Leone	1.31	Ivory Coast	17.88	Montserrat	0.16
Somalia	0.96	Madagascar	1.03	Nicaragua	8.52
South Africa	0.98	Mali	14.43	Panama	0.77
Sudan	22.19	Mauritania	4.94	St. Kitts	1.35
Swaziland	3.78	Morocco	8.58	St. Lucia	2.44
Tanzania	44.93	Niger	21.87	St. Vincent	0.62
Uganda	3.83	Rwanda	15.03	Trinidad/Tobago	0.60
Zambia	22.89	Sao Tome	0.04	Turks/Caicos	0.10
Zimbabwe	18.07	Senegal	20.35	Virgin Islands	0.01
Unspecified	17.28	Togo	3.62	Unspecified	25.08
		Tunisia	6.53		
Sub-total	**313.11**	Zaire	24.33	**Sub-total**	**145.06**
		Unspecified	17.14		
		Sub-total	**235.17**		

Asia		South America		Other Areas	
Bangladesh	105.76	Argentina	1.80	Cyprus	0.10
Bhutan	0.40	Bolivia	3.28	Fiji	0.57
Burma	3.22	Brazil	8.38	Papua New Guinea	0.79
China	13.51	Chile	4.67	Tonga	0.14
Hong Kong	0.06	Colombia	7.97	Turkey	0.22
India	90.08	Ecuador	1.58	Western Samoa	0.15
Indonesia	37.05	Guyana	2.15	Unspecified	250.71
Jordan	0.66	Paraguay	0.22		
Lebanon	1.11	Peru	16.90	**Sub-total**	**252.68**
Malaysia	3.17	Suriname	0.02		
Nepal	10.08	Uruguay	0.46		
North Yemen	0.42	Venezuela	0.11		
Pakistan	66.30	Unspecified	5.33		
Philippines	8.34				
Singapore	1.10	**Sub-total**	**197.93**		
South Korea	0.81				
South Yemen	0.12				
Sri Lanka	37.97				
Thailand	22.02				
Unspecified	8.66				
Sub-total	**410.85**				

Source: CIDA, *Annual Report,* 1984-1985

Note: All figures are in millions of Canadian dollars

STATISTICAL ANALYSIS

26. Construct a compound line graph (see Appendix 4) to illustrate the main points only of Fig. 8-7.

   a. Which sector has grown the fastest?

   b. Why do you think this is so?

27. Using the data in Fig. 8-8, shade on a world map all the countries that are listed as having received direct Canadian bilateral aid. How does the map compare with your answer to assignment 9?

28. Calculate which country's people received the largest per capita amount of bilateral aid from Canada during the period 1984–85.

Fig. 8-9
Canadian multilateral aid disbursements, 1984-85

Disbursements to UN Agencies and International Organizations

UN Development Program (UNDP)	59.00
UN Children's Fund (UNICEF)	13.25
UN Fund for Population Activities (UNFPA)	10.25
UN High Commissioner for Refugees (UNHCR)	5.50
UN Relief and Works Agency (UNWRA)	6.50
UN Voluntary Fund for the Environment (UNVFE)	1.17
World Food Program	149.90
Tropical Diseases Research Program	1.25
Onchocerciasis (River Blindness) Control Program	1.35
Commonwealth Fund for Technical Cooperation (CFTC)	14.60
International Rice Research Institute (IRRI)	2.70
International Centre for Tropical Agriculture (CIAT)	1.60
International Maize and Wheat Centre (CIMMYT)	1.55
International Potato Centre (CIP)	1.05
International Institute of Tropical Agriculture (IITA)	1.60
West African Rice Development Association (WARDA)	0.50
International Livestock Centre for Africa (ILCA)	0.50
Crops Research Institute for Semi-Arid Tropics (ICRISAT)	1.60
Cultural and Technical Cooperation Agency (ACCT)	5.17
International Atomic Energy Agency (IAEA)	0.89
International Committee of the Red Cross (ICRC)	0.75
World Health Organization (WHO)	7.08
International Labour Organization (ILO)	1.01
Food and Agriculture Organization (FAO)	2.91
United Nations Organization (UN, New York)	3.12
Pan-America Health Organization (PAHO)	4.19
Commonwealth Youth Program	0.66
Others	15.03
Sub-total	314.68

Disbursements to International Financial Institutions

International Development Association (IDA)	167.70
World Bank (IBRD)	39.96
African Development Bank (AfDB)	46.20
Asian Development Bank (AsDB)	92.00
Caribbean Development Bank (CDB)	6.87
Inter-American Development Bank (IDB)	23.46
Central American Bank for Economic Integration (CABEI)	−0.03*
Sub-total	376.16
Grand Total	**690.84**

* = repayment of loan
Source: CIDA, *Annual Report*, 1984-1985
Note: All figures are millions of Canadian dollars

Some examples of Canadian ODA are given in the following articles.

Grass Roots Radio

In 1981 farmers in Latin America learned a cheap and effective way to prevent weevils from destroying their crops. It seems that weevils have a great dislike of wood ash. Simply mixing ash in with the grain guarantees no losses during storage. When the grain is needed, the ash can be winnowed out. The idea came from farmers in Botswana and it was broadcast through the Developing Countries Farm Radio Network (DCFRN).

DCFRN was the brainchild of George Atkins, veteran CBC farm broadcaster. While traveling in the Third World in 1977, Atkins realized that modern agricultural technology often was not appropriate to developing country needs but that home-grown techniques to increase production in one part of the developing world would probably be appropriate in others. The ideas could be passed along through radio, a low-cost relatively widespread medium.

The network was originally set up in 1978 as a public service vehicle by Massey Ferguson Limited. It is now a joint project of the University of Guelph and CIDA's Institutional Cooperation and Development Services Division which is providing $150,000 between 1981 and 1983 — about 75 per cent of the necessary funds.

Atkins travels throughout Third World countries each year collecting tips on farming. These have included making compost, making harness or door hinges out of old tires, digging pit silos to store hay during the dry season, and a safe and easy way to collect honey. The latter suggestion was provided by farmers in Africa and South America who coat hollow logs with beeswax and then hang them from trees. The first swarm of bees in the vicinity usually builds a hive in one of the logs, providing a ready source of honey. Smoke is used to drive the bees away and the honey is then safely collected.

Atkins tapes the techniques he has learned in his travels and they are sent out in English, French and Spanish to 650 farm broadcasters in over 100 countries. Where necessary, local announcers translate the information into native dialects. Farmers accept the information more readily because it is presented in their own language and by broadcasters they know.

The network is a great success with an audience of over 100 million, not counting the recent addition of China which receives transmissions from Radio Australia.

Canadian International Development Agency, 1983 2

From Subsistence Land To Productive Farms

In the far southeastern corner of Nepal, along the banks of the Kankai River, 8,000 hectares of subsistence land is being turned into productive farms. An agricultural development program, with $7.9 million in funding from the Asian Development Bank, is bringing irrigation water into fields previously capable of supporting only rainy-season crops. A drainage system is being installed, roads constructed and an agricultural centre built for teaching farmers new growing techniques, supplying new seeds, and providing extension services.

The project, due for completion in 1984, is already paying dividends to some 3,300 families. Two and sometimes three rice crops a year are now taken off land that before produced only one. Yields have doubled from 1.5 to 3 metric tons per hectare. High-yielding varieties of wheat, jute, maize and potato are also being used.

Other Bank projects in irrigation, electric power and paved roads are bringing similar improvements to 6,500 families southwest of Kathmandu. In 1981–82 CIDA contributed $66.6 million to the Bank to assist in development projects in Nepal and other Asian countries.

Canadian International Development Agency, 1983 2

"Barefoot Engineers"

In Malawi CIDA is involved in a water scheme whose success is receiving international recognition. Gravity fed water is being piped from mountain streams to tap stands located in villages so that clean water is available to rural people within one kilometre of their homes.

Remarkable progress is being made and the country looks likely to achieve the mandate of the UN International Drinking Water and Sanitation Decade to provide clean water and sanitation for all of its people by 1990.

Community participation is the cornerstone of the water program. The government provides the expertise and piping and the villagers do the rest. They elect committees to direct the project, supervise construction, and to be responsible for maintenance and proper use of the system once completed.

The beauty of the system is its simplicity. It is technically uncomplicated and designed to last 100 years.

The villagers choose "barefoot engineers" who, with a little training, keep the works in good repair. The government incurs no further costs beyond supplying the piping. The villagers, through their planning, construction and maintenance, gain self-confidence and pride in contributing to their country's development.

CIDA has almost completed four water projects serving over 150,000 people at a cost of $1.5 million. Malawi is contributing $400,000. Other donors are also involved, including international organizations to which CIDA contributes, such as UNICEF, the UN Development Program and the World Health Organization.

Canadian International Development Agency, 1983 2

Trade

Increasing numbers of Third World countries have recently been asking for beneficial trade rather than more aid. These countries are looking for markets for their manufactured goods, and so they want First World countries to reduce their tariffs on such goods. They also want higher prices for their raw materials. Over the years, Third World countries have felt themselves to be at a disadvantage in both areas. They want what is called a New Economic Order to achieve these goals, but these goals will be much easier to propose than achieve. Most developed countries want to protect their manufacturing industries from competition, and they do so most commonly by means of tariffs. At the same time, in order to supply their industries with cheap raw materials, developed countries usually impose no tariffs on such imports.

For example, Japan levies no tariffs on imported cocoa beans, but a 27% tariff by value on imported chocolate. The European Economic Community levies no tariffs on imported raw cotton, but a 10% tariff on manufactured cotton fabric and a 13.7% tariff on imported cotton clothing. The USA levies no tariffs on imported hides, but a 14.4% tariff on imported leather goods.

Accordingly, many developing countries find it difficult to develop their manufacturing industries. Some countries have developed manufactures to substitute for their own imports, protecting their infant industries by high tariffs in turn. South Korea, for example, started its industrialization process with an 80% tariff on imported consumer goods. Nevertheless, if a developing country's manufacturing industries are denied access to developed countries' markets, then the tasks of industrial growth and general development are made more difficult than they would otherwise be.

The general existence of tariff barriers against manufactured products leads many developing countries to export raw materials instead. For example, 95% of all coffee exported by developing countries is in a raw state, and only 5% is processed into essences. Similarly, 62% of all cocoa is exported in bean form, and only 9% as fully processed chocolate; 88% of all phosphate is exported raw, and only 12% as processed fertilizer. It is this reliance on raw material exports that has caused the second concern for a New Economic Order, namely the call for better prices for raw material exports.

The world prices of many of the commodities exported by developing countries have declined steadily for a number of years due to overproduction by developing countries and declining demand in developed countries. For example, among a group of ten food products, four (sugar, tea, groundnut oil and palm oil) declined in price between 1960 and 1970, while as many as eight (sugar, tea, groundnuts, groundnut oil, beef, palm oil, bananas and corn) have declined in price since 1970. Declines since 1970 have also been experienced by such other raw materials as copper, iron ore, zinc, manganese, cotton and tobacco. Only the prices for petroleum, coffee, cocoa and bauxite have made any significant progress upwards since 1970.

Developing countries are thus in a difficult position, compounded by their generally large external debts caused by borrowing to finance economic development.

DISCUSSION AND RESEARCH

29. How do you think the prices of international commodities should be determined?

30. As described above, what differences exist between First and Second World reasons for giving aid to the Third World?

31. How could the Third World help itself?

32. Research the aid activities of one of the organizations listed in Fig. 8-9 as a recipient of Canadian ODA.

National Power

Only to a certain extent can disputes between nations be resolved by appeals to reason, logic or humanity. Eventually a nation may choose to ignore such appeals, and act in its own interests.

Decisions to respect or reject appeals depend upon many factors, including the relative strength of the countries concerned and their assessment of the importance of the issue. The more powerful a country is, the more independence of action it has and the more it can influence other countries. It is the weaker countries that have little influence and relatively little freedom of action under pressure.

What makes a country powerful? How can we measure its power? Power can be found in several areas. It can exist in strength of purpose, or national will. It can originate in a country's technology and industrial capacity. It can be found in the size of armed forces and stores of weapons, as well as in the country's ability to produce arms. Power can also be based in the strength of beliefs and the extent to which these beliefs can influence people's minds; capitalism, communism and religion are examples of such influential tenets. Power exists in the supply of natural resources, including population, food supplies, minerals and energy. It is impossible to say which of these sources of national power is the most important; the relative importance of the sources will vary from case to case.

There is of course no perfect or conclusive method for assessing power. Nevertheless, strategists try to do so in order to clarify the relative desirability of proposed courses of action. Planning rests upon many assumptions, most of which are impossible to predict accurately. It is often a case of asking "what would happen if . . . ?" Strategists use complex computer programs to analyze possible actions and consequences; trials of computer-run actions and consequences are called war games.

National will and strength of belief are not quantifiable, so we must restrict our choice of criteria to such items as industrial capacity, armed forces, technology and natural resources in order to obtain our "best estimates" of national power. The individual criteria for the world's most populous countries are listed in Fig. 8-10.

Fig. 8-10
National power criteria and data

	Country*	A	B	C	D	E	F	G	H	I
						National power data				
1	China	37 120	309 300	1 436 200	3 940 000		1 087 871	9 596 961	37 500 000	94
2	India	9 327	125 900	809 300	1 103 000	2 802 893	762 507	3 280 483	25 742 000	70
3	USSR	147 941	1 326 031	12 000 000	2 743 000	29 980 781	276 597	22 402 200	132 885 000	78
4	USA	101 456	2 365 062	33 410 600	2 147 494	69 800 000	238 648	9 363 123	44 592 000	389
5	Indonesia	518	7 750	560 100	269 000	291 502	167 833	1 491 564	43 000	153
6	Brazil	10 232	142 430	1 574 600	271 550	12 632	137 502	8 511 965	60 528 000	315
7	Japan	111 395	583 249	13 193 000	279 000	25 658	120 540	372 313	294 000	359
8	Bangladesh	137	2 962	30 500	78 300	2 232	102 735	143 998		56
9	Pakistan		16 068	107 900	449 000	28 093	99 841	803 493		88
10	Nigeria		7 260	65 400	138 050	138 738	91 178	923 768		192
11	Mexico	7 003	73 559	1 572 900	123 230	58 140	79 662	1 972 547	5 087 000	162
12	W. Germany	43 838	368 770	1 570 500	477 100	12 167 272	61 354	248 577	597 000	215
13	Vietnam		4 000	100 000	1 025 000	10 800	59 575	329 556		
14	Italy	26 501	181 755	1 688 400	367 900	3 519	56 505	301 225	76 000	367
15	UK	11 277	277 735	1 798 000	327 782	2 178 649	56 058	244 046	238 000	170
16	Philippines	397	19 040	369 800	108 305	33 195	55 819	300 000		173
17	France	23 176	282 480	2 686 000	526 433	7 760 141	55 108	547 026	9 100 000	396
18	Thailand	454	15 960	296 900	233 100	1 131 419	52 700	514 000	48 000	163
19	Turkey	1 700	24 100	230 800	568 000	60 109	51 259	780 576	1 424 000	227
20	Egypt	762	18 590	130 000	452 000	16 923	48 407	1 001 449	888 000	118
21	Iran	2 000	16 900	204 000	205 000	101 200	45 191	1 648 000	366 000	3
22	S. Korea	5 790	43 667	269 400	592 600	365 976	42 643	98 484	274 000	278
23	Burma		1 500	44 700	182 000	5 866	38 890	672 552		76
24	Spain	12 553	110 696	1 380 900	356 250	154 242	38 629	504 782	4 372 000	287
25	Poland	18 648	115 006	605 600	317 500	381 813	37 222	312 677	31 000	4
26	Zaire		4 560	76 400	26 000	724	33 092	2 345 409		65
27	Ethiopia		677	13 100	199 500	22 549	32 716	1 221 900		60
28	S. Africa	8 959	98 206	821 200	81 600	5 378	32 465	1 221 037	16 471 000	288
29	Argentina	2 556	39 288	879 800	175 500	250 475	30 564	2 766 889	381 000	363
30	Colombia	263	23 690	104 500	70 500	7 388	28 842	1 138 914	226 000	336
31	Canada	15 901	377 624	2 955 300	82 000	1 538 817	25 405	9 976 139	31 283 000	470

*Ranked according to population

Industrial capacity
A Steel capacity in thousands of t
B Electricity output in mkW·h
C Commercial vehicles in use

Armed forces
D Personnel in army, navy and air force

Technology
E Government Research and Development funds in US$000

Natural resources
F Total population in thousands of people
G Area in km²
H Iron ore in t
I Agricultural GNP/person in US$

Sources: UNESCO *Statistical Yearbook*, 1983
World Bank, *World Development Report*, 1984
Statesman's Year-Book, 1983-4
UN *Statistical Yearbook*, 1981
Yearbook of World Energy Statistics, 1981

STATISTICAL ANALYSIS

33. a. Calculate the mean value for each criterion in Fig. 8-10.

    b. Calculate each value as a percentage of the mean for that criterion.

    c. Add the percentages for each country across the columns to arrive at an aggregate relative power index.

    d. Rank the nations according to their aggregate relative power indices.

    e. What differences do you think the omission of national will and strength of belief makes to your final ranking?

The omnipresent radio is the single tie with the larger world in many rural areas. It can lure people away to the cities, but can also be a low-cost medium for spreading health and agricultural information.

Unicef/Joan Liftin

Clashes

The interests of the three worlds are obviously different; so are the interests of different nations within the different worlds, and of different groups within individual nations. Whenever the interests of nations or groups differ strongly there is always a risk of friction and the possibility of war. No year passes without at least several armed conflicts taking place; occasionally they flare up and are over quickly, but more frequently they are a sign of persistent tensions that in some cases have their roots in distant history.

War is fairly easy to define: it is more or less all-out continuous fighting. Friction, however, may take many forms. What can you suggest?

Clashes Within Nations

Clashes may occur within a nation or between nations. Those within a nation are usually attributable to a combination of racial, cultural and economic causes. Racial and cultural tensions exist in Britain, South Africa, Malaysia, Sri Lanka and Spain. Primarily economic clashes occur in Burma and Peru. It is important to remember, however, that racial and cultural differences tend to manifest themselves in economic differences as well, as is the case in Northern Ireland. In all cases there are components of political and social tension as well.

Frequently one of the groups involved in such disputes is stronger than the other. Because the weaker side has insufficient personnel and too few weapons, it often resorts to *terrorism*. Terrorism may take several forms: random guerrilla raids on property and people, kidnapping and hijacking. The stronger side may negotiate or make concessions to secure temporary relief from terrorism, or it may retaliate with force. Three examples of the latter are the French raid near Djibouti in 1974 to free 25 kidnapped French schoolchildren, the Israeli raid on Entebbe airport to free 100 hijacked Jewish hostages of the PLO (Palestine Liberation Organization) in 1976, and the raid by Dutch commandos in June 1977 to rescue 51 hostages from a train hijacked by nine South Moluccan terrorists. Such attempts are not always possible or successful. There are many cases where terrorists have killed without warning and rescue has

Note that terrorism can be "official" and counter-revolutionary as well as revolutionary. Nicaragua, for example, claims that the US-supported "Contra" guerrillas in El Salvador are agents of state-supported terrorism launched against the legally constituted government of Nicaragua. Other examples of state-supported terrorism could be Hitler's SS before and during World War II and Haitian President Jean-Claude Duvalier's Ton-Ton Macoute, which was abolished only when Duvalier fled to France in 1986.

been ineffective or impossible. Examples are the random shooting of passengers at both Athens and Rome airports in December 1985.

Terrorism is one of the scourges of the present world. Its victims often seem chosen at random, though its targets may be quite well defined. Since 1970 there have been over 7 000 terrorist actions in the world, mostly targeted at the First World and its supporters. It is often innocent citizens who suffer, frequently at airports. The French magazine *Le Point* has identified the major airports of risk as being Athens, Karachi, Manila, New Delhi and Tripoli, but the list is by no means exhaustive. Risks are everywhere and stepped-up security has become common. Israel has developed its own style of response: its secret service, the Mossad, tracks down known terrorists and kills them. In early 1986 the US bombed what it claimed were terrorist strongholds in Libya.

The causes of terrorism are varied. A common reason is the perceived suppression of minority rights by a majority, causing the minority to seek political independence. Examples include Armenians in Turkey, Basques in Spain, Catholics in Northern Ireland, Sikhs in India and Tamils in Sri Lanka. Such situations are often rooted in history, and are unlikely to disappear quickly or easily. A similar reason for terrorism is the desire of dispossessed groups to regain control of territory once held and now lost; the Palestinian Arabs are an example. Other terrorists operate either from a sense of religious revolution (e.g., the Islamic fundamentalist hijacking of planes in Beirut in February and June of 1985 and in Athens in June 1985) or from a sense of socio-political revolution (e.g., kidnappings of industrialists by the Red Brigade in Italy and the Baader-Meinhoff group in West Germany).

Additionally, certain states sponsor their own forms of terrorism against non-compliant or perceived problem citizens. Nazi Germany attempted to extinguish the Jews during the period 1935–45; the USSR liquidated the entrepreneurial kulaks and suppressed Ukrainian dissent by starvation in the 1920s. More recent is the terrorism of Iran's governments, both before and since the Islamic revolution. There are numerous other examples; the agency Amnesty International keeps track of them and publicizes them in the hope of exerting pressure on the governments responsible; but it has no power to prevent their occurrence.

International Frontiers

Just as there are clashes between groups within nations, so is there conflict between nations. International conflict frequently is caused by the transgression of frontiers by another country. Frontiers are the external markers of a nation's integrity and security, and most nations pay great attention to maintaining control of their frontiers. Frontiers have developed partly in response to the emotional need for some sort of national

Mountains are among the most formidable natural frontiers. This is the Jungfrau-Massive in Switzerland, approached from the west by air.

Mountains are not always regions of low population density. Where and why are there exceptions?

identity or consciousness, and partly to mark the limits of a nation's laws, privileges and security. There are two main types of frontiers: natural and artificial.

Natural Frontiers

Natural frontiers formed the earliest boundaries between countries. Natural features are generally highly visible and easily recognizable by both sides, and they require no exact surveying or map-making skills. Natural frontiers are therefore common in older settled lands, especially Eurasia.

Mountain ranges are among the most common natural frontiers. They are easy to see and generally sparsely populated. Natural communities are not split down the middle by mountains, since different communities usually develop on each side. However, the effectiveness of mountain ranges as frontiers depends to some degree upon their height and the number of passes they contain. The Pyrenees, for example, with few passes, are more effective at separating people than are the Alps, with many. The effectiveness of separation also depends upon the width of the mountain barrier. The Appalachians, although not high, proved to be a considerable barrier in the early days of European settlement in North America, simply because of their great width and numerous ridges. If the mountains are wide enough they may even be permitted by powerful neighbours to house independent buffer states such as Switzerland and Austria.

The advantages of mountains as frontiers are to some extent offset by certain disadvantages. There may be disagreements over summer grazing rights, mineral rights, trade routes and water control rights.

Deserts also have the advantages of low population density and easy recognizability. For many years they were left as uncharted wildernesses and used as natural boundaries. However, the development of underground resources, chiefly oil and water, has created friction among neighbouring nations and, with it, the need for more exact demarcation.

Rivers are often used as frontiers because they are narrow and easily recognizable. They present problems, however. Their valleys are usually areas of high population density, often peopled by a single ethnic group, meaning that frontiers established along rivers may divide the community. Rivers are important for navigation if they are wide, and they are easily crossed if they are narrow; thus it is usually desirable that both sides be under a single authority. They can be a source of disputes over fishing rights, effluent disposal, hydroelectricity generation, removal of water for irrigation, silting, bank maintenance, bridge construction, flood control, meander migration, thermal pollution and so on. These problems may occur between nations situated upstream and downstream from one another as well as those that face each other on opposite banks. West Germany and the Netherlands quibble over the Rhine waters, and Egypt and Sudan over the Nile waters as much as the USA and Mexico argue over the Rio Grande, and China and the USSR over the Amur. Rivers usually make poor frontiers. They draw things together better than they divide them.

Swamps and marshes have a low population density as a rule, but their use as frontiers may create conflict because they are a valuable source of rushes, eels, fish and birds. Marshes therefore tend to be shared by different countries, except where they are wide enough to be effective as a barrier (e.g., the Pripyat marshes between the USSR and Poland). In addition, marshes that have been drained can provide fertile soil which neighbouring countries may want to claim. Few large swamps remain in the world today, since most have been drained. However, the Chad

Which countries have frontiers in the Chad Basin swamps? In the Mato Grosso?

The International Joint Commission governs not only the Great Lakes, but also all the other waters along the Canada-US border. It has no power to order either government to act in a particular way, but its recommendations have never yet been ignored.

The Soviet nuclear-powered icebreaker *Arktika*, ice-bound in the Arctic Ocean. History, low population and ever-present ice make establishing national boundaries in the frozen polar regions especially difficult.

Basin swamps and the Mato Grosso are worthy of note. Both of these areas have low population densities so there is as yet little pressure for drainage and reclamation; conflict is thereby minimized.

Lakes may be used as boundaries, but often both sides of a lake are settled at the same time and by people of the same ethnic group. This is the case of the Indians living around Lake Titicaca, which divides Bolivia and Peru. Numerous problems occur where a lake divides a community. There are frequent border crossings for work or family visits, which increase the possibility of smuggling. Workplaces and labour supplies may be separated, people may become unhappy because of unequal taxation and social benefit policies, and national identities may become confused. There may also be many of the same problems that occur with rivers, such as effluent disposal, fishing rights and so on. The International Joint Commission governing the Great Lakes deals with problems of this type that arise between Canada and the United States.

Seas and oceans are highly visible, but are ineffective as barriers; in fact, for the last thousand years or more they have been used more as routeways than barriers. They also present the problems of demarcation and delimitation. Demarcation requires the actual surveying of a boundary line at a certain distance from the coast, but problems arise over the definition of "coast" and exactly how the line along such a coast should

Novosti Press Agency

run (e.g., headland to headland, parallel to the water line, including or excluding islands). The chief problems, however, occur with delimitation: exactly how far out from the coast, once it has been identified, should the demarcation line be drawn?

This problem is more serious now because countries are aware of the resource potential of seas and oceans. In recent years large factory fleets have moved into fishing grounds that bordering countries regard as their own. Iceland has had several encounters with the British over this matter, as has Canada with the USSR and Japan, and Ecuador with the USA. To protect "their" fisheries, the bordering states have pushed their territorial claims from the traditional cannon-shot distance of 5.56 km to 22.22 km, 370 km, and even 648 km. Such claims are naturally resisted by the nations that own the factory fleets.

The extension of territorial claims is also resisted by countries operating large merchant fleets. They prefer to maintain the traditional freedom of passage on the high seas and are concerned about the possible closure of several strategically located straits.

Maritime frontiers are also becoming more important today because of the fossil fuels and minerals found underwater. The oceans that cover about 70% of the earth's surface contain vast fuel and mineral wealth. This wealth is present not only in the rocks under the seabed, but also on the seabed itself and in the water. Although fishing rights may not have been settled yet, many countries have already agreed to divide up the continental shelves for mining operations. Furthermore, experiments in deep ocean mining are leading more countries to talk of dividing up the oceans for resource control. In fact, the entire globe is in the process of being fully claimed and divided up. Nations are pushing their frontiers into the oceans in the hope of benefiting from the tremendous potential. In this new scramble for resources, land-locked states, together with those of the developing world, feel that the wealth of the oceans should be placed in trust for all people to share.

Distances at sea are traditionally measured in nautical miles. One nautical mile equals 1.852 km (compared with a land mile that equals 1.609 km). Limits commonly described as 3 miles, 12 miles or 200 miles are in nautical miles rather than land miles, and require their own metric conversion factor. What limit does Canada claim?

For several years the UN held a series of *Law of the Sea* conferences to try to get the world's nations to agree on how to divide up the seas and seabeds. In 1984, 129 nations agreed, but some, notably the UK, USA and USSR, did not.

Artificial Frontiers

Artificial frontiers are the result of European map-making and surveying, dating from the Age of Discovery. Most early European exploration was done by sea, and so the coastlines of newly explored lands came to be known first. Interior areas remained largely unknown to the mapmakers. Faced with large blank spaces on maps of these lands, European nations often simply drew lines of latitude and longitude on the maps. Boundaries thus determined were then agreed by treaty. Many of the frontiers in Africa and the Middle East, as well as the western part of the Canada-US border, were established in this way.

One of the oddities created by artificial boundary creation is Point Roberts, a small point of land south of Vancouver, bisected by the 49th Parallel. The southern tip belongs to the USA, while the rest is Canadian. The only land connection between the US part and the rest of the USA is through Canada.

These artificial frontiers presented problems when the ground was actually surveyed. It was found that Native groups had been cut in two, that hostile cultures were packaged together and that traditional natural boundaries such as rivers and hills were totally ignored. Nevertheless, artificial frontiers offer certain advantages. They can be precisely indicated by a line of boundary markers, a fence or a wall, or a minefield with spaced gun towers. Stretches of such frontiers are characteristically very straight.

STATISTICAL ANALYSIS

34. A crude measure of the amount of conflict that may arise because of frontiers can be obtained by ascertaining the number of states crowded into a given area of land. Obviously, for a given area, if only one state has control there will be no frontier conflict; but when two states share the land, conflict is possible. The more states there are sharing the land, the greater the risk of conflict. Bearing in mind that the sizes of the

The Great Wall of China. In what senses can it be said to be either a natural or an artificial frontier?

Marilyn MacKenzie

different continents are as follows, count the number of nations in each continent and calculate the average size of a country for each continent.

	Area, km²
Africa	30 044 000
Asia, including USSR east of Urals	44 030 000
Europe, including USSR west of Urals	10 101 000
North America, north of the Rio Grande	19 166 000
Latin America, south of the Rio Grande	20 461 000

a. Is conflict more likely with a small figure or with a large figure?

b. Does population density play a part in the likelihood of conflict?

c. Where should we look for the greatest likelihood of future conflicts?

Phases of Frontier Development

Historically, the development of a frontier has followed a certain sequence. First, an isolated but growing group of people pushes a frontier into a sparsely settled territory, forming a *frontier of achievement*. This boundary marks the edge of the *ecumene*, the area settled by the expanding group. It ignores the existence of any Native peoples already living in the lands into which the expanding group is pushing. It is typical of pioneer districts in areas like the Australian outback, the Canadian north, southern Siberia and western China. The frontier of achievement is usually very ragged and discontinuous. Scattered settlements are backed by sporadic supply towns. This boundary may exist on a natural frontier. For example, the American frontier of achievement rested successively along the Appalachian mountains, the Mississippi river, the western deserts and the Pacific ocean. Where do you think it is now?

Beyond the frontier of achievement may lie the *frontier of hope*, the political frontier claimed by the state, and often extending well beyond the limits of settlement. The frontiers of the middle of South America — western Brazil, eastern Bolivia and eastern Peru, for example — are of this type. The frontiers of hope run through lands known only to Native groups and explorers; they represent the edges of territorial claims that the governments hope to take up in the future. Such frontiers of hope have more chance of being recognized by other countries if the home country occasionally "shows the flag" in the unsettled areas. Thus Canada has planned to build roads and pipelines into the Arctic, and has encouraged the Inuit to occupy some of the previously barren lands in the High Arctic. If a country fails to exercise its interest in an area the land may be claimed by another country.

The Inuit of the Canadian Arctic did not initially live as far north as many of them now do. They used to live mostly on the northern edges of the mainland, but the Canadian government persuaded many of them to move into the islands of the High Arctic in order to establish a Canadian "presence" there.

In the second stage of frontier development, expanding states will often contact one another, usually giving rise to a *frontier of conflict*. It is unlikely that languages and customs will be similar or even compatible, and still less likely that a tradition of expansion will be given up by both groups at the same time.

A prolonged period of conflict brings about a third stage of frontier development, the phase of *shifting frontiers*. For example, the boundary between France and Germany has been shifting throughout history. The movements of the frontier depend upon the relative strengths of the conflicting states. Fig. 8-11 shows how the western frontiers of Russia/ USSR have shifted during the twentieth century. Two major combatants

Fig. 8-11
Changes in the western frontier of Russian influence during the twentieth century

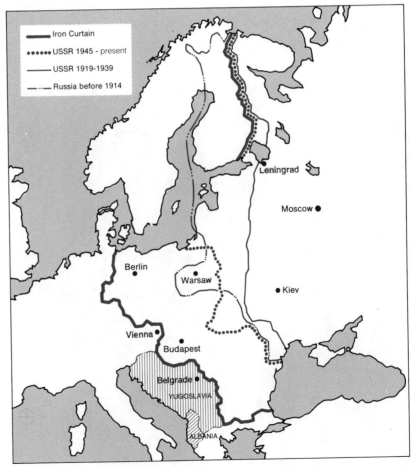

may agree to the existence of *buffer states* to minimize conflict. Paraguay and Uruguay serve as buffer states between Argentina and Brazil; Belgium and the Netherlands help to separate France and Germany; and Poland forms part of the group of countries separating the USSR and Western Europe.

The fourth phase, eventual *stability of frontiers*, may occur as the neighbouring states become less aggressive, or when the more powerful neighbour decides to end its aggression. The US-Canada frontier is an example; it is known as the longest undefended border in the world. Individual national frontiers throughout Europe are also very stable now.

After a time, neighbouring states may choose to merge their territories peacefully, producing *relic frontiers*, the fifth and last stage of frontier development. Political unification of separate kingdoms produced present-day Germany, Italy and Spain. At the present time, the same process is perhaps starting again in Western Europe, where economic union is hoped by many to be a precursor of political union. Many of the traditional frontier controls, such as passports and work permits, have already disappeared, although some others, such as currency controls, remain.

The national flag of the UK is called the Union flag (or more usually the Union Jack). It is a combination of the flags of England, Wales and Scotland. The flag of the USA is similar in principle, in that the number of stars on it has varied throughout history according to the number of states in the union.

Space is often referred to as "the last frontier." At what stage of development would you place it, and what problems do you foresee in establishing patterns for use there?

USSR Embassy Press Office / Ottawa

Co-operation

Afghans, crippled in the conflict between guerrillas and the Soviet-supported Afghan government, learn a new trade in a program sponsored by the International Red Cross in Peshawar, Pakistan.

The geopolitical picture is not completely one of trouble or potential trouble. There are an increasing number of movements for co-operation among peoples and governments. Non-governmental institutions whose purpose is to bring about international co-operation include the International Red Cross, the Salvation Army, and Oxfam. The Red Cross and the Salvation Army sponsor a variety of development projects in many countries of the world. Oxfam aims to combat hunger, injustice and inequality in the world. In addition, many church groups work internationally to help raise the living standards of the poor everywhere.

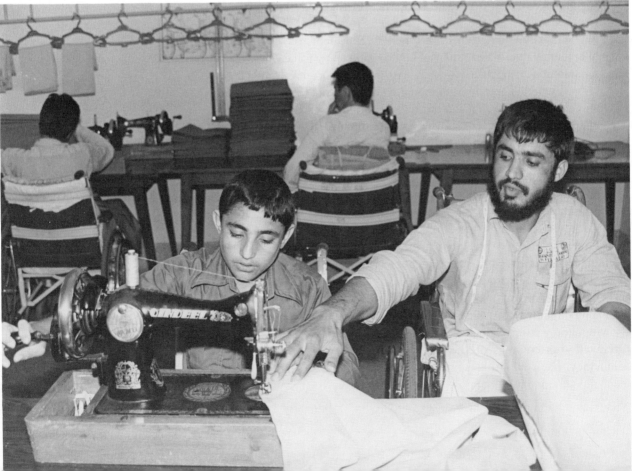

Canadian Red Cross / Lilian de Toledo

Other non-governmental groups have more specific goals, such as Pueblito, whose concern is to care for the very poor children of Latin America, and the Africa Inland Mission, which supports a variety of agricultural, rural and water development projects in Africa.

International government groups are numerous, acting chiefly as trade expediters or forums for political discussion. They include such organizations as the Latin American Free Trade Association (LAFTA), the Pacific Basin Economic Community (PBEC), the European Economic Community (EEC), the Organization for African Unity (OAU), the Organization of American States (OAS) and the specialized agencies of the UN.

The UN is an association of states that have agreed to maintain international peace and security, and to promote political, economic and social conditions that favour this purpose. The member states have no power or authority under the UN to interfere in the internal affairs of any other state, although a protest by a majority of nations may bring about a positive response.

The specialized agencies of the UN are as follows: FAO, GATT, IAEA, IBRD, ICAO, IFC, ILO, IMCO, IMF, ITU, UNESCO, UPU, WHO, WIPO, and WMO. What do all of these acronyms mean?

On the occasion of the UN's 40th anniversary, the French newspaper *Le Monde* noted (1985 6 26):

> It would be unjust to consider only the organization's failures. . . . How can we count the wars that, thanks to the UN, did not break out? Security Council meetings, however virulent, have the effect of a safety valve. The soldiers of UN peacekeeping forces have often separated warring factions. . . . Furthermore, in 1984, UN Secretary General Perez de Cuellar said, "I am sure that future historians will consider the establishment and development of the UN system of specialized agencies and world programs since 1945 as the most remarkable achievement of the international community during the second half of the twentieth century."

The specialized agencies of the UN are responsible for improved living standards, better nutrition, increased food supplies, healthier living conditions, rising literacy rates and expanded knowledge and awareness.

However, the UN has many critics who point to its failures in the political arena. It was designed to secure world peace, and yet in its first forty years it failed to prevent as many as 300 civil and regional wars and the accompanying loss of 20 000 000 lives.

One difficulty faced by the UN is that it must rely on moral suasion, allowing states to give priority to their own interests. Another of the perceived shortcomings of the UN is that it is not a representative democracy. Each nation gets one vote in the General Assembly. While

Canadian troops operate under the UN flag while serving as peace-keeping forces in the Middle East.

Canadian Armed Forces Photo

this has the advantage of ensuring that even small nations get heard, it has the disadvantage that large and powerful nations have no more say than small nations. Most of the small nations are often newly independent Third World countries, whose collective voice has thus come to dominate the Assembly. The practical result of this situation has been that the larger powers have increasingly taken their business and their problems out of the UN arena. Disarmament talks between the USA and the USSR take place elsewhere, defensive alliances such as NATO and the Warsaw Pact are built independently, and moves towards detente between China and the USA occur without reference to the UN. This inevitably weakens the moral strength of the UN, leaving it to be regarded by some as merely a Third World pressure group.

The continued existence of the UN is not really in doubt, but there are several important issues relating to its pattern of organization and style of operation to be addressed if it is to succeed in its mandate.

DISCUSSION AND RESEARCH

35. What are some of the different sorts of problems that could face minority groups?

36. What have been the causes of some recent acts of terrorism?

37. Canada's frontier of hope stretches to the North Pole. If Canada did not claim this land, who would? How does Canada try to exercise sovereignty in the Arctic? Is it challenged?

38. Research the origins of the black-white frontier in southern Africa.

39. Try to identify those areas of the world that experience **a.** frontier tension (stages 2 and 3), and **b.** frontier stability (stage 4).

40. Why do you think the western frontiers of Russian/Soviet hegemony have fluctuated more in southern and central Europe than in northern Europe, as shown in Fig. 8-11?

41. What do you think ought to happen to ocean resources?

42. Assuming that frontiers are needed, what are the properties of an ideal frontier?

43. Frontiers are the scenes of many problems. Why do nations have them? For frontiers to disappear, what would have to happen? Is this realistic?

44. Investigate the historical development of the US-Canada frontier. How far does it fit into the evolutionary stages described in the text?

45. What and where have there been disputes over water along the US-Canada border?

46. What are the components of a national identity?

47. What are the disadvantages of nationalism, once described as the "greatest curse in history"?

48. In what ways does nationalism serve a useful purpose?

49. Because the Third World often uses its majority voting strength in the UN General Assembly to pass resolutions condemning First World policies, some First World countries that contribute large amounts of money to the UN have felt that continued support of the UN is a waste of both time and money. What do you think?

50. What do you suppose the present world would be like if the UN had never existed?

CASE STUDY

SOUTH AFRICA: Apartheid and Multinationalism

South Africa used to be legally called a Union; it is now trying hard to cease to be one. Government policy, determined by a portion of the white minority, is to partition the country into politically separate areas for blacks and whites, and to further divide the black areas into separate nation-states. Inspiration for this policy is partly political, based on the philosophy of "divide and rule." To some extent, this policy is also motivated by religious belief, because of the Dutch Reformed Church's dogma that God created people separately black, brown and white, and this divine separation should not be altered. Some of the government's reasons are also economic, based on the perceived benefits to the whites of a large supply of cheap black labour. There are also historical reasons, based on the more or less simultaneous settlement by both blacks and whites in that part of southern Africa, both of whom drove out the original Khoikhoin and San from the more productive lands and into the Kalahari Desert. Another reason is the desire for a peaceful solution to the problems caused when different ethnic groups occupy the same territory. The South African government justifies its policy of separateness by pointing to the problems in other parts of the world where the peoples of two or more ethnic groups are citizens of the same state. It says that a multinational state is not workable; it wants each group to have its own state.

The policy of separate development for the different groups within South Africa is called *apartheid*. The word means "separateness." According to this policy South Africa is to be divided into a number of different and independent nation-states,

a course which the history and ethnic structure of the population are used to justify. The first European settlers were the Dutch in 1652, who pioneered the land around Cape Town. Allegedly, there were no other people in the area at that time. As the Dutch made the land productive, they needed more people; additional settlers arrived from Holland, Germany and France, and slaves were brought in from Malaya, Mozambique and East and West Africa. The Dutch prospered and sought new land beyond the Cape. Close to 1800 they encountered the Xhosa, who were slowly migrating southward along the eastern coastal plain. Fighting over the land was inconclusive and both sides came to a halt, the Dutch near the Great Fish River, the Xhosa to the north.

In the early 1800s the British seized these regions as part of their empire. They made English the official language instead of Dutch, and in 1834 abolished slavery. Both of these acts greatly upset the Dutch, who relied on slaves to support their activities. Accordingly, many Dutch moved to the interior to get away from English language and laws. The Great Trek of 1836 took them into a region that became the Orange Free State and Transvaal. Here they encountered small groups of Bantu-speaking peoples, who were migrating at about the same time from the north. There was some scattered fighting and the Dutch eventually settled in the more sparsely populated areas, far from the English on the coast. Their language developed into Afrikaans and they called themselves the Boer (farmer) people. They largely ignored the British, and were ignored in turn until 1867.

A British officer looks over the 12th Brigade and Signal Hill into the Orange Free State during the Boer War (1899–1901).

In that year British explorers discovered diamonds at Kimberley, and in 1886 gold at Johannesburg. Boer isolation ended as British industrialism pushed into the interior. In 1899 the Boers fought back, but by 1902 had been conquered. The entire region came under British control, much to the disgust of the Boers.

Meanwhile the British brought in thousands of Indians as indentured labour to work in the sugar plantations of the east coast. Most refused to return to India when their term of labour was over, despite intense repatriation propaganda by the British.

By the early years of this century the varied ethnic mixture of South Africa was basically set, and the attitudes of one group to another firmly established. The first census in 1904 showed a total population of 5 174 827, consisting of 1 117 234 *whites* and 4 057 593 *non-whites*. But these were not, nor are they yet, homogeneous groups. The

whites still are divided into mutually hostile groups of *Afrikaners* (60%) and *English* (40%). The non-whites are split into several groups: *Coloureds* (10%), the official government name for people of multiracial breeding among the early Dutch, Germans, French, Malays, local blacks and imported black slaves; *Asians* (4%), mostly the descendants of indentured Indians; and *Africans* (86%). The African segment consists of four main ethnolinguistic groups: the Nguni (Xhosa, Zulu, Ndebele and Swazi), the Sotho (Tswana, Northern Sotho and Southern Sotho), the Venda, and Tsonga.

Through the years the internal proportions of whites (60% Afrikaner, 40% English) and non-whites (86% African, 10% Coloured, 4% Asian) have remained relatively stable, but the proportions between the two major groups have altered considerably. In 1904 the proportion was one white to 3.63 non-whites, but by 1984 it was one white to 5.92 non-whites. The whites are becoming increasingly outnumbered, which may to some extent explain their developing "fortress mentality."

From the very beginnings of the legal existence of the Union of South Africa in 1910 as a Dominion in the British Empire (it changed its name in 1961 to the Republic of South Africa when it left the Commonwealth), the white government has passed a series of laws to maintain the privileges of the whites and to suppress the development of the non-whites. For example, in 1911 it passed the Native Labour Regulation Act, which discriminated against non-white wage earners; in 1913 it passed the Land Act, which reserved about 90% of South Africa's land for ownership by whites only; and in 1923 it passed the Natives (Urban Areas) Act, which banned blacks from living in white towns.

Although suppression of non-whites has been part of South Africa's history from the start, the situation began to deteriorate even more rapidly after 1948. In that year, the Afrikaners gained control of the government for the first time, running on an election platform of Save White South Africa. The

Canapress Photo Service/Stan Winer

Crossroads. This "squatter camp" has millions of inhabitants. Black men working in Capetown must return to the "homelands" to see their wives and children. Instead, they settle in these illegal squatter camps.

largely Afrikaner-supported Nationalist Party (still in power) has set out to give legal authority to the traditional Dutch Reformed Church's doctrine of white superiority. The largely English-supported opposition United Party has not won a general election since the Nationalists came to power. It contains many whites who now speak out, albeit without much effect, against the apartheid policies of the Nationalists, although it was United Party that had itself passed the earlier laws that helped to lay the groundwork for apartheid, which became official policy in 1948.

Much of the early Nationalist legislation concerned what is called "petty apartheid"; for example, in many areas blacks were forbidden to use the same restaurants, hotels and even park benches as whites. Such "petty" laws have now largely been repealed. Some other laws are much more fundamental. For example, one of the major grievances of black workers has been that they cannot gain promotion to positions that involve directing or teaching whites. In the last few years South Africa's great economic growth has put severe strains on white labour's ability to cope. There are simply not enough skilled whites to manage the growing economy, making more unjust the exclusion of blacks from many management positions.

Another major grievance has been the inferior education that is given to blacks. For example, in 1985 the annual educational expenditures were about US$1000 for a white student and only US$150 for a black student. There was one white teacher for every 16 white students, but only one black teacher for as many as 42 black students. In several different black student riots over this state of affairs in the mid-1980s, white police were used to restore order and many black students were shot and killed.

Rising protests against these and other discriminatory policies have led the South African government to implement a police state. The Nationalists passed various laws, chiefly the Pass Laws and the Terrorism Act, that in effect harass the blacks. The Pass Laws (repealed in 1986) required the blacks at all times to carry passbooks showing their identity and racial group; failure to produce it immediately upon request was cause for arrest. From 1965 to 1985 there were over 15 000 000 such arrests. Blacks were also killed in riots over passbooks, and their continued existence was a major cause of black-inspired sabotage throughout South Africa. The Terrorism Act (still in effect) has removed the principle of *habeas corpus* from the lawbooks. Therefore, people arrested under the Act can disappear without a trace for years at a time; some never reappear alive.

The existence of a police state is, however, merely the means to an end. The goal of the various policies of apartheid is, in fact, the partition of South Africa itself. The entire land area is being apportioned to the different groups so that they get rights to the regions that the South African government says they originally settled. Thus the white groups acquire rights to 87% of South Africa, including most of the arid and semi-arid interior as well as the south coast (see Fig. 8-12). The numerous black groups acquire the remaining 13%. The Coloureds and Asians get nothing, but will be permitted to reside in white South Africa, with citizenship and voting rights. The original intention of the white government was to ban black residents in South Africa — a *South Africa Without Blacks* was the slogan — but this policy was modified slightly in 1986 to permit restricted citizenship (e.g., no voting rights) to those blacks who had been born in the designated white area, who had not moved (or been moved) to their assigned areas, and who had been continuously employed for at least ten years in the white area. Partition of the territory of South Africa in this manner was a government project; it was not sought by the black groups, who regard South Africa as a single country.

The new black nations are identified and divided on the basis of differences in language (Nguni, Sotho, Venda, Tsonga), customs, physical appearance, modes of dress and ornamentation and so on. For example, the South African government's advertising supplement in the *Globe Magazine*, 1969 6 7, states that "the traditional Zulu leopard skin and beadwork are quite different from the red ochre dyed blanket of the Xhosa or the multicoloured woven blanket of the South Sotho," and "The North Sotho still love their own make of sour porridge and beer, while the South Sotho cheerfully eat horse and donkey flesh." Despite the patronizing manner in which these traditional cultural differences are described, such differences form the basis for the allocation of *homelands* (see Fig. 8-12) to the different groups of blacks. Originally, all blacks in South Africa, wherever they lived, were allocated citizenship and full voting rights in their own homelands by the South African government, though most of them had never seen a "homeland" and had no connection with one. At the same time they were deprived of the few citizenship rights they had in the newly allocated white area of South Africa. The government's intention was to have no black citizens in South Africa and to move all blacks into their new homelands, which generally occupied some of the least fertile parts of the country, and which in some cases (e.g., Bophuthatswana) existed in separated parts. The 12 000 000 or so blacks who moved to the

Fig. 8-12
South African homelands

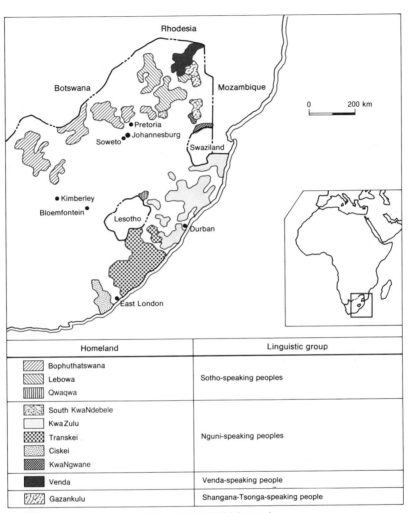

Homeland	Linguistic group
Bophuthatswana	
Lebowa	Sotho-speaking peoples
Qwaqwa	
South KwaNdebele	
KwaZulu	
Transkei	Nguni-speaking peoples
Ciskei	
KwaNgwane	
Venda	Venda-speaking people
Gazankulu	Shangana-Tsonga-speaking people

Note 1) In order to consolidate the pieces, blacks and whites are both being moved.
2) The blacks with 70% of the total population have been given rights to 13% of the land. They prefer to have either **a)** *all* the land under their control, with the whites as a minority in a black state, or **b)** independence in the homelands, but with much bigger and more consolidated homelands reflecting their 70% of the population.

new homelands, frequently at gunpoint, lost their South African citizenship, as, until 1986, did the blacks who remained in the white areas of South Africa. The latter group, along with all other blacks, lost their South African citizenship and were allocated replacement citizenship in their homelands in 1976 but had not moved (or been moved) there.

Only in 1986 did some of them regain South African citizenship, provided they applied for it in writing.

The Nationalist government generally argues that blacks remaining outside their homelands (i.e., in the white areas of South Africa), are really in a foreign country and should not expect to have the full privileges of citizenship. Various "influx

Canapress Photo Service / August Sycholt

In the homeland of Transkei. Conditions on the ''homelands'' are often desperately poor, and the land incapable of providing a livelihood for the many people forced to live there.

control" laws prevent blacks from moving easily into the rest of South Africa from a homeland, though the blacks for the most part still regard themselves as South Africans. The government sees the blacks as visitors ("temporary sojourners") because the towns and cities now occupied by white South Africans were initially founded by the Dutch or British.

The blacks, on the other hand, migrated to the towns in search of jobs many years ago, settling in confined and segregated "townships" outside the white areas. According to the government, the drift to the cities has continued because of the high rates of population growth in the homelands, the lack of jobs there and the growing number of jobs in white cities that often provide the only

source of livelihood for black workers. In general, only workers are allowed to migrate to the cities, because Afrikaners fear that allowing whole families to migrate would encourage them to stay.

Black workers contend that even though a salary is welcome, it is only about 10% of the money earned by whites doing similar work. They also complain about the "contract" nature of much of the work, whereby they agree to work for a certain length of time without striking for more wages. Nevertheless, union membership is now legally possible for blacks in South Africa, although only about 500 000 workers so far belong.

Economic growth is producing other cracks in South Africa's racial policies. The South African government has long encouraged foreign investment for economic growth, and there are now many foreign-owned companies in South Africa, a number of which are British or American. While many white people in Britain and North America resent this apparent support for the South African government, many also favour it on the grounds that disinvestment would damage the South African economy and cause more harm to the blacks than to the whites. South African blacks are divided on the issue. Some, such as Chief Buthelezi, who leads 6 000 000 Zulus, welcome investment as a source of jobs. Others, including those represented by the African National Congress (ANC), which operates from a base outside South Africa because of its revolutionary philosophy and activities, believe that continued investment provides financial and moral support to the apartheid government. The newly-formed Congress of South African Trade Unions called in 1986 for British and American firms to pull out of South Africa. Arguments on both sides are fierce, although several American firms (such as IBM, GM, Kodak and General Electric) have now pulled out, or *disinvested*.

Arguments are also fierce over the issue of sanctions. For many years there have been those who refused to buy South African products, but during the mid-1980s these people were joined by large numbers of others who think that sanctions are a necessary means to force the South African government to dismantle the apparatus of apartheid. They argue that unless sanctions are imposed by the international community South Africa will fall into civil war. These views are expressed by journalists and other citizens, by church groups, university students, trade unions and political parties. For example, the Canadian Labour Congress favours cutting all Canadian economic and diplomatic ties with South Africa. Opponents claim that sanctions have never been shown to work whenever they have been tried (e.g., US sanctions against Libya in 1985–86, UK and UN sanctions against Rhodesia — now Zimbabwe — from 1965 to 1979). In any event sanctions, they argue, will

more likely increase than decrease the risk of civil war because South Africa's economy will suffer and unemployment and discontent will rise. These views are put forward by journalists and other citizens and by some national governments, most notably those of the USA, the UK and West Germany.

Black opinion in South Africa also is divided over the issue of sanctions. Those supporting sanctions, such as Nelson and Winnie Mandela and the African National Congress, as well as Bishop Tutu, think the only way to persuade the government to end apartheid is for the international community to impose full economic and diplomatic sanctions. Others believe that sanctions will inflame an already explosive situation and argue instead for negotiation as a means to ending apartheid. Followers on both sides have been vehement in their actions in support of the opposing beliefs. The African National Congress, from its bases outside South Africa, has sponsored guerrilla actions and terrorist activities, and was joined by many disaffected young people. Much of their violence has been directed at other black people who give them less than full support, whom they consider to be puppets of the white government. The ANC has been opposed by the people belonging to Amabutho (Zulu "warriors") and Inkatha (Chief Buthelezi's political organization). Their violence was directed at the more radical black people, largely in the hope of preventing them from destroying South Africa's economy.

Many other black people are caught in the middle, disliking apartheid and violence and unsure of the effect of sanctions. The views of Barney Thusi, a truck driver from Soweto, reported in *The Toronto Star* 1986 7 20, are typical of those caught in the middle:

> I worry about the future for my children. I want to see apartheid die. I want to see my children live in freedom. But first we need jobs and food. The outside world is right to force

this government to give us our rights; they should help us gain our freedom. If sanctions can do that, maybe they are a good thing. [But] if sanctions mean some blacks will lose their jobs, that doesn't sound quite right. Outside money creates jobs for us. The little help that we get from outside countries, if it's withdrawn, we will suffer even worse. We can die of poverty.

Because black people in South Africa are not allowed to vote, they have no other way of making the government act than by taking their "politics" to the streets. Demonstrations are banned, so riots, which are forcibly suppressed, have become more common. Some opinion polls have been taken in South Africa, but their results are inconclusive and each side scoffs at results favouring the other. In 1984 a poll by a professor at the University of Natal found that blacks were opposed to disinvestment and sanctions by a margin of three to one. In 1985 a poll by *The Times* of London, England, found that 75% of the blacks thought that it would be all right for sanctions to be imposed. In 1986 a poll by the Human Sciences Research Council found that 86% of blacks in industrialized areas were opposed to sanctions, while another poll by the Community Agency for Social Enquiry found that 73% of blacks supported some form of international economic pressure against South Africa.

For its part, the Afrikaner government has also become increasingly divided during the 1980s. Those who favoured some loosening of the constraints of apartheid generally held sway until early 1986, when a strong backlash led to the formation of the Afrikaner Weerstandsbeweging (Afrikaner Resistance Movement); by mid-1986 the forces in favour of rigorous enforcement of apartheid had regained the ascendancy.

Meanwhile, a black Baptist minister from Philadelphia, Leon Sullivan, has developed a movement in the USA to apply pressure to companies with subsidiaries in South Africa to get

them to implement policies that combat apartheid. To this end Sullivan has published a number of principles to be followed by US companies in South Africa. These include nonsegregation of the races in all eating, locker room and workplace facilities; fair and equal employment practices for all races; equal pay for equal or comparable work for all races; development of training programs for supervisory and technical jobs for all non-whites; increasing the number of non-whites in supervisory positions; improving the quality of life for non-whites in such areas as housing, schooling and health care. In addition, companies agreeing to the Sullivan principles must pay at least the minimum wage and accept the rights of black workers to unionize and strike.

Many US companies have signed the *Sullivan Code*, and they are scored each year for their efforts at implementing the principles. So far, the most successful have been Ford, Monsanto, Exxon and Mobil. Firestone and Carnation have been among the significant failures.

While arguments rage internationally over the economic aspects of apartheid and its homeland policy, there are even stronger arguments over its political aspects. The government is holding to its policy despite severe objections from many blacks. Some blacks are prepared to take homeland independence now; others want nothing to do with it, seeing their future as the ultimate rulers of the entire country. Thus the nations of Transkei, Bophuthatswana, Venda, Ciskei and KwaNdebele Venda (South Ndebele) already exist; the other five have rejected the idea totally. This means that the riots and disturbances that characterize economic issues are severely compounded by wide differences in political strategy. The overriding issue is necessarily that of political power: who should have it and how should it be gained. Each group, black and white, believes it should hold the dominant political power.

In a major attempt to solidify its homelands policy, the Afrikaner-based Nationalist gov-

The township of Langa has hostels to house black men from the homelands working in Capetown, and the families of blacks born in Capetown. The arrangement of buildings makes police control of the inhabitants easy.

ernment changed the country's constitution in 1984. It set up a three-chamber parliament, weighted in favour of the whites, acknowledging for the first time the political existence of the Asians and Coloureds, but totally ignoring the Africans. The whites were given a House of Assembly with 178 seats; the Coloureds a House of Representatives with 85 seats; and the Asians a House of Delegates with 45 seats. The Africans got nothing. The move was seen by all non-whites as an attempt to provide a Coloured and Asian buffer between the whites and Africans, and to split the non-whites themselves into two factions: the recognized and the non-

recognized (the principle of divide and rule). This overt political alienation of the Africans has been the cause of much of the unrest since that time, since it highlighted for the Africans their total political unacceptability to the white government.

Support for the new constitution was mixed. Most whites accepted the granting of limited political power to some non-whites as necessary, although a large number also felt that it represented something of a surrender. Coloureds and Asians lent minimal support, a mere 20% turning out to vote in favour of the constitutional change. Africans reacted with open hostility. Riots, demonstrations, marches and strikes were put down forcefully by the whites. Many Africans were killed, but as one of them (Nthato Motlana, community leader in Soweto) said in 1984, "As long as blacks are excluded from the places where decisions are made, they are going to speak with bombs."

The recent history of South Africa has been one of growing tension, increasing radicalization of Africans and harsher suppression of unrest by the white government.

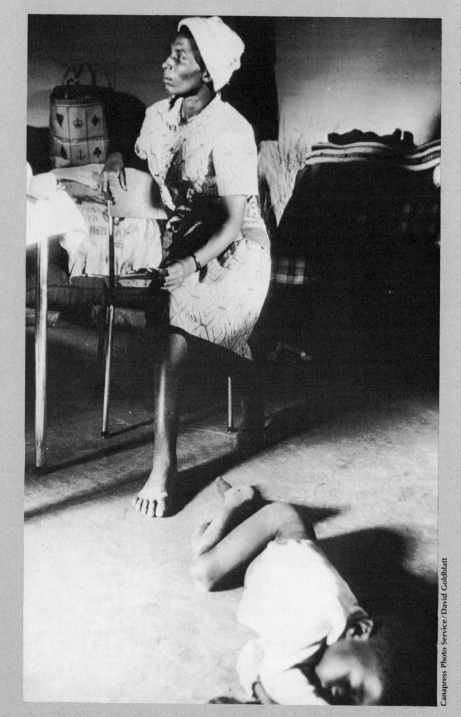

Mamokhali Setabataba in her home and shop, where she makes Basuto hats. Her husband left to work in the goldmines of Transvaal.

Canapress Photo Service/David Goldblatt

Conclusion

In this chapter, we have seen that the countries of the world are frequently classified into groups, one of the most widely accepted being the classification into three different "worlds," based on variations in population growth, food production, industrialization, energy production, quality of life and economic and political system.

The contrasts between these "worlds" exist to some extent because of ideological differences. Every nation has its own beliefs and acts according to them. Because of their different beliefs, and the actions which stem from them, nations often disagree and conflicts occur. Yet in this chapter we have also looked at some of the forms of co-operation that nations are developing within the world.

The differences in ideology, stage and type of development, and the projects based on growing international co-operation, all are components of a highly dynamic world situation. The world will not remain as it is now, and we should be aware at all times of the certainty of change and try in our analysis to recognize the trends that appear.

In all the major aspects of life and livelihood, changes have occurred at different speeds in different parts of the world, so that some countries have so far experienced great change while others have as yet experienced little. As a result, the world is enormously varied. Can we reasonably expect that cultural and economic differences will remain, or will they diminish? Is it likely that the numerous countries of the world will eventually develop into a more or less homogeneous group with similar social characteristics and standards of living? Or will differences continue? Will differences be regarded as culturally enriching, or produce fear, hostility and war?

These questions, while easy to raise, are difficult to answer. The World Bank released information in 1977 that suggested that *One World*, on the economic level, was an unattainable ideal. Figures indicated that even if the Third World countries were to double their annual growth rates, while the already industrialized countries remained unchanged, only eight would be able to close the gap within the next 100 years, and only another sixteen within the next 1000 years. The President of the

World Bank stated that policies to close the gap were unrealistic, and that the World Bank should plan instead to narrow the gap, not in monetary terms, but in terms of quality of life, nutrition, literacy, life expectancy and so on.

It appears that the world's countries will always differ in many basic respects, and the resulting problems and advantages will demand our closest attention. There is no doubt that we should occupy ourselves with the world we live in; its development to its present condition and its future prospects are probably our most vital concern.

APPENDIX 1
Principles of Ecology

The principles of ecology form the basis of the science that deals with the relationships among living organisms and their environments. Insects and reptiles are as much a part of the study of ecology as are human beings. As the particular study of the relationship between humanity and its environment, geography is therefore a part of the overall study of ecology, and the general principles of ecology accordingly underpin all geographical studies.

This Appendix presents some of the major principles of ecology, especially as they relate to the issues discussed in the text. Let us start with some basic definitions.

Definitions

Systems

A *system* is a collection of parts or events that interact with one another to produce a functioning entity. For instance, the interaction of a collection of roads, airports, cars, trucks, planes, railways, people, goods and schedules forms a functioning transportation system. Similarly the interaction of raw material production, manufacturing, transportation, construction and marketing forms a functioning industrial system. To continue functioning, all systems require inputs of energy. A *systems approach* is a way of interpreting the world, looking at a complex variety of parts and events as a single functioning, interdependent and interacting whole. It is fundamental to issues analysis.

Ecosystems

Ecosystems are the operating entities formed by the interaction of living organisms with their non-living environment. They exist in a great variety of different sizes, ranging from a single tree or a pond or a village to the whole earth. A large ecosystem may contain several smaller ecosystems, each of which may contain a number of even smaller ecosystems. All ecosystems require inputs of energy in order to continue functioning.

Populations

In ecology, the term *population* is not limited to describing only people; it can identify any group of organisms, including people, all of one kind (species) and living together in a specific area. It is possible to have a population of cows in a field, trees in a forest or people in a nation.

Communities

A *community* is made up of all the populations existing and interacting within a given ecosystem. Thus a forest community consists of all its living (*biotic*) parts — the insects, birds, reptiles, animals, people and plants — that interact with each other within the forest ecosystem.

Environments

All *environments* consist of functioning relationships between living (biotic) and non-living (*abiotic*) elements within given areas. They are similar to ecosystems.

Biomes

The world may be divided according to its major communities, such as tropical forest, temperate deciduous forest, coniferous forest, savanna, temperate grassland, tundra and desert. Such major communities are called *biomes*. The combination of all the world's biomes is called the *biosphere*, made up by all the living organisms on earth. The quantity of biotic material in a given area is called *biomass*.

Energy

Energy may be defined as the ability of a system to do work; it provides for all activity, including life itself. The source of energy for all work done by biological (biotic) systems is the sun.

Solar Radiation

The sun is a continuous thermonuclear reaction by which hydrogen is converted to helium, emitting electromagnetic energy (solar radiation) in the process. Solar energy radiates in all directions from the sun, only a tiny proportion (about 1/50 000 000) of which is received by the earth. Approximately half of this quantity is either reflected back into space from the tops of clouds or absorbed by the earth's atmosphere. The other half comes directly to the earth's surface or arrives there indirectly from scattering within the atmosphere. Small portions of the energy reaching the earth's surface are reflected back into the atmosphere from such surfaces as deserts, icefields and oceans, and some is used in heating the ground itself; some is also used to sustain life through the process of *photosynthesis*.

Electromagnetic energy from the sun comes in the form of short-wave radiation, mostly in the range 0.2 to 4.0 microns (a micron is 1/1000 mm). The visible sunlight is that part of the radiation spectrum in the range 0.39 (violet light) to 0.76 (red light) microns. Such short-wave energy generally is able to penetrate the atmosphere fairly easily, except for reflection from clouds and scatter from dust and water particles. However, a small portion of radiation with a wave length just shorter than 0.39 microns (ultraviolet radiation) is largely absorbed by a layer of ozone in the earth's upper atmosphere. Ultraviolet radiation has high energy and can break the bonds of the large organic molecules that form the living tissue of plants and other organisms. Thus the ozone layer acts as a filter for the protection of life here on earth. It permits photosynthesis to proceed.

Photosynthesis

Photosynthesis is the process whereby the radiant energy in sunlight is transformed into chemical energy stored in plants through the presence of chlorophyll. The energy is stored in the molecules and bonds of plant tissue. Without it, life as we know it could not exist.

Only plants have photosynthetic ability, or the ability to build food molecules. They are accordingly classified ecologically as *autotrophs*, or self-feeders. All other living organisms depend upon the autotrophs for the food they need to live; they are called *heterotrophs*, or other-feeders.

The First Law of Thermodynamics

The First Law of Thermodynamics states that energy can be neither created nor destroyed, that its total quantity remains constant. Its form, however, may change, so that it may exist as radiant energy, as light or heat, as chemical energy or as nuclear energy. The earth and its biosphere may thus transform the energy of electromagnetic radiation from the sun into a variety of other forms, but the energy itself cannot be destroyed. Its final form as it passes through the earth's ecosystem is heat. Unless the earth is to become hotter and hotter, the heat must be re-radiated to space. The energy received by the earth from the sun must therefore be balanced over time by an equal amount re-radiated by the earth into space. Radiation returns to space (*terrestrial radiation*) in relatively long-wave form (about 12 microns), and does not pass easily through the atmosphere. This warms the atmosphere, making it somewhat like a holding tank for heat on its way from the earth's surface to space. The increasing amount of carbon dioxide in the atmosphere from the burning of wood and various fossil fuels is causing the atmosphere to become more resistant to passing outgoing long-wave heat radiation. There is some evidence that the atmosphere is becoming warmer because of this *greenhouse effect* (short-wave energy coming in easily; long-wave energy escaping with difficulty). There is also evidence that more atmospheric particles are decreasing the prior passage of incoming short-wave radiation. It is not yet clear whether these two effects will continue to balance the level of heat energy in the earth's atmosphere. There have always been temperature fluctuations of varying durations throughout earth history and it is not easy to disentangle possible causes for these variations.

The Second Law of Thermodynamics

The Second Law of Thermodynamics states that each time energy is converted from one form to another (*interconverted*) it goes from a more organized and concentrated form to a less organized and concentrated form; this phenomenon is called *entropy*. This means there is always a loss of efficiency when energy is interconverted. The loss of efficiency is reflected in the amount of heat released in the conversion process, for heat is generally the least organized and concentrated form of energy. An electricity generating station, for example, yields large quantities of relatively useless heat; the transmission of electricity yields more "waste" heat, while the use of electricity for lighting or running motors yields even more. Solar energy is continually degraded (but not destroyed) at each conversion, eventually radiating back into space as relatively useless heat.

Food Chains

On entering an ecosystem, radiant energy is converted by photosynthesis into plant tissue, with some loss of heat in the conversion process. Plants thus form the first stage in a food chain; they are the *producers* (autotrophs), while the organisms that feed on them are the *consumers* (heterotrophs). Again, there is some loss of energy in the form of heat in the conversion from plant tissue to animal tissue. Consumers that feed only on plant tissue are called *herbivores*; those that feed on other animal tissue are called *carnivores*. Other consumers feed on plant tissue or animal tissue alike; these are called *omnivores*. In all cases the conversion process releases some stored energy in the form of heat. All producers (plants) and consumers (animals, insects, fish, birds, people) eventually die and become subject to the action of *decomposers*, again releasing some heat. Energy thus flows through an ecosystem, entering as radiation and leaving as heat, having given life to the community in its passage.

The stage at which an organism feeds in a food chain is called its *trophic level*. Producers belong to trophic level one. Consumers feeding directly on producers occupy trophic level two. Thus corn is at trophic level one; it is a producer, converting sunlight to plant tissue by photosynthesis. People who eat corn are at trophic level two, as are the insects that feed directly on corn or the cattle to whom corn may be fed. The birds that eat the insects and the people that eat the beef from the cattle are at trophic level three, for they are feeding on prior consumers. Larger birds or animals that might eat the insect-eating birds would be at trophic level four, and so on.

Trophic levels are important, because at each stage of conversion there is considerable heat loss. As much as 90% of the energy in one stage is lost as heat in the process of converting to the next higher trophic level. For example, if plant tissue in a given area contains 1000 kJ of stored chemical energy, a level two consumer will be able to derive only about 100 kJ from it. A level three consumer will derive only about 10 kJ and a level four consumer only about 1 kJ. This tendency toward a large and persistent heat loss at each higher trophic level is called the *Ten Percent Law*. It means that in practice most food chains are quite short, because at high trophic levels organisms find it difficult to find enough food to stay alive. Most food chains have only three or four levels. Moreover, there is clearly more usable energy available to those organisms occupying lower trophic levels, a fact that has led many people to decry the use of crops to feed cows and pigs as a wasteful use of resources in a world where many people are hungry.

Another characteristic of food chains is that material absorbed at one trophic level will, if not excreted or used to live, be passed up to the next higher trophic level consumer, causing increasingly high concentrations of certain substances at higher trophic levels. This process is called *biological magnification*. In this way certain pesticides and other artificial chemicals may accumulate in increasing quantities as they are passed up a food chain. Before DDT was banned in North America, for example, studies indicated that plankton at trophic level one contained about 0.04 parts of DDT per million parts of tissue, whereas gulls at trophic level four (eating big fish that ate little fish that ate plankton) had concentrations of DDT of about 75 parts per million. The tendency to biological magnification is significant to people, for they are the highest trophic level consumers in any food chain.

Cycles

While energy flows through all systems, matter does not. Matter is fixed in quantity, like energy, but it does not flow into the earth and out again; it is constantly *recycled*. The earth has a large variety of cycles, each acting as a processor of materials. The largest in terms of area and time is the geological cycle, processing the rock of the earth itself. It encompasses processes as varied as plate tectonics, mountain building, contraction and expansion of ocean basins, erosion, transportation and deposition, and involves the agencies of running water, moving ice, wind and waves. In its operation, the geological cycle produces earthquakes, volcanic eruptions, tsunamis, changing land and sea levels, floods, and related phenomena. Other major earth cycles include atmospheric wind systems that transfer heat from one part of the world to another and ocean currents that perform a similar function for ocean water. Some other important cycles are listed below.

The Water (Hydrologic) Cycle
This cycle is driven by solar energy, assisted by gravity. Water on the earth is thus constantly moving from the surface into the atmosphere and back to the surface. The portion that spends time on land in its journey back to the oceans (or back into the atmosphere again) is vital to life. And the longer it spends on land, the more useful it is. Forests and reservoirs slow down the rate of return to the oceans; deforestation and pavement speed it up. The distribution of water on the earth's land is highly uneven; areas of shortage are indicated in Fig. 3-3 in the text, and it has been one of humanity's major endeavours since early times to move water from areas of plenty to areas of shortage. Two modern schemes are illustrated in Figs. 3-4 and 3-5.

Human demand for water is considerable. The production of a single egg in North America requires about 500 l of water, while a litre of milk requires about 3 500 l of water. The production of a kilogram of beef needs about 25 000 l of water, a medium-sized car about 250 000 l of water. These quantities, although huge, are only part of the story. Since water is part of a cycle, it may be constantly re-used, making the same water usable for several different purposes. Water problems, therefore, arise not only from availability (quantity and location), but also from the deterioration of quality caused by multiple use. The chemical treatment of agricultural land and the production of toxic industrial wastes have often reduced water quality for other users. Flowing water can normally handle certain amounts of these agricultural and industrial wastes, but above a limit the wastes become unmanageable and the water is described as "polluted." Pollution is basically a problem of excess. There are four main types:

- *Thermal pollution*, caused by the release of excessive heat from electricity generating stations and industrial plants. Remember, the release of heat is a normal part of the process of energy conversion, but its large-scale concentrated release can cause problems for fish and other water organisms.
- *Cultural sedimentation*, caused by depositing in waterways the solid wastes (e.g., old tires, cans) of a culture.

– *Toxic pollution*, caused by the disposal of synthetic chemicals in the waterways. Such chemicals are often difficult for a river to break down and dilute naturally, and they tend to be absorbed into the food chain.

– *Eutrophication*, caused by excessive addition of nutrients, especially agricultural fertilizer. Large quantities of phosphorous and nitrogen cause greatly increased algae growth in the water; when the algae die, bacterial decomposition increases. Decomposition uses oxygen that fish need to survive; the fish die, further hastening the process of decomposition. Foul-smelling gases are produced and clear water becomes clogged with decaying and rotting vegetation.

Biogeochemical Cycles

Living organisms require about 30 to 40 elements for normal growth. Some, such as phosphorous and carbon, are needed in relatively large quantities; others, such as zinc and iodine, are required in only trace quantities. Since the quantity of matter is fixed, however, there is a finite supply of these elements. Their continued availability to new life thus depends upon some cycle that releases them for fresh use.

Cycles that involve a combination of *biological* organism, *geological* environment and *chemical* change are called *biogeochemical* cycles. The essence of these cycles is that a biological organism (usually a microorganism) moves an element by a process of chemical change from a geological "reservoir" (either atmosphere or lithosphere) into itself, through the food chain and back into the geological reservoir. There are two main types of biogeochemical cycle, depending upon the nature of the geological reservoir. Where the reservoir is the atmosphere, the cycles are called *gaseous nutrient cycles*; examples include the carbon, oxygen and nitrogen cycles. Where the reservoir is the lithosphere, the cycles are termed *sedimentary nutrient cycles*; examples are the phosphorous and sulphur cycles.

Elements in gaseous nutrient cycles are usually available, for the atmosphere is ever-present, while those in sedimentary nutrient cycles may be locked away in buried sedimentary rocks. The immediate availability of elements in gaseous cycles generally results in fast recycling, whereas the very slow movements of the geological cycle usually impose slow recycling speeds in the sedimentary cycles.

The nitrogen cycle is an example of a gaseous nutrient cycle. The major geological reservoir of nitrogen is the atmosphere, which consists of about 79% nitrogen. Since it is not part of any compound, but exists on its own, atmospheric nitrogen is termed "free" nitrogen. It is unusable until it has been changed from a gas into a nitrate compound by means of a process called *nitrogen fixation*. Fixation is carried out mostly by *rhizobium* bacteria living in the soil or attached to the roots of leguminous plants such as peas, beans and clover. Fixation may also occur with lightning, which converts atmospheric nitrogen into nitric acid, which is then dissolved in rainwater, carried to earth and absorbed by plants. Fixation may occur industrially in the production of nitrogenous fertilizers, where an electrical process similar to lighting is employed. Once fixation has occurred, plants take in the nitrogen through their roots and convert it to protein. Animals acquire nitrogen — and its protein — by eating plants. When the plants and animals die, or when the animals excrete wastes (urea), bacterial decay breaks the matter down into amino acids. Other bacteria change the amino acids into ammonia in a process called *aminification*. Different bacteria then change the ammonia into nitrates (*nitrification*) and more bacteria break down the nitrates into nitrogen (*denitrification*), which passes back into the atmospheric reservoir.

The phosphorous cycle is one type of sedimentary nutrient cycle. The major geological reservoir is sedimentary phosphate rock, available naturally to the basic cycle only as a result of weathering and erosion. Phosphorous itself is one of the five absolutely essential elements to life (along with oxygen, carbon, hydrogen and nitrogen) and is a vital component of genetic (DNA and RNA) and energy-producing (ATP) molecules in living tissue. The cycle begins with rock phosphates being eroded and dissolved in streams and ground water. Plants then absorb the phosphate solution through their roots, incorporating it into their tissue. Consumers acquire phosphates through eating plants. Excreted wastes and dead plant and animal matter are subsequently broken down by decomposers and phosphates returned to the soil. Much of this phosphate is washed away by rain and run-off, as was some that eroded from the sedimentary rock and was transported straight out to sea. Once in the sea, phosphates are incorporated into various marine sediments and await further geological uplift to be available for use again. The relatively small amounts of phosphorous available naturally in the cycle have caused people to seek to expand the supply artificially. Phosphates are mined in large quantities for fertilizer production, and guano and fish have proved to be valuable supplementary sources. Reliance on such additional sources is part of the present farming situation, for without these extra supplies farm productivity would rapidly diminish. It is estimated that phosphorous availability is the chief limiting factor on the earth's ability to produce food. On the other hand, some phosphorous is wasted in chemical run-off from treated fields, causing eutrophication of waterways.

Population

Population Growth

The ability of organisms to reproduce themselves under optimal conditions and cause the population to grow is called *biotic potential*. Theoretically, for example, two houseflies could generate 6 trillion houseflies within a year if there were no constraints upon breeding. Normally, however, constraints exist; these are called *environmental resistance*, and include such things as disease, starvation and competition.

A normal growth curve for a population displays a typical slanted "S"-shape, commencing with a slow initial phase (*lag phase*) followed by a period of increasingly fast growth (*logarithmic phase*) and a period of levelling off (*equilibrium phase*). At the equilibrium phase, ecologists acknowledge that the population has reached the maximum density the environment can support; this is called the *carrying capacity* of the environment.

Another fairly common growth pattern is the "J" curve, where the lag and logarithmic phases are followed by abrupt decline rather than equilibrium. The chief explanation for "J" growth patterns is that the environment for that particular population for some reason becomes almost totally unsupportive of life (e.g., by accumulation of toxic wastes, drastic temperature change or exhaustion of food production capacity).

Tolerances and Relationships

All organisms exist within certain environmental limits. They cannot exist if certain conditions are not met: corn cannot grow if there is no phosphorous in the soil (even though all other environmental factors are favourable to growth). Neither can they exist if the environment provides too much of some factor: fish cannot survive if there is too much phosphorous in the water. This aspect of environmental limits is governed by the *Law of Tolerances*, which restricts organisms to their *tolerance range*. One result is the limited geographical distribution of many organisms. Humanity has greatly extended its tolerance range artificially by its use of clothing, housing, heating, air conditioning, medical facilities and so on, and has accordingly widened its geographical distribution to cover almost the entire globe. By creating artificial environments, people have also extended the geographical distribution of many other organisms that co-exist in some sort of relationship with people.

Whenever the population of a species interacts with the population of another species (called a *symbiotic relationship*), one or both of them will change in their ability to grow and survive. The major sorts of relationships are as follows:

– *Co-operation:*   Different populations may exist in the same environment, surviving without any particular relationship, as gi-
raffes, gazelles and impalas survive in the African savannas. Each
population would continue to survive without the others, for they
have different needs, although they all may benefit if any one of
them warns of danger.

– *Mutualism:*   Two different species exist in a relationship where
each depends upon the other, as leguminous plants and nitrogen-
fixing bacteria. Each would suffer without the other. The relationship between some farmers and their specialized hybrid crops
is another example of a mutually beneficial interaction.

– *Commensalism:*   Two different species may exist together in the
same environment, but only one species benefits, the other remaining unaffected. The relationship between city people and
sparrows is an example.

– *Amensalism:*   This sort of relationship exists where one species
inhibits the growth of another species, while remaining unaffected
itself. Trees that grow in a forest may block sunlight from undergrowth, causing the undergrowth to decline but leaving the
trees unaffected.

– *Competition:*   Competition occurs when two different species (*inter-
specific competition*) or two different sets of members of the same
species (*intra-specific competition*) vie for limited environmental
resources such as living space (*territory*), sunlight and food. Both
species (or sets of the same species) are adversely affected during
the phase of competition, but sooner or later one usually pre-
dominates, taking the resources for itself and eliminating the other
in a process called *competitive exclusion*. The only way that a losing
species can survive is to change its environmental requirements
so it no longer competes with the predominant species. The
combination of environmental requirements for any species is
called its *niche*; the process of changing those requirements is
called *niche differentiation*. The use of agricultural pesticides has
represented a direct attack by humans upon the existence of
insects competing for food; many insects have responded by niche
differentiation. In former times, prairie buffalo were unable to
make such a niche differentiation and were eliminated (competitively excluded).

– *Predation:*   In this type of interaction predators survive by killing
their prey. Predators clearly benefit, for they obtain food; prey
may benefit as a group by having their numbers controlled, but
suffer individually by being killed. The lack of predators in areas

where people have introduced new animals has often caused the new animals to breed beyond the carrying capacity offered by their new environment, resulting in "J" type growth curves. The existence of predators often keeps prey growth on a more normal "S" pattern. In some cases, the growth curves oscillate up and down, as predators kill prey until their own food supply diminishes, the predators diminish in number, allowing the prey to grow again, leading to a resurgence in the number of predators, and so on in a continuing cycle. Humanity's relationship with many fish stocks is somewhat of this type, although human numbers have not declined periodically because there are usually alternative food sources available.

- *Parasitism:*   In these cases, one species (the *parasite*) feeds at the expense of the other (the *host*). There are many parasites, some that are generally harmless to the host and others that are harmful, causing weakness, disease, stunted growth and possibly death. Where there has been sufficient time for hosts to adapt to parasites, life may continue fairly normally. For example, many tropical Africans have adjusted to malaria parasites by an evolutionary development of sickle-shaped red blood cells, which are more resistant to malaria parasites than the regular round red blood cells, but which have less capacity to carry oxygen, leading to some anemia. If malaria is present, sickle-cells offer some advantage to the host; in the absence of malaria, sickle-cells are a liability to the host. If new parasites are introduced to an area previously free of them, evolutionary adaptation is not immediately possible and hosts may be destroyed, as has happened with several species of North American trees (e.g., elms) exposed to imported parasites.

Territory is that part of the environment that members of a species occupy and will defend against competing occupation by other members of the same species. The display of defensive behaviour is called *territoriality*. Generally, if the environment is bountiful, territories are relatively small; but if the environment becomes less supportive communities will usually press to expand their territory to acquire more supplies. Attempts by groups of human populations to expand their territory have occurred frequently in the past, but are of limited likelihood now because of the numerous geopolitical constraints on forceful expansionary action. Even the traditional escape valve of *migration* — the desire to find a niche in a new environment — has become less possible as political barriers have been erected around protected territory.

Communities and Equilibrium

Research into biotic communities suggests that where there is great *species diversity* there is more likelihood of ecological stability. More alternatives exist for consumers if there is a wide variety of producers; food webs develop instead of food chains. Greater variety provides a cushioning effect, so that negative disturbances in one part of the community are compensated for by positive actions elsewhere within the community. Much modern commercial farming has set up ecosystems with very limited species diversity (e.g., a single crop in a field), and in the absence of continued care such artificial ecosystems are highly unstable. A lawn is another typical and widespread example of an artificial, restricted species ecosystem; without continued intensive care, it rapidly ceases to exist as a lawn.

Stability, however, does not necessarily mean permanence. There is a natural tendency for communities to change slowly because of the process called *ecological succession*. All successions are different, but the general idea is that given new land to colonize, plants will develop in a species sequence. For example, lichens can colonize bare rock, but when they do they create small amounts of soil in which mosses can grow. The mosses force out the lichens (they *predominate*). In turn they create even more soil, with greater water-holding capacity, making conditions suitable for small seed plants, which in turn predominate. The small seed plants provide shelter for the seedlings of small shrubs and are in turn displaced. The shrubs provide good growing conditions for small trees, which soon rise above them, competing more successfully for both sunlight and root space. Through time, therefore, the ecological succession has created a series of different ecosystems, each of which is called a *seral community*, lasting until replaced by the next seral community. Finally stability (or *equilibrium*) is reached in what is called the *climax community*, usually characterized by great species diversity. Climax communities are not immune to change, since there may be environmental disasters such as floods, hurricanes, earthquakes, fires and so on, but they tend toward considerable long-term stability.

APPENDIX 2
Sample World Map

(next page)

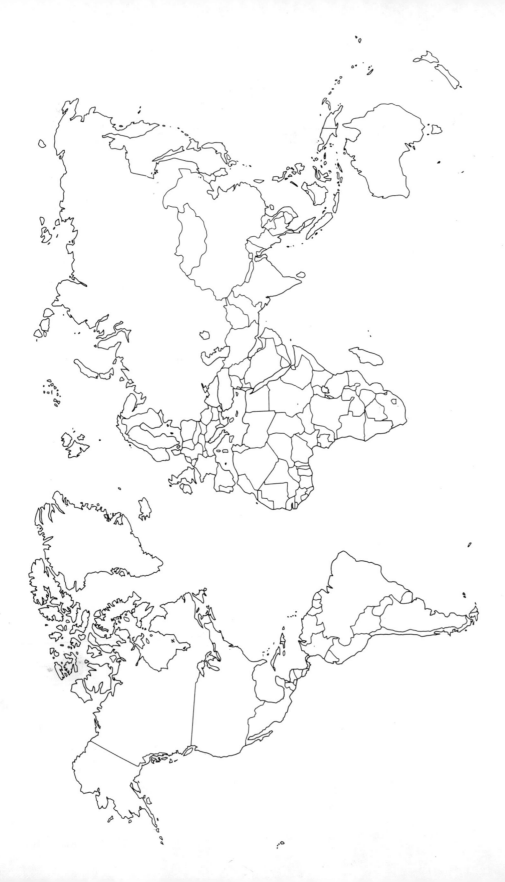

van der Grinten Projection **Equatorial Scale 1:207 000 000**

APPENDIX 3
Statistical Data

Column Headings

A Population

B Area, km^2

C Population density, people/km^2

D Birth rate, births/1000 people/y

E Death rate, deaths/1000 people/y

F Natural increase rate, birth rate minus death rate

G Life expectancy, y

H Projected rate of population increase, 1980–2000, %/y

I Average daily food intake, kJ/person/d

J Average daily food intake, g/person/d

K Average daily intake of proteins, g/person/d

L Percentage of total population employed in agriculture

M Value of international reserves, US$ millions

N Average daily food requirements, kJ/person/d

O Column I as a percentage of Column N

P Electricity production, kW·h/person/y

Q Value of manufactured output, US$/person/y

R Food production, index numbers for 1982 (1961 = 100)

S Population growth, index numbers for 1982 (1961 = 100)

T Per capita food production, index numbers for 1982 (1961 = 100)

U GNP, US$/person/y

V Percentage of total population living in urban areas

W Literacy rate, % of total population

X Energy consumption, kg/person/y

Y Percentage of total population living in rural areas

Z1 Primary activity, % of the labour force

Z2 Secondary activity, % of the labour force

Z3 Tertiary activity, % of the labour force

Note: na = not available

Sources: UN *Statistical Yearbooks*, 1980–84
UNESCO *Statistical Yearbooks*, 1983–84
UN *Demographic Yearbooks*, 1981–84
FAO *Production Yearbook*, 1982
World Population, 1983, US Department of Commerce
World Development Reports, 1984–85, World Bank

COUNTRY	A	B	C	D	E	F	G	H	I	J	K
Afghanistan	14 792 000	647 497	22.80	40.4	18.7	21.7	41.5	2.3	7 909	842	25.1
Albania	2 967 000	28 748	103.20	30.3	6.4	23.9	66.0	1.8	11 915	1 085	67.0
*Algeria	22 025 000	2 381 741	9.20	44.0	14.2	29.8	55.4	3.5	10 105	806	54.0
Angola	7 981 000	1 246 700	6.40	47.6	23.1	24.5	41.1	2.8	8 862	1 324	44.0
Argentina	30 564 000	2 766 700	11.00	25.2	8.8	16.4	68.3	1.3	14 221	1 892	119.0
Australia	15 658 000	7 686 848	2.00	15.3	7.3	8.0	74.3	1.0	13 448	2 017	117.0
Austria	7 586 000	83 849	90.50	12.4	12.3	0.1	72.6	0.1	14 679	1 898	168.0
Bangladesh	102 735 000	143 998	713.40	46.8	18.7	28.1	46.2	2.3	7 883	na	14.0
Belgium	9 879 000	30 513	323.80	12.6	11.2	1.4	71.9	0.1	16 540	2 031	191.0
Belize	161 000	22 965	7.00	39.0	5.3	33.7	47.0	3.0	11 168	na	61.0
Benin	4 033 000	112 622	35.80	48.8	19.1	29.7	45.9	3.1	9 702	1 254	58.0
Bolivia	6 195 000	1 098 581	5.60	44.8	17.5	27.3	48.7	2.4	8 761	1 104	45.0
Botswana	1 075 000	600 372	1.80	50.7	17.5	33.2	48.4	3.5	9 160	na	52.0
*Brazil	137 502 000	8 511 965	16.10	33.3	9.1	24.2	59.4	1.9	10 571	1 523	52.0
Bulgaria	8 993 000	110 912	81.10	14.5	12.2	2.3	71.3	0.2	15 279	1 475	113.0
Burkina Faso	6 907 000	274 200	25.20	47.8	22.1	25.7	31.6	2.0	8 476	691	35.0
Burma	38 890 000	676 552	57.50	38.6	14.3	24.3	52.5	2.3	9 601	790	34.0
Burundi	4 826 000	27 834	173.40	45.3	22.9	22.4	41.5	2.9	9 038	na	20.0
Cameroon	9 770 000	475 442	20.50	42.3	19.4	22.9	46.0	3.2	10 294	na	63.0
*Canada	25 405 000	9 976 139	2.50	15.5	7.2	8.3	73.9	0.9	14 104	1 969	151.0
Central African Republic	2 659 000	622 984	4.30	44.3	22.5	21.8	34.5	2.7	9 076	na	48.0
Chad	5 246 000	1 284 000	4.10	44.1	24.1	20.0	32.0	2.4	7 594	na	39.0
Chile	11 828 000	756 945	15.60	22.2	6.7	15.5	64.5	1.5	11 500	1 425	56.0
China	1 087 871 000	9 596 961	113.40	21.3	7.4	13.9	67.3	1.2	10 382	927	39.0
*Colombia	28 842 000	1 138 914	25.30	32.1	6.7	25.4	62.3	1.8	10 387	1 307	48.0
Congo	1 798 000	342 000	5.30	44.6	19.0	25.6	46.0	3.7	9 240	1 944	35.0
Costa Rica	2 761 000	50 700	54.50	29.4	4.1	25.3	68.5	2.1	11 067	1 272	66.0
Cuba	10 036 000	114 524	87.60	13.9	5.9	8.0	70.2	1.0	11 411	1 237	59.0
Cyprus	670 000	9 251	72.40	20.6	8.3	12.3	73.4	1.1	13 436	1 429	112.0
*Czechoslovakia	15 510 000	127 869	121.30	15.5	11.7	3.8	70.6	0.4	14 582	1 734	133.0
Denmark	5 109 000	43 069	118.60	10.4	11.0	-0.6	74.3	0.0	14 708	1 940	167.0
Dominican Republic	6 588 000	48 734	135.20	36.7	9.0	27.7	57.9	2.2	8 959	1 374	50.0
*East Germany	16 712 000	108 178	154.50	14.2	13.9	0.3	71.6	0.1	15 733	1 711	158.0
*Ecuador	9 380 000	283 561	33.20	41.6	9.2	32.4	60.7	2.5	8 786	1 354	54.0
*Egypt	48 407 000	1 001 449	48.30	37.8	10.1	27.7	52.7	2.0	12 390	1 341	58.0
El Salvador	4 983 000	21 393	232.90	39.7	8.2	31.5	58.5	2.6	9 085	881	47.0
Equatorial Guinea	282 000	28 051	10.10	42.3	19.4	22.9	46.0	2.4	na	na	na
Ethiopia	32 716 000	1 221 900	26.80	49.8	25.2	24.6	39.1	2.6	7 262	739	28.0
Fiji	700 000	18 272	38.30	29.6	4.2	25.4	71.3	2.1	12 117	na	80.0
Finland	4 894 000	337 009	14.50	13.2	9.1	4.1	73.4	0.3	13 133	1 872	137.0
*France	55 108 000	547 026	100.70	14.9	10.3	4.6	74.2	0.4	14 200	2 206	145.0
French Guiana	82 100	91 000	0.90	26.9	7.8	19.1	na	3.2	10 017	na	67.0
Gabon	988 000	267 667	3.70	31.2	21.3	9.9	35.0	1.0	12 113	2 254	58.0
Gambia, The	672 000	11 295	59.50	47.5	22.9	24.6	41.0	2.8	9 450	768	67.0
*Ghana	14 254 000	238 537	59.80	48.4	17.2	31.2	48.4	3.5	8 467	1 475	34.0
*Greece	10 072 000	131 944	76.30	15.4	9.1	6.3	71.9	0.4	15 242	2 041	147.0
Greenland	53 700	2 175 600	0.02	20.5	7.8	12.7	63.5	0.3	na	na	na
*Guatemala	8 206 000	108 889	75.40	41.8	7.1	34.7	54.5	2.6	8 669	851	39.0
Guinea	5 734 000	245 957	23.30	46.1	20.7	25.4	43.5	2.1	8 123	1 070	46.0
Guinea-Bissau	858 000	36 125	23.80	40.0	23.0	17.0	41.0	1.7	9 899	na	64.0
Guyana	840 000	214 969	3.90	28.3	7.3	21.0	61.0	2.0	10 429	988	47.0
Haiti	5 921 000	27 750	213.40	41.8	15.7	26.1	50.7	1.8	7 904	1 064	30.0
Honduras	4 575 000	112 088	40.80	47.1	11.8	35.3	57.7	3.0	9 135	1 041	42.0
Hong Kong	5 477 000	1 045	5 241.10	16.9	4.8	12.1	71.2	1.3	12 113	1 035	107.0
Hungary	10 670 000	93 030	114.70	13.3	13.5	-0.2	70.2	0.0	14 839	1 658	137.0

* The sample of starred (*) countries is to be used for Statistical Analysis questions throughout the text.

L	M	N	O	P	Q	Ⓡ	S	T	U	V	W	X	Y	Z₁	Z₂	Z₃
77	274	10 248	77	63	49	141	190	92	168	17	20.0	56	83	79	8	13
59	na	10 122	118	946	na	197	163	109	490	38	75.0	1 067	62	61	25	14
47	3 695	10 080	100	366	209	110	176	67	2 140	45	26.4	1 429	55	25	25	50
56	na	9 870	90	206	na	130	152	97	500	22	12.0	141	78	59	16	25
12	3 268	11 176	127	1 399	409	149	133	96	2 560	83	92.6	1 718	17	13	28	59
5	1 671	11 172	120	6 906	1 754	137	134	111	11 080	89	99.8	5 987	11	6	33	61
8	5 285	11 046	133	5 712	2 467	145	106	112	10 210	55	98.7	4 020	45	9	37	54
83	138	9 702	81	33	10	143	176	76	140	12	25.8	46	88	74	11	15 −
3	4 952	11 088	149	5 148	2 076	134	106	133	11 920	73	98.7	5 329	27	3	41	56
27	na	9 472	118	324	111	na	174	na	1 080	54	na	527	46	na	na	na
45	58	9 660	100	1	2	175	158	101	320	15	27.9	43	85	46	16	38
49	100	10 038	87	283	23	164	141	109	600	45	63.2	365	55	50	24	26
79	253	9 744	94	424	84	150	165	141	1 010	11	41.0	na	89	na	na	na
37	6 604	10 038	105	1 148	1 730	201	169	104	2 220	69	76.1	757	31	30	24	46
31	na	10 500	146	4 159	1 320	170	112	119	2 100	66	95.0	5 261	34	37	39	24
80	71	9 954	85	19	na	95	145	58	240	11	8.8	28	89	82	13	5
50	229	9 072	106	41	12	162	162	90	190	28	65.9	63	72	67	10	23 −
82	61	9 786	92	1	19	254	154	181	230	2	26.8	18	98	84	5	11
79	85	9 744	106	190	34	164	152	119	880	37	40.5	87	63	83	7	10
5	3 538	11 172	126	15 515	2 396	142	131	82	11 400	76	98.7	10 070	24	5	29	66 −
86	69	9 492	96	28	12	132	152	92	320	37	33.0	40	63	88	4	8
82	7	9 996	76	14	12	92	152	56	110	19	15.0	22	81	85	7	8
18	3 213	10 248	112	1 061	281	145	144	92	2 560	82	89.0	925	18	19	19	62
58	5 048	9 912	105	307	na	168	136	110	300	21	69.0	578	79	69	19	12 −
26	4 741	9 744	107	874	150	190	171	91	1 380	65	80.8	752	35	26	21	53
33	123	9 324	99	104	na	107	156	79	1 110	46	40.0	89	54	34	26	40
34	131	9 408	118	1 013	95	191	169	114	1 430	43	88.4	591	57	29	23	48
22	na	9 702	118	1 088	na	163	131	95	840	68	95.4	1 382	32	23	31	46 −
33	426	10 416	129	1 656	624	230	113	175	3 740	45	89.0	1 830	55	36	47	17
9	na	10 374	141	4 834	3 040	160	110	139	3 985	64	99.0	6 403	36	11	48	41
6	2 548	11 298	130	3 533	1 817	125	109	107	13 120	85	98.7	5 653	15	7	35	58
55	225	9 492	94	600	242	171	181	105	1 260	53	67.2	454	47	49	18	33
9	na	11 004	143	6 017	2 380	155	100	145	4 000	77	99.0	7 409	23	10	50	40
43	632	9 618	91	341	79	149	189	81	1 180	46	76.2	630	54	52	17	31
50	716	10 542	118	428	74	152	167	97	650	45	38.2	516	55	50	30	20
50	72	9 618	94	321	147	159	185	96	650	42	62.0	210	58	52	22	26
73	na	na	na	70	na	na	138	na	180	na	20.0	86	na	na	na	na
78	267	9 786	74	21	15	134	154	88	140	15	4.2	26	85	80	7	13 −
39	135	9 576	127	21	15	160	165	76	2 000	37	79.0	569	63	44	na	na
12	1 484	11 382	115	8 140	2 200	112	107	101	10 680	64	99.8	4 761	36	11	35	54
8	22 262	10 584	134	5 235	1 998	158	114	125	12 190	79	98.7	4 081	21	8	39	53
na	na	na	na	1 771	na	na	166	na	3 430	66	na	2 254	34	na	na	na
75	199	9 828	123	804	679	145	117	122	3 810	32	40.0	1 715	68	na	na	na
77	4	9 996	95	65	na	132	157	117	370	14	20.1	121	86	78	15	7
50	148	9 660	88	419	5	136	178	109	400	37	30.2	117	63	53	20	27
36	1 022	10 500	145	2 408	392	188	115	147	4 420	64	84.4	2 013	36	37	28	35
na	na	na	na	3 400	na	na	158	na	10 850	78	na	4 882	22	na	na	na
54	150	9 198	94	267	na	196	174	101	1 140	40	46.0	224	60	55	21	24
79	na	9 702	84	97	na	133	157	89	300	20	20.0	81	80	82	11	7
81	na	9 702	102	22	na	na	128	na	190	na	18.9	74	na	na	na	na
21	7	9 534	109	522	94	154	161	108	720	30	91.6	855	70	na	na	na
65	24	9 492	83	64	38	127	151	92	300	26	22.3	66	74	74	7	19
62	101	9 492	96	209	132	209	192	111	600	37	56.9	237	63	63	20	17
2	na	9 618	126	2 584	619	128	130	94	5 100	91	77.3	1 487	9	3	57	40
16	na	11 046	134	2 261	581	190	105	150	2 100	55	98.9	3 809	45	21	43	36

COUNTRY	A	B	C	D	E	F	G	H	I	J	K
Iceland	241 000	103 000	2.30	18.6	7.1	11.5	76.7	0.9	12 655	1 650	126.0
*India	762 507 000	3 280 483	232.40	33.2	15.1	18.1	45.6	1.8	8 392	720	30.0
*Indonesia	167 833 000	1 491 564	112.50	33.6	16.2	17.4	47.5	1.9	9 643	789	36.0
*Iran	45 191 000	1 648 000	27.40	44.4	13.6	30.8	57.5	3.0	12 230	928	60.0
ˋIraq	15 507 000	434 924	35.70	47.0	13.0	34.0	55.2	3.4	11 101	1 137	41.0
ˆIreland	3 617 000	70 283	51.50	21.9	9.7	12.2	71.2	1.0	15 809	2 156	140.0
*Israel	4 094 000	20 700	197.80	24.3	6.8	17.5	73.9	1.6	12 789	1 979	108.3
Italy	56 505 000	301 225	187.60	11.2	9.7	1.5	72.8	0.1	15 301	1 976	139.0
Ivory Coast	9 472 000	322 463	29.40	47.5	18.2	29.3	46.0	3.6	11 017	1 548	56.0
*Jamaica	2 403 000	10 962	219.20	27.0	5.8	21.2	64.7	1.4	10 794	1 361	63.0
*Japan	120 540 000	372 313	323.80	13.0	6.1	6.9	76.1	0.5	12 109	1 478	80.0
Jordan	3 641 000	97 740	37.30	29.3	10.5	18.8	52.3	3.8	10 067	1 474	54.0
Kampuchea	6 249 000	181 035	34.50	30.9	29.4	1.5	30.2	na	7 539	995	20.0
*Kenya	20 177 000	582 646	34.60	53.8	14.4	39.4	49.1	3.9	8 631	1 053	37.0
Kuwait	1 870 000	17 818	105.00	37.5	3.9	33.6	69.0	3.5	14 377	na	na
Lao(Laos)	3 819 000	236 800	16.10	44.1	20.3	23.8	43.6	2.5	7 795	779	24.0
Lebanon	2 619 000	10 400	251.80	30.1	8.7	21.4	65.2	1.2	10 483	1 472	63.0
Lesotho	1 512 000	30 355	49.80	39.8	16.3	23.5	50.3	2.6	10 256	na	30.0
Liberia	2 232 000	111 369	20.00	48.7	14.0	34.7	44.9	3.1	10 391	1 311	56.5
Libya	3 885 000	1 759 540	2.20	42.2	12.7	29.5	55.4	4.1	14 356	1 181	118.0
Luxembourg	367 000	2 586	141.90	12.0	11.1	0.9	69.8	0.0	na	2 031	na
Madagascar	9 909 000	587 041	16.90	45.0	18.0	27.0	37.9	3.1	10 231	1 096	28.0
Malawi	7 056 000	118 484	59.60	51.1	19.1	32.0	42.6	3.1	9 320	802	39.0
Malaysia	15 664 000	329 749	47.50	33.1	7.9	25.2	69.9	2.0	11 130	925	47.0
Mali	7 735 000	1 240 000	6.20	49.4	22.2	27.2	42.2	2.5	8 383	806	41.0
Malta	362 000	316	1 145.60	15.0	8.6	6.4	71.0	0.6	12 793	1 272	108.0
Mauritania	1 656 000	1 030 700	1.60	50.2	22.3	27.9	42.2	2.6	8 614	1 039	54.0
Mauritius	1 034 000	2 045	505.60	27.3	7.8	19.5	63.0	1.6	11 353	902	70.0
Mexico	79 662 000	1 972 547	40.40	38.3	6.4	31.9	65.4	2.3	11 773	1 092	63.0
Mongolia	1 912 000	1 565 000	1.20	37.1	8.3	28.8	62.6	2.4	11 386	1 063	89.0
Morocco	24 258 000	446 550	54.30	45.4	13.6	31.8	55.4	2.4	11 134	837	50.0
Mozambique	13 994 000	783 030	17.90	44.8	19.0	25.8	46.0	2.9	7 942	1 331	31.0
Namibia	1 146 000	824 292	1.40	43.5	15.1	28.4	51.3	3.0	9 341	na	66.0
Nepal	16 996 000	140 797	120.70	43.7	20.7	23.0	43.3	2.6	8 039	744	26.5
Netherlands	14 501 000	40 844	355.00	12.5	8.1	4.4	75.7	0.4	14 658	2 051	174.0
*New Zealand	3 162 000	268 676	11.80	25.8	8.0	17.8	72.0	0.7	14 746	2 043	152.0
Nicaragua	3 030 000	130 000	23.30	46.6	12.2	34.4	55.3	3.0	9 593	1 152	52.0
Niger	6 495 000	1 267 000	5.10	51.4	22.4	29.0	42.2	3.2	9 311	855	36.0
Nigeria	91 178 000	923 768	98.70	49.8	17.8	32.0	37.0	3.3	9 815	1 362	52.0
North Korea	20 082 000	120 538	166.60	32.5	8.3	24.2	62.6	2.1	12 482	1 083	31.0
North Yemen (Arab Rep)	6 067 000	195 000	31.10	48.6	24.1	24.5	41.3	2.8	9 542	697	36.0
Norway	4 159 000	324 219	12.80	12.8	9.9	2.9	75.7	0.3	13 810	1 853	147.0
Oman	1 041 000	212 457	4.90	48.9	18.6	30.3	51.3	2.9	na	na	na
*Pakistan	99 841 000	803 943	124.20	43.1	15.0	28.1	51.3	2.4	9 660	979	43.0
Panama	2 145 000	75 650	28.40	27.7	6.0	21.7	65.9	1.9	9 618	1 320	56.0
Papua New Guinea	3 449 000	461 691	7.50	42.5	15.7	26.8	50.3	2.1	9 601	na	38.0
Paraguay	3 722 000	406 752	9.20	36.7	7.6	29.1	64.2	2.2	12 188	1 810	79.0
*Peru	20 273 000	1 285 216	15.80	38.6	10.6	28.0	54.1	2.2	9 097	1 400	44.0
*Philippines	55 819 000	300 000	186.10	35.1	8.6	26.5	60.8	2.1	9 723	898	33.0
Poland	37 222 000	312 677	119.00	18.9	9.2	9.7	70.2	0.7	14 889	na	128.0
*Portugal	10 082 000	92 082	109.20	16.3	9.9	6.4	68.7	0.5	13 423	1 799	107.0
Puerto Rico	3 368 000	8 897	378.60	22.8	4.8	18.0	72.9	3.3	na	1 567	na
Romania	22 930 000	237 500	96.50	18.0	10.4	7.6	69.8	0.6	14 263	1 483	100.0
Rwanda	6 036 000	26 338	229.20	49.6	19.3	30.3	45.9	3.4	9 244	1 560	14.0
Saudi Arabia	11 152 000	2 149 690	5.20	45.9	14.4	31.5	53.1	3.6	12 134	985	72.0

* The sample of starred (*) countries is to be used for Statistical Analysis questions throughout the text.

L	M	N	O	P	Q	R	S	T	U	V	W	X	Y	Z₁	Z₂	Z₃
11	230	11 172	113	13 061	na	124	125	101	12 860	45	99.0	4 905	55	28	26	46
62	4 693	9 282	90	186	32	142	154	87	260	24	34.1	199	76	71	13	16
57	5 014	9 072	106	51	44	201	156	108	530	22	56.6	242	78	58	12	30
36	na	10 122	121	433	292	167	171	97	1 986	52	36.2	874	48	39	34	27
39	na	10 122	110	465	147	203	190	104	1 561	70	30.0	595	30	42	26	32
20	2 651	10 542	150	3 175	786	141	117	118	5 230	59	98.0	3 206	41	18	37	45
6	3 497	10 794	118	332	343	200	159	136	5 160	90	87.9	2 255	10	7	36	57
10	20 134	10 584	145	3 257	1 386	133	111	112	6 960	70	93.9	3 273	30	11	45	44
78	18	9 702	114	229	113	232	172	115	1 200	42	35.0	155	58	79	4	17
19	85	9 408	115	1 047	118	113	141	92	1 180	48	96.1	1 632	52	35	18	47
10	28 208	9 828	123	4 957	3 163	118	120	108	10 080	78	98.8	3 575	22	12	39	49
24	1 087	10 332	97	368	136	95	189	67	1 620	60	67.6	740	40	20	20	60
73	na	9 324	81	26	na	46	134	33	90	10	48.0	3	90	na	na	na
77	231	9 744	89	99	2	159	194	91	420	15	47.1	129	85	78	10	12
2	4 068	na	na	7 079	1 512	na	417	na	20 900	91	59.6	4 548	9	2	34	64
73	na	9 324	84	302	na	242	158	125	80	14	43.6	68	86	75	6	19
9	1 516	10 416	101	673	90	216	138	160	1 142	77	76.0	934	23	11	27	62
82	43	9 576	107	4	1	106	148	112	540	13	52.0	na	87	87	4	9
68	7	9 702	107	539	61	149	172	101	520	34	21.0	366	66	70	14	16
13	9 003	9 912	145	1 806	1 020	199	193	123	8 450	58	39.0	2 134	42	19	28	53
6	na	11 080	na	3 319	2 003	na	108	na	15 910	68	99.8	11 813	32	6	46	48
82	na	9 534	107	47	19	134	166	94	330	20	50.0	67	80	87	4	9
82	49	9 744	96	70	4	208	162	123	200	10	25.0	49	90	86	5	9
45	4 098	9 366	119	662	211	302	177	136	1 840	30	58.5	987	70	50	16	34
86	17	9 870	85	15	na	113	172	66	190	19	9.4	27	81	73	12	15
5	1 026	10 206	125	1 508	643	184	107	141	3 600	64	85.0	1 372	36	na	na	na
82	162	9 702	89	61	23	102	160	59	460	26	17.4	169	74	69	8	23
27	35	9 534	119	454	120	140	137	104	1 270	44	79.0	301	56	29	28	43
34	4 074	9 786	120	1 033	77	180	186	96	2 250	68	82.7	1 687	32	36	26	38
46	na	10 206	112	1 023	na	113	176	73	750	53	95.0	1 611	47	55	22	23
50	230	10 164	110	256	98	169	184	111	860	42	21.4	339	58	52	21	27
62	na	9 828	81	353	na	126	155	111	170	9	33.2	91	91	66	18	16
47	na	9 576	98	na	na	178	137	147	1 960	23	na	na	77	na	na	na
92	202	9 240	87	15	11	108	160	85	150	4	19.2	11	96	93	2	5
5	9 339	11 298	130	4 547	2 264	171	119	130	11 790	76	98.6	5 652	24	6	45	49
9	674	11 088	133	7 254	1 096	132	125	90	7 700	85	98.8	3 274	15	10	34	56
40	na	9 450	102	394	149	142	196	94	860	55	57.5	319	45	39	14	47
87	105	9 870	94	11	na	144	174	67	330	14	9.8	44	86	91	3	6
51	3 895	9 912	99	91	88	131	171	76	870	21	34.0	220	79	54	19	27
44	na	9 828	127	1 965	na	177	164	95	570	63	85.0	2 666	37	49	33	18
74	962	10 164	94	13	5	109	158	73	460	14	8.6	96	86	75	11	14
7	6 253	11 256	123	22 627	2 035	145	112	121	14 060	54	98.6	5 950	46	7	37	56
60	1 138	na	na	1 049	415	na	173	na	5 920	20	50.0	794	80	na	na	na
52	721	9 702	100	190	48	196	177	111	350	29	20.7	221	71	57	20	23
33	120	9 702	99	1 607	307	194	180	108	1 910	53	87.1	923	47	33	18	49
81	454	9 576	100	422	77	161	153	104	840	17	32.1	293	83	82	8	10
48	806	9 702	126	247	162	181	188	89	1 630	40	80.1	159	60	49	19	32
38	1 209	9 870	92	536	29	133	175	91	1 170	66	72.5	595	34	40	19	41
45	2 199	9 492	102	364	104	186	178	87	790	38	88.6	353	62	46	17	37
29	na	11 004	135	3 394	270	128	118	125	2 500	58	98.8	4 507	42	31	39	30
25	544	10 290	130	1 515	119	91	122	na	2 520	32	71.0	1 250	68	28	35	37
3	na	na	na	4 219	1 679	84	165	64	3 350	67	87.8	3 270	33	21	19	60
45	404	11 130	128	3 020	na	184	121	123	2 540	51	98.0	4 420	49	29	36	35
69	173	9 744	95	33	41	163	170	86	250	5	49.7	18	95	91	2	7
59	32 236	10 164	119	966	1 709	45	189	116	12 600	69	24.6	1 680	31	61	14	25

COUNTRY	A	B	C	D	E	F	G	H	I	J	K
Senegal	6 755 000	196 192	34.40	47.8	22.1	25.7	42.2	2.9	10 034	882	62.0
Sierra Leone	3 909 000	71 740	54.50	45.5	19.2	26.3	45.9	2.3	−8 845	1 016	56.0
Singapore	2 561 000	581	4 407.90	17.0	5.3	11.7	71.6	1.0	12 995	1 183	80.0
Somalia	6 542 000	637 657	10.30	46.2	19.9	26.3	42.5	3.0	− 8 950	876	80.0
*South Africa	32 465 000	1 221 037	26.60	37.9	10.3	27.6	60.3	2.7	11 869	1 126	63.0
South Korea	42 643 000	98 484	433.00	23.4	6.6	16.8	65.9	1.4	12 289	1 046	36.0
South Yemen (PDR)	2 211 000	332 968	6.60	47.6	20.9	26.7	44.1	2.4	− 8 833	816	51.0
Spain	38 629 000	504 782	76.50	14.1	7.6	6.5	72.4	0.6	13 999	1 838	131.0
Sri Lanka	16 206 000	65 610	247.00	27.6	6.1	21.5	65.9	1.8	9 454	868	46.0
*Sudan	21 682 000	2 505 813	87.00	45.8	18.4	27.4	46.5	2.8	9 958	1 275	67.0
Suriname	377 000	163 265	2.30	25.4	7.2	18.2	64.6	1.3	10 366	908	56.0
Swaziland	671 000	17 363	38.60	47.5	19.1	28.4	45.9	2.1	10 496	na	55.0
Sweden	8 338 000	449 964	18.50	11.3	11.1	0.2	75.5	0.1	13 259	1 910	145.0
Switzerland	6 491 000	41 288	157.20	11.6	9.3	2.3	73.3	0.0	14 805 −	2 124	163.0
Syria	10 423 000	185 180	56.30	46.4	8.9	37.5	56.6	3.4	12 025	1 286	77.0
Taiwan	19 511 000	35 759	545.60	23.0	5.0	18.0	69.5	1.9	na	1 108	na
*Tanzania	21 902 000	945 087	23.20	46.3	15.8	30.5	50.5	3.4	−8 518	1 349	33.5
*Thailand	52 700 000	514 000	102.50	32.3	8.9	23.4	56.2	1.7	9 664	918	25.0
Togo	3 003 000	56 000	53.60	47.8	18.9	28.9	35.1	3.2	− 8 845	1 452	35.0
Trinidad & Tobago	1 247 000	5 128	243.20	24.6	6.5	18.1	66.1	1.7	11 348	1 176	67.0
*Tunisia	7 386 000	163 610	45.10	34.9	11.1	23.8	57.9	2.2	11 554	1 004	77.0
Turkey	51 259 000	780 576	65.70	34.9	10.2	24.7	53.7	1.9	12 453	1 562	65.0
Uganda	14 732 000	236 036	62.40	44.7	14.4	30.3	52.6	3.3	7 820	1 570	31.0
*UK	56 058 000	244 046	229.70	13.4	11.8	1.6	70.8	0.0	13 923	1 888	149.0
United Arab Emirates	1 682 000	83 600	20.10	30.5	7.3	23.2	61.6	3.7	15 082 •	na	na
Uruguay	2 936 000	177 508	16.50	18.3	9.5	8.8	68.6	0.7	12 046	1 645	105.0
*USA	238 648 000	9 363 123	25.50	15.9	8.6	7.3	73.0	0.7	15 338 −	2 216	169.0
*USSR	276 597 000	22 402 200	12.30	18.7	10.3	8.4	69.0	0.7	14 234 ▲	1 837	97.0
*Venezuela	19 120 000	912 050	21.00	36.9	6.1	30.8	67.4	2.6	11 126	1 313	69.0
Vietnam	59 575 000	329 556	180.80	40.1	16.1	24.0	52.7	2.4	− 8 471	924	24.0
West Germany	61 354 000	248 577	246.80	10.1	11.7	− 1.6	73.0	− 0.1	14 855 −	2 033	163.0
Western Sahara	91 000	266 000	0.30	20.4	4.5	15.9	na	2.9	na	na	na
Yugoslavia	23 165 000	255 804	90.60	16.7	9.0	7.7	67.8	0.6	14 818 •	1 543	107.0
*Zaire	33 092 000	2 345 409	14.10	46.2	18.7	27.5	46.0	3.1	− 8 959	1 744	36.0
*Zambia	6 770 000	752 614	9.00	49.2	17.2	32.0	48.4	3.3	− 8 366	808	39.0
Zimbabwe	8 952 000	390 580	22.90	47.3	8.1	39.2	53.6	3.6	8 026	893	45.4

* The sample of starred (*) countries is to be used for Statistical Analysis questions throughout the text.

L	M	N	O	P	Q	R	S	T	U	V	W	X	Y	Z_1	Z_2	Z_3
73	9	9 996	100	120	28	85	160	71	430	34	10.0	195	66	77	10	13
64	16	9 660	92	66	13	149	158	103	320	23	15.0	87	77	65	19	16
2	7 549	9 660	135	2 844	1 501	675	144	277	5 240	100	88.9	4 515	0	2	39	59
79	31	na	na	15	na	157	222	104	280	32	6.1	93	68	82	8	10
28	666	10 290	115	3 179	411	189	162	136	2 770	50	50.0	2 694	50	30	29	41
36	2 682	9 870	125	1 128	447	168	149	91	1 700	61	87.6	1 416	39	34	29	37
57	255	10 122	87	97	na	129	172	93	460	38	27.1	604	62	45	15	40
15	10 805	10 332	135	2 926	755	168	121	130	5 640	76	92.4	2 397	24	14	40	46
53	327	9 324	101	111	27	205	149	54	300	24	86.0	109	76	54	14	32
76	17	9 870	101	53	24	189	178	119	380	23	32.0	89	77	78	10	12
17	207	9 492	109	4 025	245	312	159	126	3 030	na	65.0	2 882	na	na	na	na
71	104	9 744	108	314	99	237	169	128	760	8	55.2	na	92	na	na	na
5	3 601	11 298	117	11 569	2 229	124	109	122	14 870	88	98.7	5 156	12	5	34	61
5	13 979	11 298	131	7 501	na	139	115	104	17 430	59	98.7	3 488	41	5	46	49
47	291	10 416	115	365	185	219	192	86	1 570	49	40.0	836	51	33	31	36
34	na	na	na	na	na	na	na	na	1 300	na	85.0	na	na	34	37	29
80	19	9 744	87	38	16	168	172	102	280	13	73.5	48	87	83	6	11
74	1 732	9 324	104	316	155	189	169	91	770	17	78.6	333	83	76	9	15
67	152	9 660	92	28	26	144	167	84	380	21	15.9	130	79	67	15	18
15	3 348	10 164	112	1 546	649	77	130	111	5 670	22	92.2	5 601	78	10	39	52
38	536	10 038	115	432	113	162	171	96	1 420	54	38.0	662	46	35	32	33
52	1 285	10 584	118	513	71	180	159	98	1 540	44	68.8	702	56	54	13	33
80	na	9 786	80	48	1	140	167	90	220	9	52.3	23	91	83	6	11
2	15 238	10 584	132	5 043	1 515	140	105	145	9 110	91	99.0	4 641	9	2	42	56
5	3 202	na	na	5 921	5 322	na	244	na	24 660	79	53.5	7 558	21	na	na	na
11	430	11 214	107	1 137	90	114	119	95	2 820	84	93.9	895	16	11	32	57
2	18 924	11 088	138	10 251	3 063	160	122	105	12 820	78	99.5	10 204	22	2	32	66
15	na	10 752	132	4 837	1 066	151	120	132	2 600	63	99.8	5 738	37	14	45	41
17	8 164	10 374	107	2 166	279	218	182	113	4 220	84	76.5	3 153	16	18	27	55
69	na	9 072	na	71	na	168	154	96	150	19	87.0	148	81	71	10	19
4	43 719	11 214	132	5 980	3 869	140	107	116	13 450	85	98.6	5 614	15	4	46	50
na	na	na	na	550	na	na	183	na	na	41	na	540	59	na	na	na
35	1 597	10 668	139	2 617	161	177	119	133	2 790	44	87.5	2 290	56	29	35	36
73	152	9 324	96	165	1	175	140	124	210	38	54.5	74	62	75	13	12
65	56	9 702	86	1 493	63	127	176	87	600	45	49.0	373	55	67	11	22
58	141	10 038	80	597	55	153	180	111	870	24	68.8	552	76	60	15	25

APPENDIX 4
Statistical Techniques

Arithmetic and Logarithmic Scales
Multiple and Compound Line Graphs
Linear Dispersion Diagrams
Proportional Circles
Triangular Graphs
Correlations: Scattergraphs
Correlations: The Phi (ϕ) Coefficient
Correlations: Rank Correlation
Correlations: Grouped Data Technique
Correlations: Standard Deviation Technique
Percentage Deviation from the Group Mean
Coefficient of Determination
Moving Averages
Index Numbers
Rank-Size Rule

Most of the statistical techniques explained here may be examined in Arkin and Colton, *Statistical Methods*, 1968.

Arithmetic and Logarithmic Scales

For all practical purposes the scales used in graphing may be classified into two groups: arithmetic and logarithmic.

Arithmetic scales are the most generally used of the two types. They are employed when there is a need to represent on a map or graph a certain distance or quantity in the real world. For example, a map with a scale of 1 cm = 1 km (1:100 000) has an arithmetic scale; so does a graph with a vertical scale of 1 cm = 1 000 000 t of product. Arithmetic scales, whether on maps or graphs, always have consistently equal divisions. Thus, if 1 cm = 10 years is the scale along the horizontal axis of a graph, then 1 cm always represents 10 years along that same axis; it does not suddenly change to equal 5 years or 20 years.

Logarithmic scales are more unusual. They are used whenever there is a need to show *rates of change* accurately. Arithmetic scales are unable to do this; they yield a false visual impression. For example, in Graph 4-1, line C appears to represent the slowest-growing quantity, while line A represents the fastest-growing quantity. Graph 4-2 seems to show a sharp change in the rate of increase at point X.

Graph 4-1

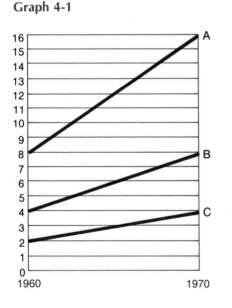

Graph 4-2

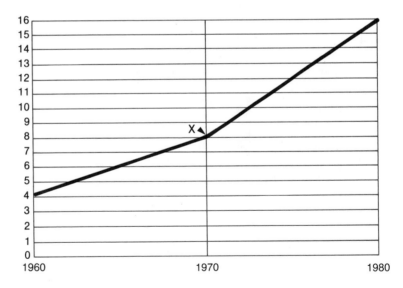

Graphs 4-1 and 4-2 are plotted on arithmetic scales; as a result they convey incorrect impressions of rates of change. If we examine the figures being plotted we see that in *all* cases there is a doubling of the data between the beginning and end of each time period. All the *rates* of change shown in the two graphs are in fact identical. If we are to give the correct visual impression we cannot therefore use arithmetic scales.

We must use logarithmic scales, which have diminishing distances between scale lines as quantities increase, as shown in Graph 4-3.

Graph 4-3

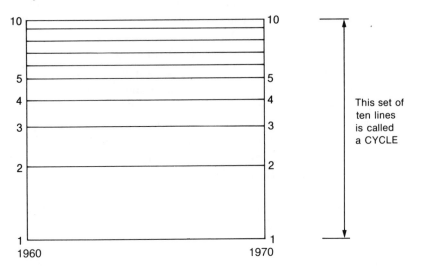

This set of
ten lines
is called
a CYCLE

Graph 4-4

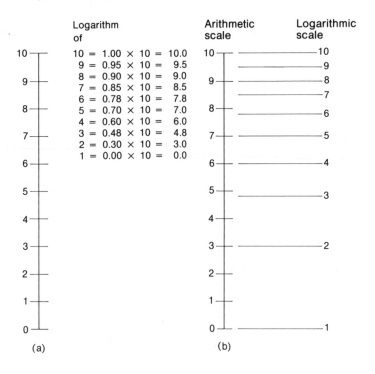

	Logarithm of		
10 =	1.00 × 10 =	10.0
9 =	0.95 × 10 =	9.5
8 =	0.90 × 10 =	9.0
7 =	0.85 × 10 =	8.5
6 =	0.78 × 10 =	7.8
5 =	0.70 × 10 =	7.0
4 =	0.60 × 10 =	6.0
3 =	0.48 × 10 =	4.8
2 =	0.30 × 10 =	3.0
1 =	0.00 × 10 =	0.0

Arithmetic scale

Logarithmic scale

(a)

(b)

The spacing and value of the lines in a cycle are determined by plotting the logarithms (multiplied by ten) of the numbers from one to ten on a standard arithmetic scale. In Graph 4-4, (a) is an arithmetic scale set up to represent numbers from zero to ten. If the logarithms of the numbers from one to ten are multiplied by ten and plotted against the arithmetic scale, they will appear as in (b); these numbers determine the basic spacing of the lines in a cycle.

Notice that there is no zero on a logarithm (log) scale. The reason for this is that there is no logarithm for zero. This means that the scale may be extended to infinity, both upward and downward, simply by inserting more cycles as needed. (Each set of ten lines is called a cycle). Graph 4-5 shows just two cycles, along with lines A, B, and C from Graph 4-1. Notice that the lines are now all parallel, indicating identical rates of change. Graph 4-6 shows the data of Graph 4-2 on a 2 cycle log scale; note that the line is completely straight, indicating no change in the rate of increase from one time period to the next.

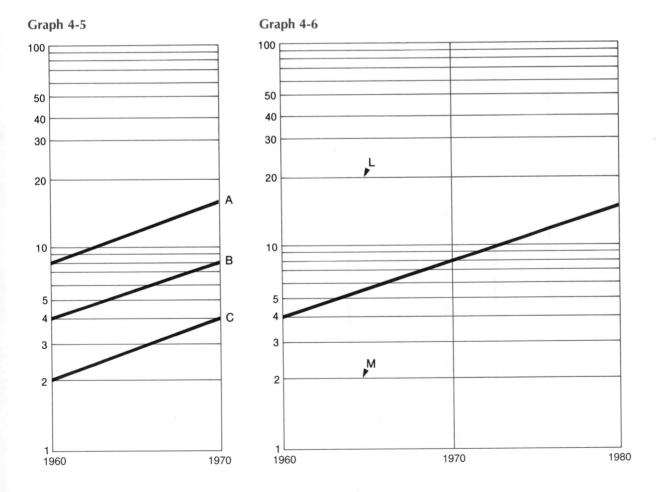

Graph 4-5

Graph 4-6

The numbering of the vertical axis on a log scale graph is done according to powers of ten. The bottom line of a cycle is *always* some power of ten, such as

$$10^9 \quad (= 1\ 000\ 000\ 000)$$
$$10^6 \quad (= 1\ 000\ 000)$$
$$10^3 \quad (= 1\ 000)$$
$$10^2 \quad (= 100)$$
$$10^1 \quad (= 10)$$
$$10^0 \quad (= 1)$$
$$10^{-1} (= 0.1)$$

Graph 4-7
Log scales: sample cycle frequencies and sizes

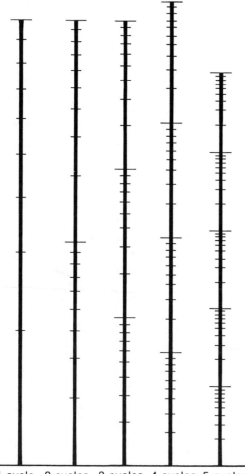

1 cycle   2 cycles   3 cycles   4 cycles   5 cycles

According to this system of numbering, each cycle has a value ten times as large as that of the cycle below it, and each line in a cycle is ten times larger than the equivalent line in the next cycle below. Thus in Graph 4-6 line L has a value ten times that of line M.

Log scales can be of any actual size. Thus a single cycle (representing quantities as diverse as, say, 1 to 10 or 1 000 000 to 10 000 000) can be the size shown in Graph 4-3, or it can be as large as a football field. Graph 4-7 gives you a selection of cycle frequencies (1 cycle to 5 cycles) as well as a choice of cycle sizes (a single cycle being progressively smaller in the sequence of 1 cycle to 5 cycle log scales). Notice that all these log scales fit neatly on a normal page.

Notice that Graphs 4-3, 4-5, and 4-6 have log scales on the vertical axis only. They have a normal arithmetic scale representing quantities of time along the horizontal axis. Such graphs, with a log scale on the vertical axis and an arithmetic scale on the horizontal axis, are called *semi-log graphs*. They are used whenever time is plotted on the horizontal axis and a log scale is required for the vertical axis. Time, in other words, is always plotted on an arithmetic scale. It is worth noting that any graph with time plotted along the horizontal axis is called a *time-series graph*, because it shows a series of plots over a period of time.

Multiple and Compound Line Graphs

These graphs offer two different methods of presenting information. The multiple line graph is more versatile in that it can accommodate either related or unrelated material, either to the same scale or to different scales, including log scales. The compound line graph is restricted to showing variations in the components of a total, always on an arithmetic scale. The following table, which shows the numbers of passengers carried by different Fiction City Transportation modes, 1960–1983, may be illustrated by either type of graph, as shown in Graph 4-8.

Mode	1960	1970	1975	1980	1983
Streetcar	860	909	790	783	786
Trolley bus	112	238	249	332	393
Bus	182	565	738	810	959
Subway	—	106	263	418	503

Graph 4-8
Multiple and compound line graphs of the same information

Graph 4-9
A linear dispersion diagram

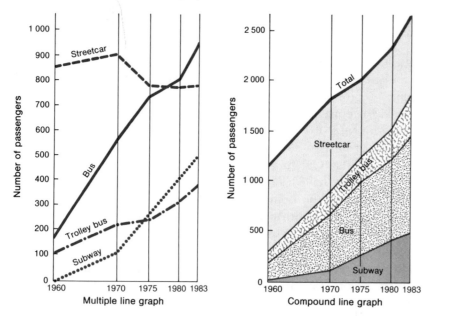

Multiple line graph

Compound line graph

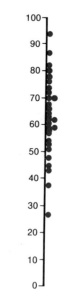

Linear Dispersion Diagrams

These diagrams are a simple way of showing the distribution of data along a continuum. For example, in a geography class in Edmonton a few years ago, the final marks for thirty students were 27, 48, 76, 94, 72, 68, 57, 59, 63, 82, 45, 53, 61, 64, 74, 43, 54, 62, 60, 59, 38, 70, 62, 87, 51, 78, 80, 67, 58, 70. Graph 4-9 is a linear dispersion diagram showing the distribution, or dispersion, of the marks on a scale of 0–100.

Proportional Circles

A circle is the most compact means of enclosing an area, and thus on maps, where space is scarce, it is often desirable to use circles to represent data. Proportional circles provide two important pieces of information. First, the *position* of the circle on the map indicates geographical location. Second, the *size* of the circle shows the quantity found in a particular area.

Since different quantities are represented by different circle sizes (e.g., large quantities are represented by large circles), it is essential to calculate the circle sizes carefully. In order to make the sizes proportional to the quantities being mapped, we must first obtain the square roots of these quantities. Square roots are required because it is the *area* of the circle that represents the quantity, and the area of a circle is given by the formula πr^2. In all cases π is constant and may be ignored when comparing circle sizes. Variations in circle sizes are therefore caused by variations in r^2. Since r^2 represents the quantity to be mapped it is possible to find r (the radius of the circle) by obtaining the square root of the quantity to be mapped.

North and Central America, for example, produces 28.6%, or 2 597 808 000 tce, of the world's energy. If we are going to plot the latter quantity on a world map, then we need to know the square root of 2 597 808 000. It is 50 969 (i.e., $r = \sqrt{2\ 597\ 808\ 000} = 50\ 969$). This particular figure is, however, much too big to use as the radius of a circle; we must divide it by a number that will bring it down to a useful size. By *useful size* we mean a figure that, in appropriate units, can be used as the radius of a circle on a map. For assignments in the text, the map we will likely use is the world map in Appendix 2; thus we need to find a radius for a circle that will fit well over North America on a map of similar size. If we divide 50 969 by 2 000 we get a figure of 25.48, which we can round to 25. A radius of 25 mm would be suitable. Of course, in order to keep the comparisons valid, we must divide the square roots of all the other data in the same set by 2 000.

Each data set will have to be processed differently. It may be necessary to divide the square roots of the data in some sets by only two or three; in other sets, the square roots may have to be multiplied by a common number to become a useful size. Sometimes we may be able to use the square roots of the figures in the data set just as they are. It is always up to us to decide the best radius sizes for the proportional circles.

Triangular Graphs

These graphs are used for showing patterns in data whenever three components of a whole are given in percentage terms. For example, the employment categories for Canada are: primary (8.4%); secondary (26.8%); and tertiary (64.8%). These figures may be plotted on a triangular graph in the manner shown in Graph 4-10.

The location of plotted data on the triangular graph is important. A position close to the centre of the triangle indicates that all three components are more or less equal, whereas a position near one of the sides means that one of the components makes up only a small portion of the whole in relation to the other two components. A position close to two of the sides (i.e., near a corner) indicates that two components constitute a small part of the whole, while the remaining component makes up a large part.

Graph 4-10
A triangular graph

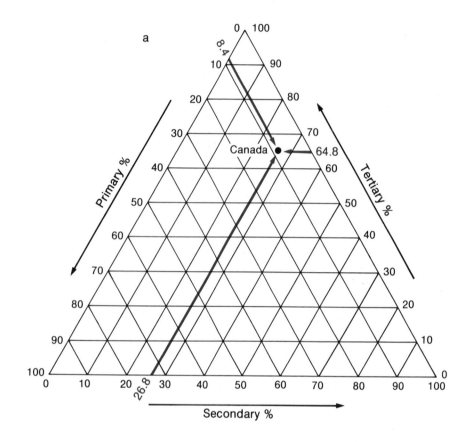

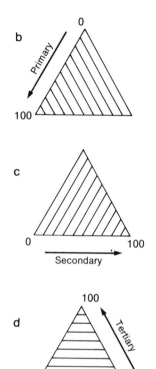

Triangular graphs are used chiefly for plotting data for several countries. The resulting groupings or clusters are then analyzed; deviations must also be accounted for.

Correlations: Scattergraphs

A scattergraph shows the correlation between two variables. It is often impossible to tell from a mass of data whether or not two variables go well together; we can find this information quickly on a scattergraph. For example, if we wish to discover the extent of relationship between the two hypothetical data sets shown below, then we can construct a scattergraph like Graph 4-11, which clearly provides the information.

Student #	Data set x Final mark %	Data set y Initial job earnings $K (K = thousands)
1	68	15.3
2	54	13.2
3	38	9.3
4	55	16.2
5	68	19.4
6	84	27.3
7	46	10.2
8	34	9.3
9	62	18.5
10	35	17.0
11	67	21.5
12	98	24.3
13	82	18.7
14	27	9.2
15	63	18.2
16	71	12.7
17	65	21.0
18	78	25.2
19	59	12.2
20	16	14.3

We can tell from the graph that a relationship exists, because there is a pattern made by the plotted data. We observe that the relationship is fairly strong, but not perfect, because the data fall into a fairly narrow band. If the relationship were perfect then the dots would form a line rather than a band.

The line that can be drawn through the middle of the plotted data, so that distances between the line and data are minimized, is known as the *line of best fit*. It is a representative of the data being plotted. The farther any dots are from the line of best fit, the less typical they are of the displayed correlation. We should always try to discover reasons for such deviations. The line of best fit also clearly shows whether the relationship is positive or negative. The relationship in Graph 4-11 is positive (i.e., one variable rises as the other one does), because the line of best fit slopes up to the right.

Graph 4-11
A scattergraph

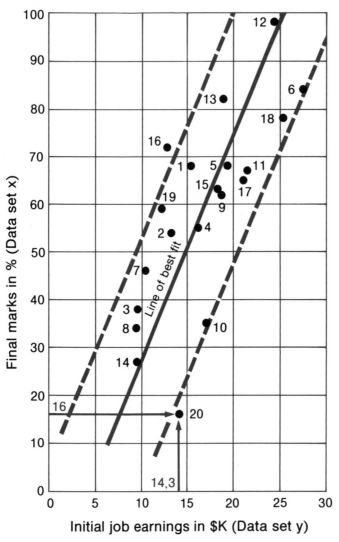

Occasionally the range of data is so great that a normal arithmetic scale cannot accommodate it. At such times it is customary to use appropriate log scales along one axis or both. Graph 4-12 illustrates a scattergraph frame that has log scales along both axes; in this case each axis has a 3 cycle log scale. It is possible to construct *log-log graphs* like this one with as many cycles as desired along either axis. Thus there can be three or four cycles along the vertical axis if needed, with one or two along the horizontal axis. The number of cycles used depends upon the range of data being plotted.

Graph 4-12
A 3 × 3 log-log graph

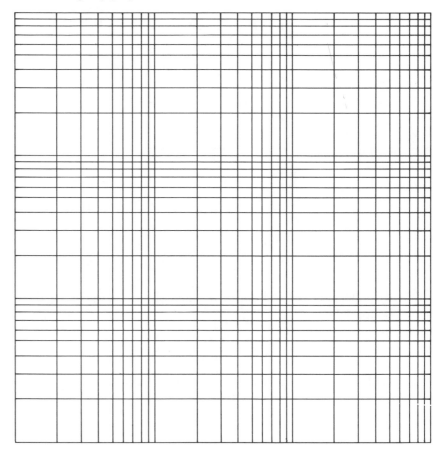

Correlations: The Phi (φ) Coefficient

The phi coefficient gives us a mathematical indication of the nature and degree of correlation between two variables. This indication is not difficult to obtain. For example, we can examine the correlation between average daily food intake and agricultural population (Columns I and L of Appendix 3). First we divide the data in Column I into two graphs; daily per capita food availability of 10 000 kJ and under, and food availability of over 10 000 kJ. We then merely count the number of countries in each group. The next step is to divide the countries in each of these groups into two further groups: the first group consists of those countries with 50% or less of the population engaged in agriculture, the second group, of those nations with over 50% of the people in agriculture. Again, we simply count the number of countries in each category. We then set up a two by two table as shown below, and insert the numbers we have counted in the appropriate boxes.

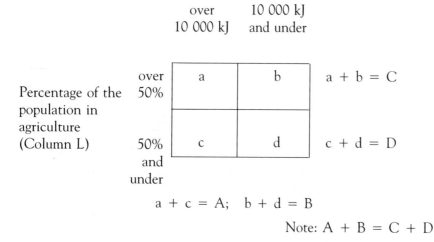

Daily per capita food availability (Column I)

	over 10 000 kJ	10 000 kJ and under	
Percentage of the population in agriculture (Column L) over 50%	a	b	a + b = C
50% and under	c	d	c + d = D

a + c = A;   b + d = B

Note: A + B = C + D

Add the numbers across and down, as shown by the letters, and then apply the formula:

$$\phi = \frac{(a \times d) - (b \times c)}{\sqrt{A \times B \times C \times D}}$$

For example, if we had thirty countries distributed as follows,

a 5	b 8	5 + 8 = 13 (C)
c 10	d 7	10 + 7 = 17 (D)

5 + 10 = 15 (A)   8 + 7 = 15 (B)

then the formula would read:

$$\phi = \frac{(5 \times 7) - (8 \times 10)}{\sqrt{15 \times 15 \times 13 \times 17}}$$

$$= \frac{35 - 80}{\sqrt{49725}}$$

$$= \frac{-45}{223}$$

$$= -0.2$$

In this example the coefficient is negative, indicating an *inverse* relationship. It is also quite small, indicating a weak relationship. The maximum range of coefficients is from $+1.0$ to -1.0; the first value reveals a perfect positive relationship, and the second, a perfect negative (inverse) relationship. A coefficient of zero (0.0) indicates no relationship at all.

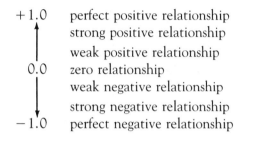

$+1.0$	perfect positive relationship
	strong positive relationship
	weak positive relationship
0.0	zero relationship
	weak negative relationship
	strong negative relationship
-1.0	perfect negative relationship

Since a correlation may never be more than perfect, it is impossible to obtain correlation coefficients that fall outside the designated range.

Correlations: Rank Correlation

The rank correlation technique is an attempt to obtain a correlation coefficient through a comparison of the rank positions of any item (such as a country) in two different data sets. Actual quantities are not involved. The technique involves arranging the items in each data set in order from highest to lowest. Because of the large number of countries in the world we recommend that you use only those marked with an asterisk (*) in Appendix 3. If you had to find the rank correlation coefficient for the relationship between, say, average daily food intake and electricity production (Columns I and P in Appendix 3), then you would proceed as follows:

Step 1. Rank the sample countries (*) according to their per capita food value in Column I; the country with the largest value will be first. Write in the countries' rank (1, 2, 3, etc.) in the first column, and set up another three columns.

Step 2. Assess their rank (1, 2, 3, etc., the largest first) in the matter of electricity generation (Column P) and write the appropriate rank for each country in the second column.

Step 3. Find the difference d in each pair of ranks. For example, if a country ranks 3 in the first column and 8 in the second, then the difference d is 5. If another country ranks 12 in the first column and 3 in the second, then the difference d is 9. Write the difference in the third column.

Step 4. Square the difference d, producing d². Write the answer in the fourth column, and add (Σ) all these d² answers to produce the sum of d² (Σd²) at the bottom of the fourth column.

Step 5. Apply the rank correlation formula

$$\rho = 1 - \frac{6(\Sigma d^2)}{n(n^2 - 1)}$$

where ρ (rho) is the *rank correlation coefficient*, whose range of values and method of interpretation are identical with those of the ϕ (phi) coefficient explained in the preceding section. The number $6(\Sigma d^2)$ is Σd^2 multiplied by 6, and n is the number of countries in the sample.

Step 6. Analyze the value of ρ. This means you must explain why the two variables exhibit the degree of relationship shown.

Correlations: Grouped Data Technique

The calculation of a correlation coefficient can be laborious if we do it for 150 or so countries individually; this is why we often restrict our examination to a sample of countries. As an alternative to taking a sample, we can use the *grouped data technique*, in which we study countries by groups rather than individually. The steps are as follows:

Step 1. Set up a correlation table, as in Graph 4-13.

Step 2. Examine the data and decide on appropriate *class intervals* for both sets. Classification is the arranging of large amounts of data into groups. Incomes, for example, may be arranged in groups of $5 000: $0 to $4 999, $5 000 to $9 999, $10 000 to $14 999, and so on. The size of the group selected is called the class interval. For our example we will use the hypothetical data in Fig. 1, and group both sets into ten classes.

Step 3. Write in the class intervals that have been decided upon, in the manner shown in Graph 4-14.

Step 4. In the boxes of the f rank, insert the number of students classified in each marks category. In the f column, insert the number of students grouped into each earnings class. Now, enter in the central boxes the number of times a given combination of variables occurs. Consider, for example, the students whose earnings fall into the $8–9.9K category. There are nine students in this class; of the nine, only one has final marks in the 0–9% class. Thus a combination of a final mark between 0 and 9% and an initial income of $8–9.9K occurs only once, so 1

Graph 4-13
A correlation table for data grouped into ten classes

Class interval ⟶														Totals ▼	$f(d_x d_y)$
Frequency f ⟶		f_x													
Deviation d ⟶		d_x													
fd ⟶	fd_x														
f_y	d_y	fd_y	fd^2												
Totals ⟶											$\Sigma\,[f(d_x d_y)] =$				

is entered in the appropriate central box, as shown in Graph 4-14. From the graph we also see that an income of \$8–9.9K combines with a final mark of 10–19% once, with a mark of 20–29% twice, and with a mark of 30–39% five times. The double classification right through two data sets that is required in this step must be completed with care.

Step 5. Add all the numbers in the f rank (f_x) to obtain the frequency total for data set x. Similarly, add the numbers in the f column (f_y) to get the frequency total for data set y. Make sure that the sum of f (Σf) equals the number (n) of items in your data, and that $\Sigma f_x = \Sigma f_y$.

Step 6. For deviations, count the lowest class in each data set as zero and insert the value (0) in the d space opposite the lowest class. Count each class above the lowest as one deviation, and

Graph 4-14
A completed correlation table for the data in Fig. 1

Variable x: Final marks of 58 students

— 10 spaces for 10 classes —

Variable y: Initial earnings in $K of 58 students — 10 spaces for 10 classes

Class intervals					0-9	10-19	20-29	30-39	40-49	50-59	60-69	70-79	80-89	90-99	Totals	$f(d_x d_y)$
Frequency f				f_x	1	3	2	8	4	11	17	6	4	2	58	
Deviation d				d_x	0	1	2	3	4	5	6	7	8	9		
			fd →	fd_x	0	3	4	24	16	55	102	42	32	18	296	
	f_y	d_y	fd_y	fd^2	0	3	8	72	64	275	612	294	256	162	1 746	
26-27.9	3	9	27	243									${}_{72}2^{144}$	${}_{81}1^{81}$		225
24-25.9	2	8	16	128								${}_{56}1^{56}$		${}_{72}1^{72}$		128
22-23.9	3	7	21	147							${}_{42}1^{42}$	${}_{49}2^{98}$				140
20-21.9	4	6	24	144							${}_{36}3^{108}$		${}_{48}1^{48}$			156
18-19.9	11	5	55	275						${}_{25}2^{50}$	${}_{30}7^{210}$	${}_{35}1^{35}$	${}_{40}1^{40}$			335
16-17.9	6	4	24	96				${}_{12}1^{12}$			${}_{20}1^{20}$	${}_{24}3^{72}$	${}_{28}1^{28}$			132
14-15.9	7	3	21	63		${}_{3}1^{3}$				${}_{12}2^{24}$	${}_{15}1^{15}$	${}_{18}3^{54}$				96
12-13.9	6	2	12	24					${}_{6}1^{6}$		${}_{10}4^{40}$		${}_{14}1^{14}$			60
10-11.9	7	1	7	7		${}_{1}1^{1}$			${}_{3}1^{3}$	${}_{4}2^{8}$	${}_{5}3^{15}$					27
8-9.9	9	0	0	0	${}_{0}1^{0}$	${}_{0}1^{0}$	${}_{0}2^{0}$	${}_{0}5^{0}$								0
Totals	58		207	1 127											$\Sigma [f(d_x d_y)] =$	1 299

Fig. 1
Final marks and initial job earnings
of 58 students, hypothetical data

	Data set x	Data set y
Student #	Final mark %	Initial job earnings $K
1	68	15.3
2	54	13.2
3	38	9.3
4	55	16.2
5	68	19.4
6	84	27.3
7	46	10.2
8	34	9.3
9	62	18.5
10	35	17.0
11	67	21.5
12	98	24.3
13	82	18.7
14	27	9.2
15	63	18.2
16	71	12.7
17	65	21.0
18	78	25.2
19	59	12.2
20	16	14.3
21	68	15.7
22	73	22.1
23	64	20.0
24	23	8.0
25	58	19.2
26	66	18.9
27	77	22.0
28	46	15.0
29	63	18.3
30	68	23.9
31	30	13.2
32	45	15.2
33	47	11.1
34	71	18.2
35	60	18.7
36	81	21.4
37	55	12.4
38	63	15.2
39	57	14.3
40	59	10.2
41	50	18.7
42	82	26.1
43	63	16.7
44	16	8.2
45	51	10.4
46	33	9.0
47	57	10.5
48	35	11.1
49	58	13.7
50	18	10.0
51	63	16.2
52	8	8.2
53	68	16.7
54	93	27.5
55	72	16.6
56	33	9.1
57	61	18.0
58	31	9.5

insert those values (1, 2, 3, etc.) in the appropriate d spaces (d_x and d_y).

Step 7.   Multiply the d_x and d_y values by the corresponding f value; i.e., d_x by f_x and d_y by f_y. Enter your answers in the fd rank (fd_x) and column (fd_y).

Step 8.   Add (Σ) the fd_x figures and enter the answer (Σfd_x) to the right in the totals box, where the figure of 296 is entered in Graph 4-14.

Step 9.   Add (Σ) the fd_y figures and enter the answer (Σfd_y) below the column in the totals box, where 207 is located in Graph 4-14.

Step 10.   Square all individual d values (d_x and d_y) and multiply the squares by the appropriate f value (d_x^2 by f_x and d_y^2 by f_y). Enter the answers in the fd^2 rank (fd_x^2) and column (fd_y^2). Sum (Σ) the fd_x^2 figures and enter the answer to the right, where 1 746 is entered; then sum the fd_y^2 figures and enter the answer under the column where 1 127 is shown.

Step 11.   For each central box of the correlation table in which data are classified, multiply the apropriate d numbers; i.e., d_x multiplied by d_y. Enter the answer in the lower left corner of each box.

Step 12.   Multiply the $d_x d_y$ values just obtained by the frequency (f) figures already inserted in the central boxes. Enter the answer, $f(d_x d_y)$, in the upper right corner of each box. For example, in Graph 4-14 for the combination of marks in the class 60–69% and earnings in the class $18–19.9K, the frequency (f) is 7; the class deviation of marks (d_x) is 6 and the class deviation of earnings (d_y) is 5, so $d_x d_y = 30$. This figure can be seen in the lower left corner of the box. The frequency (7) multiplied by the $d_x d_y$ figure of 30 produces an $f(d_x d_y)$ figure of 210, which can be seen in the upper right corner of the box.

Step 13.   Add the $f(d_x d_y)$ figures across, and put each rank's total in the extreme right hand column. Thus 144 and 81 add up to 225, and so on.

Step 14.   Add (Σ) the figures in the right hand column. Enter the answer, $\Sigma f(d_x d_y)$, at the foot of the column.

Step 15.   Apply the formula for the *coefficient of correlation* (r):

$$r = \frac{\theta}{\sigma_x \sigma_y}$$

where

$$\theta = \frac{\Sigma[f(d_x d_y)]}{n} - \left(\frac{\Sigma(fd_x)}{n}\right)\left(\frac{\Sigma(fd_y)}{n}\right)$$

$$\sigma_x = \sqrt{\frac{\Sigma(fd_x^2)}{n} - \left(\frac{\Sigma fd_x}{n}\right)^2}$$

$$\sigma_y = \sqrt{\frac{\Sigma(fd_y^2)}{n} - \left(\frac{\Sigma fd_y}{n}\right)^2}$$

In the case of our example in Graph 4-14 the appropriate values are

$$\theta = \frac{1\ 299}{58} - \left(\frac{296}{58}\right)\left(\frac{207}{58}\right)$$

$$= 22.3966 - (5.1034)(3.5690)$$

$$= 22.3966 - 18.2140$$

$$= 4.1826$$

$$\sigma_x = \sqrt{\frac{1\ 746}{58} - \left(\frac{296}{58}\right)^2}$$

$$= \sqrt{30.1034 - 26.0447}$$

$$= 2.0146$$

$$\sigma_y = \sqrt{\frac{1\ 127}{58} - \left(\frac{207}{58}\right)^2}$$

$$= \sqrt{19.4310 - 12.7378}$$

$$= 2.5871$$

Substitution of these values in the formula indicates that

$$r = \frac{4.1826}{2.0146 \times 2.5871}$$

$$= \frac{4.1826}{5.2120}$$

$$= 0.8025$$

Our example yields a correlation coefficient of 0.8025. This is high. The full range of possibilities for this coefficient is the same as that for the coefficient described in the section on phi coefficients above.

Correlations: Standard Deviation Technique

Most plotted data tend to be distributed in such a way that the majority cluster around a middle point; this tendency is illustrated in the linear dispersion diagram in Graph 4-9. There is also, of course, a range of deviation from this central point. In statistics there are various methods of measuring the extent of such deviation; one of the most commonly used is the *standard deviation* (σ) *technique*. A comparison of standard deviations between two sets of data enables us to arrive at a widely used measure of correlation. In order to determine such a correlation between, for example, data sets in Columns H and V of Appendix 3 (annual rate of natural increase and percentage of population that is urban), we would proceed as follows:

Step 1. Select the sample. These are the countries marked with an asterisk (*) in Appendix 3.

Step 2. Set up a table with five empty columns. Write the names of the selected countries down the left side, outside the five columns. Alphabetical order will do.

Step 3. Write the appropriate data from Column H of Appendix 3 in the first column of your table; call them data set x.

Step 4. Square these data and write the answers (x^2) in the second column.

Step 5. Write the appropriate data from Column V in the third column; call them data set y.

Step 6. Square these data and write the answers (y^2) in the fourth column.

Step 7. Multiply the x data by the y data, and write the answer (xy) in the fifth column.

Step 8. Calculate the mean ($\bar{x}$) of the x data.

Step 9. Calculate the mean ($\bar{y}$) of the y data.

Step 10. Add the figures in the second column to give a total, Σx^2.

Step 11. Add the figures in the fourth column to give a total, Σy^2.

Step 12. Add the figures in the fifth column to give a total, Σxy.

Step 13. Apply the standard deviation correlation formula

$$r = \frac{\theta}{\sigma_x \sigma_y}$$

where

r = standard deviation correlation coefficient

$$\sigma_x \text{ (standard deviation of x data)} = \sqrt{\frac{\Sigma x^2}{n} - \bar{x}^2}$$

$$\sigma_y \text{ (standard deviation of y data)} = \sqrt{\frac{\Sigma y^2}{n} - \bar{y}^2}$$

$$\theta = \frac{\Sigma xy}{n} - \overline{xy}$$

Step 14. Interpret the result in the manner shown at the end of the section on phi correlations.

Percentage Deviation from the Group Mean

A fairly simple way of determining the extent of variation within a group of data is to calculate the mean of the data and then see how far each item deviates from the group mean. When different magnitudes of data are being compared it is better to use proportions rather than absolute quantities; hence percentage deviations are a useful tool. Consider, for example, the following values for one criterion (x) for twenty sample countries (n = 20):

162	150
173	226
98	191
42	175
263	138
117	104
84	88
37	209
427	191
349	112

Total (Σx) 3 336

These values yield a mean ($\bar{x}$) of 166.8 ($\bar{x} = \dfrac{\Sigma x}{n} = \dfrac{3\ 336}{20} = 166.8$).

Each individual term *deviates* from the mean, and we can assess the degree of such deviation by a simple percentage calculation, giving the mean a value of 100 in all cases. The item 98 deviates from the mean of 166.8 to the degree of 41 percentage points, rounded to the nearest whole number (98 is 58.75% of 166.8; 58.75 subtracted from 100 is 41.25; 41.25 rounded to the nearest whole number is 41). Therefore the percentage deviation of the item 98 from the group mean of 166.8 is 41.

Coefficient of Determination

There is often a need to ascertain the extent to which variations in one variable may cause (or determine) variations in another. For example, to what degree does a high rate of population increase cause starvation? We can obtain some idea by calculating the coefficient of determination (r^2) as follows. We will use the sample countries marked by an asterisk (*) in Appendix 3, because the calculations would be laborious if we were to perform them for all countries listed. The number of countries in the sample = n.

Country	F (Column F data – Natural increase rate)	$F - \bar{F} = f$	f^2	I (Column I data – Average daily food intake)	$I - \bar{I} = i$	i^2	fi
Algeria Brazil Canada etc.							
	$\bar{F} = \dfrac{\Sigma F}{n}$		$\Sigma f^2 =$	$\bar{I} = \dfrac{\Sigma I}{n}$		$\Sigma i^2 =$	$\Sigma fi =$ $(\Sigma fi)^2 =$

Step 1. Set out columns as shown.

Step 2. Add (Σ) the data for the sample in Column F and calculate the mean ($\bar{F}$).

Step 3. Add (Σ) the data for the sample in Column I and calculate the mean ($\bar{I}$).

Step 4. Subtract the mean $\bar{F}$ from each actual item of F data, to give f. Some answers will be negative; mark them so.

Step 5. Subtract the mean $\bar{I}$ from each actual item of I data, to give i. Again, be sure to show negative values.

Step 6. Square the f answers and the i answers to give f^2 and i^2 respectively.

Step 7.   Add the f^2 column (Σf^2).

Step 8.   Add the i^2 column (Σi^2).

Step 9.   Multiply f (not f^2) by i (not i^2), to give fi in the last column. Some of these figures may be negative.

Step 10.   Add (Σ) the fi figures (Σfi), remembering to subtract any negative values, and square the result to give Σfi^2. You now have all the information you need to obtain the coefficient of determination, also known as r^2. Do it by applying the following formula:

$$r^2 = \frac{(\Sigma fi)^2 / \Sigma f^2}{\Sigma i^2}$$

Step 11.   Interpret your result. The answer should be between 0 and 1. The closer it is to 1, the stronger the causality. In our example, for instance, a result of 0.8314 indicates that 83.14% of starvation is caused by the high rate of population increase. On the other hand, a result of merely 0.1796 indicates that 17.96% of starvation is caused by high rates of population increase. The answer, as with many statistical answers, is likely to be more precise than the truth warrants. Such accuracy is often called *spurious accuracy*; an example of this is a statistical item showing an average family size of 2.483 children. While statistics accurate to two or three decimal places are too precise to be truthful, they nevertheless help to quantify phenomena and causes that may otherwise exist only as vague ideas and statements.

Moving Averages

These are a way of looking at a set of data over a long period of time and obtaining the long-term trends by eliminating all the minor fluctuations. Moving averages are frequently used for unemployment statistics; people often speak of these figures as being "seasonally adjusted."

The technique is very simple, and can be easily illustrated with unemployment data. Let us assume that the unemployment rates for each month in the past year were as follows:

January	9.7%
February	9.9%
March	9.8%
April	9.3%
May	8.7%
June	8.1%

July	7.2%
August	6.3%
September	7.4%
October	8.0%
November	8.6%
December	8.9%

In such a case the average for the whole year may be obtained by adding all the rates and dividing by 12. The annual average is 8.5%. We may therefore say that 8.5% unemployment was the norm for the year, and that some months were above the norm and some below. When the unemployment figure for the following January comes in, a figure of 9.5%, we again perform the calculations, replacing the first January figure with the most recent one.

The twelve month sequence now reads:

Feburary	9.9%
March	9.8%
April	9.3%
May	8.7%
June	8.1%
July	7.2%
August	6.3%
September	7.4%
October	8.0%
November	8.6%
December	8.9%
January	9.5%

The average for this new sequence is just under 8.5%; consequently a situation arises in which some people say that unemployment is 9.5% while others say that it is only 8.5% "seasonally adjusted." If moving average calculations are performed for a long period of time, they effectively eliminate all minor fluctuations. Long-term trends may thereby be established.

Index Numbers

Index numbers are a device for measuring changes in data over a period of time. They are based on a percentage system, so that comparisons are possible between data of different magnitudes. The calculation of an index number proceeds as follows:

Step 1. Examine the information at the start of the period of time for which the index number is to be calculated. Consider, for example, the data series below:

1970	1971	1972	1973	1974	1975	1976	
1 350	1 225	1 150	1 125	980	1 000	1 120	Canada's fishery catch, t
205	210	240	320	285		290	390	Landed value of fishery catch, $ millions

(Source: Fisheries and Environment Canada)

If we wish to compare both sets of data from the period 1970 to 1976, then 1970 becomes what is called the *base year* and its data are assigned an index value of 100 (1970 = 100).

Step 2. To find the index numbers for the data in 1976, divide them by the appropriate 1970 data and multiply the answer by 100. For instance, 1 120 divided by 1 350 is 0.83, and 0.83 multiplied by 100 is 83. Similarly, 390 divided by 205 is 1.90, and 1.90 multiplied by 100 is 190. The 1976 index numbers for Canada's fishery catch in tonnes and landed value in dollars are, respectively, 83 and 190 (1970 = 100).

Step 3. Interpret the results. The 1976 index numbers indicate that, compared with those of 1970, the catch had gone down a little while the value had risen considerably.

Rank-Size Rule

The rank-size rule is based on generally observed phenomena. It states essentially that the size of a city (in population) is the reciprocal of its rank. Thus the population of the second-ranked city would be about half that of the first-ranked city, the population of the third-ranked city one-third the size of the first-ranked city and so on.

It is a general rule that if the rank (first, second, etc.) of cities is plotted against their size on a log-log graph, the pattern will appear as a fairly straight line. Rank is measured along the horizontal axis, so that up to one hundred cities can be accommodated on a 2 cycle log scale. Size is measured along the vertical axis in appropriate units (thousands, millions, etc.).

Index